THE UNIVERSITY OF CHICAGO
ORIENTAL INSTITUTE PUBLICATIONS
VOLUME 120

Series Editors
Thomas A. Holland
and
Thomas G. Urban

ORIENTAL INSTITUTE PUBLICATIONS • VOLUME 120

EXCAVATIONS AT THE PREHISTORIC MOUND OF CHOGHA BONUT, KHUZESTAN, IRAN

SEASONS 1976/77, 1977/78, AND 1996

by

ABBAS ALIZADEH

with contributions by

Naomi F. Miller, Richard W. Redding, *and* Arlene Miller Rosen

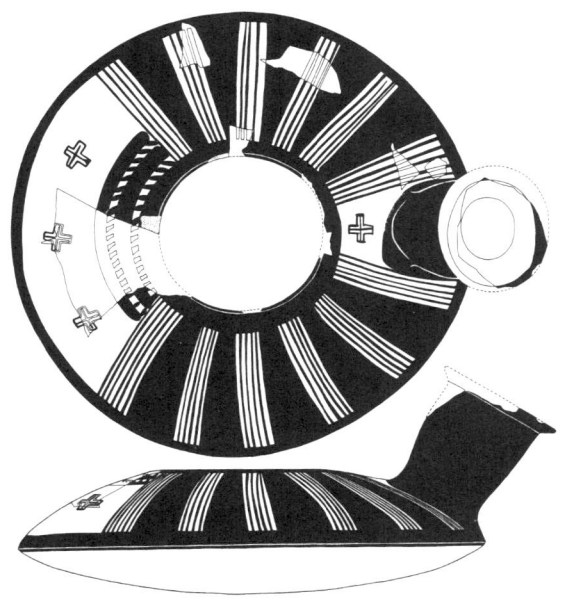

THE ORIENTAL INSTITUTE OF THE UNIVERSITY OF CHICAGO

CHICAGO • ILLINOIS

In Association with the Iranian Cultural Heritage Organization

Library of Congress Catalog Card Number: 2003107043

ISBN: 1-885923-23-6

ISSN 0068-3367

The Oriental Institute, Chicago

©2003 by The University of Chicago. All rights reserved.
Published 2003. Printed in the United States of America.

Series Editors' Acknowledgments

The series editors acknowledge the assistance of Adam Miglio, Leslie Schramer, and Alexandra Witsell in the production of this volume.

Title Page Illustration:

Middle Susiana Tortoise Vessel (B I-1; fig. 20), drawn by W. Raymond Johnson

Printed by McNaughton & Gunn, Saline, Michigan

The paper used in this publication meets the minimum requirements of American National Standard for Information Sciences—Permanence of Paper for Printed Library Materials, ANSI Z39.48–1984

This book is dedicated to the warm and hospitable people of rural Khuzestan, especially those from the villages of Upper Bonut, Qale Khalil, and Dolati.

TABLE OF CONTENTS

LIST OF ABBREVIATIONS	xi
LIST OF FIGURES	xiii
LIST OF PLATES	xv
LIST OF TABLES	xvii
BIBLIOGRAPHY	xix
PREFACE	xxxi
CHAPTER 1. INTRODUCTION	1
BACKGROUND OF CURRENT RESEARCH	1
THE QUESTION OF THE ORIGINS OF DOMESTICATION IN IRAN	5
Ganj Darreh	5
Tappeh Asiab	5
Tappeh Ali Kosh	6
Tappeh Tuleii	7
SUSIANA AND DEH LURAN IN THE EARLY NEOLITHIC PERIOD	8
DISCUSSION AND CONCLUSION	8
CHAPTER 2. KHUZESTAN ENVIRONMENT	13
ARID ZONE	13
SEMI-ARID ZONE	13
DRY ZONE	14
RIVERS	14
CHAPTER 3. RESULTS OF 1976/77, 1977/78, AND 1996 EXCAVATIONS	17
EXCAVATION METHODS AND STRATEGIES	17
Analytical Methods	17
Subsistence Production	17
Craft Specialization	17
Inter-regional Connection	17
Storage, Residential Segregation, and Social Complexity	17
Recording System and Excavation Procedures	18
EXCAVATION RESULTS	19
STRATIGRAPHIC TRENCH	21
CHIPPED STONE INDUSTRY	21
STONE OBJECTS	22
CLAY FIGURINES	22
FLORA AND FAUNA	22
CHAPTER 4. POST-ARCHAIC ARCHITECTURE AT CHOGHA BONUT	23
LATE SUSIANA 2 PHASE	23
LATE MIDDLE SUSIANA PHASE	24
Architectural Phase *B*	24
Large Circular Structure	25
Building I	25
Buildings II and III	26
Architectural Phase *A*	26
Building IV	26
Building V	26
Kilns and Ovens	27
INTERPRETATION	28

CHAPTER 5. ARCHITECTURE OF THE ARCHAIC, FORMATIVE, AND ACERAMIC SUSIANA	33
ARCHAIC SUSIANA 0 (BONUT F, ARCHITECTURAL PHASE 5)	33
FORMATIVE SUSIANA (BONUT B–E, ARCHITECTURAL PHASES 1–4)	33
THE REMAINS OF ACERAMIC SUSIANA (BONUT A)	35
SUMMARY	40
CHAPTER 6. POTTERY	43
INTRODUCTION	43
Inter-regional Connection	45
POTTERY SEQUENCE AND TYPOLOGY	45
Late Susiana 2	45
LATE MIDDLE SUSIANA	46
ARCHAIC AND FORMATIVE SUSIANA	47
CHAPTER 7. SMALL OBJECTS	67
CLAY SPINDLE WHORLS	67
CLAY HUMAN FIGURINES	67
T-shaped Figurines	67
Figurines with Abbreviated Anatomical Features	67
Other Abstract Figurines	68
ANIMAL FIGURINES	68
BONE OBJECTS	68
SHELL OBJECT	69
STONE OBJECTS	69
Tools	69
Miscellaneous	69
CHAPTER 8. ADMINISTRATIVE TECHNOLOGY	85
INTRODUCTION	85
MIDDLE SUSIANA PERIOD	85
ARCHAIC, FORMATIVE, AND ACERAMIC PERIODS	88
CHAPTER 9. CHIPPED STONE INDUSTRY	91
INTRODUCTION	91
GROUP 1: MICRO-BLADES	91
GROUP 2: BLADES WITH STRAIGHT BULBAR SURFACE	92
GROUP 3: BLADES WITH CURVED BULBAR SURFACE	92
GROUP 4: BLADE CORES	92
CHAPTER 10. PLANT REMAINS FROM THE 1996 EXCAVATION. *Naomi F. Miller*	123
SAMPLING AND FLOTATION	123
Character of the Assemblage	123
TAXA	123
Cereals	124
Pulses and Other Legumes	125
Wild and Weedy Plants	127
INTERPRETATION	127
POTENTIAL FOR FUTURE RESEARCH	127
CHAPTER 11. PRELIMINARY PHYTOLITH ANALYSES. *Arlene Miller Rosen*	129
METHODS	129
RESULTS	129
SINGLE-CELL PHYTOLITHS	129

MULTI-CELL PHYTOLITHS	131
DISCUSSION	131
CHAPTER 12. FIRST REPORT ON FAUNAL REMAINS. *Richard W. Redding*	137
QUANTIFYING THE DATA: MEASURING ABUNDANCE	137
METHODOLOGY	138
MATERIAL FROM CHOGHA BONUT	139
DISCUSSION	141
CONCLUSION	142
APPENDIX 1. RADIOCARBON DATING OF THE SUSIANA SEQUENCE	149
APPENDIX 2. INDEX OF FEATURES AND LAYERS FROM THE 1996 SEASON	151
APPENDIX 3. INDEX OF LOCI FROM THE 1976/77 AND 1977/78 SEASONS	153
INDEX OF GEOGRAPHICAL NAMES	159
PLATES	161

LIST OF ABBREVIATIONS

cf.	*confer*, compare
cm	centimeter(s)
CMT	Chogha Mami Transitional
D.T.	deep trench
E	east
e.g.	*exempli gratia*, for example
ext.	exterior
el.	elevation (above sea level)
fig(s).	figure(s)
gm	gram
hl	half life
ICHO	Iranian Cultural Heritage Organization
i.e.	*id est*, that is
indet.	indeterminate
int.	interior
IS	inside surface, diameter of
m	meter(s)
MB	meat bearing
mm	millimeter(s)
N	north
NA	not available
NISP	number of identified specimens
NMB	non-meat bearing
n(n).	note(s)
no(s).	number(s)
OS	outside surface, diameter of
pl(s).	plate(s)
p(p).	page(s)
S.T.	stratigraphic trench
Tr.	trench
unident.	unidentified

LIST OF FIGURES

1. Selected Sites in the Ancient Near East 2
2. Map Showing the Location of Chogha Bonut in Susiana 3
3. Contour Map and Elevations of Chogha Bonut and Its Immediate Vicinity 4
4. 1978 Contour Map of Chogha Bonut 7
5. Composite Plan of Middle, Archaic, and Formative Susiana Architecture from the 1977/78 Excavations and Square M10 Trench (with Deep Trench Indicated) and Stratigraphic Trench from the 1996 Excavations at Chogha Bonut 20
6. Plan of Late Middle Susiana Architectural Phase *b* from the 1977/78 Excavations and Square M10 Trench (with Deep Trench Indicated) and Stratigraphic Trench from the 1996 Excavations at Chogha Bonut 24
7. Plan of Late Middle Susiana Architectural Phase *a* from the 1977/78 Excavations and Square M10 Trench (with Deep Trench Indicated) and Stratigraphic Trench from the 1996 Excavations at Chogha Bonut 27
8. Plan of Late Middle Susiana Building I 28
9. Section Drawing and Top Plan of Late Middle Susiana Pottery Kiln K10:209 29
10. Plan of Archaic Susiana 0 Architecture from the 1977/78 Excavations and Square M10 Trench (with Deep Trench Indicated) and Stratigraphic Trench from the 1996 Excavations at Chogha Bonut 34
11. Plan of Formative Susiana Architecture from the 1977/78 Excavations and Square M10 Trench (with Deep Trench Indicated) and Stratigraphic Trench from the 1996 Excavations at Chogha Bonut 35
12. Plan of Layer 1 and Feature 7 in Square M10 and Plan of Layer 1 and Layer 11 in Square M10 36
13. Plan of Feature 14 in Square M10 and Plan of Feature 15 in Square M10 36
14. Plan of Feature 18 in Square M10 and Plan of Feature 28 in Square M10 37
15. Plan of Features 31 and 34 in Square M10 37
16. Section Drawing of the West Balk in Square M10 (1996) 38
17. Section Drawing of the South Balk in Square M10 (1996) 38
18. West Section Drawing of the 1996 Stratigraphic Trench 39
19. Stratigraphic Sequence in Square M10, Based on Modified Harris Matrix 41
20. Middle Susiana Tortoise Vessel 49
21. Various Types of Middle and Late Susiana Pottery 51
22. Various Types of Middle Susiana Pottery 53
23. Formative Susiana Pottery: Straw-tempered Soft Ware 55
24. Formative Susiana Pottery: Smeared-painted Ware, Orange Buff Plain Ware, Black-on-Cream Painted Ware, Maroon-on-Cream Painted Ware, Red-slipped Straw-tempered Ware, and Maroon-on-Red Painted Ware 57
25. Archaic Susiana 0 Pottery: Maroon-on-Cream Painted Ware 59

26.	Various Archaic Susiana Pottery Types: Maroon-on-Cream Painted Ware, Black-on-Cream Painted Ware, and Broad Band-painted Ware	61
27.	Archaic Susiana Pottery: Painted-burnished Variant Ware	63
28.	Archaic Susiana Pottery: Painted-burnished Variant Ware	65
29.	Stone Vessel Fragments	71
30.	Anthropomorphic Figurines	73
31.	Animal Figurines	75
32.	Abstract Figurines/Tokens	77
33.	Various Stone, Shell, and Clay Objects	79
34.	Various Stone Objects	81
35.	Various Bone Objects	83
36.	Various Types of Tokens	87
37.	Administrative Devices and Spindle Whorls	89
38.	Various Types of Flint Micro-Blades	115
39.	Various Types of Flint Blades with Straight Bulbar Surface	117
40.	Various Types of Flint Blades with Curved Bulbar Surface	119
41.	Bullet-shaped and Tongue-shaped Flint Blade Cores	121
42.	Pisum/Vicia/Lathyrus Diameter	125
43.	CB-97-2 Phytolith of *Phragmites* sp. Stem and CB-97-1 Phytolith from *Phragmites* sp. Leaf	132
44.	CB-97-1 Wheat Husk Phytolith and CB-97-1 Barley Phytolith	133
45.	Percentages of Phytoliths from Different Grass Sub-families and Plant Parts	134
46.	Percentages from Two Samples of Multi-cell Phytoliths	135
47.	Percentage of Cells Per Silica from Wheat Husk Phytoliths	135

LIST OF PLATES

1. Staff of the 1996 Season of Excavation at Chogha Bonut, the Late Haj Qapuni (our majordomo) and His Extended Bakhtiari Family, and Three Boys from the Village of Upper Bonut

2. Panoramic View of Chogha Bonut, View West; Panoramic View of Chogha Bonut, View East; and Test Trench at the Eastern Base of Chogha Bonut

3. Square M10 Prior to Excavation, View Southeast; Excavations in Square M10, View Northwest; and Excavations in Square M10, View Southeast

4. *In situ* Dry-sieving in Square M10 and Members of the 1996 Expedition in the Process of Flotation at Susa Castle

5. Straw-tempered Mudbrick Fragment from Aceramic Level in Square M10, Piece of Red Ochre on Feature 28, and an Early Neolithic Circular Fire Pit with Rocks in Feature 34

6. Top View of Feature 28 Showing Articulated Sheep/Goat Legs and a Circular Fire Pit, Close-up of Sheep/Goat Horn on Feature 28, and Close-up of Articulated Sheep/Goat Legs and Horn on Feature 28

7. Sheep/Goat Horns from Feature 28 and Top View of Feature 18 with Fire Pits and Root/Animal Holes

8. Feature 31 Showing Patch of White Ash and Unexcavated Fire Pits, View West; and Features 31 and 34 with Southern Balk of Square M10, Showing Deep Trench

9. View of the Stratigraphic Trench, View West and Northern Balk of Square M10

10. Samples of Reeds from the Vicinity of Chogha Bonut and Reed Impressions on the Northwestern Corner of Feature 28

11. Middle Susiana Building I, View South; and Kiln J10:209 and Building I, View East

12. Late Middle Susiana Kilns in Building I, View South; and Late Middle Susiana Kiln K10:209

13. Late Middle Susiana Oven K10:205, View South; and Late Middle Susiana Circular Structure K9:201, View South

14. Long, Cigar-shaped Mudbricks of Archaic Susiana 0 Building in L11, View East

15. Various Stone Objects

16. Stone Objects and Bullet-shaped Flint Cores

17. Various Small Clay Objects, Small Stone Objects, and Stone Vessel Fragments

18. Clay Figurines and Horn-like Clay Object

19. Various Clay Tokens

20. Late Middle Susiana Administrative "Tablets"

21. Various Types of Formative Susiana Pottery

22. Formative Susiana Straw-tempered Soft Ware

23. Formative Susiana Smeared-painted Ware

24. Archaic Susiana Painted-burnished Variant Ware

25. Flint Blades, Painted-burnished Variant Ware, and Maroon-on-Cream Painted Ware

26. Late Middle Susiana and Late Susiana 2 Pottery

LIST OF TABLES

1.	Average Monthly Precipitation at Abadan, Ahvaz, and Dezful	13
2.	Chogha Bonut Sequence	22
3.	Relative Chronology of Prehistoric Sites in Iran and Mesopotamia	31
4.	List of Flint Blades, Obsidian Blades, and Blade Cores by Type and Findspot	93
5.	Inventory of Flotation Samples from 1996 Excavation	124
6.	Miscellaneous Non-botanical Items	125
7.	Plant Remains from Chogha Bonut	126
8.	Phytolith Counts and Percentages	130
9.	NISP for Mammal Taxa Other than Gazella, Ovis, and Capra Presented by Body Part and Provenance	142
10.	NISP for Gazelle, Sheep, and Goat for Square M10 Presented by Body Part and Provenance	143
11.	NISP for Gazelle, Sheep, and Goat for the 1996 Stratigraphic Trench Presented by Body Part and Level	143
12.	Fusion Data for Ovis-Capra Bones	144
13.	Fusion Data for Gazella Bones	144
14.	Measurements for Bones	145
15.	List of Radiocarbon Dates from Chogha Bonut	149
16.	List of Radiocarbon Dates from Chogha Mish	150

BIBLIOGRAPHY

Adams, Robert McC.

1962 "Agriculture and Urban Life in Early Southwestern Iran." *Science* 136: 109–22.

Alizadeh, Abbas

1988 "Socio-economic Complexity in Southwestern Iran During the Fifth and Fourth Millennia B.C.: The Evidence from Tall-i Bakun A." *Iran* 26: 17–34.

1992 *Prehistoric Settlement Patterns and Cultures in Susiana, Southwestern Iran: The Analysis of the F. G. L. Gremliza Survey Collection*. Museum of Anthropology, Technical Report 24. Ann Arbor: University of Michigan.

1997a "Excavations at Chogha Bonut: The Earliest Village in Susiana, Iran." *The Oriental Institute News & Notes* 153: 1–4.

1997b "Iranian Prehistoric Project." In *The Oriental Institute 1996–1997 Annual Report*, edited by William M. Sumner, pp. 49–56. Chicago: The Oriental Institute.

Alley, Richard B., and Michael Bender

1998 "Greenland Ice Cores: Frozen in Time." *Scientific American* 278: 80–85.

Amiet, Pierre

1971 "La glyptique de l'Acropole (1969–71): Tablettes lenticulaires de Suse." *Cahiers de la Délégation archéologique française en Iran* 1: 217–33.

Bak, Per, and Ken Chen

1991 "Self-Organized Criticality." *Scientific American* 264: 46–53.

Bakkar, J. W., et al.

1956 *The Development of Khuzestan's Land and Water Resources*. Rome: Food and Agricultural Organization of the United Nations.

Bar-Yosef, O., and Mordechai Kislev

1989 "Early Farming Communities in the Jordan Valley." In *Foraging and Farming: The Evolution of Plant Exploitation*, edited by David R. Harris and Gordon C. Hillman, pp. 632–42. One World Archaeology 13. London: Unwin Hyman.

Bar-Yosef, O., and Richard H. Meadow

1995 "The Origins of Agriculture in the Near East." In *Last Hunters, First Farmers: New Perspectives on the Prehistoric Transition to Agriculture*, edited by T. Douglas Price and Anne Birgitte Gebauer, pp. 39–94. Santa Fe: School of American Research Press.

Baykal-Seeher, Ayse, and Julia Obladen-Kauder

1996 *Demircihüyük: Die Ergebnisse der Ausgrabungen 1975–1978*, Band 4: *Die Kleinfunde*. Mainz: Verlag Philipp von Zabern.

Beck, Lois C.

    1986   *The Qashqaii*. St. Louis: Washington University.

Binford, Lewis R.

    1971   "Post-Pleistocene Adaptations." In *Prehistoric Agriculture*, edited by Stuart Struener, pp. 22–49. New York: Natural History Press.

Bökönyi, Sandor

    1973   "Some Problems of Animal Domestication in the Middle East." In *Domestikationsforschung und Geschichte der Haustiere*, edited by J. Matolcsi, pp. 69–75. International Symposium in Budapest 1971. Budapest: Akadémiai Kiadó.

    1976   "Development of Early Stock Rearing in the Near East." *Nature* 264: 19–23.

    1977   *Animal Remains from the Kermanshah Valley, Iran*. British Archaeological Reports, Supplementary Series 34. Oxford: British Archaeological Reports.

Bottema, S., and Willem van Zeist

    1981   "Palynological Evidence for the Climatic History of the Near East, 50,000–6,000 B.P." In *Préhistoire du Levant*, edited by J. Cauvin and P. Sanlaville, pp. 111–32. Paris: Centre national de la recherche scientifique.

Braidwood, Linda S.; Robert J. Braidwood; Bruce Howe; Charles A. Reed; and Patty Jo Watson; editors

    1983   *Prehistoric Archeology along the Zagros Flanks*. Oriental Institute Publications 105. Chicago: The Oriental Institute.

Braidwood, Robert J.

    1967   *Prehistoric Man*. Second edition. Glenview: Scott Foresman.

Braidwood, Robert J., and Bruce Howe

    1960   *Prehistoric Investigations in Iraqi Kurdistan*. Studies in Ancient Oriental Civilization 31. Chicago: University of Chicago Press.

Braidwood, Robert J.; Bruce Howe; and Charles A. Reed

    1961   "The Iranian Prehistoric Project." *Science* 133: 2008–10.

Braidwood, Robert J.; Halet Çambel; W. Schirmer; et al.

    1981   "Beginnings of Village-Farming Communities in Southeastern Turkey: Çayönü Tepesi, 1978 and 1979." *Journal of Field Archaeology* 8: 249–58.

Briggs, John, and F. David Peat

    1989   *The Turbulent Mirror: An Illustrated Guide to Chaos Theory and the Science of Wholeness*. New York: Harper and Row.

British Naval Intelligence, Admirals Division

    1944   *Geography Handbook Series: Iraq*. London: British Naval Intelligence.

Broman Morales, Vivian

    1983   "Jarmo Figurines and Other Clay Objects." In *Prehistoric Archeology along the Zagros Flanks*, edited by Linda S. Braidwood, Robert J. Braidwood, Bruce Howe, Charles A. Reed, and Patty Jo Watson, pp. 369–424. Oriental Institute Publications 105. Chicago: The Oriental Institute.

    1990   *Figurines and Other Clay Objects from Sarab and Çayönü*. Oriental Institute Communications 25. Chicago: The Oriental Institute.

Cauvin, Jacques

    1979   "Les fouilles de Mureybet (1971–1974) et leur signification pour les origines de la sédentarisation au Proche-Orient." In *Archaeological Reports from the Tabqa Dam Project — Euphrates Valley, Syria*, edited by David Noel Freedman, pp. 19–48. Annual of the American Schools of Oriental Research 44. New Haven: American Schools of Oriental Research.

Chase, P. G., and R. A. Hagaman

    1986   "Minimum Number of Individuals and Its Alternatives: A Probability Theory Perspective." *Ossa* 13: 75–86.

Coveney, Peter, and Roger Highfield

    1995   *Frontier of Complexity: The Search for Order in a Chaotic World*. New York: Fawcett Columbine.

Davidson, Iain

    1993   Review of *The Roots of Civilization: The Cognitive Beginnings of Man's First Art, Symbols and Notation*, by Alexander Marshack. *American Anthropologist* 95: 1027–28.

Delougaz, Pinhas, and Helene J. Kantor

    1996   *Chogha Mish: The First Five Seasons of Excavations, 1961–1971*. Edited by Abbas Alizadeh. Oriental Institute Publications 101. Chicago: The Oriental Institute.

Dittmann, Reinhard

    1984   *Eine Randebene des Zagros in der Frühzeit: Ergebnisse des Behbehan-Zuhreh Surveys*. Berliner Beiträge zum vorderen Orient 3. Berlin: Dietrich Reimer.

Dollfus, Geneviève

    1975   "Les fouilles à Djaffarabad de 1972 à 1974, Djaffarabad, périodes I et II." *Cahiers de la Délégation archéologique française en Iran* 5: 5–220.

    1978   "Djaffarabad, Djowi, Bendebal: Contribution à l'étude de la Susiane au Ve millénaire et au début du IVe millénaire." *Paléorient* 4: 141–68.

    1983   "Djowi et Bendebal, deux villages de la plaine centrale du Khuzistan (Iran), 5e millénaire avant J.-C. Travaux de 1975, 1977, 1978." *Cahiers de la Délégation archéologique française en Iran* 13: 17–285.

Driesch, Angela von den

    1976   *A Guide to the Measurement of Animal Bones from Archaeological Sites*. Peabody Museum Bulletin 1. Cambridge: Peabody Museum.

Forest, J.-D.

1991 "L'architecture de la phase de 'Oueili-Obeid 0: Travaux de 1983–1985." In *'Oueili: Trauvaux de 1985*, edited by Jean-Louis Huot, pp. 17–158. Éditions du Centre national de la recherche scientifique 89. Paris: Centre national de la recherche scientifique.

Fukai, Shinji; Kiyoharu Horiuchi; and Toshio Matsotani

1970 *Telul eth-Thalathat: The Excavation of Tell II*. Tokyo: Yamakama Publishing.

Ghirshman, Roman

1938 *Fouilles de Sialk près de Kashan,* Volume 1: *1933, 1934, 1937*. Paris: Musée du Louvre.

Gleick, James

1988 *Chaos: Making a New Science*. New York: Penguin Books.

Goodwin, Brian, and Peter Saunders, editors

1989 *Theoretical Biology: Epigenetic and Evolutionary Order from Complex Systems*. Edinburgh: Edinburgh University Press.

Gould, Stephen J., and N. Eldredge

1977 "Punctuated Equilibria: The Tempo and Mode of Evolution Reconsidered." *Paleobiology* 3: 115–51.

Grayson, D. K.

1984 *Quantitative Zooarchaeology*. New York: Academic Press.

Hall, Nina, editor

1994 *Exploring Chaos: A Guide to the New Science of Disorder*. New York: W. W. Norton.

Hansman, John

1967 "Charax and the Karkheh." *Iranica Antiqua* 7: 21–58.

Harris, David R.

1989 "An Evolutionary Continuum of People-Plant Interaction." In *Foraging and Farming: The Evolution of Plant Exploitation,* edited by David R. Harris and Gordon C. Hillman, pp. 11–24. London: Unwin Hyman.

Harris, David R., and Gordon C. Hillman, editors

1989 *Foraging and Farming: The Evolution of Plant Exploitation*. London: Unwin Hyman.

Harris, Edward

1989 *Principles of Archaeological Stratigraphy*. New York: Academic Press.

Helbaek, Hans

1969 "Plant Collecting, Dry-farming, and Irrigation Agriculture in Prehistoric Deh Luran." In *Prehistory and Human Ecology of the Deh Luran Plain: An Early Village Sequence from Khuzistan, Iran,* edited by Frank Hole, Kent V. Flannery, and James A. Neely, pp. 383–428. Memoirs of the Museum of Anthropology 1. Ann Arbor: University of Michigan.

Henry, Donald O.

1989 *From Foraging to Agriculture: The Levant at the End of the Ice Age*. Philadelphia: University of Pennsylvania Press.

Hesse, Brian

1978 Evidence for Husbandry from the Early Neolithic Site of Ganj Dareh in Western Iran. Ph.D. dissertation, Columbia University.

Higgs, E. S., editor

1972 *Papers in Economic Prehistory: Studies by Members and Associates of the British Academy Major Research Project in the Early History of Agriculture*. Cambridge: Cambridge University Press.

Hillman, Gordon C.

1984 "Interpretation of Archaeological Plant Remains: The Application of Ethnographic Models from Turkey." In *Plants and Ancient Man*, edited by W. van Zeist and W. A. Casparie, pp. 1–41. Rotterdam: Alkema.

Hillman, Gordon C., and M. E. Davies

1990a "Domestication Rates in Wild-Type Wheats and Barley under Primitive Cultivation." *Biological Journal of the Linnaean Society* 39: 39–78.

1990b "Measured Domestication Rates in Wild Wheats and Barley under Primitive Condition, and Their Archaeological Implications." *Journal of World Prehistory* 4: 157–222.

Hilzheimer, M.

1941 *Animal Remains from Tell Asmar*. Studies in Ancient Oriental Civilization 20. Chicago: University of Chicago Press.

Hole, Frank

1974 "Tepe Tula'i, an Early Campsite in Khuzistan, Iran." *Paléorient* 2: 219–42.

1977 *Studies in the Archaeological History of the Deh Luran Plain: The Excavation of Chogha Sefid*. Memoirs of the Museum of Anthropology 9. Ann Arbor: University of Michigan.

1983 "Symbols of Religion and Social Organization at Susa." In *The Hilly Flanks and Beyond: Essays on the Prehistory of Southwestern Asia Presented to Robert J. Braidwood, November 15, 1982*, edited by T. Cuyler Young, Jr., Philip E. L. Smith, and Peder Mortensen, pp. 315–34. Studies in Ancient Oriental Civilization 36. Chicago: The Oriental Institute.

1987 *The Archaeology of Western Iran: Settlement and Society from Prehistory to the Islamic Conquest*. Edited by Frank Hole. Smithsonian Series in Archaeological Inquiry. Washington, D.C.: Smithsonian Institution Press.

1999 "Revisiting the Neolithic." In *The Iranian World: Essays on Iranian Art and Archaeology Presented to Ezat O. Negahban,* edited by Abbas Alizadeh, Y. Majidzadeh, and S. Malek Shahmirzadi, pp. 13–27. Tehran: Iran University Press.

Hole, Frank; Kent V. Flannery; and James Neely

1969 *Prehistory and Human Ecology of the Deh Luran Plain*. Memoirs of the Museum of Anthropology 1. Ann Arbor: University of Michigan.

Hopf, Maria

    1969   "Plant Remains and Early Farming in Jericho." In *The Domestication and Exploitation of Plants and Animals*, edited by Peter J. Ucko and Geoffrey W. Dimbleby, pp. 355–59. London: Duckworth.

Horgan, John

    1997   *The End of Science*. New York: Broadway Books.

Howe, Bruce

    1983   "Karim Shahir." In *Prehistoric Archeology Along the Zagros Flanks*, edited by Linda S. Braidwood, Robert J. Braidwood, Bruce Howe, Charles A. Reed, and Patty Jo Watson, pp. 23–154. Oriental Institute Publications 105. Chicago: The Oriental Institute.

Jarman, H. N.

    1972   "The Origins of Wheat and Barley Cultivation." In *Papers in Economic Prehistory: Studies by Members and Associates of the British Academy Major Research Project in the Early History of Agriculture*, edited by E. S. Higgs, pp. 15–26. Cambridge: Cambridge University Press.

Jarman, M. R., and P. F. Wilkinson

    1972   "Criteria of Animal Domestication." In *Papers in Economic Prehistory: Studies by Members and Associates of the British Academy Major Research Project in the Early History of Agriculture*, edited by E. S. Higgs, pp. 83–96. Cambridge: Cambridge University Press.

Johnson, George

    1996   *Fire in the Mind: Science, Faith, and the Search for Order*. New York: Vintage Books.

Kaboli, Mir Abedin

    2000   *Archaeological Survey in Qomrud*. Tehran: Iranian Cultural Heritage Organization.

Kempisti, Andrzej

    1990   "Relics of Architecture." In *Nemrik 9: Pre-Pottery Neolithic Site in Iraq (General Report, Seasons 1985–1986)*, edited by Stefan K. Kozlowski, pp. 45–53. Wydawnictwa: University of Warsaw.

King, A. R.

    1973   Review of *The Roots of Civilization*, by Alexander Marshack. *American Anthropologist* 75: 1897–1900.

Kirkby, Michael J.

    1977   "Land and Water Resources of the Deh Luran and Khuzistan Plains." In *Studies in the Archaeological History of the Deh Luran Plain*, edited by Frank Hole, pp. 251–88. Memoirs of the Museum of Anthropology 9. Ann Arbor: University of Michigan.

Kislev, Mordechai E.

    1989   "Pre-Domesticated Cereals in the Pre-Pottery Neolithic A Period." In *People and Culture Change*, edited by I. Hershkovitz, pp. 147–52. British Archaeological Reports, International Series 508. Oxford: British Archaeological Reports.

1992 "Agriculture in the Near East in the VIIth Millennium B.C." In *Préhistoire de l'agriculture*, edited by P. C. Anderson, pp. 87–93. Paris: Centre national de la recherche scientifique.

Kouchoukos, Nicholas

1998 Landscape and Social Change in Late Prehistoric Mesopotamia. Ph.D. dissertation, Yale University.

Kozlowski, Stefan K.

1990 *Nemrik 9: Pre-Pottery Neolithic Site in Iraq (General Report, Seasons 1985–1986)*. Wydawnictwa: University of Warsaw.

Kramer, Carol

1979 "An Archaeological View of a Contemporary Kurdish Village: Domestic Architecture, Household Size, and Wealth." In *Ethnoarchaeology: Implications of Ethnology for Archaeology*, edited by C. Kramer, pp. 139–63. New York: Columbia University Press.

1983 "Spatial Organization in Contemporary Southwest Asian Villages and Archaeological Sampling." In *The Hilly Flanks and Beyond: Essays on the Prehistory of Southwestern Asia Presented to Robert J. Braidwood, November 15, 1982*, edited by T. Cuyler Young, Jr., Philip E. L. Smith, and Peder Mortensen, pp. 347–68. Studies in Ancient Oriental Civilization 36. Chicago: The Oriental Institute.

Le Breton, Louis

1947 "Note sur la céramique peinte aux environs de Suse et à Suse." In *Archéologie susienne*, by R. de Mecquenem, Louis Le Breton, and M. Rutten, pp. 120–219. Mémoires de la Mission archéologique en Iran 30. Paris: Presses Universitaires de France.

Lees, G. M., and N. L. Falcon

1952 "The Geographic History of the Mesopotamian Plains." *Geographical Journal* 118: 24–39.

Legge, A. J.

1975 "Appendix B. The Fauna of Tell Abu Hureyra: Preliminary Analysis." *Proceedings of the Prehistoric Society* 41: 74–77.

Lorenz, Edward

1993 *The Essence of Chaos*. Seattle: University of Washington Press.

Masson, Vadim Mikhailovich, and Victor Ivanovich Sarianidi

1972 *Central Asia: Turkmenia before the Achaemenids*. Ancient Peoples and Places 79. New York: Praeger.

Malek-Shahmirzadi, Sadegh

1977 Tepe Zagheh: A Sixth Millennium B.C. Village in the Qazvin Plain of the Central Iranian Plateau. Ph.D. dissertation, University of Pennsylvania, Philadelphia.

1980 "Tepe Zaghe and the Problem of the Fugitive Painted Pottery." *Survey and Excavations* 3: 13–21.

2002 *The Ziggurat of Sialk: Report* No. 1. Tehran: Iranian Cultural Heritage Organization.

Marshack, Alexander

- 1972a *The Roots of Civilization: The Cognitive Beginnings of Man's First Art, Symbol and Notation.* New York: McGraw-Hill.
- 1972b "Upper Paleolithic Notation and Symbol." *Science* 178: 817–28.

Masuda, Seiichi

- 1972 "Excavations at Tappeh Sang-e Chakhmaq." In *Proceedings of the First Annual Symposium on Archaeological Research in Iran,* edited by F. Bagherzadeh, pp. 1–5. Tehran: Iran Bastan Museum.
- 1974 "Excavations at Tappeh Sang-e Chakhmaq." In *Proceedings of the Second Annual Symposium on Archaeological Research in Iran,* edited by F. Bagherzadeh, pp. 23–33. Tehran: Iran Bastan Museum.

McCorriston, Joy, and Frank Hole

- 1991 "The Ecology of Seasonal Stress and the Origins of Agriculture in the Near East." *American Anthropologist* 93: 46–69.

Mellaart, James

- 1987 "Common Sense vs. Old fashioned Theory in the Interpretation of the Cultural Development of the Ancient Near East." In *Studies in the Neolithic and Urban Revolutions: The V. Gordon Childe Colloquium,* edited by Linda Manzanilla, pp. 261–70. British Archaeological Reports, International Series 349. Oxford: British Archaeological Reports.

Miller, Naomi F.

- 1996 "Seed-Eaters of the Ancient Near East: Human or Herbivore." *Current Anthropology* 37: 521–28.
- 1997 "Farming and Herding Along the Euphrates: Environmental Constraint and Cultural Choice (Fourth to Second Millennia B.C.)." In *Subsistence and Settlement in a Marginal Environment,* edited by Richard L. Zettler, pp. 123–32. Museum Applied Science Center for Archaeology, Research Papers in Science and Archaeology 14. Philadelphia: University of Pennsylvania.

Moore, A. M. T.

- 1975 "The Excavations of Abu Hureyra in Syria: A Preliminary Report." *Proceedings of the Prehistoric Society* 41: 50–77.

Moore, A. M. T., and Gordon C. Hillman

- 1992 "The Pleistocene to Holocene Transition and Human Economy in Southwest Asia: The Impact of the Younger Dryas." *American Antiquity* 57: 482–94.

Negahban, Ezat O.

- 1973 "Preliminary Report of the Excavation of Sagzabad." *Marlik* 1: 1–9.
- 1977 "Preliminary Report of Qazvin Expedition: Excavations at Zaghe, Qabrestan, and Sagzabad 1971–72." *Marlik* 2: 26–44.

Oates, Joan

- 1969 "Choga Mami 1967–68: A Preliminary Report." *Iraq* 31: 115–52.

1978 "Ubaid Mesopotamia and Its Relation to Gulf Countries." In *Qatar Archaeological Report: Excavations 1973*, edited by Beatrice de Cardi, pp. 39–52. Oxford: Oxford University Press.

Oates, Joan; T. E. Davidson; D. Kamilli; and H. McKerrell

1977 "Seafaring Merchants of Ur?" *Antiquity* 51: 221–34.

Oberlander, Theodor M.

1968 "Hydrology." In *The Cambridge History of Iran: The Land of Iran*, Volume 1, edited by William B. Fisher, pp. 264–79. Cambridge: Cambridge University Press.

Pabot, H.

1961 *The Native Vegetation and Its Ecology in the Khuzistan River Basins.* Khuzistan Development Service, Ahwaz, Iran. (Mimeographed)

Pollock, Susan

1983 "Style and Information: An Analysis of Susiana Ceramics." *Journal of Anthropological Archaeology* 2: 354–90.

Price, Theron Douglas, and Birgitte Gebauer, editors

1995 *Last Hunters, First Farmers: New Perspectives on the Prehistoric Transition to Agriculture.* Santa Fe: School of American Research Press.

Redding, Richard W., Jr.

1981 Decision Making in Subsistence Herding of Sheep and Goats in the Middle East. Ph.D. dissertation, University of Michigan.

1984 "Theoretical Determinants of a Herder's Decisions: Modeling Variation in the Sheep/Goat Ratio." In *Animals and Archaeology: Early Herders and Their Flocks*, edited by J. Clutton-Brock and C. Grigson, pp. 161–70. British Archaeological Reports, International Series 202. Oxford: British Archaeological Reports.

1991 "The Role of the Pig in the Subsistence System of Ancient Egypt: A Parable on the Potential of Faunal Data." In *Animal Use and Culture Change*, edited by P. J. Crabtree and K. Ryan, pp. 20–30. Museum Applied Science Center for Archaeology, Research Papers in Science and Archaeology, Supplement to Volume 8. Philadelphia: University of Pennsylvania.

Reed, Charles A.

1983 "Archeozoological Studies in the Near East: A Short History (1960–1980)." In *Prehistoric Archeology Along the Zagros Flanks*, edited by Linda S. Braidwood, Robert J. Braidwood, Bruce Howe, Charles A. Reed, and Patty Jo Watson, pp. 511–36. Oriental Institute Publications 105. Chicago: The Oriental Institute.

Ringrose, T. J.

1993 "Bone Counts and Statistics: A Critique." *Journal of Archaeological Science* 20: 121–57.

Rosen, Arlene Miller, and S. Weiner

1994 "Identifying Ancient Irrigation: A New Method Using Opaline Phytoliths from Emmer Wheat." *Journal of Archaeological Science* 21: 132–35.

Rosenfeld, André

1971   Review of *Notation dans les gravures du paléolithique supérieur*, by Alexander Marshack. *Antiquity* 45: 317–19.

Ruelle, David

1991   *Chance and Chaos*. Princeton: Princeton University Press.

Safar, Fuad; Mohammad Ali Mustafa; and Seton Lloyd

1981   *Eridu*. Baghdad: Ministry of Culture.

Schmandt-Besserat, Denise

1974   "The Use of Clay Before Pottery in the Zagros." *Expedition* 16: 11–17.

1977a   "An Archaic Recording System and the Origin of Writing." *Syro-Mesopotamian Studies* 1: 1–32.

1977b   "The Beginnings of the Use of Clay in Turkey." *Anatolian Studies* 27: 133–50.

1978   "The Earliest Precursor of Writing." *Scientific American* 238: 50–59.

1992   *Before Writing: From Counting to Cuneiform*. Two volumes. Austin: University of Texas.

Schwanitz, F.

1966   *The Origin of Cultivated Plants*. English edition. Cambridge: Harvard University Press.

Shimabuku, Daniel M.

1996   "The Ground Stone Tools from Chogha Mish." In *Chogha Mish: The First Five Seasons of Excavations, 1961–1971*, by Pinhas Delougaz and Helene J. Kantor (edited by Abbas Alizadeh), pp. 261–78. Oriental Institute Publications 101. Chicago: The Oriental Institute.

Shroeder, J. W.

1953   *Interim Report to the Government of Iran on the Geology of the Karkheh River Basin*. Rome: Food and Agricultural Organization of the United Nations.

Smith, Philip E. L.

1968   "Ganj Dareh Tepe." *Iran* 6: 158–60.

1972a   "Ganj Dareh Tepe." *Iran* 10: 165–68.

1972b   "Prehistoric Excavations at Ganj Dareh Tepe in 1967." In *The Memorial Volume of the Vth International Congress of Iranian Art and Archaeology*, Volume 1 (Tehran-Isfahan-Shiraz, 11th–18th April 1968), edited by Firuz Bagherzadeh, pp. 183–93. Tehran: Ministry of Culture and Arts.

1974   "Ganj Dareh Tepe." *Paléorient* 2: 207–09.

1975   "Ganj Dareh Tepe." *Iran* 13: 178–80.

1976   "Reflections on Four Seasons of Excavations at Tappeh Ganj Dareh." *Proceedings of the Fourth Annual Symposium on Archaeological Research in Iran*, edited by Firuz Bagherzadeh, pp. 11–23. Tehran: Iran Bastan Museum.

Stampfli, Hans R.

    1983   "The Fauna of Jarmo, with Notes on Animal Bones from Matarrah, the 'Amuq and Karim Shahir." In *Prehistoric Archeology along the Zagros Flanks*, edited by Linda S. Braidwood, Robert J. Braidwood, Bruce Howe, Charles A. Reed, and Patty Jo Watson, pp. 431–84. Oriental Institute Publications 105. Chicago: The Oriental Institute.

Stewart, Ian

    1995   *Nature's Numbers: The Unreal Reality of Mathematics*. New York: Basic Books.

Stout, Margaret E.

    1977   "Clay Sling-Bullets from Tell Sweyhat." *Levant* 9: 63–65.

Vanden Berghe, Louis

    1970   "La nécropole de Kalleh Nisar." *Archéologia* 32: 64–73.

    1973   "Le Luristan avant l'âge du bronze: La nécropole de Hakalan." *Archéologia* 57: 49–58.

    1987   "Luristan, Pusht-i-Kuh au chalcolithique moyen (les nécropoles de Parchinah et Hakalan)." In *Préhistoire de la mésopotamie: La mésopotamie préhistorique et l'exploration récente du djebel Hamrin,* edited by J.-L. Huot, pp. 91–126. Paris: Éditions du Centre national de la recherche scientifique.

Voigt, Mary

    1983   *Hajji Firuz Tepe, Iran: The Neolithic Settlement*. University Museum Monograph 50. Philadelphia: The University Museum, University of Pennsylvania.

Watson, Patty Jo

    1979   *Archaeological Ethnography in Western Iran*. Viking Fund Publications in Anthropology 57. Tucson: University of Arizona Press.

Weiss, Harvey

    1976   Ceramics for Chronology: Discriminant and Cluster Analyses of Fifth Millennium Ceramic Assemblages from Qabr Sheykheyn, Khuzistan. Ph.D. dissertation, University of Pennsylvania.

Wilkinson, Tony J.; Belinda H. Monahan; and David J. Tucker

    1996   "Khanijdal East: A Small Ubaid Site in Northern Iraq." *Iraq* 58: 17–50.

Wright, Henry T.; Naomi F. Miller; and Richard W. Redding

    1980   "Time and Process in an Uruk Rural Center." In *L'archéologie de l'Iraq: Perspectives et limites de l'interprétation anthroplogique des documents*, edited by Marie-Thérèse Barrelet, pp. 265–84. Colloques internationaux du Centre national de la recherche 580. Paris: Centre national de la recherche scientifique.

Wright, Henry T.; Richard W. Redding; and Susan M. Pollock

    1989   "Monitoring Interannual Variability: An Example from the Period of Early State Development in Southwestern Iran." In *Bad Year Economics*, edited by P. Halstead and J. O'Shea, pp. 106–13. Cambridge: Cambridge University Press.

Wright, Herbert E., Jr.

> 1983 "Climatic Change in the Zagros Mountains — Revisited." In *Prehistoric Archeology along the Zagros Flanks*, edited by Linda S. Braidwood, Robert J. Braidwood, Bruce Howe, Charles A. Reed, and Patty Jo Watson, pp. 369–424. Oriental Institute Publications 105. Chicago: The Oriental Institute.

Zeist, Willem van

> 1967 "Late Quaternary Vegetation History of Western Iran." *Review of Palaeobotany and Palynology* 2: 301–11.

> 1970 "The Oriental Institute Excavations at Mureybit, Syria: Preliminary Report on the 1965 Campaign, Part 3: The Paleobotany." *Journal of Near Eastern Studies* 29: 167–76.

> 1988 "Some Aspects of Early Neolithic Plant Husbandry in the Near East." *Anatolica* 15: 49–68.

Zeist, Willem van, and Johanna Bakker-Heeres

> 1979 "Some Economic and Ecological Aspects of the Plant Husbandry of Tell Aswad." *Paléorient* 5: 161–69.

> 1982 "Archaeobotanical Studies in the Levant, 1. Neolithic Sites in the Damascus Basin: Aswad, Ghoraifé, Ramad." *Palaeohistoria* 24: 165–256.

Zeist, Willem van, and Gerrit Jan de Roller

> 1991/92 "The Plant Husbandry of Aceramic Çayönü, Southeast Turkey." *Palaeohistoria* 33/34: 65–96.

Ziegler, Charlotte

> 1953 *Die Keramik von der Qal'a des Hajji Mohammed*. Ausgrabungen der Deutschen Forschungsgemeinschaft in Uruk-Warka 5. Berlin: Verlag Gebr. Mann.

Zohary, Daniel

> 1989 "Domestication of the Southwest Asian Neolithic Crop Assemblage of Cereals, Pulses and Flax: The Evidence from the Living Plants." In *Foraging and Farming: The Evolution of Plant Domestication*, edited by David R. Harris and Gordon Hillman, pp. 358–73. London: Unwin Hyman.

> 1992 "Domestication of the Neolithic Near Eastern Crop Assemblage." In *Préhistoire de l'agriculture*, edited by P. C. Anderson, pp. 81–86. Paris: Centre national de la recherche scientifique.

Zohary, Daniel, and Maria Hopf

> 1988 *Domestication of Plants in the Old World*. Oxford: Clarendon Press.

> 1993 *Domestication of Plants in the Old World*. Second edition. Oxford: Clarendon Press.

Zohary, Michael

> 1963 "On the Geobotanical Structure of Iran." *Bulletin of the Research Council, Israel, Supplement* 11: 1–113.

> 1973 "Man and Plants through the Ages." In *Geobotanical Foundations of the Middle East*, Volume 2, edited by Michael Zohary, pp. 608–54. Stuttgart: Gustav Fischer Verlag.

PREFACE

The Oriental Institute excavations at Chogha Mish not only provided a long, uninterrupted sequence of prehistoric Susiana, they also yielded evidence of cultures much earlier than what had been previously known, pushing back the date of human occupation on the plain by at least one millennium. The discovery of the Archaic Susiana period with its distinct repertoire of ceramics, objects, and architecture shed considerable light on the evolution of human societies in southwestern Iran. The sophistication of the artifacts and architecture of even the earliest phase of the Archaic period showed that there must have been a stage of cultural development antecedent to the successful adaptation to and adoption of village life in southwestern Iran, but surveys and excavations had failed to reveal one.

It was not until 1976 that evidence for an earlier, formative stage of the Archaic Susiana period was accidentally discovered. In that year, news of the destruction of a small mound, some six kilometers to the west of Chogha Mish, reached Helene Kantor, who was at that time working at Chogha Mish. Always a passionate guardian of archaeological sites and monuments, Kantor rushed to the site to see a bulldozer razing it to the ground. Overcoming the resistance of the bulldozer operator, she valiantly stopped further destruction of the mound, two meters of which had already been removed in an attempt to level the plain for a multimillion dollar agribusiness project. Knowing that the destruction would resume as soon as she left the site, Kantor contacted some government officials in Tehran and received a permit to conduct a salvage operation at the site. That site is Chogha Bonut, which was destined to make a major contribution to the prehistoric sequence of Susiana, thereby increasing our knowledge of the formative stages of the village life in southwestern Iran.

Kantor worked at Chogha Bonut for two seasons. The 1976/77 season was primarily devoted to clearing the destruction debris and salvaging whatever had been removed by the bulldozer, and to preparing the site for excavation. Systematic work began in 1977/78, when solid evidence for the initial stages of village life in Susiana was recovered. The results of the second season of excavations at Chogha Bonut were so promising that there was no question as to the continuation of the project.

In the chaos that ensued the 1979 revolution in Iran, all archaeological activities in Iran were indefinitely interrupted and most of the documents and archaeological materials from Chogha Bonut and Chogha Mish that were kept in the archives of the dig house at the small village of Qaleh Khalil, between Chogha Bonut and Chogha Mish, either were destroyed or have disappeared. The difficulty in working with incomplete and fragmentary records imposed severe limitations on a coherent presentation of the materials excavated by Kantor. Nevertheless, in the present publication I have made use of the partial records, photographs, and drawings to reconstruct and interpret the two periods, the Archaic Susiana and Middle Susiana, that are not the focus of my own investigations of Chogha Bonut.

The materials from both the Archaic and Middle Susiana periods are briefly dealt with here for two reasons. First, both periods are well known and documented at Chogha Mish and are published in great detail (Delougaz and Kantor 1996), and therefore extensive treatment of the materials in this volume would be redundant. Second, in the absence of pertinent data, and despite the clear differences between the overall architectural plans of the Archaic and Middle Susiana settlements at Chogha Bonut and Chogha Mish, it is impossible to speculate about any specific aspects of these two settlements. Therefore, the sections on the Archaic Susiana 0 and Middle Susiana must be viewed with this caveat in mind.

During the 1977/78 season the Oriental Institute of the University of Chicago was the sole sponsor of the Chogha Mish project. The representative of the Iranian Center for Archaeological Research, now the Iranian Cultural Heritage Organization, was Miss Fatemeh Pajuhandeh. Other staff members were Dr. Guillermo Algaze, Miss Mansureh Niamir, and Mr. James Simon, archaeologists; Mrs. Diana Olson-Rasche, photographer; and Dr. W. Raymond Johnson, artist. During the Nawrouz holiday, the excavations were augmented by Dr. Yousef Majidzadeh of Tehran University and Dr. Robert Gordon of Damavand College, Tehran.

When in 1993 I was assigned to the task of completing Kantor's monumental volume (co-authored by Pinhas Delougaz) on the excavations at Chogha Mish, I became intrigued by and much interested in the earliest stage of cultural development in southwestern Iran. From Kantor's short reports and private discussions, I knew that Chogha Bonut was a potentially promising site to address the issue of the initial colonization of the Susiana plain. That possibility was too important to ignore, and the only way to find out was to excavate the site again since almost all the materials from the two seasons of excavation at the site in the 1970s are either missing or destroyed.

Several years after the Iranian revolution, some sporadic archaeological activities, primarily rescue operations, were conducted exclusively by the Iranian archaeologists of the Iranian Cultural Heritage Organization (ICHO). Even Tehran University's Department of Archaeology and Institute of Archaeology were not able to obtain a permit to resume their annual field classes in the Qazvin plain. Under these conditions, there seemed to be no hope for an academic staff of an American university to secure a permit and initiate archaeological investigation in Iran, but I applied, nevertheless. When in 1994 I was informed that I would be allowed to conduct an archaeological survey in the summer pasture of the nomadic Qashqaii tribe in northwestern Fars, I became hopeful that I could convince the authorities of the importance of Chogha Bonut and persuade them to allow me to examine the site.

From Kantor's report, I knew Chogha Bonut displayed what she called the "Formative" stage of the lowland Susiana phase, and that the site could contain an even earlier aceramic phase of the early occupation of Susiana in the eighth millennium B.C. The excavation was conducted with the hope of substantiating Kantor's claim and thereby increasing our understanding of the processes of the initial colonization of lowland Susiana. Thus, the focus of this report is primarily on Aceramic and Formative aspects of Susiana; while the material from the Middle Susiana period at Chogha Bonut has been included to provide additional evidence to the already massive database from this period (for detailed analyses, see, e.g., Alizadeh 1992; Delougaz and Kantor 1996; Dollfus 1975, 1978, 1983; Hole 1977, 1987; Hole, Flannery, and Neely 1969).

With the kind and enthusiastic support of Mr. Seraj al-Din Kazerouni, the then Director of the ICHO and his Research Deputy, Mr. Jalil Golshan, I was able to obtain a permit to excavate Chogha Bonut on behalf of the Oriental Institute and the ICHO in September and October 1996. Mr. Naser Noruzzadeh-Chegini, the Director of Archaeological activities at the ICHO, was instrumental in the process of securing the dig permit and in obtaining permission to ship to the States fauna and flora samples for analysis.

To accommodate the ICHO's desire for training students of archaeology and some of its representatives, save for a few occasions, we did not hire local workers. I had with me Messrs. Abbas Moqadam, Gabriel Nokandeh, Hamidreza Tabrizian, and Farhad Jafary, four talented and enthusiastic graduate students of archaeology at Tehran University. The ICHO representatives were Messrs. Hasan Rezvani, Bahman Kargar, Behrouz Omrani, and Farukh-Ahmadi (pl. 1:A). I owe a debt of gratitude to all these individuals, particularly to Mr. Rezvani, a seasoned archaeologist, for the smooth operation of the dig.

In addition to the individuals just mentioned, a number of others were instrumental in the operation of the dig. Professor Sadeq Malek-Shahmirzadi was always an inexhaustible source of encouragement and helped with the selection of the staff. Mr. Muhammad Tamadun, an avid amateur archaeologist and my former classmate at Tehran University, was instrumental in the preparation for the dig. My brother, Hasan Alizadeh, perhaps a frustrated archaeologist, participated in the first week of the operation and did much footwork in the preparation.

The enthusiasm of the local people was overwhelming. Haj Qapuni, the former worker and local guard at Chogha Mish, acted as our unofficial majordomo, visited us almost daily, and kept the crew happy with unlimited supply of watermelons, cucumbers, bread, and yogurt, and occasionally invited us over to have lunch with his large, extended family of settled Bakhtiari nomads (pl. 1:B). We were extremely sad to hear that he was killed in a car accident shortly after we left the field. The residents at the nearby village of Upper Bonut visited us daily and offered their help. Among them were three young boys who showed so much interest in our work and so much intelligence that they became unofficial members of the crew, giving us an extra hand in the excavation and in so many other intangible ways (pl. 1:C).

Mrs. Diana Olson-Rasche, the professional photographer of the 1977/78 season of excavations at Chogha Bonut, kindly printed *pro bono* the selected photographs from that season. Other photographs were taken by Mr. Farhad Jafari, a student member of the staff, and myself. I owe a debt of gratitude to all these individuals without whose help our project would not have been possible.

CHAPTER 1
INTRODUCTION
BACKGROUND OF CURRENT RESEARCH

The primary objective of the 1996 season of excavations at Chogha Bonut (3567695 N, 264950 E) was to investigate the problems of the initial colonization of lowland Susiana during the early Holocene period. The focus of this publication therefore is primarily to present and analyze the materials from the initial stages of occupation in Susiana. The theoretical significance of the project lies in the fact that the paradigm of the "hilly flanks" of the Fertile Crescent can no longer account for a number of recent archaeological discoveries in Syria, Jordan, and Anatolia. Briefly, the "hilly flanks" hypothesis proposes that evidence for the initial processes of domestication should be sought in the natural habitat of the early domesticates in the piedmont of the Zagros Mountains (Braidwood 1967; Braidwood and Howe 1960).

The last three decades of archaeological investigation in the ancient Near East have witnessed the discovery of an increasing number of year-round occupied large sites with no apparent morphological evidence of domesticated species, as well as sites with evidence of morphologically domesticated cereals and/or animals in regions not suspected to be the locus of the domestication of wheat, barley, sheep, and goats. As a result, it is becoming apparent that the "hilly flanks" hypothesis may no longer explain the processes of domestication of animals and plants and the adoption of sedentary village life in the ancient Near East. Combined recent archaeological and climatological evidence as well as improved techniques in radiocarbon dating have provided a large database that would allow processes of domestication of wild species of animals and cereals and sedentarization of human communities in the Near East to be better interpreted to include "anomalies" not fitting in the prevailing paradigm. The excavation of Chogha Bonut was undertaken in part to test the validity of the new emerging picture of the Neolithic Revolution in the Near East.

As mentioned above, we conducted excavations at Chogha Bonut primarily to study the early stages of village life in southwestern Iran. Nevertheless, we would feel remiss not to include the remnant of the materials from the Archaic and Middle Susiana periods that were excavated by Helene Kantor in 1978, particularly since chances of returning to the site for a thorough investigation of Chogha Bonut's later occupation are slim.

Chogha Bonut is to date the oldest lowland village in southwestern Iran (figs. 1–2). It is a small mound; in its truncated and artificially rounded state, it has a diameter of ca. 50 m and is about 5 m high (figs. 3–4; pl. 2:A–B). Chogha Bonut was first occupied sometime in the second half of the eighth millennium B.C., before the invention of pottery. The site continued to be occupied for much of the seventh millennium B.C., until the beginning of the Archaic period (the earliest period attested at Chogha Mish, some 6 km to the east), when it was deserted for at least one millennium. Then, sometime in the fifth millennium (Late Middle Susiana),[1] it was reoccupied and remained inhabited into the early fourth millennium (Late Susiana 2), when it was deserted once again.

I have argued elsewhere (Alizadeh 1992) that the change in the ceramic tradition of the Late Middle Susiana phase seems to coincide with, or was the result of, changes in settlement pattern and some regional developments. Chogha Bonut, perhaps a specialized center for manufacturing pottery and a satellite of the much larger site of Chogha Mish, seems to have suffered the same fate as did Chogha Mish, which as a regional center was abandoned after the conflagration of its "Burnt Building," marking the end of the Middle Susiana period. As at Chogha Mish, Chogha Bonut was resettled sometime during the Late Susiana 2 phase, when Susa had already been established as a regional center. Of Chogha Bonut's most recent occupation during the Late Susiana 2 phase, we have only a deep well (K10:202; fig. 6); the summit of the mound that may have contained architectural remains was removed by a bulldozer.

Evidence from archaeological surface surveys indicates that during the period between the desertion of Chogha Mish and Chogha Bonut and the founding of Susa, no one site attained, as far as size is concerned, a central position, as did Chogha Mish before and Susa later. Moreover, there was a slight decrease in the size of the regional population and a general tendency for the settlements to move to the west of the plain (Hole 1987, pp. 85–86; Alizadeh 1992).

---

1. For a detailed discussion on the subdivision of the Middle and Late Susiana periods into Early Middle Susiana, Late Middle Susiana, Late Susiana 1, and Late Susiana 2, see Alizadeh 1992, pp. 22–26, and Alizadeh in Delougaz and Kantor 1996, pp. xxiii–iv, 280–84, 298–300.

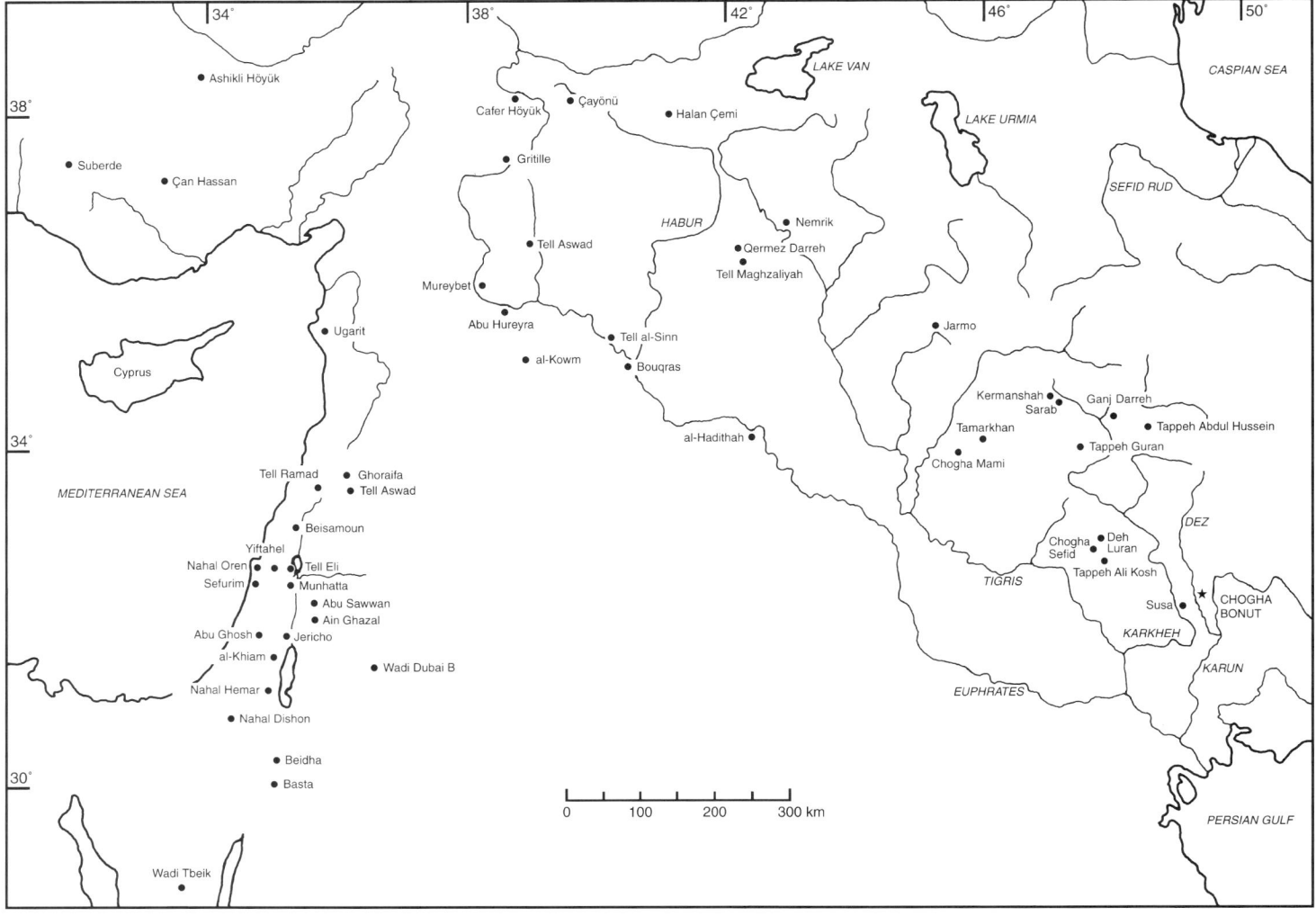

Figure 1. Selected Sites in the Ancient Near East

If, as I have argued elsewhere (Alizadeh 1992), we are justified in stretching the initial settlement of Susa earlier than usually accepted, then it is reasonable to suggest that when Chogha Mish was deserted following a regional upheaval, its inhabitants sought to resettle in a less volatile region away from the troubled area, and so founded Susa on the western part of the plain, soon, if not immediately, after they left Chogha Mish.[2] This suggestion also helps to explain the initial large size of Susa and its associated socio-economic eminence from the onset, a development that must have started prior to the founding of Susa, whether at Chogha Mish or at some as yet undiscovered site.

During the Early Middle Susiana phase, there was still an inter-regional pottery tradition since close parallels still existed between the ceramics of Susiana, Deh Luran (Khazineh phase; Hole 1977), and southern Mesopotamia (Ubaid 2/Haji Mohammad and Eridu XII–IX; Ziegler 1953; Safar, Mustafa, and Lloyd 1981). The Middle Susiana period was a time of population increase in southwestern Iran, as indicated by a number of regional surveys (Adams 1962; Dittmann 1984; Hole 1987; Alizadeh 1992). It was also a period of expansion/migration in Mesopotamia to more marginal regions, such as those along the Persian Gulf coast (Oates 1978; Oates et al. 1977). By the middle of the period, the number of sites reached a maximum. Chogha Mish grew to be the largest settlement and, perhaps as a consequence, Chogha Bonut was reoccupied, this time it seems as a center for manufacturing pottery.

The Middle Susiana period might have ended in violence, as suggested by the evidence of fire at Chogha Mish. This large Middle Susiana center, along with Chogha Bonut and some other contemporary sites, was abandoned, not to be re-occupied for perhaps several generations. Similar developments occurred in Deh Luran. Helbaek (1969, p. 364) used botanical analysis to look for environmental factors in the termination of the Bayat phase in Deh Luran. Helbaek postulates that millennia of land-use in the area had caused salinization which forced the population to search for new

---

2. This does not mean that in such an early stage of historical development only one site (Chogha Mish) dominated the whole plain of Susiana, although it may well have. There might have been other major Middle Susiana sites, as yet unexcavated, that were probably centers of local polities.

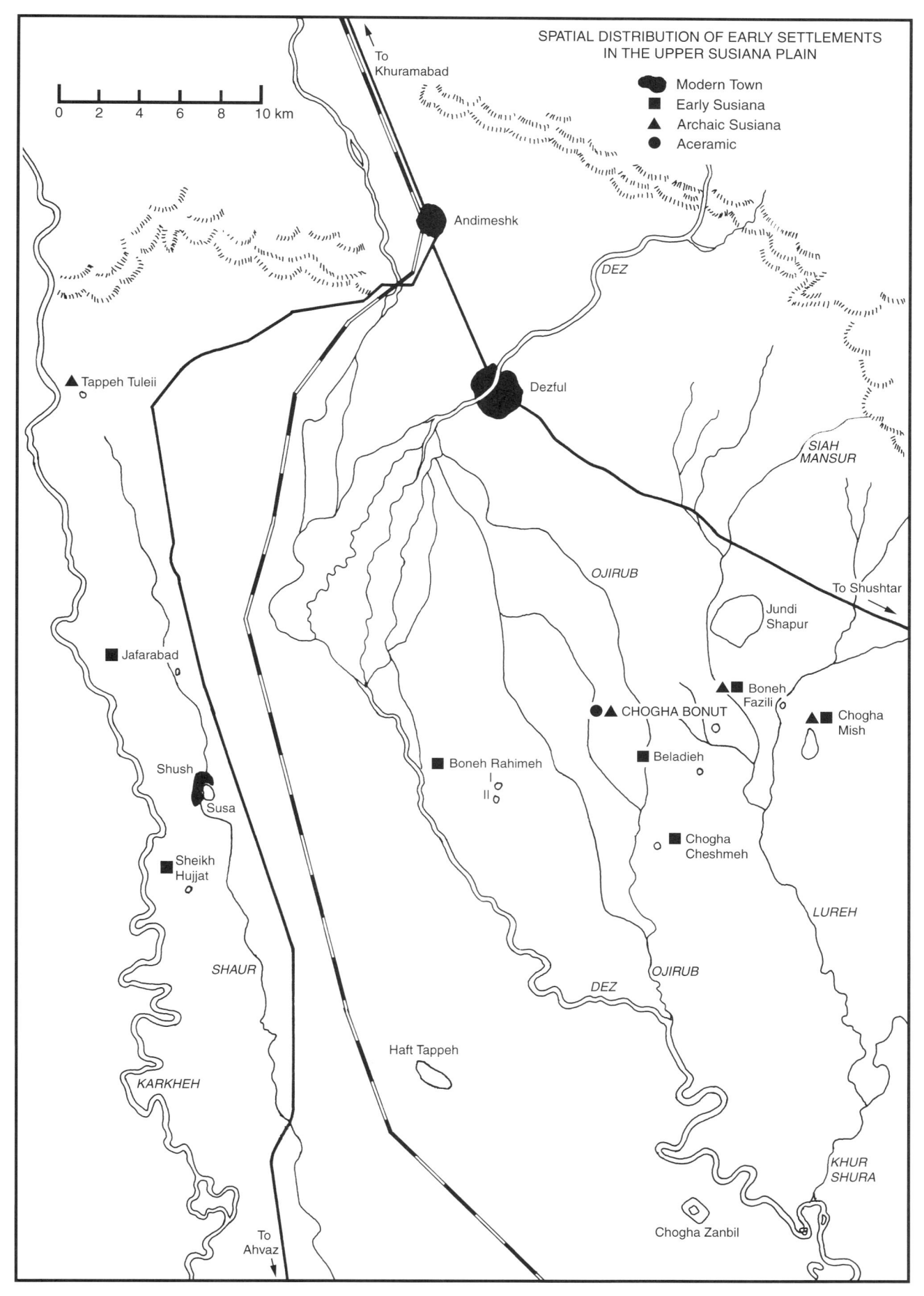

Figure 2. Map Showing the Location of Chogha Bonut in Susiana

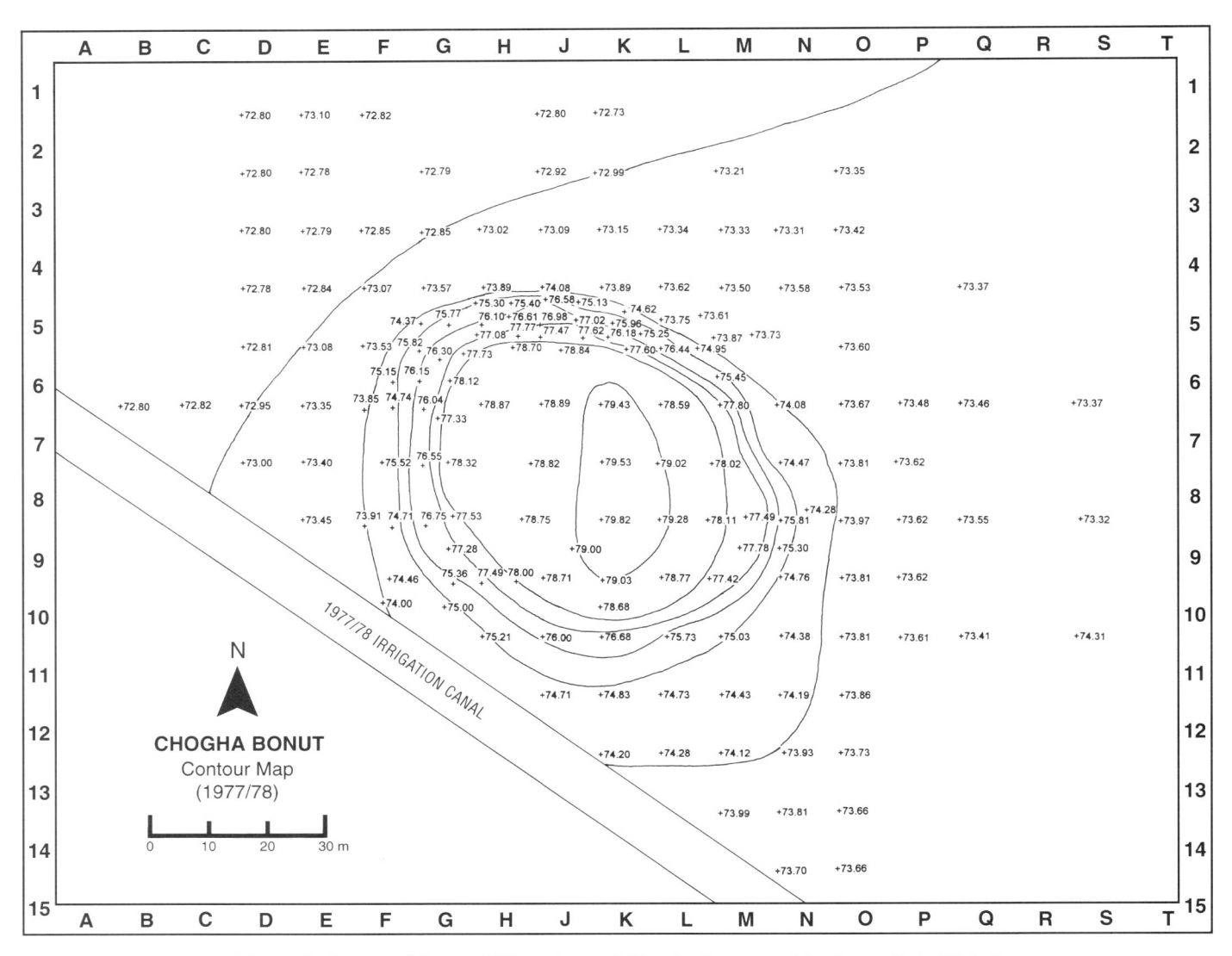

Figure 3. Contour Map and Elevations of Chogha Bonut and Its Immediate Vicinity

lands. Kirkby (1977, p. 255), however, argues that the plain was not subject to drastic salinization. Whatever the local causes for the desertion of some sites in the Susiana and Deh Luran plains, there must have been some inter-regional factors that contributed to such developments in the mid-fifth millennium in southwestern Iran.

Stylistic pottery changes indicate that by the end of the Middle Susiana period, the inter-regional contact between southwestern Iran and Mesopotamia ceased. There appears to have been a re-orientation in the inter-regional contact. The Late Susiana was a period of increasing contact with the resource-rich highland, as suggested by the general similarities among the regional ceramics of southwestern Iran. In fact, the dot motif, one of the most prominent diagnostics of the Late Susiana 1 pottery assemblage, has even been found in surveys around Qum (Kaboli 2000) and at Tappeh Sialk during the recent excavations by Malek-Shahmirzadi (2002).

A general westward shift of settlements in Susiana also occurred at the end of the Middle Susiana period. The large cemeteries of Hakalān and Parchineh in the Zagros Mountains appeared during this period (Vanden Berghe 1970, 1973, 1987). These cemeteries are not associated with any settlement and are located in areas unsuitable for grain agriculture, suggesting their use by prehistoric mobile pastoralists. Similar cemeteries of later historical periods in this region reinforce this attribution (Vanden Berghe 1973). It is, therefore, tempting to link the desertion of Chogha Bonut and Chogha Mish, the westward movement of the population in the lowland, the similarities among the regional ceramics in southwestern Iran, and the appearance of the isolated highland cemeteries to the crystallization of mobile pastoralist groups in southwestern Iran, ultimately leading to state societies there.[3] The presumed correlation between

---

3. The presumed westward shift of the Dez and Karkheh Rivers has also been considered as a major contributing factor in the taphonomy of the landscape in Susiana (Kouchoukos 1998).

the increased activities of mobile pastoralists and the westward shift of Susiana settlements becomes more plausible when we note that the eastern part of the Susiana plain traditionally has been, and still is, the locus of the winter pasture for the mobile pastoralists of the region. If this environmental niche was also used in antiquity, as one might expect, then the westward shift of Susiana settled communities could also indicate an increase in the activities of such mobile pastoralist groups in the area.

THE QUESTION OF THE ORIGINS OF DOMESTICATION IN IRAN

Except for Tappeh Ali Kosh, located in the Deh Luran plain north of Susiana, all aceramic Neolithic sites in Iran are situated in the Zagros Mountains. These early Neolithic sites are informative about the beginnings of village life in southwestern Iran, but unlike Chogha Bonut and Tappeh Ali Kosh, these early villages were located in the presumed natural habitat of the early domesticates and most were occupied presumably after the domestication[4] of some species of cereals and animals had already been well underway.

Before the 1996 investigations at the basal levels of Chogha Bonut, in the nearby Deh Luran plain Tappeh Ali Kosh was the earliest lowland village thought to have been established at or soon after the eve of animal and plant domestication. The location of Tappeh Ali Kosh was considered special because it lay outside of the presumed natural realm of the major domesticated species of wheat, barley, sheep, and goats and as such was taken as evidence for the early Holocene agricultural revolution. The assumption was that after initial steps toward domestication were taken in the highland, the presumed natural habitat of some species of plants and animals, population increase forced some communities to split and move to more marginal areas where their survival depended on an economic strategy of farming and herding animals mixed with hunting and gathering. Before discussing the characteristics of the early Neolithic settlement at Tappeh Ali Kosh, it is useful to discuss Ganj Darreh and Tappeh Asiab, the two early highland sites assumed to have been occupied at a time considered transitional between the collecting of food and the producing of it. In addition, it is also useful to discuss briefly the finds from the small mound of Tappeh Tuleii in northwestern Susiana.

GANJ DARREH

Ganj Darreh and Tappeh Asiab, both located in the Zagros Mountains at an elevation of ca. 1330–1350 m above sea level, are known to be the precursors of Tappeh Ali Kosh. The small mound of Ganj Darreh with an elevation of ca. 1350 m above sea level is located some 37 km from the provincial center of Kermanshah. Notwithstanding a single sherd (perhaps intrusive), the 0.5–1.0 m deposit of the lowest level (Level E), dated to ca. 8400 B.C., is aceramic (Smith 1968, 1972a, 1972b, 1974, 1975, 1976). As with Tappeh Asiab and Chogha Bonut, no architecture was found in this early level, but a number of fire pits, some containing fire-cracked rocks, were discovered. The lithic industry throughout the phase is indistinguishable, as at Tappeh Asiab, Chogha Bonut, and Tappeh Ali Kosh, and comparable to the lithic assemblages at these early sites. But unlike Tappeh Ali Kosh and perhaps Tappeh Asiab and Chogha Bonut, virtually no obsidian is reported. Simple lightly baked clay animal and human figurines found at Ganj Darreh are also common at all early Neolithic sites. No morphologically domestic species of animals were found at Ganj Darreh, but Brian Hesse (1978) argues for some kind of human control over sheep and goats. No information on Ganj Darreh flora is available.

TAPPEH ASIAB

Tappeh Asiab is an open-air site on the Qara Su River, 5 km east of Kermanshah. The 2.5–3.0 m of deposits consist of alternating layers of clay, stones, ashes, and a number of circular fire pits, some containing fire-cracked rocks. A large circular depression, presumed to have been a subterranean chamber and two burials, containing one flexed and one extended body covered with red ochre, were also found (Braidwood, Howe, and Reed 1961). The community that

---

4. Throughout this study "domestication" is defined not as the culmination of the processes that resulted in the inability of certain animals and plants to survive without human aid — a stage reflected in the morphological changes readily discernible by botanists and zoologists — but rather as the intensification of those processes prior to the universal appearance of morphologically domesticated species of plants and animals. For a detailed treatment of the subject, see Harris and Hillman 1989, pp. xxxi–7; Harris 1989.

frequented Tappeh Asiab hunted wild goats (presumably in the early stage of domestication; see Bökönyi 1973, 1976, 1977), sheep, pigs, cattle, gazelle, and onager; the fauna also include red deer, badger, red fox, hare, and birds. No information on the flora is available.

The lithic industry at Tappeh Asiab seems to be undifferentiated throughout the sequence. While microlith blades, bipolars, discoids, and amorphous blades as well as cores with single platform and pyramidal shapes are abundant, lunates, semilunates, and celts are absent. The few obsidian blades seem to be intrusive. Both animal and abstract human figurines are also reported. Objects traditionally considered ornaments are simple and rare.

TAPPEH ALI KOSH

Tappeh Ali Kosh is located in the Deh Luran plain northwest of Khuzestan. At an elevation of about 170 m above sea level, this mound lies at the foothills of the Zagros Mountains and is surrounded by the rivers of Dawairij and Meimeh and shallow marshes (Hole, Flannery, and Neely 1969). The entire deposit is divided into three stratigraphic zones (A–C), of which zones C–B (Buz Murdeh and Ali Kosh phases) are aceramic, and zone A (Mohammad Jaffar phase) yielded pottery.

The chipped stone industry, though richer than those reported from Tappeh Asiab, Ganj Darreh, and Chogha Bonut, exhibits similar conservatism observed at other early highland sites, as well as at Chogha Bonut. It consists of numerous micro-blades, double and single backed blades, notched blades, scrapers, and bullet-shaped flint cores. Grinding stones and querns are rare. As with the other sites, no celts are reported and no geometric microliths have been found. The numerous obsidian blades (347 pieces; Hole, Flannery, and Neely 1969, table 8) found at Tappeh Ali Kosh far exceed the few found at Chogha Bonut and Tappeh Asiab, a feature with possible chronological implications as obsidian blades become more frequent later in the Neolithic period.

Both animal and human figurines of slightly baked clay are reported from Tappeh Ali Kosh. The typical animal figurines and the highly abstract finger-shaped figurines from Tappeh Ali Kosh are also known from other early Neolithic sites of Chogha Bonut, Ganj Darreh, Tappeh Asiab, Sarab, and Jarmo, as are simple shell and bone personal ornaments. But the typical T-shaped figurines make their first appearance in the ceramic Mohammad Jaffar phase.

The early inhabitants of Tappeh Ali Kosh practiced a mixed economy of hunting-gathering and animal husbandry and farming. Domestic emmer wheat (*Triticum decoccum*), domestic einkorn (*T. monococcum*), wild einkorn (*T. boeticum*), wild two-row barley (*Hordeum spontaneum*), and domestic six-row barley (*H. vulgare* var. *nudum*) were among the identified flora. Domestic sheep and goats were in abundance. Also present were gazelle, onager, pig, gerbil, and birds.

The presence of architecture in the initial settlement (Buz Murdeh phase) suggested a permanent village in this early stage (Hole, Flannery, and Neely 1969, pp. 33–40, figs. 6–9). The building in the initial phase of occupation (Buz Murdeh phases C2 and C1) consisted of simple mudbricks measuring $15 \times 25 \times 5$–10 cm. But in the next phase of occupation (Ali Kosh phases B2 and B1), long, cigar-shaped mudbricks so typical of the Susiana Archaic period appear. This type of brick first appeared at Ganj Darreh Level D and Chogha Bonut Formative Susiana and continued throughout the Archaic Susiana period.[5]

The two early phases of occupation at Tappeh Ali Kosh (Buz Murdeh and Ali Kosh phases) are aceramic. As at Jarmo, pottery at Tappeh Ali Kosh appears suddenly in the Mohammad Jaffar phase in at least three categories: "Jaffar plain," "Jaffar painted," and "Khazineh red," a development that suggests pottery was introduced into the Deh Luran plain, most probably from Susiana. In addition, at Chogha Sefid (Hole 1977), some 13 km northwest of Tappeh Ali Kosh, another type of pottery, "Sefid red-on-cream" appears late in the Mohammad Jaffar phase. This pottery, known at Chogha Bonut as "maroon-on-cream" painted ware, is well attested in Susiana at Chogha Bonut, Chogha Mish, and Tappeh Tuleii, ca. 15 km south of Andimeshk (Hole 1974). This particular pottery class seems to have appeared earlier at Chogha Bonut than it did at Tappeh Ali Kosh because the painted burnished variant that gradually replaced maroon-on-cream at Chogha Bonut does not occur at Tappeh Ali Kosh, but it appears in abundance with a few pieces of the painted burnished variant ware at Chogha Sefid (Hole 1977, figs. 43–44, especially 44:bb).

---

5. The earliest examples of this type of mudbrick are reported from the basal levels of Tell el-'Oueili (Forest 1991, figs. 9, 15–16, 27, 30, 33, pls. 3–4) and somewhat later at Chogha Mami (Oates 1969, p. 116, pl. 22:c).

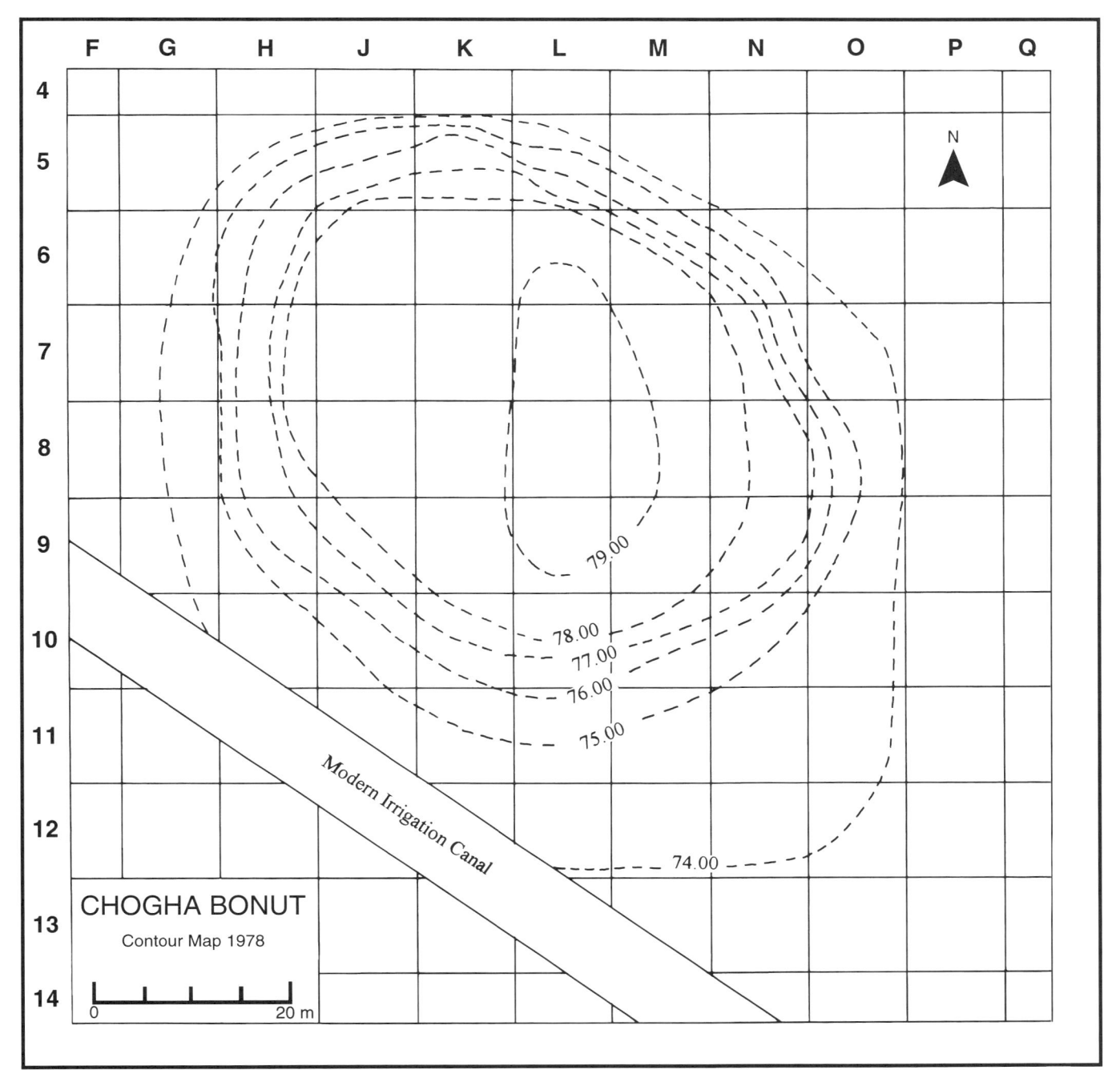

Figure 4. 1978 Contour Map of Chogha Bonut

TAPPEH TULEII

Tappeh Tuleii, situated in northwestern Khuzestan, almost halfway between Chogha Bonut and Tappeh Ali Kosh, is a small early Neolithic mound. Both spatially and chronologically, the site is situated almost halfway between Tappeh Ali Kosh and Chogha Bonut. Tappeh Tuleii (named after an edible tuber that grows on the site) was considered a campsite by the excavator (Hole 1974), though this is not certain.

Tappeh Tuleii was established after the processes of domestication were well underway. Judging from the pottery and other artifacts, the site could have been occupied soon after Chogha Bonut was deserted for the first time, and perhaps shortly before Chogha Mish was occupied. The pottery and other materials recovered from Tappeh Tuleii are unquestionably Susian and their closest parallels come from the Formative and Archaic 0 phases of Chogha Bonut and Chogha Mish, though the excavator has treated the material with Deh Luran in mind.

Aside from the animal and human T-shaped figurines, so typical of the Archaic period, three classes of painted pottery put the site in a transitional phase between the Formative and Archaic 0 phases as defined at Chogha Mish (Delougaz and Kantor 1996, pp. 227–47) and Chogha Bonut (see *Chapter 6*, below).

SUSIANA AND DEH LURAN IN THE EARLY NEOLITHIC PERIOD

Radiocarbon dates reported from the sites just discussed and similar sites in the highland put all the early Neolithic aceramic sites in western Iran within the 8000–7000 B.C. range. However, considering the problems with radiocarbon dates, these dates alone are not sufficient to be used as definite criteria to establish chronological priority of any of these early sites, even though some (Tappeh Asiab and Ganj Darreh) yielded morphologically wild species of the plants and animals that at Tappeh Ali Kosh and Chogha Bonut are considered morphologically domesticated and presumably later.

A comparative study of the materials and the sites just mentioned indicates that the economies of the chipped stone industry of the Susiana and Deh Luran aceramic phases seem almost identical and therefore not suitable for chronological studies. Nevertheless, as mentioned earlier, there are a number of elements that may put the initial phase of the occupation of Susiana earlier than that of Deh Luran.

The chronological position of the Chogha Bonut Aceramic period vis-à-vis the Buz Murdeh phase in Deh Luran has theoretical implications in terms of the occupation of the lowland on the eve of domestication. However, the paucity of excavated materials dating to the initial phases of the Neolithic prevents us from proposing a chronological framework without the use of radiocarbon dating. Nevertheless, comparative analyses of the pottery sequences from the early villages in Susiana and Deh Luran indicate that, at least in southwestern Iran, pottery manufacture began earlier in Susiana than it did in Deh Luran and continued to influence Deh Luran for several millennia. Moreover, the culture-specific T-shaped figurines, so characteristic of the early Neolithic sites in western southwestern Iran (Sarab, Chogha Bonut, Chogha Mish, Tappeh Ali Kosh) and northeastern Iraq (Jarmo), occur from the beginning of the occupation at Chogha Bonut but appear later in the Mohammad Jaffar phase at Tappeh Ali Kosh. Admittedly, such a conclusion is based on uncertain grounds. It is perfectly possible that Chogha Bonut and Tappeh Ali Kosh are contemporary, but given the present evidence from Chogha Bonut, it seems highly unlikely that Tappeh Ali Kosh, or any other early Neolithic sites in Iran (with the possible exception of Tappeh Asiab) would be earlier. The implication is that during the eighth millennium B.C., the environmental conditions were favorable in Iran (if not the whole Near East) to allow the establishment of early villages in a number of environmental niches suitable for the transition from collecting and hunting food to producing it.

The early ceramic assemblages as reported from Chogha Bonut, Chogha Mish, and Tappeh Tuleii consist of classes of pottery vessels with a number of distinct shapes and painted designs that seem to represent an unbroken and evolutionary sequence from the Formative to the Archaic Susiana 3 phase, during which the close-line ware, or the Chogha Mami Transitional ware as it is known in Deh Luran, was introduced in the sequence. Specific in the Susiana early pottery assemblage are the Formative maroon-on-cream painted ware, the Archaic Susiana 0 painted burnished variant ware, and the Archaic Susiana 1 painted-burnished ware. These wares are well attested at Chogha Bonut, Tappeh Tuleii, and Chogha Mish, but poorly represented in Deh Luran.

Environmental conditions suitable for practicing agriculture and animal husbandry are of course of great importance in the early stages of the development of domestication in the Near East. Iran, with its geographic features and a large number of different environmental niches, must have had a number of climates and cultural regions so prominent in the later Neolithic period. Unfortunately, comparatively little research in the late Pleistocene/early Holocene epoch climates has been conducted in Iran; and prior to the excavations at Chogha Bonut, the environmental and climatic conditions of the early Neolithic period in Susiana were extrapolated from the data pertinent to the Deh Luran region. Important additional evidence against the primacy of the highland in the initial phase of the Neolithic period comes from the results of the analysis of the flora (*Chapter 10*), phytoliths (*Chapter 11*), and fauna (*Chapter 12*) from Chogha Bonut. The results of these analyses indicate that in the eighth millennium B.C., Susiana was a rather wet grassland and perhaps contained a number of marshes with attending characteristic fauna and flora. This is expected since if the Younger Dryas climate event had any effects in southwestern Iran, it may have ushered in a warmer and wetter environment in the lowland, as suggested by the results of the analyses in *Chapters 10–12*.

DISCUSSION AND CONCLUSION

The results of the Deh Luran expedition not only raised this obscure region in southwestern Iran to an international status as the earliest locus of permanent villages in southwestern Iran, but they also provided convincing evidence for the proposed mechanism of domestication of plants and animals in the wider context of the Fertile Crescent. Since the publication of Tappeh Ali Kosh (Hole, Flannery, and Neely 1969) and the nearby site of Chogha Sefid (Hole 1977), the discovery of a number of sites in Syria, Jordan, and Anatolia, coupled with new technology in radiocarbon dating and insight from more reliable climatic studies, serious questions have been raised about the prevailing paradigm for the origins and dynamics involved in the processes of domestication and initial village life in the Near East (e.g., Moore et al. 2000; Cauvin 1977).

Paradigm shifts usually occur when a case is overstated and contradictory evidence accumulates. The more the position of Tappeh Ali Kosh and its predecessors (such as Jarmo and Ganj Darreh) was emphasized, the more sites were discovered in areas presumably unsuitable for the transition from hunting-gathering and incipient farming communities to fully sedentary farming villages. Most of these "white elephants" (to use Mellaart's [1987, p. 265] label for pieces of evidence that do not fit) are located in the Levant and Syria. Chogha Bonut with its early aceramic deposit is the only site so far known in southwestern Iran that can at least challenge the idea of a vertical highland-lowland progression and development of farming and animal husbandry and initial village life in southwestern Iran.

In science, technological advances and improvements often lead to new discoveries and improvement of knowledge whereby prevailing paradigms are challenged, leading to their refinement and/or replacement by new insights. Improvements in excavation techniques in the last three decades have resulted in relatively tremendous stratigraphic control of archaeological deposits. Controversies surrounding the relative reliability of radiocarbon dating and the circumstances involving various organic samples notwithstanding, improvements in radiocarbon analysis with the aid of accelerator mass spectrometry (AMS), scanning electron microscopy (SEM), and the techniques of wood cellulose and bone collagen extraction, as well as a number of other sophisticated techniques, have increased our ability to address questions of the origins of food-producing techniques and the development of village life in the Near East.

Thus, in searching for the origins of agriculture and domestication of animals, archaeologists have questioned the "hilly flanks" hypothesis (Binford 1971, for example). Some scholars, for example, believe that southwestern Iran, particularly the highland, was cold, dry, and mostly uninhabited between 11000 and 9000 B.C., and that the domestication of cereal grains took place not in the mid-altitude of the Zagros Mountains, but in the oases in the Levant, Jordan, and Syria (van Zeist 1988; Zohary 1989; Bar-Yosef and Meadow 1995; Moore et al. 2000). When this sudden spell of cold and dry weather (known as the Younger Dryas climate event, ca. 11,000–10,000 B.P.) gradually came to an end, the uninhabited regions of the Near East were colonized by groups of people who already were practicing a mixed economy of food producing and food gathering (Hole 1999; McCorriston and Hole 1991; Moore and Hillman 1992). If this were the case, then one would expect to find such sites in warmer, lower altitudes more suitable for practicing agriculture than in cooler, higher altitudes.

Some investigators have proposed that although the progenitors of the domesticated species of plants and animals ranged throughout the entire Fertile Crescent, only a small area known as the Levantine Corridor was the locus of domestication of cereals, and that it was from this area that agriculture spread to other parts of the Near East (Henry 1989; Hole 1999; Moore et al. 2000). This proposition is primarily based on pollen analysis, the evidence of the first appearance of morphologically domestic cereal grains, and the chronological primacy of the evidence as indicated by radiocarbon dating. Though this new proposition, which competes with the "hilly flanks" hypothesis, has improved our understanding of some of the processes that led to the development of agriculture and animal husbandry as a control mechanism over food supply, it need not be extended to the entire Near East as an explanation of the origins of agriculture.

Despite recent advances in the field, the dispute over the characteristics and attributes of the early domesticates is still alive,[6] and perhaps specialists can not reach a consensus unless the problem is addressed with a different approach. Although the presence of morphologically domestic cereal grains and animal skeletal remains obviously points to the genetic changes and mutation due to some control mechanism on the part of humans, the absence of such evidence is not synonymous with a hunting-gathering way of life. The chronological primacy of the evidence of plant domestication in the Levant and Syria is based on the interpretation of radiocarbon dating. To use radiocarbon determinations to anchor our discussions of chronological primacy of the processes of domestication in a given region, though useful in general, remains questionable until we can no longer arbitrarily discern such datings as either too young or too old (see Braidwood et al. 1983, pp. 12–13). Similarly, the presence of morphologically wild cereal grains and animal bones from post-Pleistocene sites in the Near East does not necessarily mean that the inhabitants of such sites did not practice animal husbandry and/or grain cultivation. Addressing this problem, Herbert Wright (1983, p. 508) argues against "any specula-

---

6. See Hillman and Davies 1990a; idem 1990b; Kislev 1989; idem 1992; Zohary 1992.

tion on the length of time required for genetic changes to be recorded in certain grain morphology."[7] The same is true about our reliance on the statistically derived conclusions based on the ratio of adult to immature animals, and the rate of genetic changes that occur in the process of animal domestication. Charles Reed (1983, p. 516) warns that "We do not know how many generations of animals have to be protected from natural selection before changing gene frequencies produce recognizably different phenotypes in the skeleton, but presumably the rate of morphological variation would be different for different species and certainly would vary relative to the kind and degree of control exerted upon the domesticates by the domesticators."[8]

In what is now considered by some scholars (e.g., Bar-Yosef and Meadow 1995; Henry 1989; Hole 1999) the center for domestication of cereals, there are a number of anomalies that are difficult to explain with the current hypothetical reconstructions of the events. While the inhabitants of Pre-pottery Neolithic B (PPNB) Mureybet practiced grain agriculture, no evidence of domesticated animals is reported from the site. Conversely, at the nearby contemporary Abu Hureyra we have evidence of domesticated species of sheep and goats (Legge 1975).[9] On the other hand, domestic cereals are reported to be present at Jericho (Hopf 1969), Nativ Hagdud (Bar-Yosef and Kislev 1989; Zohary and Hopf 1988), and Tell Aswad (van Zeist and Bakker-Heeres 1979), but the contemporary Pre-pottery Neolithic A (PPNA) Mureybet lacks any evidence of similar domestic cereals (McCorriston and Hole 1991, p. 51).

With all the archaeological evidence pertaining to the processes of domestication of certain species of plants and animals, our assumptions and hypotheses not withstanding, we would still be very hard pressed to point to a single region as the primary locus for the development of agriculture and animal husbandry. We may continue to be eluded as long as we think *a priori* that there was a *center* out of which the knowledge of domestication spread throughout the Near East. In fact the available evidence indicates that perhaps there were a number of loci in which domestication of plants and animals took place. A multi-center approach would be more consistent with the evidence because all the mobile inhabitants of the Upper Palaeolithic Near East had accumulated experiences and faced similar environmental factors that contributed to the domestication of plants and animals. Given the fact that hunting and gathering was the primary mode of subsistence for much of the history of the human species, such intimate knowledge of environment must have existed in the cultural traditions of the inhabitants of the ancient Near East for a long time. The same is true of the post-Pleistocene hunter-gatherers of the New World where domestication occurred independent of the Old World, indicating that domestication of plants and animals need not, of course, evolve around wheat, barley, sheep, goat, pigs, and all other early domesticates of the Near East or occur as a result of climatic changes alone since such changes occurred many times prior to the Upper Palaeolithic period. Whenever the exact time of such a momentous development, the universal occurrence of the strategic change from collecting food to producing it seems to have been an inevitable response to a myriad of conditions, some, if not most, of which may never be known to us.

The situation outlined above and the fact that a genuine transition site with attending indisputable transitional morphologies of the domesticated species of plants and animals on the eve of domestication still eludes us, it is warranted to look at the problem with a different approach from other disciplines.

The ideas in the fields of chaos and complexity, the maddeningly slippery nature of these concepts notwithstanding,[10] may be drawn upon to suggest that initial conditions in the processes of adopting agriculture and animal husbandry as a new way of life and economy need not be major, and thus easily detectable, particularly in archaeological records. This pessimism, if justified, has major consequences in our search for understanding the causes of domestication and in our attempt to reconstruct the processes through which it passed.

---

7. Schwanitz (1966) also notes "Do wild species, if they are grown by man, turn directly into cultivated plants? By no means. The plants remain wild plants even when they are grown under improved conditions of cultivation, showing better development and a higher yield than those plants gathered in the fields and forests. They still have not lost any of the properties that mark them as wild plants and have not yet taken on any characteristics that make them more useful or desirable than wild plants, and so they do not differ in any way from the wild form. They are as useful as gathered plants, but can in no way be considered true cultivated forms, for a genuine cultivated plant always differs from its wild ancestor in certain of its hereditary characters."

8. Stampfli (1983, p. 453) also expresses his concern with the difficulty of the objective assessment in the distinction between domestic and wild animals.

9. Explaining away such anomalies in terms of varied exploitation and local availability of resources (Bar-Yosef and Meadow 1995, p. 84) seems like adding Ptolemaic epicycles to a system.

10. So many scientists and journalists define chaos and complexity in so many different ways and in so many overlapping terms that the two have become virtually synonymous. Nevertheless, the term "edge of chaos" with which some scientists refer to complexity seems to be more descriptive if the end-product of a system is used as a general criterion, though there can be many more. For example, systems with high degrees of order and stability (such as crystals) produce nothing novel in terms of complexity; on the other hand, completely chaotic, aperiodic systems (such as turbulent fluids, hot gases) are too formless and are in the actual realm of chaos. Truly complex systems such as amoebas, stock markets, and socio-cultural systems

Human societies are, of course, complex adaptive systems. As such, they respond to a myriad of environmental stimuli (including physical, material, and cultural) by changing, adapting to, and adopting new strategies and courses of action. Though this much is clear, the initial conditions that force a system to change its behaviors are impossible to know, particularly in the case of historical events. Equally difficult to know is at what historical junction such conditions manifested themselves.

Looking at human societies as complex adaptive systems, we may be justified in borrowing ideas from the fields of chaos and complexity as a general explanatory model, though the following is by no means intended as a full presentation, but a brief discussion as to the utility of such a model.[11]

A central theme of chaos and complexity is the idea of "attractor," the final shape a system assumes after undergoing a series of changes triggered by initial conditions.[12] From the shape of an attractor (in this case, domestication) we may *deduce* some conditions (particularly when they do not involve material objects) that contributed to its shape, but we may never be able to *know* relevant initial conditions which shaped the slope of the attractor that determines what types of dynamics would occur, particularly in historical events. Many historical events are addressed implicitly or explicitly by a process akin to what is known as reverse engineering, in other words, the starting point is the finished product. Domestication metaphorically is a starting engine for agriculture and animal husbandry that has been shaped and reshaped for thousands of years, so much so that it is now impossible to determine the initial shape of this powerful engine and the dynamics involved in its development.

Another pivotal idea in these fields is what Per Bak, the Danish physicist, refers to as "self-organized criticality" (Bak and Chen 1991). Bak uses the analogy of a sandpile to describe this notion: as sand is added to the pile, it reaches the critical state in which the addition of even a single grain of sand can trigger an avalanche down the pile's sides. It must be noted that self-organized criticality, like punctuated equilibrium (Gould and Eldredge 1977), is not a theory[13] but a description useful to formulate ideas. It is in this general sense that such mathematical theories and abstract notions may provide insights into cultural phenomena of which domestication is a major one. In this sense, domestication of animals and plants can be thought of as an attractor to which, under certain initial conditions, human societies are driven regardless of the type of flora and fauna available to them. Since domestication has occurred several times and in a number of places, no particular series of factors and variables may be marshaled as the cause that steered a given society towards domestication (attractor).

In explaining events and phenomena, we explicitly, or often implicitly, take what we consider the final shape of their underlying systems — which, in terms of complexity, are attractors — and then try to marshal the initial conditions to which the system is sensitive and responsive. In the fields of chaos and complexity such attractors are, of course, mathematical abstractions of a certain shape the system assumes once it has settled. In this sense, attractors can be thought of as basins with slopes. The properties of these slopes are such that the systems which are attracted to their center need not take similar paths, or trajectories, to reach the destination point. In our case the attractor is the adaptation to permanent villages and full control over food supply. Looking at the problem from this angle, we may more effectively approach the different processes (paths) that led to the domestication of plants and animals worldwide as different paths leading to the same destination.

We may even extend the analogy to the questions of urban development and state formation. Once a complex adaptive system finds its attractor, by definition, it need not stay forever in that position since the assumption of a new position generates feedback, the accumulation of which, in time, forces the system to settle in another position. In this sense, the development of cities and formation of states, among other major socio-cultural transformations, can also be treated as attractors, the pathways of which, depending on the socio-economic and cultural structure of a given society, were different for different systems in different regions, leading to various political structures and systems such as complex chiefdoms, city-states, bundesrepubliken, empires, democracies, or dictatorships.

---

happen at the border between rigid order and randomness (see Horgan 1997, pp. 191–97). Moreover, practitioners in the fields of chaos and complexity believe that many phenomena in nature are "emergent," in other words, properties that cannot be predicted and/or understood by examining the systems' parts, an obvious anti-reductionist idea.

11. "Model" here is taken to be an abstraction of a situation that is not observable, but in which a number of events are *believed* to have happened in certain ways.

12. For general discussions of the fields of chaos and complexity, see, for examples, Gleick 1988; Briggs and Peat 1989; Ruelle 1991; Lorenz 1993; Hall 1994; Coveney and Highfield 1995; Stewart 1995 (chapter 9); Horgan 1997 (chapter 8); and Johnson 1996.

13. In the sense that a theory, by definition, must provide a well-defined framework within which one may make predictions.

If we consider agriculture and domestication of animals as the emergent property of thousands of years of hunting and gathering and accumulated experience, then domestication could have occurred, as it did, not in one but in a number of regions in the world, though not necessarily at the same time. If the eye, certainly one of the most complex products of evolution, could have evolved not just once but more than fifty times,[14] then it is perfectly conceivable that, as an inevitable response of human communities to a myriad of environmental, cultural, and historical conditions that seem to have evolved by the late Upper Palaeolithic period ushering in a major era in the history of the human species, the domestication of plants and animals happened not just once and not just in one locus, as it did.

Looking at the problem from this angle, the domestication of certain species of plants and animals seems to have a certain propensity to occur, though not always spurred by the same sets of variables. Although almost all the theories advanced to explain the origins of domestication have a kernel of truth, their narrative descriptions of the processes that were involved are highly conjectural since the fundamental units of the processes are either elusive and/or unknowable (unobservable). This seems to be inevitable given the fact that, to paraphrase Heisenberg's caveat, what we are learning about the past is not the past but the version of the past that is exposed to our methods of inquiry;[15] and what passes as bits and pieces of data/reality is primarily the creation of our measurement. Nevertheless, as in any intellectual endeavor, even if we never form a consensus on the question of the origins of domestication, it is the journey that matters.

---

14. For a detailed discussion on the independent development of the eye, see Goodwin and Saunders 1989, p. 50.

15. Quoted in Johnson 1996, p. 147.

CHAPTER 2
KHUZESTAN ENVIRONMENT

The geography of Khuzestan was a major factor in the development and shaping of its prehistoric and even historic cultures and civilizations. Several detailed studies of the geology and geography of the region have been carried out and published.[16] Here, it suffices to give only an overview of the Khuzestan environment.

The alluvial plain of Khuzestan lies in southwestern Iran. It is surrounded by the Zagros Mountain range to the north and east, the Persian Gulf to the south, and the Iraqi border to the west. Khuzestan can be divided into three climatically different zones (Pabot 1961, pp. 9–14):

1. Arid, with less than 200 mm rainfall, covering an area of ca. 20,000 km^2
2. Semi-arid, with a rainfall between 200 and 300 mm, covering an area of ca. 15,000 km^2
3. Dry, with rainfall ranging from 300 to 900 mm, covering an area of ca. 25,000 km^2

Table 1. Average Monthly Precipitation in mm at Abadan, Ahvaz, and Dezful*

Month	Abadan	Ahvaz	Dezful
October	2.7	2.5	0
November	25.0	31.2	55.6
December	34.6	51.5	78.5
January	37.1	54.7	82.2
February	33.8	47.0	52.1
March	16.2	18.0	52.0
April	14.5	17.7	33.1
May	6.1	1.8	22.4
June	0	0	2.3
Annual average	ca. 155	ca. 230	ca. 378

*Taken from Bakkar et al. 1956, tables 10–11.

ARID ZONE

This region covers the alluvial plain south and southwest of Ahvaz. It consists of fine silt with no hard rocks or sand dunes. Large areas of this zone are covered with saline marshes, which partially dry up in summer. The soil is mostly saline, especially in the southeastern part, with severely limited agricultural possibilities. The arable lands are constantly reduced by active erosion. Outside the marshes, the land is desert-like with very poor flora (Pabot 1961, p. 19).

SEMI-ARID ZONE

The southwestern limit of the semi-arid zone is the region of Susangerd and Ahvaz; its northern limit lies some 10–15 km south of Dezful and Shushtar and at the foot of Agha Jari Hills (Pabot 1961, p. 20). This zone is much less homogeneous than the arid zone. It is mostly silty, with large saline areas and some marshes. It also contains all the sandy areas and dunes of Khuzestan, as well as low sandstone or marl-gypseous hills (Pabot 1961, p. 20). Erosion is very active in the region east of Ahvaz and south of Shushtar. Although this region is the thoroughfare of major rivers, loaded with silt from the Zagros Mountain range, the degradation of ancient irrigation systems and lack of drainage

---

16. See, for example, Lees and Falcon 1952; Schroeder 1953; Bakkar et al. 1956; Pabot 1961; Hansman 1967; Oberlander 1968; Helbaek 1969; and Kirkby 1977.

have brought so much salt to the surface that extensive stretches of once cultivated land have been deserted. The flora in this region is much richer than in the arid zone (Pabot 1961, p. 20). Because of the high content of minerals, such as salt, gypsum, and calcium carbonate, and intense evaporation and poor drainage, over-irrigation may have caused irreversible salinization (Kirkby 1977, p. 253). My own observations in Khuzestan, however, indicate that salinization could not have been a major problem in this region, particularly in areas where water is available, farmers repeatedly inundate and drain saline land to "wash" it. The whole process may take a few weeks.

DRY ZONE

Extending from the middle of the Karkheh River valley up to the east of Gachsaran, this zone contains some conglomerate and sandstone, but gypseous marls are predominant. Erosion is prevalent throughout this zone, especially in the southeast where the rains are more violent and irregular. The dry zone has relatively few silty areas with somewhat stony ground. The natural flora, of at least five hundred species, is much richer than in the other zones (Pabot 1961, p. 24). In general, there is no precipitation in the summer, and the winter precipitation comes in the form of torrential rains that saturate the soil quickly. Thus much of the water is lost as runoff (Bakkar et al. 1956, p. 52).

RIVERS

The Karkheh, Dez, and Karun Rivers, the three major rivers along with the smaller streams that irrigate Khuzestan, drain ca. 100,000 km^2 of the Zagros Mountains (Kirkby 1977, p. 251). These streams, created by high precipitation in the mountains (400–800 mm), are vital since dry farming is marginal even in the rainy winter season (Kirkby 1977, p. 253). Despite this observation, large areas south of Shushtar, and especially east of the Gargar, a branch of the Karun, are still under dry agriculture.

The rivers follow the lines of three major northwest-southeast geological ridges resulting from vertical tectonic movements that had considerable impact on the hydrology and drainage of the plain (Lees and Falcon 1952, pp. 24 ff.). The areas between these ridges form a series of independent plains. Immediately below a ridge, the soil is less saline and has coarser sediments with, accordingly, better drainage (Schroeder 1953, p. 12). According to statistics, the flow of water in the three major upper Susiana rivers is out of phase with the agricultural regime, in other words, the maximum river discharge occurs in mid-spring, when the crops are ready to be harvested and are thus most susceptible to damage by flooding. Minimum discharge occurs in late fall/early winter and late summer when water is most needed (Oberlander 1968, p. 267). Unlike the major rivers, the Shaur (see fig. 2), a small river flowing west of Shush and originating from a perennial spring and seepage of the Karkheh, has its maximum and minimum discharge respectively in November and in April/May. Because the Shaur has its maximum discharge in the dry seasons, it is very heavily tapped, especially for summer crops.

Among the rivers that irrigate Khuzestan, the least saline is the Dez and the most saline are the lower Khuzestan rivers of Jarrahi and Hendijan. The major alluvial fan, which is neither too saline nor too silty for irrigation, lies in the region between Dezful and Susa, or between the rivers of Karkheh and Dez (Bakkar et al. 1956, pp. 263–66). This region is mainly irrigated by the low saline waters of the Dez. Its relative high summer flow also allows summer irrigation. Although the Karun has similar advantages, most of its waters are used in the south in the region of Ahvaz, with large areas of flat lands. In recent years, however, major canal and dam constructions have provided the local farmers in the Dimcheh and Shushtar areas with plenty of freshwater from the Karun.

The Karkheh is more saline and has less summer flow; thus, it suffices for the summer irrigation of only small areas. River fans experience minor floods annually, but major floods also occur. The sediments deposited by these floods cover existing saline surfaces, creating non-saline surfaces. Such conditions encourage winter cultivation, which in antiquity probably influenced the choices of settlements above the plain level on the already existing mounds, an important environmental factor in the formation of many high mounds with long history of occupation in Khuzestan (Bakkar et al. 1956, p. 266).

As the data in table 1 indicate, the Dezful area receives the highest precipitation and thus is the least risky region for dry agriculture in Susiana. This situation must have prevailed in prehistory since the three earliest settlements (Chogha Bonut, Chogha Mish, and Tappeh Tuleii) in the Susiana plain are located in this area, with Chogha Bonut and Tappeh Tuleii marking the southern and northern boundaries, respectively (fig. 2). Needless to say, the earliest colonizers of Susiana must have spent sufficient time in the region prior to choosing the locus of Chogha Bonut for their settlement. This environmental knowledge might have been gained initially through a combination of seasonal migration and changing of temporary campsites, of which the basal levels at Chogha Bonut may once have been. In a recent (2002) joint ICHO-University of Chicago (Oriental Institute and the Department of Anthropology) expedition in Khuzestan, we found at least two Archaic settlements south of Shushtar. Thus dry farming or its alternative, flood irrigation agriculture, must have been, as today, possible from the beginning of settled life in Khuzestan.

CHAPTER 3
RESULTS OF 1976/77, 1977/78, AND 1996 EXCAVATIONS
EXCAVATION METHODS AND STRATEGIES

ANALYTICAL METHODS

The analysis of archaeological data is, of course, an undertaking designed to discover and to understand the significance of variation in the archaeological record. Theoretically, there can be infinite dimensions along which variation can be organized, but in practice dimensions of variability are selected in response to the questions and problems addressed by any particular research endeavor. In any case, variation may involve either the formal or the structural properties of the archaeological record, but the most significant patterns of variation often involve both formal and structural properties. For present purposes, formal properties are defined as the measurable attributes of tangible archaeological things: buildings, installations, features, or objects; while structural properties are the intangible relationships among such things, or the relationships of such things to some larger context such as regional environment. Thus, for example, the diachronic distribution (structural) of stylistically defined ceramic types (formal) can be a powerful chronological tool. With these general observations in mind, the following sections outline some of the analytical programs that were either followed in the 1996 season of excavation and/or will be followed in future investigations at the site.

SUBSISTENCE PRODUCTION

Subsistence production can be explored in terms of the changing character and environmental context of settlement patterns. Such factors as the availability of various sources of water, good agricultural land, natural pastures, and the relative clustering or dispersal of settlements are important in light of our understanding of traditional farming and animal husbandry.[17] Few archaeological surveys in Susiana were primarily designed to find low, early sites. Such early sites can also be buried under several meters of deposits of later periods, thus making them extremely difficult to find, but not impossible. Therefore, additional intensive survey of the Dezful area in the future may provide the necessary data to address this problem.

CRAFT SPECIALIZATION

We hoped and expected the evidence of craft specialization to come from the raw materials, by-products such as pottery wasters, kilns, and concentration of special tools and objects such as spindle whorls, pounders, blades, jewelry, and the presence of planned architecture.

INTER-REGIONAL CONNECTION

The presence at Chogha Bonut of a variety of materials not found locally and of pottery with characteristics shared in other regions was taken to be indicative of inter-regional contacts, though not necessarily direct.

STORAGE, RESIDENTIAL SEGREGATION, AND SOCIAL COMPLEXITY

The storage activity is indicated by the presence of architectural units or simple pits with plastered walls suitable for such activity. One can also expect to find pottery vessels suitable for storing goods. The possible evidence of residential segregation and functionally different quarters, studied in light of the nature of the material culture and variations in the plan and quality of residential units, could be used to reconstruct processes of socio-cultural development.

---

17. See, for example, Watson 1979; Kramer 1979, 1983; Beck 1986.

If the symbolic analysis of the painted ceramics indicates a specific pattern of spatial distribution of certain motifs, that evidence is also taken as an indication of social ranking (Hole 1983; Pollock 1983).[18] Such observations could not have been made in our short and limited 1996 season of excavations, but we hope in the future to be able to investigate such problems.

As part of our future plan, assessing the site variability due to socio-economic changes through time is one of the most important objectives of the project. Some of the lines of evidence that may be discovered include patterns of food consumption, patterns of animal slaughter, variations in the ratio of goats to sheep, variations and frequency in the consumption of wild game, diachronic and synchronic stylistic variations in ceramics, patterns of distribution of architectural units with specific functions, and variations in the material culture of each architectural unit and/or graves. To ensure the ideal retrieval of archaeological materials, the following general procedures were and are being closely followed:

1. Changes in subsistence technique and strategies would be derived from a sequence of floral and faunal remains. The establishment of age-sex structure of faunal remains is crucial in understanding the transition from a pastorally based economy to one based on agriculture.

2. Changes in the quantities of exchanged/traded material may provide a measure for inter-regional trade.

RECORDING SYSTEM AND EXCAVATION PROCEDURES

Since the 1996 season of excavation was primarily designed to study the earliest occupation at Chogha Bonut, save for some observations we made on the site concerning the stratigraphic relations between Middle Susiana and Formative and Archaic remains, we did not deal with levels later than the Archaic period. This gap is filled with the extant results of the 1977/78 excavations conducted by Helene Kantor. Every effort is made to provide an accurate presentation of the architecture and artifacts dating to the Middle Susiana and Late Susiana periods. In addition, we have included architecture and artifacts from the Formative and Archaic periods that we deemed important in enhancing our knowledge of the early Neolithic phase at Chogha Bonut.

In preparing the material for publication, we had to exclude a number of pieces of evidence of which the stratigraphic information was lost. Even so, some pieces seemed to us important enough to be included. These pieces are marked in the descriptive index of objects with the abbreviations NA (not available).

Objects from the 1976–1978 seasons can be distinguished from those recorded in the 1996 season by their registration numbers. Field registration numbers of the 1996 season are prefixed with CB (Chogha Bonut), while those from the 1976–1978 seasons are prefixed with B (Chogha Bonut). The latter may be followed by either arabic numerals (e.g., B 1234) or roman I or II (e.g., B I-345) indicating that the object was found either in the first season (1976/77) or in the second (1977/78). The provenances mentioned from the 1976/77 and 1977/78 seasons are all locus numbers. These numbers consist of the square designation followed by three digits, the first of which indicates the season; thus L11:201 is the first locus dug in the second season (1977/78) in Square L11. The initial letter should not be confused with the 1996 system of recording where F stands for *Feature* and L stands for *Layer* (see below). The stratigraphic sequence in Square M10 is illustrated in figure 19 using a modified version of the Harris Matrix (Harris 1989). The lowest levels are represented as a square marked D.T. L35–L39 (fig. 19). These levels were excavated with arbitrary 20 cm levels in a 1 × 1 m trench to reach virgin soil and therefore no feature numbers are assigned.

The objectives of the project demanded detailed stratigraphic control and observations and careful retrieval of materials to study subtle changes in material culture and organic remains that are of utmost importance to this project. As a general procedure, we used a layer (L) and feature (F) system to control the stratigraphic information (see *Appendix 2: Index of Features and Layers from the 1996 Season*). A feature is defined as anything shaped and/or built purposefully by humans or animals, such as walls, floors, ovens, pits, animal burrows, and so on. A layer is defined as the fillings of such features — a dump on a surface is considered a layer(s) if no effort was made to contain it in a defined space such as a pit or a bin. In some cases, where we realized we were dealing with a feature rather than a layer, the designation of a layer was changed to feature as in Features 14, 28, 31, and 34.

---

18. My own analysis of the grammar of designs and the spatial distribution of certain designs (forthcoming) of the Bakun pottery suggests a relation between certain vessels and painted motifs with socio-economic status as observed at Tall-e Bakun; see also Alizadeh 1988.

It was absolutely critical to screen soil samples intensively if propositions and hypotheses about changes through time were to be tested effectively. To ensure a maximum retrieval of materials, deposits from some primary contexts (predominantly fire pits) and organic-looking debris were completely sifted and wet-sieved. From secondary and tertiary contexts only one-fifth of the deposit was sifted. To increase the usefulness of the screened and flotation samples, the volume in cubic meters of earth screened should be recorded for each unit. Unfortunately, the exigencies of the excavation prevented us from doing so.

We retrieved the seeds by dry sieving at the site and flotation in the camp (pl. 4:A–B). Samples were taken when dry-sieving in the field suggested charred remains would be recovered in at least moderate quantities. The contents of fire pits were floated in their entirety. Up to one-fifth of large features and layers were also taken. Charred material was retrieved through manual flotation. Soil was poured into a 1 mm mesh and immersed in water; then it was gently stirred. Floating material was collected with a metal spoon. The soil remaining in the mesh (heavy fraction) was spread on newspaper to dry. Anything visible with a magnifying glass that was burnt or looked like a seed was added to the sample.

The evidence of chipped stone industry is dealt with in a rudimentary fashion. To compensate for this, we have provided line drawings (figs. 38–41) and photographic samples (pls. 15–16) of all the types in the assemblage. To provide the interested reader with information for analytical study, a comprehensive index of all the whole pieces is also provided (table 4).[19]

EXCAVATION RESULTS

The first, brief, season of the rescue excavations at Chogha Bonut in 1976/77 proved that the occupation of the site was discontinuous. After a settlement of long duration in very early times, Chogha Bonut was deserted until about the late sixth millennium B.C., when it was resettled during the Late Middle Susiana phase. The site was deserted again at the end of the Middle Susiana period and was briefly resettled sometime during the Late Susiana 2 phase. These results were obtained by test excavations on the bulldozed eastern part of the mound, where some early structures and small segments of Late Middle Susiana walls were discovered in a narrow pit with occupation debris (figs. 6–9). In the 1977/78 season most of the area excavated was in the middle part of the mound, including a relatively small part that had not been torn down quite as low as the rest of the mound.

Our special interest in Chogha Bonut was its aceramic deposit that would make the site unique among the early sites in large alluvial plains in Iran. Since the Archaic and later periods were known from Chogha Mish (Delougaz and Kantor 1996) and Tappeh Tuleii (Hole 1974), northwest of Chogha Mish, we were eager to reach the basal levels during our excavations. Our main objectives in the 1996 season were to obtain a stratigraphic profile of the earliest deposits at Chogha Bonut and to provide a narrative description of the cultural development of the initial phase of colonization of the Susiana plain. To do this, given our limited time, budget, and manpower, we had to select an area on the mound where we could have a representative profile of the site's early deposits, easily accessible without having to excavate thick erosion layers and later Middle and Late Susiana deposits. This proved to be a difficult task because Chogha Bonut has been bulldozed twice. In addition, two seasons of excavations had produced a large amount of debris that had been dumped over the eastern slopes of the mound, but the exact location of which was unknown to us. Finally, eighteen years of rain and trampling by farmers, pastoralists, and their animals made it difficult to distinguish, without trial excavation, the disturbed and undisturbed areas of the mound.

At the base of the mound, we tested three areas on the southern and eastern sectors of the mound (fig. 5; pls. 2:C, 3:A). Although all these areas showed signs of disturbance, we decided that the eastern sector of the mound with its numerous ashy lenses visible just above the surrounding plain would be the most suitable spot to reach the lowest levels. We then opened a 5 × 5 m trench in Square M10 (figs. 5–7; pl. 3:B–C). After removing about one meter of bulldozer-disturbed deposit, we reached undisturbed layers, though the bulldozer's blades had penetrated even deeper in parts of the area not shown on the section drawings (figs. 16–17). The bulldozing and the fact that the area was pierced with animal and root holes caused a few pieces of pottery to penetrate into deeper aceramic levels.

---

19. I am very grateful to Mr. Abbas Moqadam, a student member of the 1996 season, for taking time to provide a first draft of the index in Tehran.

From the beginning we encountered in Square M10 aceramic layers accumulated in an area that seemed to have been an open court or a campsite, although this interpretation is by no means certain. In this area, we found successive surfaces with layers of alternating ash and clay, the latter occasionally contained some artifacts but was otherwise very clean, as if deposited naturally and rapidly. The surfaces were made usually of beaten earth and were primarily furnished with round- and oval-shaped hearths, ranging in diameter from 30 to ca. 90 cm and from 10 to 50 cm in depth; most of these fire pits contained fire-cracked rocks, very typical of the early Neolithic period (pl. 5:C). We found no solid architecture in Square M10, but the presence of fragments of straw-tempered mudbricks (pl. 5:A) indicated that mudbrick architecture or structures existed in the aceramic levels elsewhere in the mound.

We did not find any plastered floor. Some surfaces consisted of beaten earth and could be easily recognized as living surfaces by their composition, horizontal distribution of artifacts, and the hearths that were dug into them. These surfaces were rather poor in terms of artifacts. Exceptions are Features 14 and 15 with a number of fire pits and concentrations of flint blades and especially clay tokens and figurines (fig. 13:A–B). Both Feature 14 and Feature 15 had a concentration of small to medium rocks of the same type used in the fire pits. Nonetheless, no particular patterns in their spatial distribution on the floors were present. One of the most interesting yet enigmatic surfaces was Feature 28 (fig. 14:B), which contained a large (F26/L32) and a small (F27/L33) fire pit (pl. 6:A).

In the northwestern and northern part of Feature 28 we found two sheep/goat horns (pl. 7:A) accompanied by five articulated bones of five sheep/goat lower legs. The cluster between F26/L32 and F9/L12 was flanked by small to me-

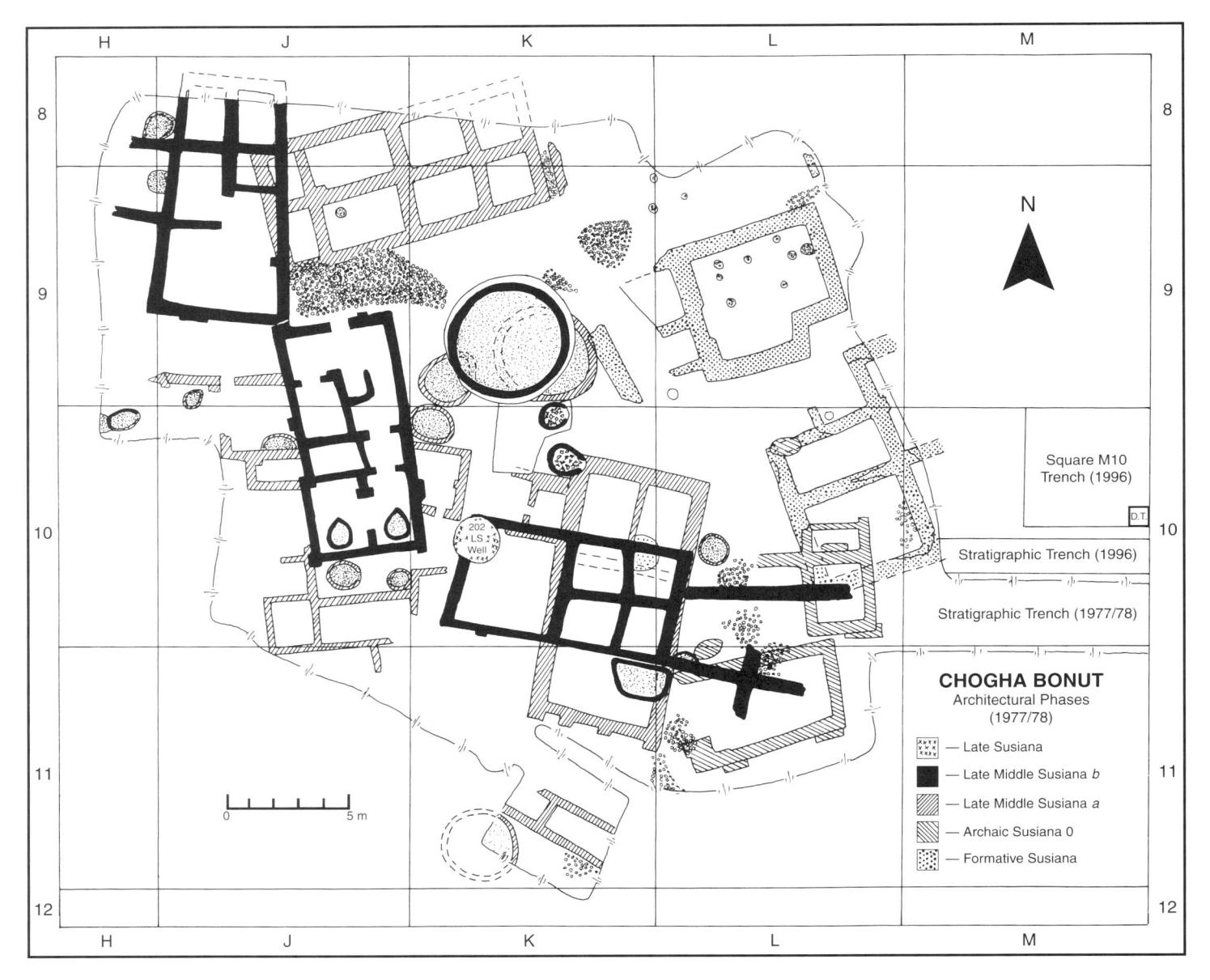

Figure 5. Composite Plan of Middle, Archaic, and Formative Susiana Architecture from the 1977/78 Excavations and Square M10 Trench (with Deep Trench [D.T.] Indicated) and Stratigraphic Trench from the 1996 Excavations at Chogha Bonut

dium rocks, and close to the northern cluster was found a large chunk of red ochre (fig. 14:B; pl. 5:B). If this deposit has any significance, it escapes us.

The analysis of the flora samples indicates to Naomi Miller (see *Chapter 10*) that animal dung probably was not the primary source of fuel. In addition, Arlene Miller Rosen's analysis of phytolith samples (see *Chapter 11*) indicates the presence of reeds that were perhaps used either in construction of fences, shelters, and perhaps as fuel. On several occasions we encountered reed impressions embedded onto various surfaces (pl. 10:B). These impressions perfectly match the type of reeds still growing on the banks of rivers, streams, irrigation canals, and marshes in Khuzestan (pl. 10:A).

From the beginning our intention was to excavate the entire area down to virgin soil, but the tedious work of carefully excavating and separating numerous thin layers prevented us from achieving this goal without extending the season to two months or more. To obtain a general picture of the basal levels, however, we opened a 1 × 1 m trench (D.T.) on the southeastern corner of Square M10 (fig. 17; pl. 8:B). Here, after excavating ca. 80 cm of alternating layers of ash and clay we reached virgin soil, a surprisingly small accumulation of alluvial sediment in at least 9,000 years. Level numbers 35–39 were retroactively assigned to the five distinct levels found in this trench. The shallowness of Chogha Bonut basal levels suggests the early colonizers of Susiana chose high ground for settlement. Although further investigations at the site's perimeter are needed to support this observation, the results of phytolith analysis point to a wet, marshy environment during the Aceramic period (see *Chapter 11*). This conclusion is further supported by the faunal evidence (see *Chapter 12*) that indicates the presence of the giant Indian gerbil (*Tatera indica*), a species adapted to a much wetter environment than that of Susiana today.

STRATIGRAPHIC TRENCH

Since we opened our trench at the lowest possible slope of the mound, it could not give us a profile of stratification of Chogha Bonut from the Aceramic to the beginning of the Archaic period. To develop this profile, we opened a stratigraphic trench one meter south of Square M10 and excavated it to virgin soil (figs. 5–7, 10–11, 18; pl. 9:A). It was here that we found several classes of pottery not previously known in Susiana. Because of the exigencies of the excavation, we decided not to excavate this trench by features and layers but by arbitrary 20 cm levels, the artifacts of which were kept separate. From the beginning (el. 77.60) we encountered architectural features made of the typical long cigar-shaped mudbricks. Five architectural phases (Bonut B–F; fig. 18; table 2) were recorded in this area, the earliest of which (Bonut B, el. 75.85) corresponds with the appearance of pottery. The assignment of these architectural levels to the Susiana cultural phases is based both on their stratigraphic positions and the stylistic analysis of the pottery.

Below the earliest architectural phase (Bonut B), the deposit (Bonut A; fig. 18; table 2) is very similar to that excavated in Square M10, in other words, a series of ashy and greenish layers separated by rather thick layers of clayish soil down to virgin soil. These clayish layers, as in Square M10, were mostly devoid of artifacts, erosion lenses, and streaks of ash (figs. 16–18; pl. 9:B). Our recent observations in Khuzestan indicate that this type of stratification may represent a seasonal camp, rather than a permanent, year-round occupation.[20]

CHIPPED STONE INDUSTRY

The most numerous artifacts at Chogha Bonut, as was expected, were flint tools and stone objects (figs. 29, 33:A–B, E, J, 34; pls. 15–16, 17:F, L, Q, T–W). The lithic industry at Chogha Bonut is advanced and is basically a blade industry (figs. 38–41). It is virtually undifferentiated from the beginning of the settlement to the end of the Aceramic period, a situation comparable to a number of early Neolithic sites in the Zagros Mountains. The presence of various high-quality flint cores, not found locally, indicates some sort of regional exchange. However, the assemblage is comparatively small and we suspect that the area of excavation was not the locus of manufacture, as the paucity of flakes also indicates. Obsidian blades were rare particularly in the aceramic layers. Altogether twenty-six blades and microblades were discovered; eight came from the aceramic levels and the remainder from the ceramic period. The majority of the blades are greenish gray in color, but some blackish gray also occur. The rarity of obsidian blades in the Chogha

---

20. During the 2002 Joint Oriental Institute/ICHO expedition at Dar Khazineh, southeast of Shushtar, we observed similar stratification.

Bonut aceramic levels is in sharp contrast to the aceramic levels of the Buz Murdeh and Ali Kosh phases at Tappeh Ali Kosh where 449 pieces are reported (Hole, Flannery, and Neely 1969, table 8). This difference may have chronological implications if the Chogha Bonut collection is representative, a question that at present cannot be satisfactory addressed as the area of excavation was rather small, though it must be noted that the excavation area at Tappeh Ali Kosh was only five square meters larger than our 5 × 5 m trench.

Table 2. Chogha Bonut Sequence

Period	Terrace	Square M10 (1996)	Stratigraphic Trench
Late Susiana 2	K10:202 (Well)	—	—
Late Middle Susiana	Buildings I–V	F9/L12 (Pit)	—
Early Middle Susiana	—	—	—
Early Susiana	—	—	—
Archaic Susiana 3	—	—	—
Archaic Susiana 2	—	—	—
Archaic Susiana 1	—	—	—
Archaic Susiana 0	L10:204–205; L11:203	—	Bonut F, Architectural phase 5 (77.75–78.00)
Formative Susiana	L9:201; L10:203, L10:207	—	Bonut B–E, Architectural phases 1–4 (75.75–77.25)
Aceramic Susiana	—	All Levels and Features, except L1 and F9/L12	Bonut A (72.80–75.70)

STONE OBJECTS

Although we did not find complete stone vessels and bracelets, the fragments we found illustrate the skill and sophistication of the early inhabitants of the Susiana plain (figs. 29, 34:A–B, E). The rarity of stone mortars and large stone tools may be an accident of discovery since the area of excavation was rather small, a situation similar to the basal aceramic levels at Ganj Darreh in the Zagros Mountains (Smith 1968, 1972b, 1975; Howe 1983, p. 117).

CLAY FIGURINES

Numerous clay objects with either mat or cloth impressions on one side indicate the use of clay tokens/sealings at this early stage of Susiana cultural development (figs. 31–32). A number of clay and stone figurines were found throughout the sequence (figs. 30–31; pls. 16:C, F–H; 17–18). The typical T-shaped figurines (figs. 30:A–C; pl. 18:A–D, F) were limited to the upper levels of the aceramic deposit and continued into the ceramic period. Crudely shaped clay zoomorphic figurines were found throughout the basal levels of the Aceramic period (fig. 31).

FLORA AND FAUNA

Our most precious and potentially more informative materials are the bones and carbonized seeds that we collected from every layer and feature. The bones were not in good condition and they were often covered with a thick layer of salt crystals. The faunal samples were analyzed by Richard Redding of the University of Michigan (*Chapter 12*).

The floral samples were analyzed by Naomi Miller of the Museum Applied Science Center for Archaeology, University of Pennsylvania. According to Miller, the types represent a small range; most of the material comes from cereals, primarily barley (*Hordeum vulgare*) and emmer wheat (*Triticum dicoccum*). Einkorn (*T. monococcum*), bread/hard wheat (*T. aestivum/durum*), and lentil (*Lens*) are also present. Seeds from several wild and weedy taxa, notably leguminous types, grasses, and a few others were found in the samples (see *Chapter 10*).

Soil samples for phytolith analysis were studied by Arlene Miller Rosen of the Institute of Archaeology, University College London (see *Chapter 11*).

CHAPTER 4
POST-ARCHAIC ARCHITECTURE AT CHOGHA BONUT

The results obtained during the 1976/77, 1977/78, and 1996 seasons have greatly advanced our knowledge of the site and are presented here period by period, beginning with the latest. Salvage excavations in 1977/78 uncovered a series of buildings dating to the Middle Susiana, Archaic, and Formative Susiana periods (figs. 5–8; table 3). Save for a deep well, architectural remains of the Late Susiana 2 phase were completely destroyed by the bulldozer. Two phases of architecture represent the Middle Susiana period (figs. 6–7); the pottery from these phases, however, falls within the range of the Late Middle Susiana phase (figs. 20–22; pl. 26). An erosion level, 20–80 cm thick, separates the remains of the Middle Susiana period from those of the Archaic and Formative periods.

LATE SUSIANA 2 PHASE

During the first season, as many sherds as possible were collected from the destruction debris pushed off the upper part of the mound in the hope of determining the latest period of the occupation. As no typical Late Susiana sherds were retrieved, it was assumed that the period did not exist on the mound. This conclusion was disproved by a feature that was discovered at the beginning of the 1977/78 season, when work began to enlarge the previously excavated area toward the west. Immediately below the destruction level of the bulldozer in Square K10, there appeared a circle of dark gray soil almost two meters in diameter (202 LS Well; fig. 5). The soft soil was strikingly different from the surrounding hard brown or brownish red bricky detritus.

As work proceeded in the feature K10:202, it became clear that it was a pit lined with hard clay and filled with soft gray earth alternating with thick caps of clay. The thornbush roots had grown downwards in a circular pattern by following the interstices between the hard clay caps and the lining of the pit. The pit was excavated to a depth of about 5.50 meters (from el. 79.68 to 74.25) without reaching the bottom. For reasons of safety and convenience it was deemed impractical to go deeper. It is likely that the pit was a well that went down to the ancient water table. In the 1996 season, we encountered a similar Middle Susiana pit (F9/L12, mostly destroyed by bulldozer) in Square M10 of perhaps similar function because the pit was almost free of material refuse.

The fill of K10:202 was consistent throughout. It contained a considerable amount of carbonized grain (now lost) but relatively few sherds, mostly of fine painted ware (pl. 26:C). These were all consistently different from the sherds found at the same level outside of K10:202 and can be dated without question to the later part of the Late Susiana period.[21] The coherence of the fill was indicated by joining sherds found from various levels in the fill. Presumably, after the well had served its primary use some time during the Late Susiana period, it was filled at one time. The thick layers of hard clay might have been inserted in order to consolidate what would otherwise have been a soft, insecure fill. Admittedly, this is pure speculation and the true nature of the feature and its fill remains unknown.

Only rather small sherds were found in K10:202. They do not represent the full range of Late Susiana 2 ceramics but consist of fragments of fine painted vessels. The lower part of a typical Late Susiana 2 beaker with a flat base is decorated with dotted horizontal lines. Fragments of a convex-sided bowl painted on the exterior have narrow and wide bands bordered by loops and, at the lip, a petal-like frieze. The sherds of a large fine ware beaker are decorated with several registers of abstract butterfly and small V-motifs (pl. 26:C), typical of the Late Susiana period.

Since K10:202 was dug down from a level that was completely destroyed by the bulldozing of the upper part of the mound, it was impossible to ascertain the original context of the well. We may speculate that it was dug between Late Susiana houses. Although K10:202 remains at present the only evidence for a Late Susiana settlement at Chogha Bonut, it is a feature that implies the existence of a settlement there during that period.

---

21. Specifically the Late Susiana 2 phase; see Alizadeh 1992, pp. 21–27, 57–58.

LATE MIDDLE SUSIANA PHASE

The disturbed condition of Chogha Bonut provided some special excavation problems, during both the 1970s and 1996 excavations. In some spots high ridges of loose soil had been heaped up on the artificial destruction surface; elsewhere soil had been secondarily compacted or pushed into the straight slashes cut in the surviving structures by the earth-loosening rods of the bulldozer. When the destruction of the mound was stopped, a relatively small part of the central section still stood somewhat higher than the outer portions, where, as revealed in 1978, very little was left of Middle Susiana levels. The investigation of this "island" of less destroyed remains has revealed Middle Susiana structures with varying floor levels. The superimposition of several buildings is used as evidence of at least two distinct architectural phases: Late Middle Susiana phase *a* and phase *b*, phase *a* being earlier.

Contemporary structures need not all be on the same level and installations such as kilns must have been short-lived, with superimposed examples following each other in rapid succession. Nevertheless, where the evidence of superimposition is lacking, available absolute levels are used as the primary criteria for the subdivision of isolated features.

ARCHITECTURAL PHASE *B* (FIG. 6)

The uppermost Middle Susiana remains are directly at the destruction surface; they consist of considerable patches of hard clay and brick material, in spots showing individual brick outlines, and the floors of some approximately circular structures whose context might have been destroyed. This whole complex may have stood on a platform, parts of which were still visible in 1978. This feature consisted of a bricky material that was discontinuous but sometimes en-

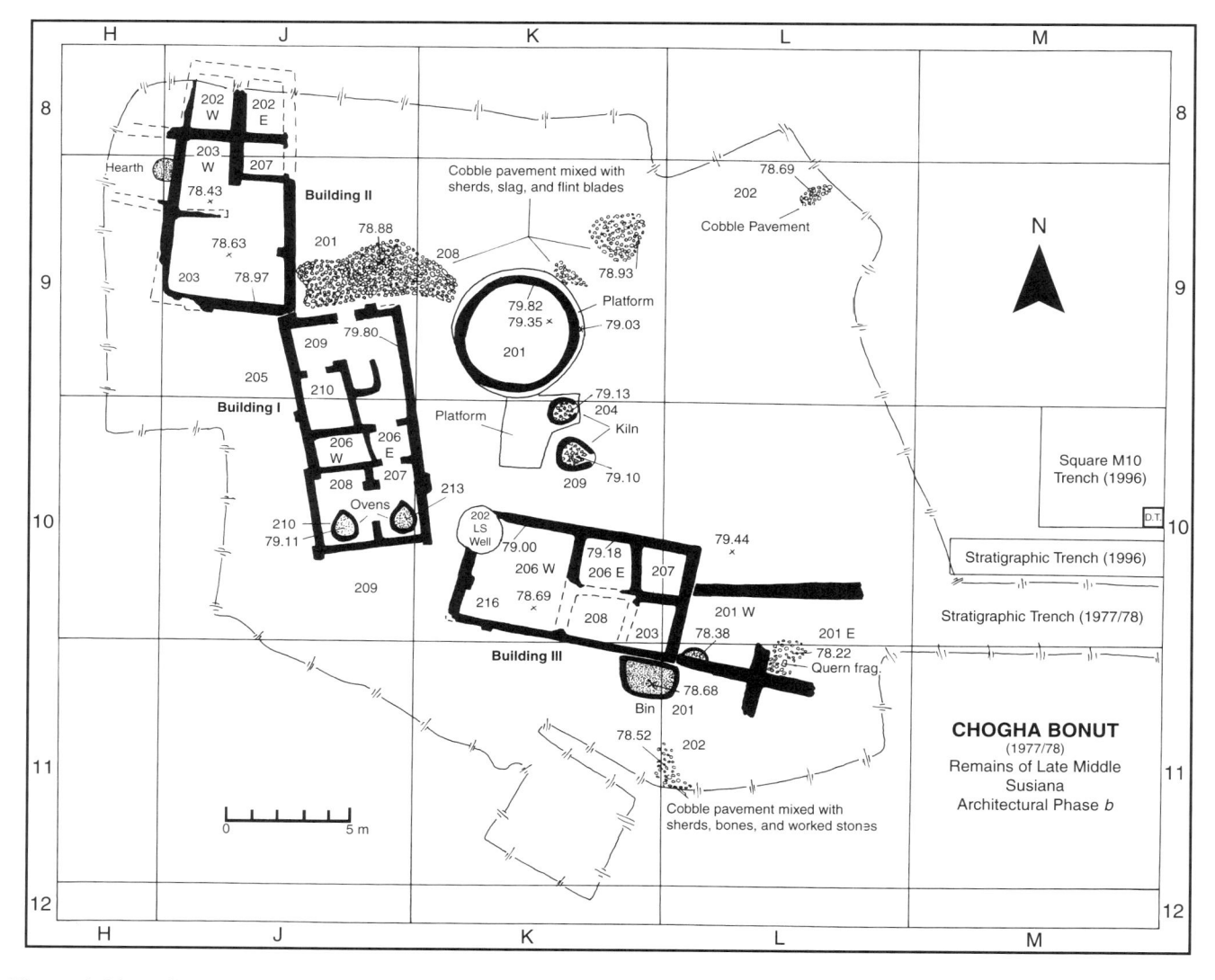

Figure 6. Plan of Late Middle Susiana Architectural Phase *b* from the 1977/78 Excavations and Square M10 Trench (with Deep Trench [D.T.] Indicated) and Stratigraphic Trench from the 1996 Excavations at Chogha Bonut

closed patches of softer earth without showing wall faces. No articulated bricks were distinguished in 1978 and our attempt to do so in 1996 failed to reveal any individual mudbricks.

Underlying the uppermost levels are a number of kiln floors and a carefully constructed pavement, approximately 7.00 × 2.50 m in size, consisting of a layer of hard-packed earth on top of small pebbles (J9:201; fig. 6). A similar, but less preserved pebble pavement, about 2.00 × 2.30 m in size, was revealed in Squares K9 and L9. If anything remained of the associated architectural contexts of either pavement we could not find it in the available excavation record. However, from the fact that all these three patches of pavement are approximately at the same level and no remains of architecture were reported above them, we may deduce that they may have all been part of a much larger pavement covering the open space around the large circular structure (K9:201) and the smaller K10:204 and K10:209.

The floors of several rooms of Building I in Squares J8 and J9 (J8:202 and 203; fig. 6), are approximately at the same level of those in Building I and presumably contemporary. Building I is the only one so far found at Chogha Bonut, the plan of which is completely preserved (figs. 6, 8; pls. 11, 12:A); it is described in more detail below. To the west of Building I scattered installations at a lower level probably belonged to the earlier phase of the Late Middle Susiana phase.

Large Circular Structure

The highest preserved Middle Susiana feature is K9:201, which is a circular area, about 4.5 meters across at its largest point, delimited by a pisé wall varying in thickness from 20 to 40 cm (fig. 6; pl. 13:B). This wall was preserved on the north side to a height of 47 cm above floor level. In the surviving remains there is no trace of an entrance or hole. Much of the exterior was bordered by a lower step or foundation platform. On the interior both the wall and the floor of K9:201 had been carefully plastered with a thin, hard coat of mud.

Parts of a wall of a presumably similar structure are reported to project toward the east from underneath K9:201 (K9:202; fig. 7; pl. 13:B). Apparently the walls of this second large circle had been destroyed almost to floor level when K9:201 was built. There were no finds on the floor of K9:201 to suggest its function. Neither did the floor have ashes and intense black and red color characteristic for kilns. There were only scattered traces of burning, which seem to be secondary. Both K9:201 and the earlier K9:202 (fig. 7) are considerably larger than the many kilns that have been identified at Chogha Bonut, so it seems unlikely that they were kilns. Perhaps the structures served as granaries or depots for some kind of commodity, but this is by no means certain.

Building I

In the highest preserved area of Chogha Bonut, the southern part of Square J9 and the eastern side of Square J10, plastered mudbrick walls provide a coherent plan (figs. 6, 8; pls. 11, 12:A). The building consists of three rooms to the north and either an open court or, less likely, two rooms to the south. The one major uncertainty in the plan is the location of the entrance, despite the preserved height of the walls. The most likely place for it is in the northern wall, which has been badly damaged. Field notes indicate some cracks in it, which may represent an original doorway secondarily filled, but this could not be established with certainty. The three interior doorways are well preserved so that the interior circulation pattern is clear.

The main rooms appear to be on the north, namely the L-shaped room J9:209 enclosing the smaller room J9:210 on two sides. In the eastern part of J9:209 two irregular narrow walls formed a partition delimiting a bin. The doorway in the south end of J9:209 led into a room, J10:206, the eastern end of which served as a passageway connecting with J10:207. The western part of J10:206 was set off by a narrow partition wall and was presumably a storage area. The numerous buttresses built against the walls of this structure suggest that the building may have had an upper level, for which no direct evidence is available. There are some problems as to the interpretation of the back part of the building. Its enclosing walls are clear, but it is not altogether certain that J10:207 and J10:208 form an open court. This is probable, however, since the "walls" between them are irregular, thick, and too far apart to form a doorway comparable to those in the other parts of the building. These projections may well be secondary.

At the south end of J10:207 and 208 it is striking how the two kiln/oven floors, which are 40 cm higher than the house floor, fit within the circuit of the walls (pls. 11–12). We can only presume that they belonged to a later stage of the same building. All the evidence presently at hand, when taken together, suggests that the back part of the building was an open courtyard with two kilns/ovens. If these two structures were ovens used for domestic purposes (primarily baking bread), it seems unusual to have two ovens side by side in a single house, a situation that is not presently observed in the region. Alternatively, these structures could have been industrial kilns of a craftsman, assuming that this unit was a living space for a nuclear family. Given the number of kilns and ovens in such a small area (ca. 90 sq. m of exposure) it is equally possible that the whole complex was a regional workshop, although no direct evidence for this assumption is available.

Buildings II and III

These two buildings, just to the northwest and southeast of Building I, are not well preserved (fig. 6). Nonetheless, their plan and size are very similar to Building I. The western and northeastern parts of Building II were destroyed by the bulldozer and therefore we are not certain about the overall plan of the building. As in Building I, no clear entrance to the building was noted, nor were any doorways between rooms discovered. A hearth with no walls but with a sunken burnt floor and covered with ash in the northern part of Squares H9 and J9 must have been located inside a room, now destroyed. No other installation was found in this building.

To the southeast of Building I lies Building III. The plan of this building is almost identical to that of Building II, provided the projection of the walls is correct, in that it has a presumably rectangular open court leading to four chambers in the back of the building. The northwest corner of the building was destroyed by the Late Susiana well. A rather large bin with walls made of pisé abuts the building's southern wall, and a small oven lies just to the southeast corner of the building. Whereas there is no question of the contemporaneity of this bin with Building III, it is impossible to ascertain whether the small oven belonged to this phase. This oven is built against a northeast-southwest wall that seems to be a continuation of the southern wall of Building III. The two roughly parallel walls that intersect the eastern wall of Building III may represent an even earlier stage of Middle Susiana architecture at Chogha Bonut, but no further evidence is provided in the notebooks and the heavy erosion at the site prevented us from further investigation in the 1996 season.

ARCHITECTURAL PHASE *A*

The area on the west side of excavation had been destroyed below the level of Building I. Bits and pieces of walls discovered in this section are associated with floors ranging from el. 78.49 to 78.24; they are the earliest Late Middle Susiana structures recovered at Chogha Bonut (fig. 7). Unfortunately, they are not as well preserved as Building I, but the presence of a number of kilns and ovens suggests a similar function for this earlier complex. As in the later phase, a centrally located large circular structure lies in the middle of the complex, surrounded with at least four architectural units (K9:202; fig. 7). Patches of preserved cobble pavement in K10, L10, L11, and K11 suggest continuity in the architectural technique and perhaps in the function of the complex in both phases.

Building IV

Located to the north of the circular structure, this building was partly destroyed by the bulldozer, as was another building just to its east, of which only a fragmentary wall is preserved (fig. 7). The preserved portion of Building IV consists of at least eight rectangular and square rooms, the largest of which is provided with a raised and apparently open hearth. Aside from this hearth, no other evidence is found to suggest a domestic use for this building. The absence of doorways makes it difficult to reconstruct communication patterns between rooms. Unlike Buildings II and III, Building IV does not seem to have had an open court.

Building V

This building is situated just to the south of the central circular structure (fig. 7). The size and plan of this building are similar to those of Buildings I–IV. Unlike Building IV, Building V seems to have had an open court (K10:201; fig. 7), an assumption based on its size and the absence of any partition wall in K10:201. But since the inner face of the building's western and eastern walls is damaged and eroded, our interpretation remains tentative. This building differs from the rest of the Middle Susiana buildings at Chogha Bonut in that it is provided with a vestibule or foyer (K10:205 E; fig. 7) leading to K10:204 S, though no doorway connecting the two has been found.

Belonging to the same phase or perhaps an even earlier architectural phase of the Late Middle Susiana phase at Chogha Bonut are scattered walls, floors, and cooking installations discovered in the south and west of the excavation area (fig. 7; pl. 13:A). Given the available information, it is difficult to reconstruct the plan of these badly damaged architectural units and their relationship to Buildings IV and V.

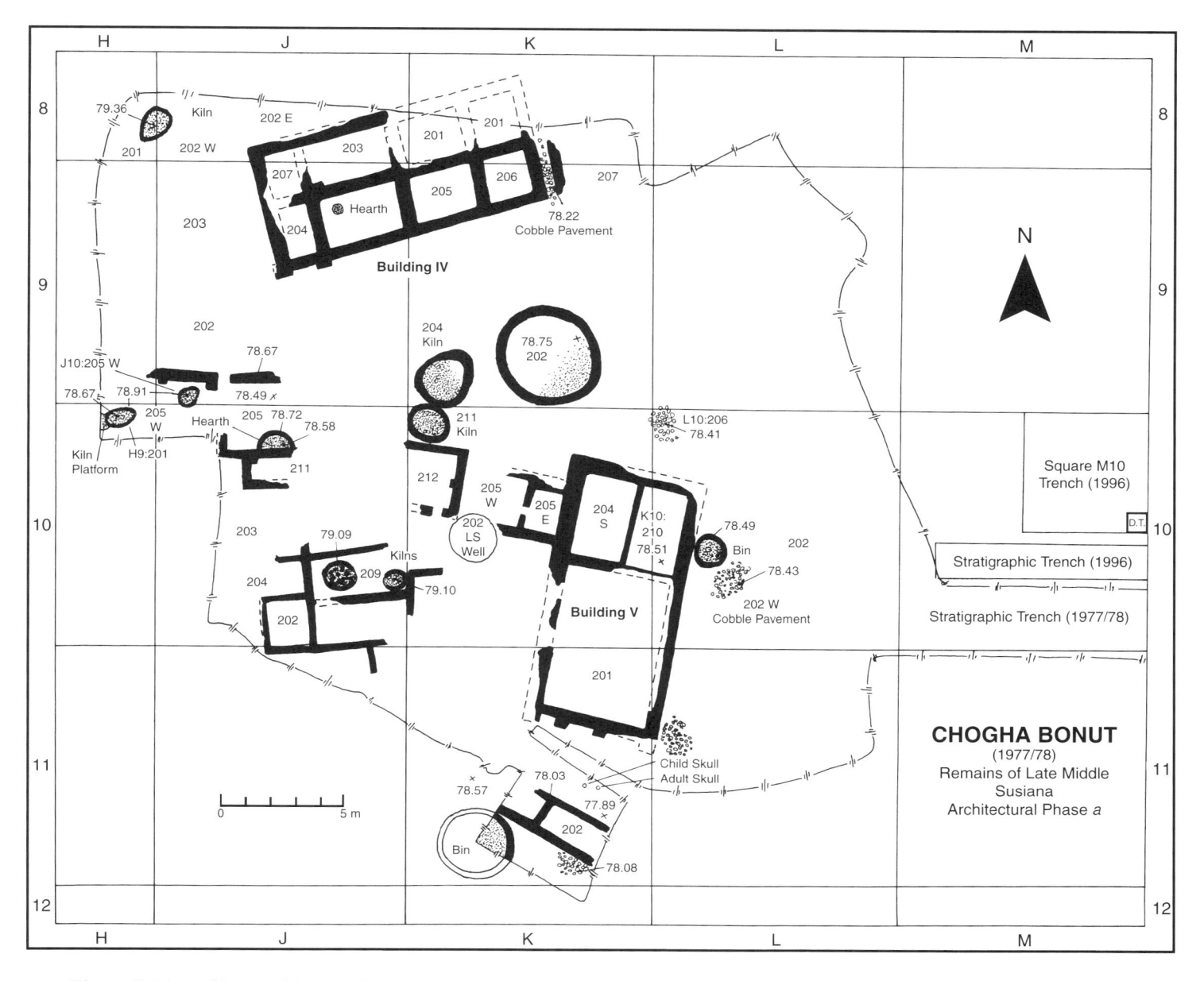

Figure 7. Plan of Late Middle Susiana Architectural Phase *a* from the 1977/78 Excavations and Square M10 Trench (with Deep Trench [D.T.] Indicated) and Stratigraphic Trench from the 1996 Excavations at Chogha Bonut

Kilns and Ovens

Even when little remained of the walls of these structures, there was no problem in identifying them as kilns because ashes, wasters, and burnt earth were immediately above their floors. The greatest dimensions of the kilns range from 2.40 m (K9:204; fig. 7) to 0.90 m (J10:209 E; fig. 7). The shapes of the kilns vary from a fairly regular circle to a definite oval. The two best kilns (K10:204 and K10:209; fig. 6) belong to the earlier phase *a*, and are found in Building I. It is uncertain whether or not they had an aperture. The walls of J10:210 and J10:213 are reported to be continuous. Judging by the kilns preserved to much higher elevation, most of the kilns seem to have had an opening at the level of the floor. There was a tendency to narrow the kiln at the aperture, thus producing the ovoid shape. Accordingly, we can assume that the twin kilns or ovens at the rear of Building I (J10:210 and J10:213; fig. 6), whose floors were at the destruction level, had originally opened at their northern end even though traces of their stoke holes were not preserved. The interiors of the kilns were plastered with mud on the sides and floor. Below the plaster there was frequently a flooring of sherds as in the two small kilns south of the large circular structure (K10:204 and K10:209; fig. 6). K10:209 (fig. 9) of phase *b* is a good example of an ovoid kiln; it has a well-preserved sherd floor and its 40 cm high wall stumps are sufficient to suggest the shape of the complete structure.

CHOGHA BONUT
Late Middle Susiana House

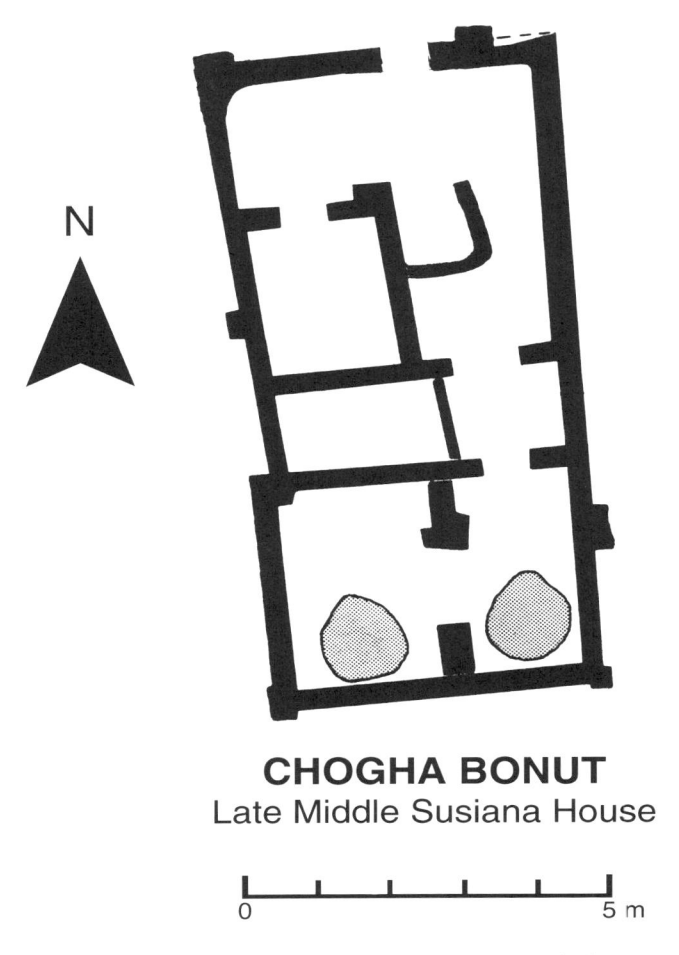

Figure 8. Plan of Late Middle Susiana Building I

The structure L10:202 of phase *a* and its associated pebble pavement (fig. 7) were apparently of different character. The feature is an approximately circular area of pebbles embedded side by side in a thin layer of clay mixed with straw. The pebbles were clearly selected for flatness and perhaps also for size — they range in length only from 14 to 5 cm. There was no surrounding wall and there were traces of burning so that the structure could have been associated with preparation of some kind food or commodity. Next to this pavement, at the same level, was a low-walled bin of uncertain function (L10:202; fig. 7), also fire blackened.

INTERPRETATION

The five surviving Middle Susiana buildings at Chogha Bonut are remarkably similar in size, general plan, and architectural details. They are rectangular in plan with presumably a courtyard (with the exception of Building IV) beyond which a series of square or rectangular chambers provided living and/or storage space. Except for a room in Building IV with a small circular oven, these architectural units have no other specific domestic installation. Moreover, little material that would point to domestic use was found on the floors of these buildings. In contrast, the area surrounding the architectural units were strewn with huge amounts of potsherds mixed with large patches of dark ash.

The Middle Susiana settlement at Chogha Bonut was small, even if we make allowance for a few more buildings that might have been destroyed by the bulldozer, though this seems unlikely because one would expect to find traces of their foundations among the buildings that survived. In contrast, numerous pottery kilns and at least two large circular storage facilities were found within and without the surviving buildings. By any standard, the number of industrial installations is proportionally much higher than the number of buildings and certainly far exceeds the domestic requirement for food preparation and/or pottery manufacture. In addition, as noted, Middle Susiana levels at Chogha Bonut contained masses of potsherds and pottery wasters (pl. 26:A) mixed with layers of ash and soot. Together, these pieces of evidence suggest that Chogha Bonut could have been a special center for manufacturing pottery during the Middle Susiana period when Chogha Mish, as a regional center, dominated the plain of Susiana. This interpretation, however, does not imply that Chogha Bonut was solely used as a workshop. Rather, the site does not seem to have been prima-

CHOGHA BONUT
Late Middle Susiana Kiln K10:209

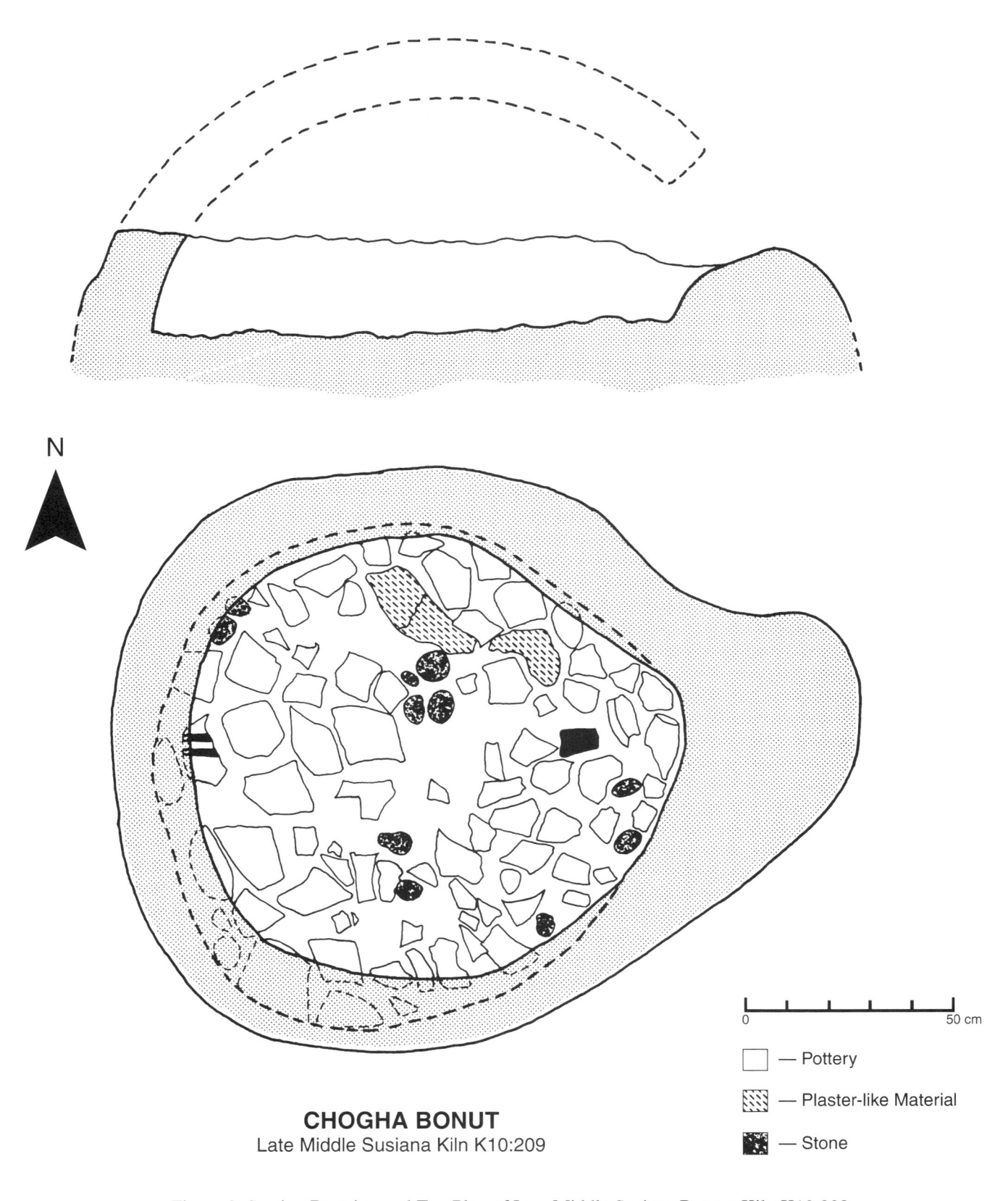

Figure 9. Section Drawing and Top Plan of Late Middle Susiana Pottery Kiln K10:209

rily a typical rural village with subsistence economy. Middle Susiana was the most populated prehistoric period in Susiana with hundreds of sites scattered in the northern part of the region, creating a high demand for pottery and other goods. The sophisticated and highly artistic Middle Susiana pottery shows little, if any, regional variation, suggesting a well-established pottery tradition, which could have been manufactured in specialized sites such as Chogha Bonut. The archaeological evidence from Chogha Bonut notwithstanding, chemical analysis of pottery and study of the grammar of the designs and their spatial distribution will have to be conducted before one can address the question of craft specialization during the Middle Susiana period.

Table 3. Relative Chronology of Prehistoric Sites in Iran and Mesopotamia

DATE B.C.	SUSIANA PERIOD	SUSIANA SITE	DEH LURAN	ZAGROS MOUNTAINS	FARS PERIOD	FARS SITE	CENTRAL PLATEAU PERIOD	CENTRAL PLATEAU SITE	MESOPOTAMIA PERIOD	MESOPOTAMIA SITE NORTH	MESOPOTAMIA SITE SOUTH
3800	Late Susiana 2	Chogha Mish Jafarabad 1–3 Susa Acropole 25–26 Bandebal III (Level 10)		Godin VI	Late Fars	Tall-e Bakun A	Late Plateau	Ghabrestan III	Ubaid 4	Tepe Gawra XII Tepe Gawra XIV–XIV	Eridu V–IV Eridu VII–VI
4000											
4200				Godin VII							
4400	Late Susiana 1	Susa Acropole 27? Bandebal II (Levels 11–17) Qabr-e Sheikheyn	Frukhabad A23–31, B32–47			Tall-e Gap	Middle Plateau	Ghabrestan I (Levels 13–11) Hessar I–A Ghabrestan I (Levels 19–17)	Ubaid 3		al-Ubaid
4600											
4800	Late Middle Susiana	Jafarabad 3m–n Chogha Mish	Bayat	Godin VIII	Middle Fars						
5000	Early Middle Susiana	Jawi I Bandebal I Chogha Mish	Mehmeh			Tall-e Bakun B				Arpachiyah H3–H4	
5200			Khazineh	Godin IX					Ubaid 2		Haji Mohammad
5400							Early Plateau	Cheshmeh Ali Upper			
5600	Early Susiana	Jafarabad 6–4 Chogha Mish	Tappeh Sabz		Early Fars	Shamsabad			Ubaid 1	Arpachiyah H1	Eridu XIX
5800				Godin X							
5900	Archaic Susiana 3	Chogha Mish	Chogha Sefid CMT			Jari		Cheshmeh Ali Lower	Ubaid 0		Tell el-'Oueile 11–19
6100						Mushki				Samarra es-Sawwan I	
6300	Archaic Susiana 2	Chogha Mish	Surkh	Haji Firuz	Archaic Fars	?	Archaic Plateau	Tappeh Sialk / Tappeh Zagheh	Hassuna	Hassuna 1a	
6500	Archaic Susiana 1	Chogha Mish	Chogha Sefid					Tappeh Sang-e Chakhmaq		Um Dabaghieh IV	?
6700	Archaic Susiana 0	Chogha Bonut F Tuleii	Mohammad Jafar	Abdul Husein/ Guron					Jarmo		
6900	Formative Susiana	Chogha Bonut B–E	Tappeh Ali Kosh		Aceramic Fars		Aceramic Plateau	?		Late Jarmo Early Jarmo	
7200	Aceramic Susiana	Chogha Bonut A	Buz Murdeh							Maghzalieh	
				Asiab Ganj Dareh E							

CHAPTER 5
ARCHITECTURE OF THE ARCHAIC, FORMATIVE, AND ACERAMIC SUSIANA

The architectural remains of the early period at Chogha Bonut can be divided into two distinct phases (Archaic Susiana 0 and Formative Susiana). Based on the stratigraphic observations and stylistic analysis of the pottery in the stratigraphic trench (fig. 18; table 2), Formative Susiana is divided into four architectural phases (Bonut B–E).

In the first season at Chogha Bonut the walls of a very early structure were found almost immediately below the lowest courses of badly destroyed Middle Susiana walls (L10:205 and L11:203; figs. 5, 10). In Square L11, just below Middle Susiana walls and a 10 cm erosion level, the upper part of two wide walls made of long, cigar-shaped mudbricks typical for the Archaic Susiana was reached. These early walls are dated not only by their typical Archaic Susiana bricks, but also by sherds of completely different style and manufacture from those of the Middle Susiana period.

The architectural remains of the Archaic period are found only in the eastern part of the excavation area. This area is the most heavily damaged by bulldozer and therefore the remaining architectural features do not yield a coherent plan of the settlement. The concentration of Archaic features on the eastern part of the mound does not seem to be accidental. In 1996, we opened a test trench on the western slope of the mound in Square H9 in an attempt to find remains of Archaic levels there below the Middle Susiana deposit. We excavated this exploratory trench to a depth of three meters with no traces of any object or architecture datable to the Archaic period. At ca. el. 75.50, we abandoned the trench. In addition, our intensive surface survey of the mound in 1996 indicated that pre-Middle Susiana sherds are limited to the eastern part of the mound. A test trench at the southern part of the mound, dug to virgin soil, also failed to reveal any traces of Archaic or Formative Susiana, and traces of Middle Susiana occupation here rested on virgin soil. Taken together, the evidence indicated to us that at Chogha Bonut Archaic remains are limited to the eastern part of the mound and that the settlement was very small, perhaps consisting of only a few houses.

ARCHAIC SUSIANA 0 (BONUT F, ARCHITECTURAL PHASE 5)

The latest architectural unit of this phase was found in Square L11 (fig. 10; table 2). The plan is incomplete and consists of a rectangular structure with three walls made of the typical long cigar-shaped mudbricks. The bricks are laid in stretchers with the exception of the southwestern part of the southern wall where a series of headers provides what seems to be a platform of unknown function (pl. 14). The same wall is reinforced by two low buttresses made of the same type of bricks. The inner face of these walls is well preserved and shows no sign of partition walls. Thus, L11:203 could have been an open court of a building, the western part of which is completely destroyed. A shallow bin and a fragment of a cobble pavement on the north side of the northern wall could have belonged to this building, judging by their stratigraphic position and artifacts, as well as the fact that the beaten earth surface on which the pavement rests abuts the northern wall of this building.

Another building (L10:204 and L10:205; fig. 10), smaller but better preserved, was found to the northeast of L11:203. This building, too, was constructed with long, cigar-shaped mudbricks. Much of the building is destroyed and the preserved parts consist of a rectangular room with a large patch of burnt floor next to its eastern wall (L10:205). To the north of this room, a small, rectangular chamber was found (L10:204). Except for what seems to be a bench constructed on its southern wall, no other feature was found in this room. The fragmentary walls oriented north and west could have belonged to rooms that contained a mud-plastered shallow bin (L10:203). In the stratigraphic trench, architectural phase 5 (Bonut F) is assigned to this phase on the basis of absolute level and the similarities of its ceramics to those found in L10:204–205 and L11:203.

FORMATIVE SUSIANA (BONUT B–E, ARCHITECTURAL PHASES 1–4)

Below the level of Archaic 0 buildings, two buildings were found (figs. 5, 11). The attribution of these two buildings to an earlier period rests on the type of artifacts associated with them and their stratigraphic position. The southern

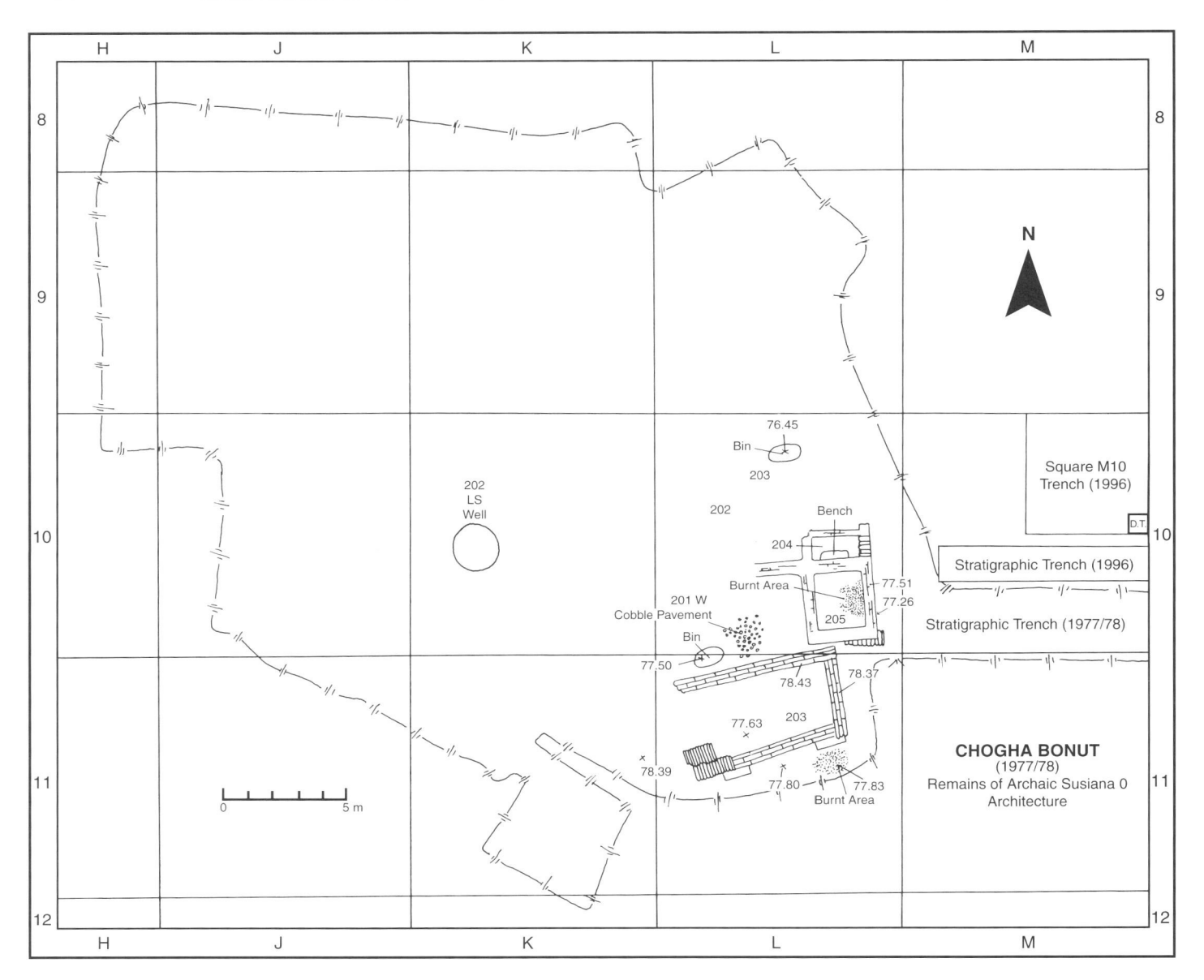

Figure 10. Plan of Archaic Susiana 0 Architecture from the 1977/78 Excavations and Square M10 Trench (with Deep Trench [D.T.] Indicated) and Stratigraphic Trench from the 1996 Excavations at Chogha Bonut

building, L10:203 S and L10:207, was heavily damaged by the bulldozer and perhaps by natural erosion, as it is located on the eastern edge of the mound. The best-preserved part of this building is a rather thick northwest-southeast wall with heavily damaged partition walls jutting out from it.

The second building (L9:201) is much better preserved. It consists of an almost square room with a number of small, circular fire pits containing fire-cracked rocks, so typical of the early Neolithic sites in the Zagros Mountains. The eastern corner of its southern wall is offset, presumably to accommodate the existing wall of L10:203 S. A niche is provided in the inner face of the western wall; the outer face of this wall is furnished with at least two fragmentary partition walls that originally may have joined an isolated fragmentary wall to the west. This wall fragment might have been the western outer wall of this building, but there is no direct evidence to support this reconstruction. Whatever the complete plan of this building, the numerous fire pits dug in its floor suggest a non-domestic function for this room; it is also possible that L9:201 was an open court of a larger building now destroyed.

In the stratigraphic trench, four architectural levels (Bonut B–E) are assigned to the Formative period (fig. 18; table 2). Only small portions of stratified walls made of long mudbricks and intervening deposits were found in this area, a situation that makes it difficult to determine the nature of the architecture in these early phases. Nonetheless, the evidence from the stratigraphic trench provides an unbroken architectural sequence from the end of the Aceramic period to the end of Archaic 0.

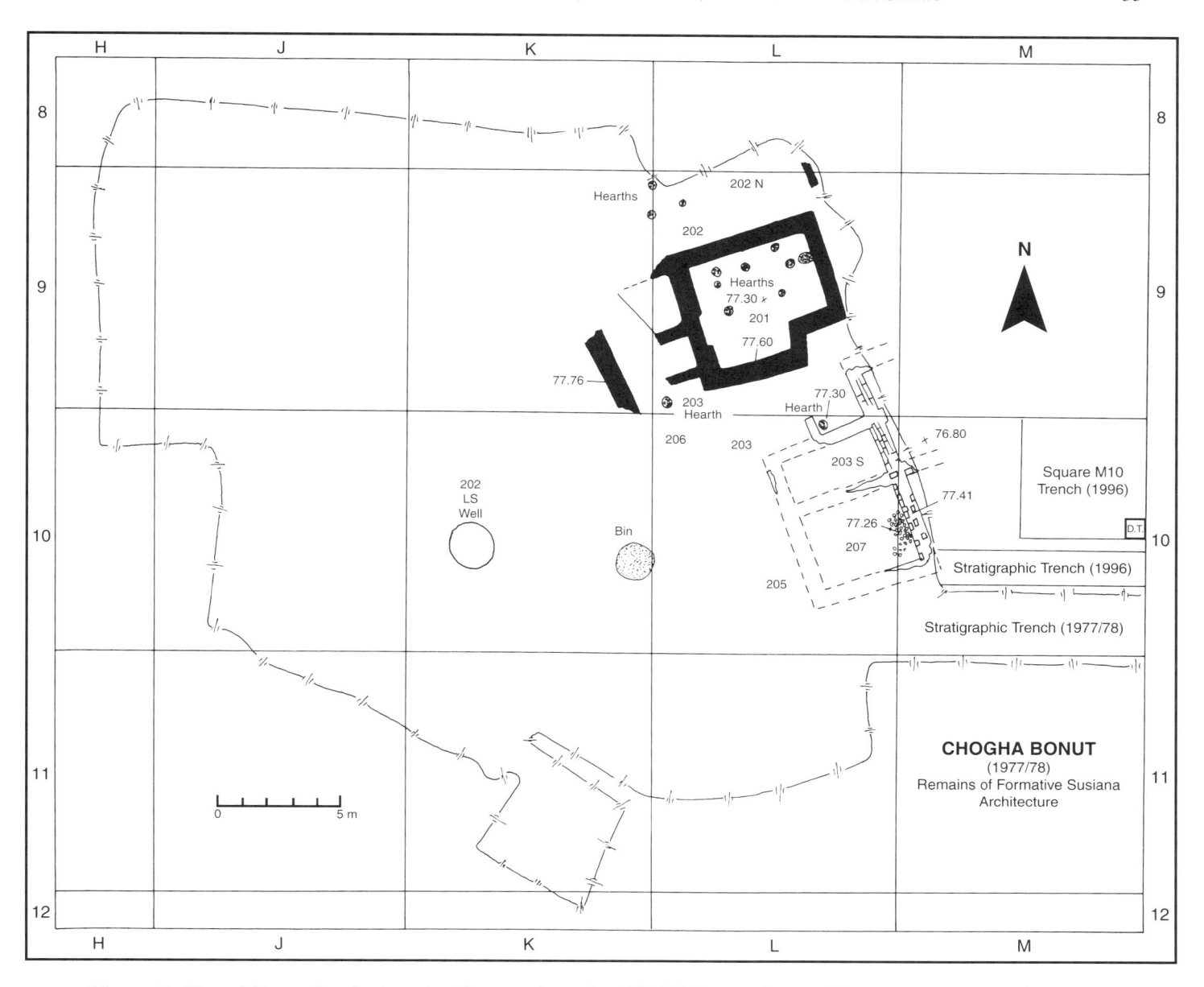

Figure 11. Plan of Formative Susiana Architecture from the 1977/78 Excavations and Square M10 Trench (with Deep Trench [D.T.] Indicated) and Stratigraphic Trench from the 1996 Excavations at Chogha Bonut

THE REMAINS OF ACERAMIC SUSIANA (BONUT A)

From Kantor's notes and our own intensive survey of the site, we knew that the concentration of the archaic architecture and sherds was on the eastern half of Chogha Bonut. We therefore selected this part of the mound to reach the basal levels. Here we found a series of superimposed beaten earth floors with associated fire pits that continued down to the sterile soil. No architectural units were discovered from the aceramic layers, but the presence of a few fragments of straw-tempered mudbricks (pl. 5:A) suggests that solid architecture may exist in other parts of the mound.

The top level in our 5 × 5 m trench (Layer 1; fig. 12) consisted of topsoil and accumulation of bulldozed debris left from 1978 that capped an erosion layer with mixed Archaic, Middle Susiana, and Late Susiana sherds. At el. 75.10 we reached a beaten earth surface (F7) with three fire pits (F1, F4, and F5; fig. 12a). Associated with these fire pits were two post holes (F3/L6, F6/L9) and two circular patches of slightly burnt surface on the preserved northern part of F7 (fig. 12:A).

The beaten earth surface, F7, had been formed on top of a 10 cm occupational debris (L11) that consisted of soft light brown soil mixed with bones, stone blades, and debitage (fig. 12b). Another floor (F14) was reached at el. 74.80. Four circular fire pits (F10/L15, F11/L16, F16/L19, and F17/L20) with fire-cracked rocks were associated with this floor (fig. 13:A). Material remains on this floor consisted of two clusters of rocks, some smeared with red ochre, some bone and stone tools, and a few possible clay tokens.

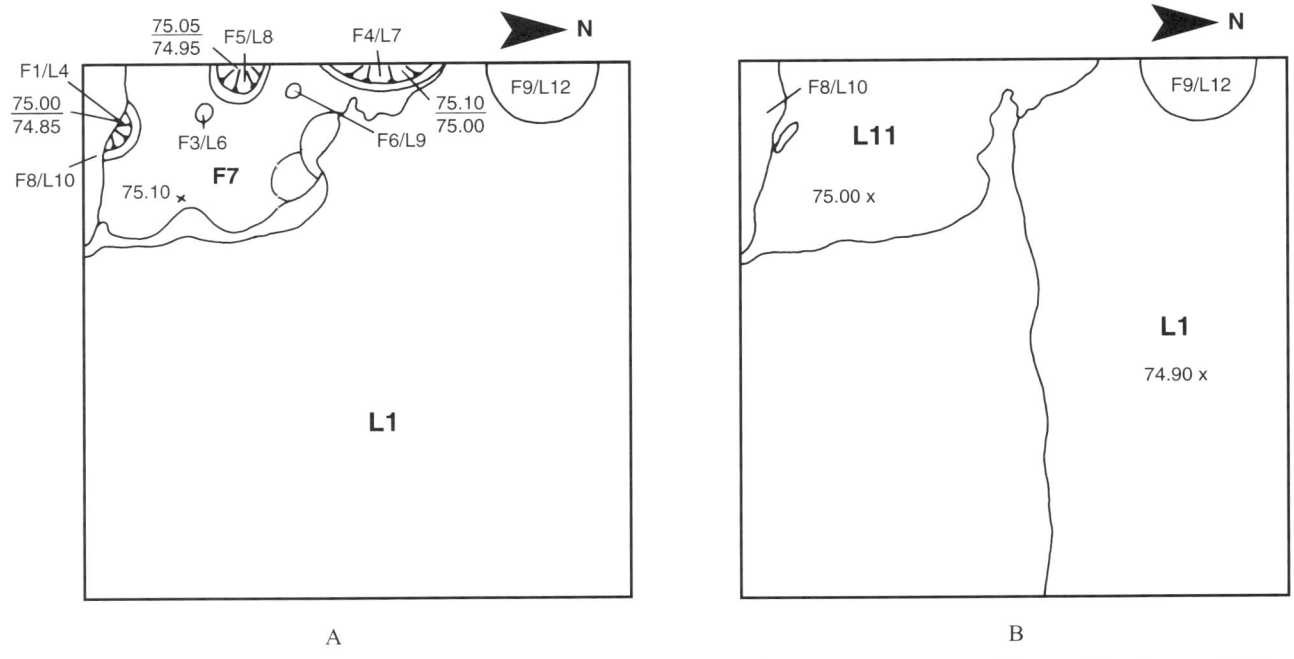

Figure 12. (A) Plan of Layer 1 and Feature 7 in Square M10 (B) Plan of Layer 1 and Layer 11 in Square M10

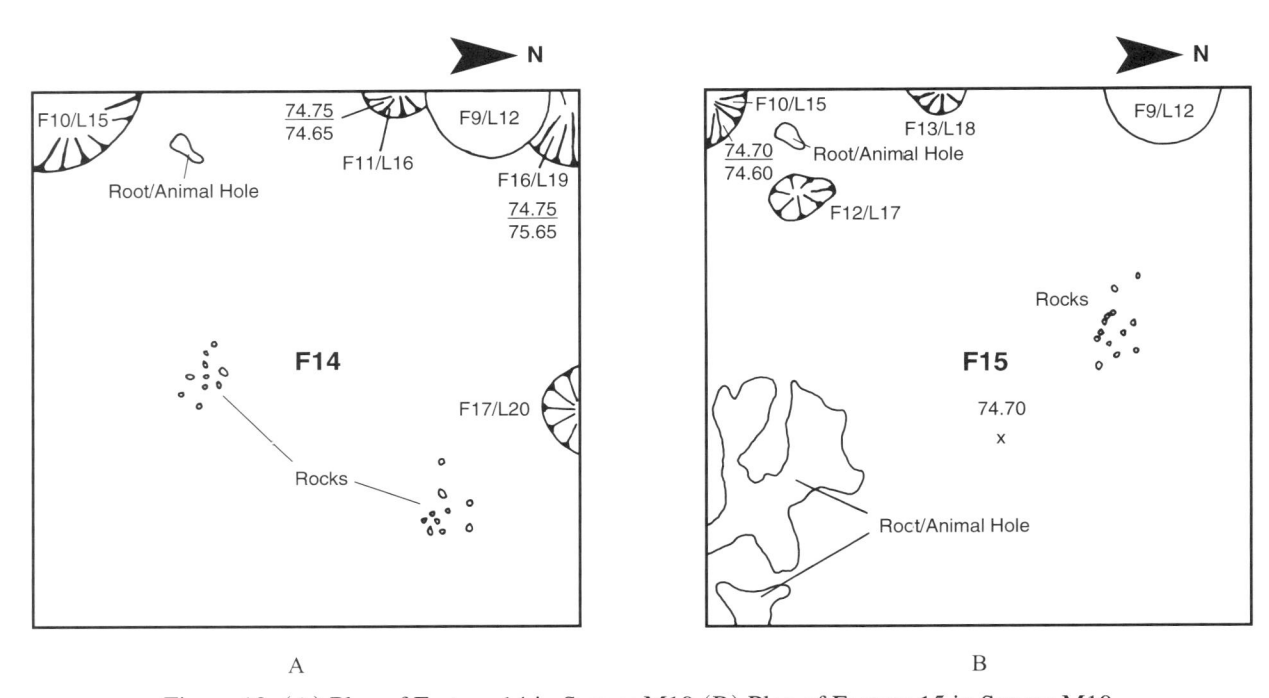

Figure 13. (A) Plan of Feature 14 in Square M10 (B) Plan of Feature 15 in Square M10

Another beaten earth floor (F15) was found immediately below F14 at el. 74.70 (fig. 13:B). The southeastern corner of this floor was pierced and heavily damaged by animal and root holes. The fire pit F10/L15 had penetrated into this floor. Two fire pits, one elliptical (F12/L17) and one circular (F13/L18), were the only installations on this floor. Another cluster of rocks mixed with very soft ash was found on the northern part of the square. Numerous flint blades, bullet-shaped cores, and debitage were scattered across this surface with no apparent spatial pattern.

Six elliptical and circular fire pits with fire-cracked rocks had been dug into the underlying beaten earth floor Feature 18 (fig. 14:A, pl. 7:B). Except for a stone hammer, some bones, and flint blades and cores no other material remains were found on this floor. Twelve centimeters below F18, another beaten earth floor (F28) was reached (fig. 14:B). Two circular fire pits, one large (F26/L32) and one small (F27/L33), were found on this floor. Other finds included articulated sheep/goat legs, two goat horns, a large lump of red ochre, and a number of stone hammers (fig. 14:B).

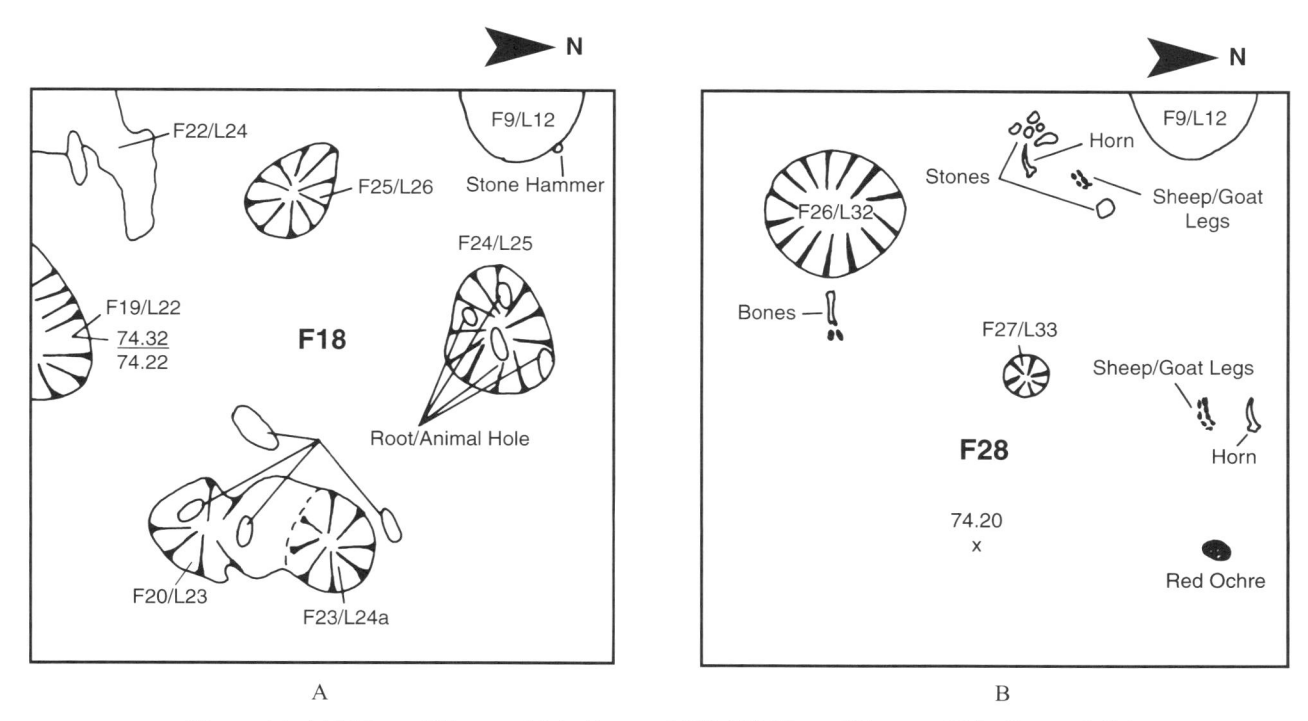

Figure 14. (A) Plan of Feature 18 in Square M10 (B) Plan of Feature 28 in Square M10

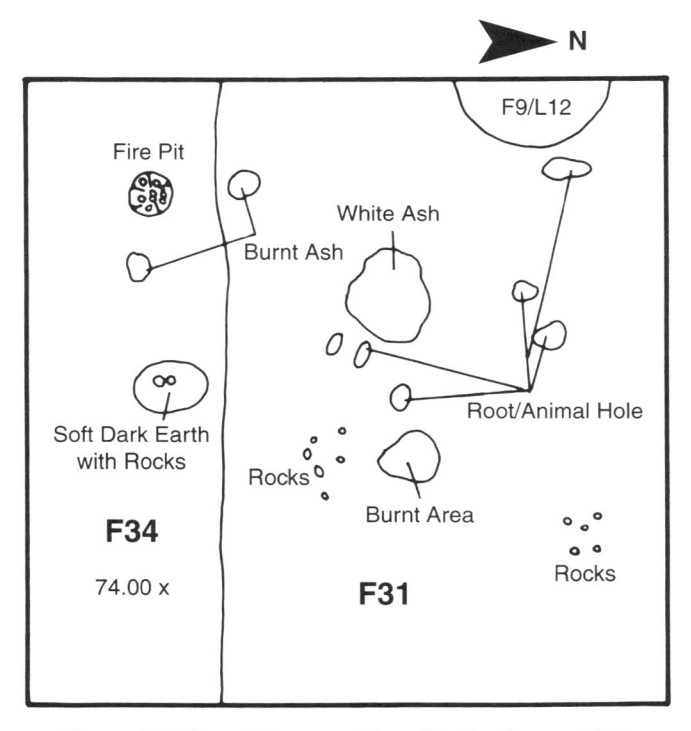

Figure 15. Plan of Features 31 and 34 in Square M10

The next floor (F31) contained a fire pit, an elliptical burnt area, and a circular heap of white ash that was surrounded by animal holes (fig. 15, pl. 8:A). Two clusters of rocks, some smeared with red ochre, were found to the north and south of the elliptical burnt area in the middle of the square. No other feature was associated with this floor.

Because of insufficient time, we did not complete the removal of F31. Instead we chose to excavate the southern part of it to reach the lower layers. Here (fig. 15) we reached an occupational level consisting of greenish tan earth and some light gray ash mixed with bones and flint blades. This debris was accumulated on another beaten earth floor (F34) at el. 74.00. A small circular fire pit filled with fire-cracked rocks was located on the western part of this strip (fig. 15). In the middle, a circular patch of dark soft earth mixed with rocks was found.

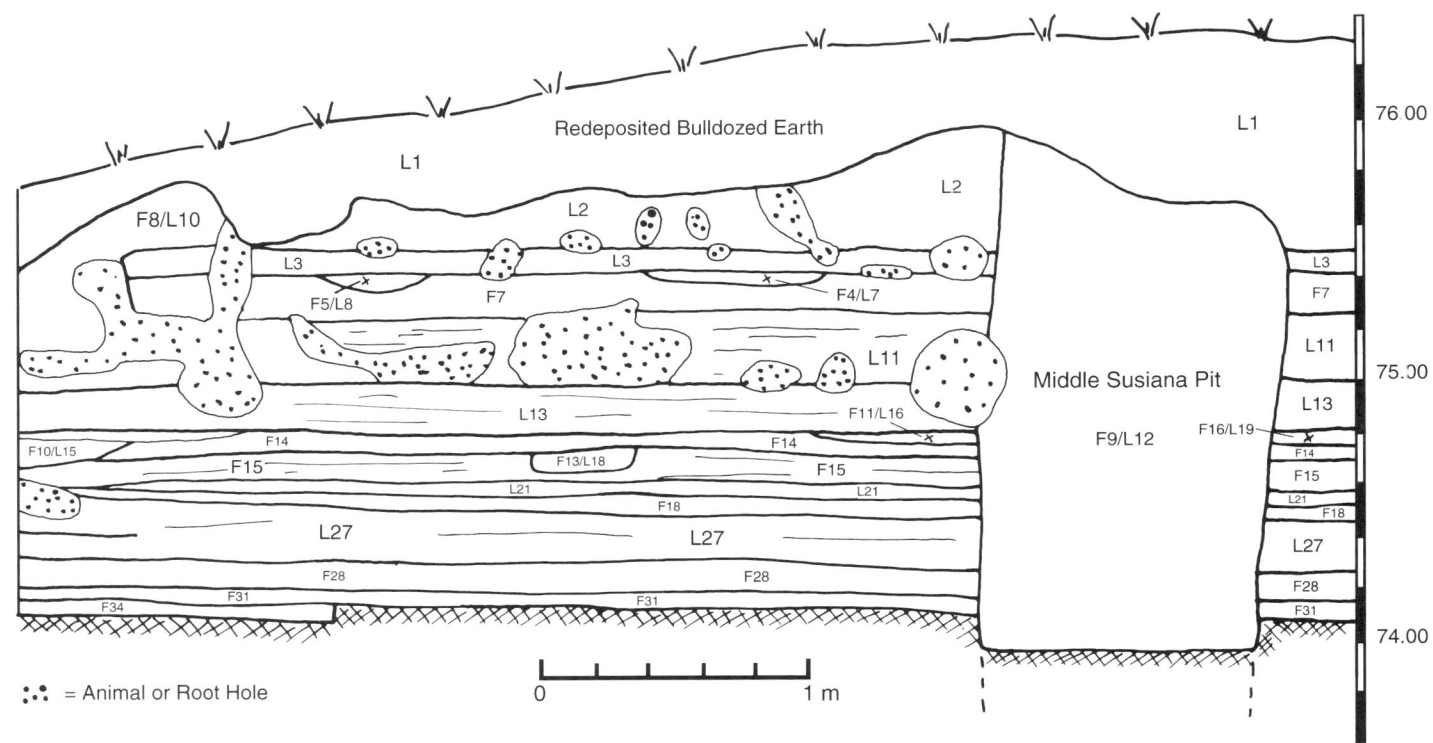

Figure 16. Section Drawing of the West Balk in Square M10 (1996)

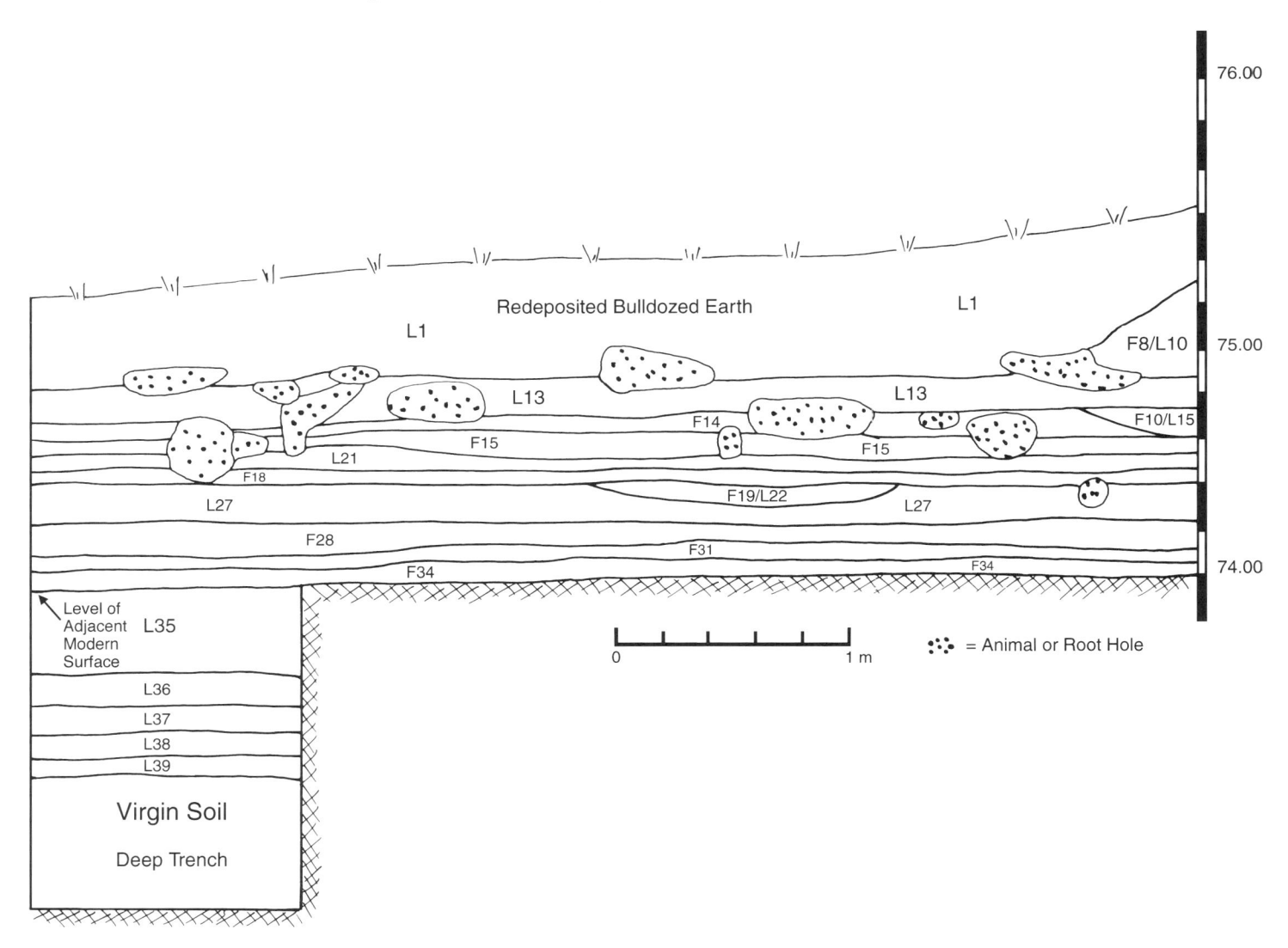

Figure 17. Section Drawing of the South Balk in Square M10 (1996)

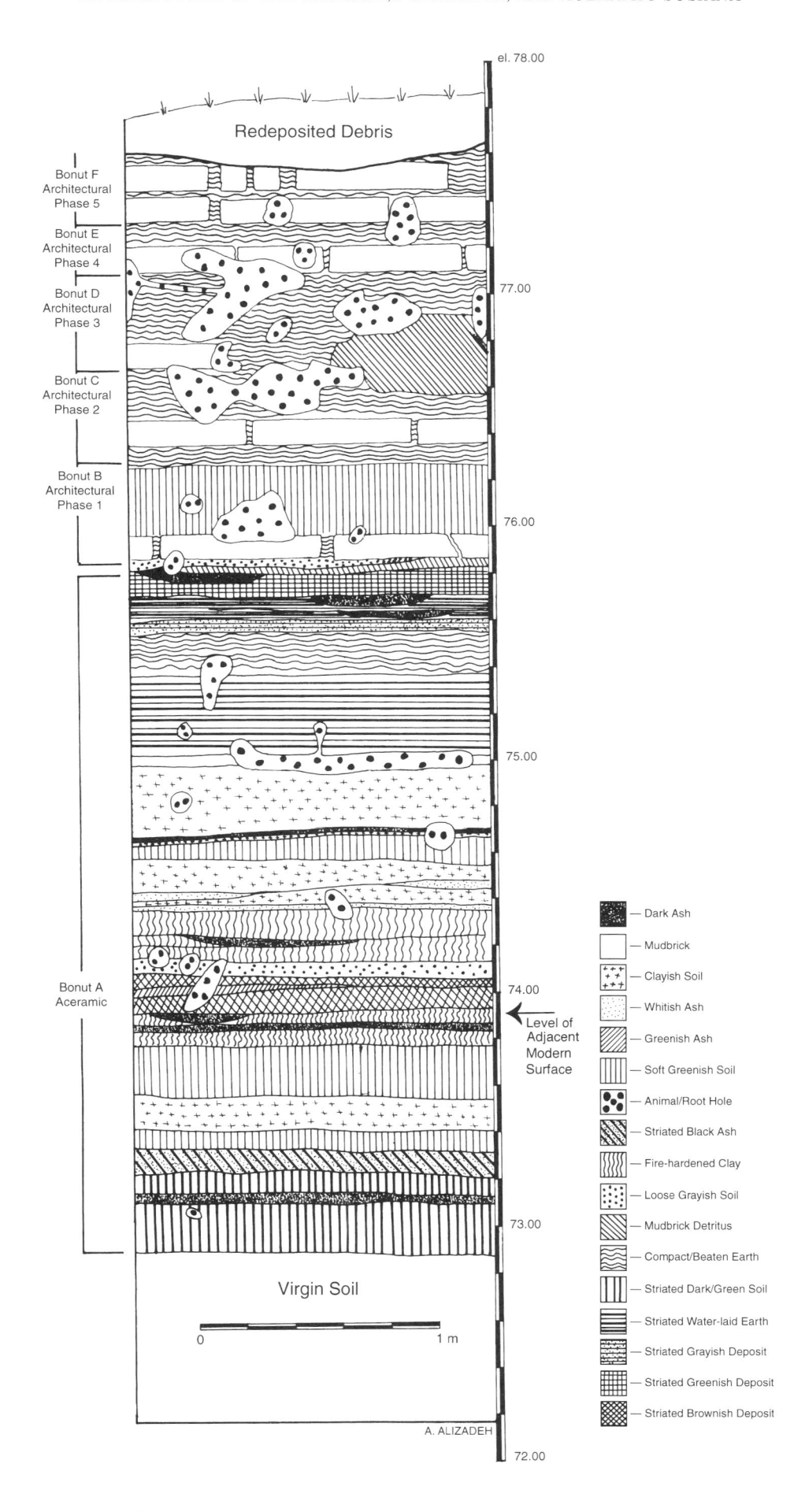

Figure 18. West Section Drawing of the 1996 Stratigraphic Trench

To reach the sterile soil we opened a 1 × 1 m area (D.T.) on the southeastern corner of Feature 34. Here, after excavating a series of superimposed levels of alternating clayish soil, muck, dark ash, and striated dark green soil (figs. 17–18), we reached sterile soil, which we excavated for another meter. This sterile soil consisted of a homogeneous light brown clay deposit devoid of any cultural material. Thus from the beginning of the occupation of Chogha Bonut, only 120 cm of alluvial deposit had been accumulated in this part of lowland Susiana, indicating a very stable environment.

SUMMARY

The eastern part of Chogha Bonut was the most heavily damaged sector of the site. Our surface survey of the site in 1996 and the results of the excavations of 1976/77, 1977/78, and 1996 indicated that primarily the eastern part of the mound was occupied during the Aceramic, Formative, and Archaic periods. As a result, the architectural remains of the Formative and Archaic periods sustained heavy damage.

The surviving architectural remains of the Archaic 0 phase consist of two separate buildings, the complete plans of which cannot be restored. A rather large rectangular structure in Square L11 is all that is left of a building that, based on its rather large size, must have been a hall or courtyard of a much larger structure. The three surviving walls are neatly made of long, cigar-shaped mudbricks laid as stretchers. Two platforms or buttresses, made of the same material, were built against the outer face of its southern wall. The western portion of this building, where presumably the living quarters were located, is entirely destroyed, but the presence of two rows of headers, one slightly higher than the other, may have provided access to the rooms on this side (pl. 14). The other, smaller building in Square L10 is better preserved. The building material is the same as the larger building, but the neat division of space and straightness of its walls indicate a degree of architectural sophistication even in this early phase in Susiana. A wall fragment that lies under the southeastern corner of this building certainly belongs to the earlier Formative Susiana period (fig. 10).

Two partially preserved buildings are dated to the Formative Susiana period. Both buildings are made of long, cigar-shaped mudbricks mixed with bricks of smaller size, as indicated on the plan. Whereas the more heavily damaged building in Squares L10 and M10 may be considered a residential unit, the better-preserved building in Square L9 may have had a different function. Only a largish "hall" of this building remains intact (L9:201; fig. 11). The outer faces of the northern, eastern, and southern walls are perfectly preserved, indicating that no partition walls were built against them. Remains of at least two partition walls perpendicular to the western wall, however, indicate the presence of subsidiary chambers in this section of the building. The interior of the same wall is furnished with a niche and shows traces of mud plaster. The floor of the large "hall" consists of compact, beaten earth into which at least eight fire pits had been dug, although not necessarily at the same time. The shape of the building and the presence of numerous fire pits, certainly uncharacteristic for domestic use, suggest non-domestic use for this building, the nature of which can only be speculated.

As with the pottery, architectural development must have been indigenous at Chogha Bonut, as the successive architectural phases discovered in the stratigraphic trench of the 1996 season indicate (fig. 18; table 2). Furthermore, although no architecture was discovered from the aceramic levels, the presence of mudbrick fragments indicates that the early inhabitants of Chogha Bonut had knowledge of this architectural component. In addition, the use of the characteristic long cigar-shaped mudbricks along with smaller mudbricks in the Formative Susiana period may be considered an intermediate stage, prior to which perhaps smaller mudbricks were used in the Aceramic period, a suggestion that requires further investigation at the site.

Judging by the ephemeral character of the occupation, it is perfectly possible that the Aceramic period at Chogha Bonut may represent a seasonal occupation by people who practiced a mixed economy based on farming and animal husbandry and occasional hunting of animals.

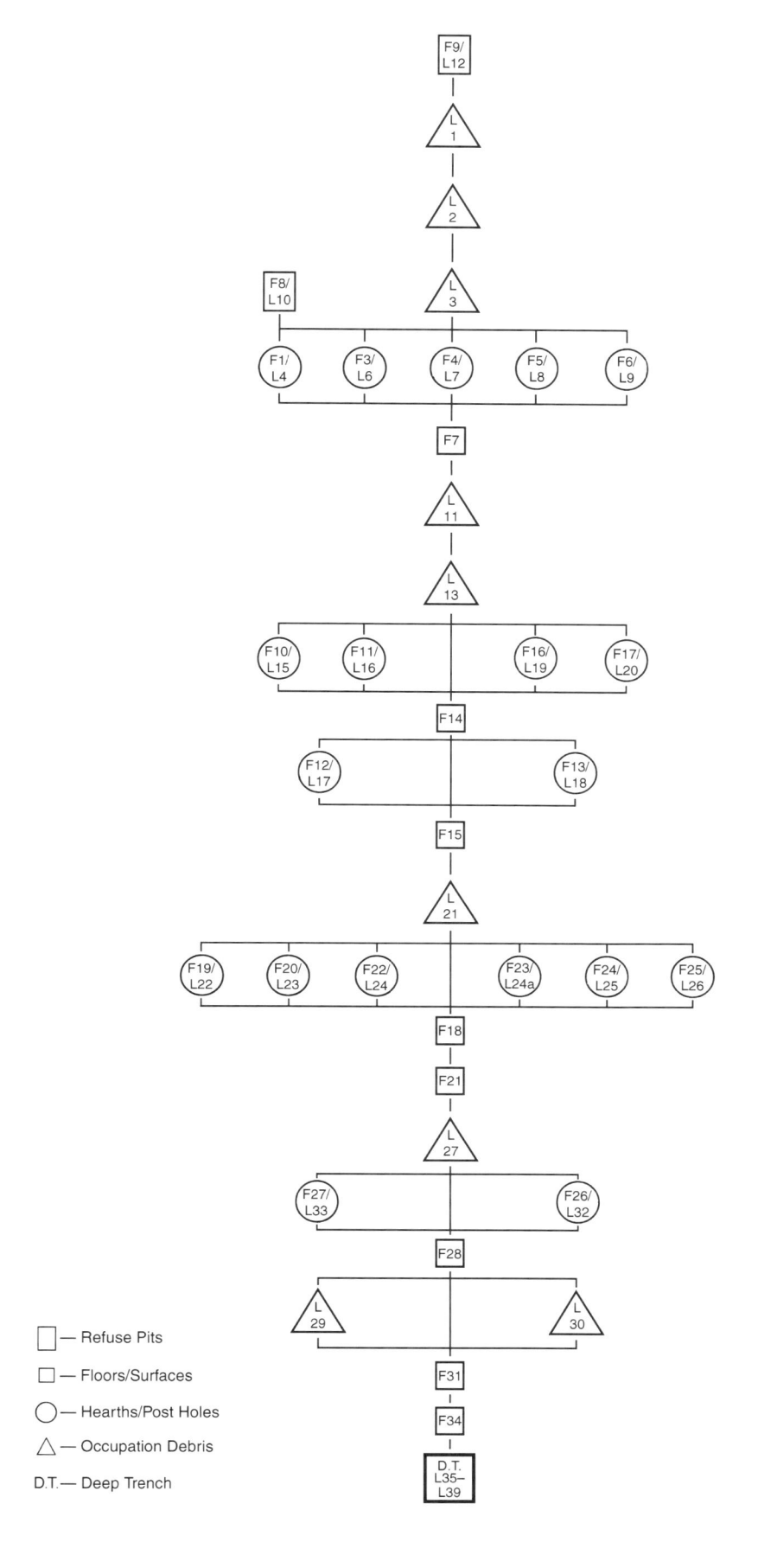

Figure 19. Stratigraphic Sequence in Square M10, Based on Modified Harris Matrix

CHAPTER 6
POTTERY
INTRODUCTION

Only the ceramics of the Formative period and Archaic Susiana 0 phase are analyzed in detail here. For a detailed analysis of the ceramics of other phases that occur at both Chogha Bonut and Chogha Mish, see Kantor and Delougaz 1996.

The pottery was recovered mainly as fragments; there were very few relatively complete examples. Occasionally there were clusters of sherds such as that found just below the destruction level in the area above K10:208. The cluster consisted of fragments of high-necked jars and of a large convex-sided bowl, found covering a small, unpainted jar (Chogha Bonut II-11). The fabrics of the Middle Susiana pottery range from buff to a variety of red wares. Many of the fragments were unpainted and may have belonged not necessarily to plain vessels but to the lower part of jars with a painted upper body. The soil of Chogha Bonut is saline so that often the paint of decorated vessels has become loose and remains lying in the ground, however carefully a sherd is removed. Nonetheless, the designs can be recovered and used for dating. The 1977/78 season pottery strongly suggests that the Middle Susiana occupation at Chogha Bonut belongs to the final phase of the period (figs. 20–22; pl. 26:A–B, D–E).

Among the painted vessels, one of the most prominent types is the large convex-sided bowl decorated with arcs outside and a variety of designs inside. Small painted bowls and cups are also quite common. Often their decoration consists only of horizontal bands and simple geometric motifs (fig. 21); occasionally caprine animals painted with sweeping lines, so characteristic of the Late Middle Susiana phase, occur (fig. 22:F). Another representational motif is the leopard, which occurs on the sherds of a large jar (not illustrated, Ch. B. 1010). The unpainted pottery is represented by a large number of lipsherds and other body fragments in fine, standard, and coarse buff ware. Unfortunately, the majority of the sherds are too small to permit the reconstruction in drawing of the complete forms. It is clear, however, that a considerable variety of shallow and deep bowls was in use. One complete shallow bowl of coarse ware was found in K10:203 and the sherds of a standard ware bowl were recovered from K10:207 (fig. 21:M). Specialized forms occur among the sherds. One is a bowl so shallow that its only practical use would have been as a lid. Others consist of a stand(?) (fig. 21:R), a tortoise vessel (fig. 20), and the lips of coarse ware bowls which are frequently coated outside with a hard mud plaster; such vessels may well have served for some specific function.

The dating of the early levels at Chogha Bonut depends upon the small finds, above all on the pottery. Because of the inaccessibility to the materials excavated in the 1970s, no detailed analysis of the ceramics is possible at present, but some significant facts are already clear. No level at Chogha Bonut is characterized only by sherds of the painted-burnished variant ware diagnostic of the basal levels at Chogha Mish. Rather, the latest architectural phase is characterized by the relatively primitive types of painted-burnished variant vessels and sherds. Furthermore, in most of the early loci at Chogha Bonut, this type is accompanied by other varieties of pottery, some of which are unknown at Chogha Mish. Outstanding are sherds of maroon-on-cream painted ware. Maroon-on-cream painted ware in turn occurs in the earliest architectural phase at Chogha Bonut and is accompanied by smeared-painted ware and almost no painted-burnished variant. In our stratigraphic trench of the 1996 season, the smeared-painted ware continued to the depth of el. 76.50, 30 cm below the lowest architectural phase, in successive occupational levels with no evidence of architecture.

The ceramic evidence can be interpreted in terms of cultural development as follows. The straw-tempered soft ware (fig. 23; pl. 22) and the various types of pottery associated with it, such as smeared-painted ware (pl. 23), represent a stage of development earlier than any known at Chogha Mish. Parallels for the painted-burnished variant ware (pl. 24) and maroon-on-cream painted ware (pl. 25:E–K) have been found at Tappeh Tuleii (Hole 1974, figs. 11–14), northwest of Chogha Bonut, and at Chogha Sefid in Deh Luran (Hole 1977, figs. 43–44). Thus, the evidence from these sites can now be fitted into the early cultural sequence of central Khuzestan as established by the combined finds from Chogha Mish and Chogha Bonut.

Helene Kantor introduced the term Formative Susiana and applied it to those levels at Chogha Bonut with the characteristic painted-burnished variant and some other types of pottery unknown from Chogha Mish. Based on our stratigraphic observations and the stratified sequence of the various types of pottery we found at Chogha Bonut, there seems to have been a pottery phase earlier than that characterized by the presence of the maroon-on-cream painted and painted-burnished variant wares. However, there does not seem to exist any stratigraphic hiatus between this phase and the succeeding Archaic Susiana period. The maroon-on-cream painted ware persisted for a time along side the developing painted-burnished variant ware. It was at this point, in the initial phase of the Archaic Susiana 1, when Chogha Bonut was abandoned to lie deserted for many centuries until it was resettled in the Middle Susiana period.

The ceramic evidence from Chogha Bonut now indicates that at Chogha Mish (in Tr. XXV; see Delougaz and Kantor 1996, pl. 228) a very early phase of Archaic Susiana 1 is represented. In fact, it is probably necessary to subdivide Archaic Susiana 1 phase into two subphases, the initial one represented at Chogha Bonut, and the following phase characterized by standard painted-burnished ware found only at Chogha Mish (Delougaz and Kantor 1996, pls. 223–26). This conclusion now does away with one of the difficulties we have had in considering the painted-burnished ware an extremely wide variation in the type of decoration. The answer is that the painted-burnished variant and the standard painted-burnished ware (not found at Chogha Bonut), although they may have overlapped for a short time, constitute two subphases of the Archaic Susiana 1 phase, hence Archaic Susiana 0.

A typical pottery that precedes the painted-burnished variant ware and overlaps with it for a short time at Chogha Bonut is the maroon-on-cream painted ware, a cream-slipped ware with rows of superimposed triangles as primary design (fig. 25:A–C; pl. 25:E–K). Three sherds of this highly characteristic type from Chogha Mish (Delougaz and Kantor 1996, pl. 228:G–I) indicate that the earliest occupation at Chogha Mish was perhaps for a short time contemporaneous with Chogha Bonut before it was deserted.

With the realization that at Chogha Bonut we are dealing with at least three successive chronological phases represented by distinctive ceramic assemblages, the assumption of a continuous development, one leading steadily to the other, is warranted. In addition to the evidence of pottery, Chogha Bonut has also provided examples of T-shaped figurines analogous to those found in the basal levels at Chogha Mish, indicating initial contemporaneity of Chogha Mish with Chogha Bonut.

As noted above, at Chogha Bonut the painted-burnished variant ware is frequently accompanied by sherds of maroon-on-cream painted ware. In our 1996 stratigraphic trench, we did not find any evidence of a stratigraphic break between the layers marked by the presence of painted-burnished variant and maroon-on-cream painted ware, nor did we find any break between these and those layers that contained smeared-painted ware, suggesting an uninterrupted development of local pottery.

The smeared-painted ware was known from the 1977/78 season. Helene Kantor termed this characteristic ware "film-painted ware" to underline the fact that on some of the examples the paint is so thin that the underlying surface can be seen. But the term seems to be misleading, and in any case, most of the sherds of this type have thick paint, hence the descriptive term "smeared-painted." We chose the term "smeared" to describe its highly characteristic technique of painting. As can be seen on plate 23, the paint is smeared on the surface of the vessel using fingers, the impressions of which are still clearly visible (fig. 24:I–K, M).

The smeared-painted ware itself overlaps for a short time with an earlier simple straw-tempered soft ware and a chaff/straw-tempered red-burnished ware of the initial ceramic period at Chogha Bonut (figs. 23–24; pls. 22–23). Thus one of the major problems at Chogha Mish, namely, the antecedent for the already sophisticated ceramics of the Archaic Susiana period, can now be addressed.

For the initial ceramic period characterized by the coarse straw-tempered and red-burnished wares at Chogha Bonut, we suggest the term "Formative Susiana," formerly used by Helene Kantor for the phase characterized by the painted-burnished variant ware. The stratified evidence from our stratigraphic trench at Chogha Bonut indicates that the painted-burnished variant ware was preceded by at least two distinct earlier ceramic phases and therefore the term "Formative" cannot apply to the cultural stage characterized by the painted-burnished variant ware, clearly a late comer. Based on our understanding of the pottery sequence at Chogha Bonut and Chogha Mish, we suggest the term Formative Susiana for the period characterized by the coarse, straw-tempered, and smeared-painted wares. The latter seems to have been an experimental stage in manufacturing painted pottery as it appears to have been short-lived and so far has been found only at Chogha Bonut.

As we mentioned before, a distinct phase characterized by maroon-on-cream painted ware follows the Formative period, preceding and overlapping with the phase characterized by the painted-burnished variant. To avoid confusion by introducing yet another term, we suggest Archaic 0 for this phase and reserve Archaic Susiana 1 for the phase characterized by both the painted-burnished variant and standard painted-burnished wares, both present at the basal levels at Chogha Mish. At Chogha Bonut the remains of the Formative period rest on layers with ashy deposits, hearths, flint implements, and animal bones, but not pottery. We propose Aceramic Susiana for this initial phase of the colonization of the Susiana plain.

INTER-REGIONAL CONNECTION

The combined finds from Chogha Bonut and Chogha Mish provide excellent links with other areas. In the Susiana plain not far from Susa, agricultural operations brought to life and partly destroyed the site of Tappeh Tuleii with shallow deposits containing sherds comparable to Chogha Bonut Archaic Susiana 0 (Hole 1974, figs. 11–14). Since then at least two more settlements of the Formative period have been found, one a few kilometers south of Chogha Bonut and another in the Mianab region south of Shushtar. Farther afield in Deh Luran, Chogha Sefid provides close parallels for the maroon-on-cream painted ware (Hole 1977, fig. 43), but here this ware is associated with the later standard painted-burnished ware (Hole 1977, fig. 44:bb), which is the hallmark of the Archaic Susiana 1 phase at Chogha Mish.

Another element connecting Chogha Sefid with Chogha Bonut and Chogha Mish is the T-shaped figurines, which occur in great quantity at Deh Luran sites (Hole, Flannery, and Neely 1969, fig. 98, pl. 38:I; Hole 1977, fig. 91). Remarkably similar figurines have been found very far away in northwestern Iran at Jarmo (Broman Morales 1983, fig. 164:7a–11) and Sarab (Broman Morales 1990, pl. 15:T–AB) in the Zagros Mountains and at the site of Tappeh Sang-e Chakhmaq (Masuda 1974, fig. 3:10, 12) in the Iranian central plateau. Tappeh Sang-e Chakhmaq has also provided straw-tempered bowls of simple shapes decorated with panels strongly reminiscent of those typical for the painted-burnished variant. Similar pottery is also reported from the early Neolithic site of Jeitun in Turkmanestan (Masson and Sarianidi 1972, fig. 7). A further link with northwestern Iran is hinted at by the presence of the specific long, cigar-shaped mudbricks from Jeitun (Masson and Sarianidi 1972, p. 36, pl. 7). In view of the normal situation in Iran, where local cultures developed in the individual plains and valleys, it is indeed remarkable to find at this early period such relatively strong similarities of materials so far apart. The circumstances raise many questions as to the possibility of a relatively simple cultural tradition lying at the root of many more elaborate and differentiated periods.

Can these close parallels from widely separated sites in southern Turkmanestan (Jeitun; ibid., p. 36, fig. 7), the central plateau (Tappeh Sang-e Chakhmaq), the Zagros Mountains (Jarmo and Sarab), Deh Luran (Tappeh Ali Kosh and Chogha Sefid), and Susiana be interpreted as regional variations of a single incipient cultural horizon which can be taken as the common ancestor of many later regional traditions in Iran? It should be noted, however, that the problem in accepting such a proposal is that we do not have any representatives of an analogous cultural phase in any known geographically intervening sites. For example, at Tappeh Sialk the early straw-tempered pottery of levels 1 and 2 is quite different (Ghirshman 1938, pp. 11–14, pls. 4–6). In the northwest, at Tappeh Zagheh, nothing has been published antedating the Zagheh phase that appears to be contemporary with the Late Archaic/Early Susiana period (Negahban 1973, 1977). In the northwest, the Neolithic site of Haji Firuz has nothing similar, although it has produced primitive pottery (Voigt 1983). Accordingly, the comparisons for the transitional Formative/Archaic Susiana phase can give us hints that it may have been a widely distributed primeval culture. If such was actually the case, then it can be taken as the common ancestor of many of the regional cultures in Iran.

Unlike a number of early Neolithic sites, such as Jarmo and Sarab in the Zagros Mountains and Tappeh Ali Kosh in lowland Deh Luran, pottery appeared at Chogha Bonut in its initial, rudimentary form and developed through time until it reached its zenith by the end of the Late Susiana period. Thus it is tempting to consider Susiana as the primary locus for the invention of pottery in southwestern Iran. But such an assertion must be supported by more evidence than we have at present.

POTTERY SEQUENCE AND TYPOLOGY

LATE SUSIANA 2

Late Susiana pottery comes in many types and shapes; the following descriptions are only of the types found at Chogha Bonut.

Type 1: Standard Buff Ware

The greater part of the Late Susiana pottery was made of what is basically a single ware, standard buff ware, even though it exhibits a great range of gradations from relatively coarse to extremely fine (pl. 26:C). The paste is dense and tempered with mineral inclusions, normally so small and evenly diffused through the paste as to be hardly noticeable. Thicker, coarser variations have visible grits and sometimes traces of vegetal tempering. The color varies considerably, ranging from brown to apricot or pink tones, but buff shades are the most common. Greenish buff examples are relatively rare. There are no gray cores.

The vessels are well manufactured, even in the cases where the vessel is large and thick. Very regular horizontal striations sometimes occurring on necks suggest that such specimens were turned rather rapidly on some kind of a wheel, but on the whole the pottery is still handmade. The paint varies in color from purplish brown to almost black (fig. 21:I). It tends to be glossy, although matt versions also appear. In places where the paint has flaked away, its traces can be clearly seen on the surface.

Type 2: Red Wares

There is a considerable diversity among the specimens of red ware. Nonetheless, all varieties resemble each other in having a dense paste and in being highly fired, often with a metallic ring. Sometimes a few scattered small grits and air pockets occur, but often there is no visible tempering. The interior and exterior colors of the paste vary through many shades of buff, brown, brownish red, orange, or pale red. Based on the presence or absence of gray or black core, and despite their basic identity, the red ware sherds can be divided into two main categories. The sherds of the latter group have a thick dark core with only a thin layer of red on each side, except for some examples where the red layers are thicker. The dark core does not seem to be indicative of low firing; such sherds have a high ringing clink.

Dark core ware occurs either with or without a red wash. The surfaces of the uncoated group can be either matt or stroke burnished. The stroke burnishing usually leaves a typically rippled surface and sometimes has produced a very high sheen. Such sherds occur in red or in a light tan or cream variant. In the coated group of the dark core ware, the red wash is usually fairly dense, but frequently uneven. Sometimes the wash is only thinly smeared. Dark core, red-washed sherds were sometimes burnished, either so slightly as to be hardly apparent or enough to produce a considerable sheen.

Type 3: Gray Ware

Gray ware is very rare. It is uniformly dense and usually without visible tempering. Both the interior and exterior surfaces of bowls are burnished with irregular horizontal strokes.

LATE MIDDLE SUSIANA

Sherds and vessels belonging to the Late Middle Susiana phase are the most numerous at Chogha Bonut. The following is the description of the types available for analysis and does not include the entire range of Middle Susiana pottery repertoire at Chogha Bonut.

Type 1: Standard Buff Ware

The paste of standard buff ware varies in color from various shades of brownish yellow, through cream, to greenish buff (pl. 26:A–B, D–E). The mineral inclusion varies in both the amount of grit and the size of the individual grains. Sometimes larger grits, though scattered rather sparsely in the paste itself, were worked up to the surface in clusters during the shaping and smoothing of the vessels. The texture of the paste varies from granular to dense.

The vessels are handmade and frequently show marks of shaping and scraping. In some cases surfaces remain relatively rough; in others there has been smoothing, though usually not enough to obliterate all the scrape marks or to produce a polish. Often smoothing of still moist vessels produced a self slip difficult to distinguish from actual slips added separately unless the latter are of a different shade than the paste.

The color of the paint ranges from brown to black and not infrequently has a definite greenish tinge, due perhaps to overfiring and/or chemical agents. The thickness of the paint also varies considerably. The thicker paint is darker in color, often granular, and tends to flake.

Type 2: Fine Buff Ware

The finer range of buff ware is distinguishable by a dense paste, the absence of any visible tempering, and thin body walls, about 6 mm or less. The ware tends to be more highly fired than the standard varieties. This type usually has a creamy buff slip on both the interior and exterior surfaces.

Type 3: Straw-tempered Buff Ware

Rare at Chogha Bonut, straw-tempered buff ware is a variant of the standard buff ware and is distinguished by its vegetal tempering and also by the relative thickness of the walls of the vessels. The ware was used for some of the coarser domestic vessels, which are usually unpainted.

Type 4: Plain Red Ware

Plain red ware is another rare Middle Susiana type at Chogha Bonut, but it is relatively common at Chogha Mish. The paste is dense, granular, and the mineral tempering is often too fine to be easily visible. Apart from the usual sand or very fine grits, mica or white particles can also be seen in larger vessels. Vessels and sherds of this type are high fired and as a result have a clinky ring. The basic color is bricky red, but light orange-red and brown shades occur. Though not common, examples of a gray core do occur.

Type 5: Gray Ware

Gray ware is a rare type represented by a few sherds characterized by their dense, uniformly gray paste, with only occasional scattered grits visible. The surfaces of the vessels are burnished. The gray ware seems to be typical for the Late Middle Susiana phase and, though rare at both Chogha Bonut and Chogha Mish, it is known from several sites in central Khuzestan.[22]

ARCHAIC AND FORMATIVE SUSIANA

Nine major types of pottery are distinguished at Chogha Bonut, described below in the order of their stratigraphic position, beginning with the earliest.

Type 1: Straw-tempered Soft Ware

Straw-tempered soft ware is the earliest type at Chogha Bonut (fig. 23; pls. 21:A–D, 22), occurring for the first time at a depth of el. 75.60 in the stratigraphic trench just below the first earliest evidence of solid architecture with long, cigar-shaped mudbricks. The color of the paste ranges from yellowish (10YR 7/1 on the Munsell scale) to brownish (10YR 5/3) to grayish buff (10YR 5/2) with usually a gray core (10YR 5/1) either gradually or abruptly changing to the color of the surface. The specimens are heavily straw tempered and sometimes include medium to large grits. Some pieces seem to have either a wash of fugitive red ochre or are decorated with a simple band of fugitive red paint. A finer version (fig. 23:M–O) has a smooth face, is less friable, and continues throughout the sequence. The surface of the earlier specimens is usually mottled red and/or gray and pitted as a result of the burning-out of straw (pl. 22:B–D). The shapes are simple and consist of dimple base open, hemispherical bowls with simple blunt or beaded lip, straight-sided shallow trays, and hole-mouth jars. Impressions of over-two, under-two twilled baskets on a few pieces (pl. 22:A) indicate that in the beginning of the sequence baskets were used to shape the pottery.

Type 2: Red-slipped Straw-tempered Ware

Red-slipped straw-tempered ware has a denser paste than straw-tempered soft ware (type 1). The color of the paste ranges from orange buff to light orange to buff with a gray core usually at or close to the thicker base. Sometimes a gray core is sandwiched between two layers of orange buff and/or buff (fig. 24:R). The surface is usually smoothed and has a red or maroon wash and is occasionally burnished.

Type 3: Smeared-painted Ware

Smeared-painted ware is rather well baked. Fine straw or, more frequently, chaff is used as the tempering agent. The paste is usually orange buff and occasionally the gray core changes gradually or abruptly to buff or orange buff. A brownish buff or light maroon slip or wash (sometimes thick and uneven) is usually applied to both interior and exte-

---

22. Jafarabad, Levels 3m and n (Dollfus 1975, fig. 53:11–13); Bendebal, Levels 16, 14–13 (Dollfus 1983, figs. 68:3–4, 8; 79:8 and 83:3, 5); Susa (Le Breton 1947, fig. 33:7); and Qabr-e Sheikheyn (Weiss 1976, fig. 11). For presumably analogous burnished-black ware, see Deh Luran, Tappeh Sabz, Bayat Phase (Hole, Flannery, and Neely 1969, pp. 168–69).

rior surfaces. The exterior surface is usually painted with a pigment ranging in color from red to maroon to brown and apparently applied with fingers. The simple forms consist of hemispherical bowls with beaded or blunt lips and dimple base and hole-mouth jars (fig. 24:A–B, D, J, L; pls. 21:E–J, X, 23).

Type 4: Orange Buff Plain Ware

Orange buff plain ware is an undecorated variety of smeared-painted ware (type 3; fig. 24:C, E–H; pl. 21:K–M, U–W, Y–Z).

Type 5: Maroon-on-Cream Painted Ware

Maroon-on-cream painted ware (figs. 24:P–Q, S–T, 25, 26:A–B, D, I; pls. 21:N–T, 25:E–K) is a well-baked type that has fine vegetal tempering mixed with occasional sand or medium grits. The color of the paste is usually uniformly pale red, but sometimes a dark to light gray streak is sandwiched between pale red layers; some specimens have a completely gray core. The surface treatment consists of a cream slip/wash both on the interior and exterior surfaces over which maroon to reddish brown paint is applied. The painted designs primarily consist of horizontal rows of superimposed triangles with their apexes pointing down and occasionally of checkered pattern. The whole surface is usually burnished, but the painted area has a higher luster. Rare variations of this type are pieces with thinner walls and dark paint, though not fugitive, but applied so thin and perhaps not well baked that if rubbed hard, the paint can be removed leaving a shade on the surface.

Type 6: Black-on-Cream Painted Ware

Essentially the same as maroon-on-cream painted ware (type 5), black-on-cream painted ware differs in painted decoration. It accompanies maroon-on-cream painted ware and overlaps with the painted-burnished variant ware. Type 6 decoration consists of a horizontal row of reserved triangles hanging from the lip and painted chevrons (figs. 24:N–O; 26:C, E, G–H). This type seems to be limited to the Susiana area and is also found at Tappeh Tuleii.[23]

Type 7: Broad Band-painted Ware

Perhaps related to black-on-cream painted ware, broad band painted ware is a straw-tempered buff ware with usually a light gray core or a streak of gray near the base. The color of the interior surface varies from yellowish orange to bright rose orange to light brownish buff. The exterior surface is usually mottled from tan to orange. Both interior and exterior surfaces are burnished. The single broad band with uneven lower edge and characteristic trickles ranges in color from dark brown to reddish brown to maroon (fig. 26:I–L). Examples of this type were found at Chogha Mish and Chogha Sefid.[24]

Type 8: Maroon-on-Red Painted Ware

Only two pieces of maroon-on-red painted ware were found in a disturbed context. The dense paste is light red in color with a streak of gray and tempered with fine chaff. The exterior is covered with a red slip over which a geometric design is painted with a deep maroon pigment. The entire surface is burnished to a high luster (fig. 24:U–V).

Type 9: Painted-burnished Variant Ware

The paste and surface treatment of this prominent ware (figs. 27–28; pls. 24, 25:B–D) are very similar to those of maroon-on-cream painted ware (type 5). The color of the paste varies from light buff to yellowish tan, brown, or orange. It often has a marked gray or dark core. The usual straw face is either self slipped or has a thin coating of the same kind of clay that was mixed with straw to form the paste. Sometimes straw cavities show through on the surface. The color of the surface is either orange or, more often, mottled orange and yellowish buff. Unlike the standard painted-burnished ware, the burnished surface of this type is not always shiny. This is particularly noticeable on the paint, which sometimes has relatively little sheen and, when worn, none at all.

---

23. Compare Hole 1974, figs. 13:h–k, 14:d.

24. Delougaz and Kantor 1996, pl. 228:J–K; Hole 1977, fig. 46:a–g.

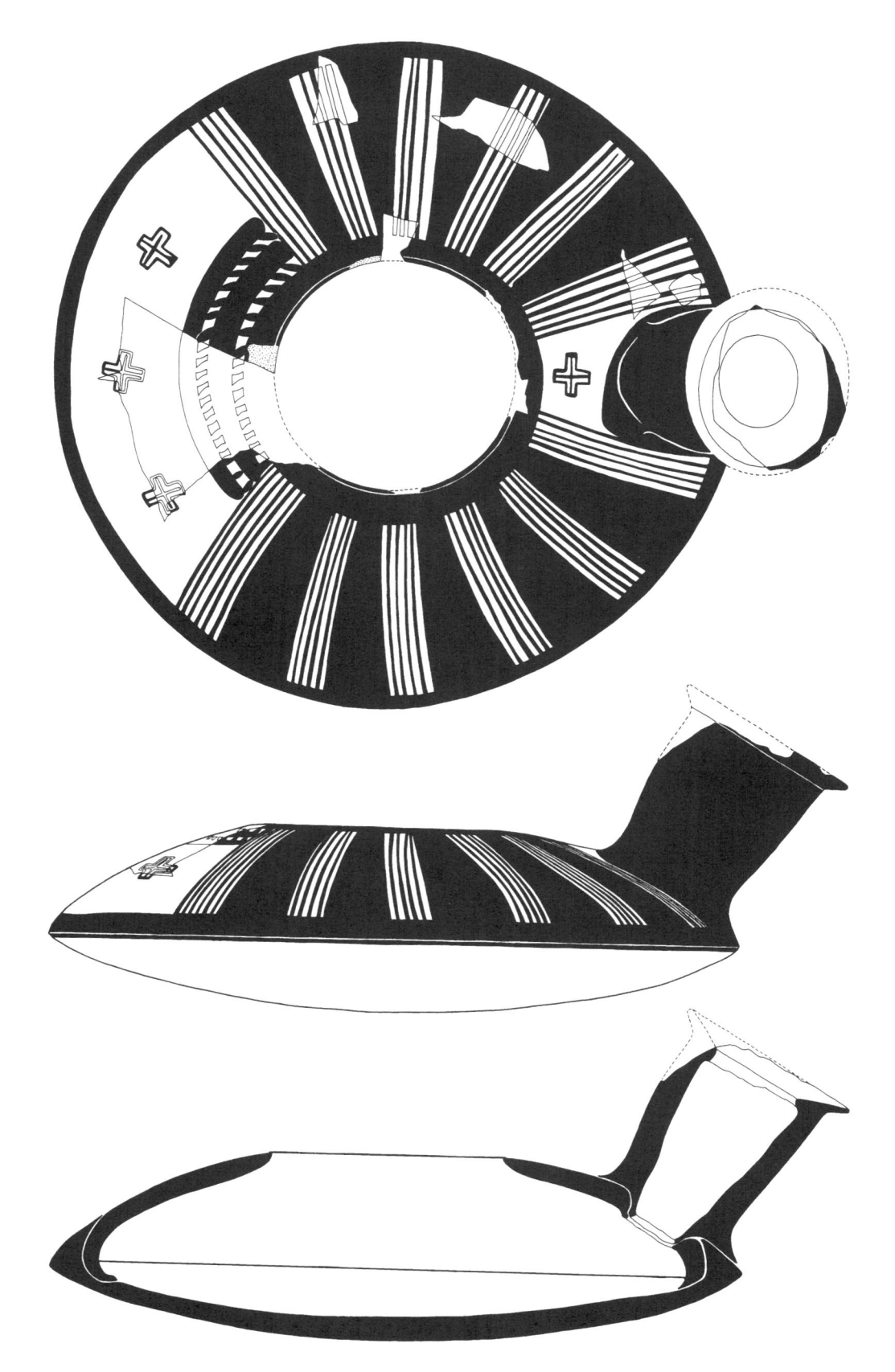

Field Number	Findspot	Elevation	Description
B I-1	NA	Surface	Middle Susiana standard ware: Warm buff clay. Fine mineral inclusion. Buff slipped. Dark paint

Figure 20. Middle Susiana Tortoise Vessel. Scale 2:5

Figure 21. Various Types of Middle and Late Susiana Pottery. Scale 2:5

	Field Number	Findspot	Elevation	Description
A	B 1091	NA	NA	Middle Susiana standard ware: Greenish buff clay, some very fine grits included. Slipped. Dark paint
B	B 1188	M9:101	NA	Middle Susiana standard ware: Body sherd probably belonging to a tortoise vessel. Yellowish buff paste with some medium size grits. Perhaps creamy buff slipped. Granular dark brown paint
C	B 1174	NA	NA	Middle Susiana standard ware: Yellowish buff clay with some small grits. Yellowish buff slipped. Dark brown paint
D	B 1175	NA	NA	Middle Susiana fine ware: Buff clay with no visible inclusion. Creamy buff slipped. Black paint
E	B 1191	L10:101	78.41	Middle Susiana standard ware: Greenish buff clay grading to reddish. Dense paste with few scattered grits and air pockets. Dark brown to black paint
F	B 1187	M10:101	NA	Middle Susiana standard ware: Dense reddish buff clay grading to greenish buff with small to medium grits. Creamy green slip on the interior; light creamy buff slip on the exterior. Black flaky paint
G	B 2030	NA	NA	Middle Susiana standard ware: Dense buff greenish clay with small grit tempering. Both surfaces smoothed and probably slipped. Thick greenish brown paint, in some places vitrified
H	B 2029	NA	NA	Middle Susiana standard ware: Light brownish buff clay with no visible inclusion. Wet-smoothing is apparent from finger marks on the exterior. Thick granular dark paint
I	B 2026	K10:202	78.57	Late Susiana standard ware: Creamy buff clay with no visible inclusion. Slipped all over. Dark paint
J	B 1007	NA	NA	Middle Susiana gray ware: Gray paste grading to black with no visible inclusion. Surface burnished gray-black with horizontal and diagonal burnishing strokes still visible. Two shallow grooves near the exterior lip
K	B 1185	L9:102	78.78	Middle/Late Susiana 1 standard ware: Dense yellowish buff clay with some scattered fine grits. Wet-smoothed with approximately horizontal striations on the interior. Flaky dark brown to black paint
L	B 1314	L11:103	79.17	Middle Susiana fine ware: Creamy buff paste with few visible small grits. Probably light cream slip on the exterior, light cream buff on the interior. Black paint grading to dark brown
M	B II-24	K10:207	78.28	Middle Susiana standard ware: Dense buff paste with medium to large grits. Interior wet-smoothed, exterior somewhat rough with drag marks visible
N	B 1240	M10:101	NA	Middle Susiana standard ware: Creamy buff paste with some medium size grits. Light creamy buff slip on the exterior and interior surfaces. Dark brown paint grading to reddish brown
O	B 2036	K10:205	79.28	Middle Susiana standard ware: Fragment of a ladle handle; dense yellowish buff paste with no visible inclusion. Dark brown paint
P	B I-2	NA	NA	Middle Susiana standard ware: Dense greenish buff paste with no visible inclusion. Surface color varies from greenish to yellowish buff. Olive green paint, slightly granular where thicker
Q	B 2039	K10:205	79.28	Middle Susiana fine ware: Dense greenish buff paste with no visible inclusion. Possibly self slipped or greenish to yellow slip applied to the exterior surface. Flaky, granular black paint
R	B 1193	L9:102	78.78	Middle Susiana standard ware: Dense, yellowish buff paste with scattered small grits. Roughly horizontal striation marks on the interior; on the exterior some scoring marks. Creamy buff with pink tinge near top. Brown paint

POTTERY 51

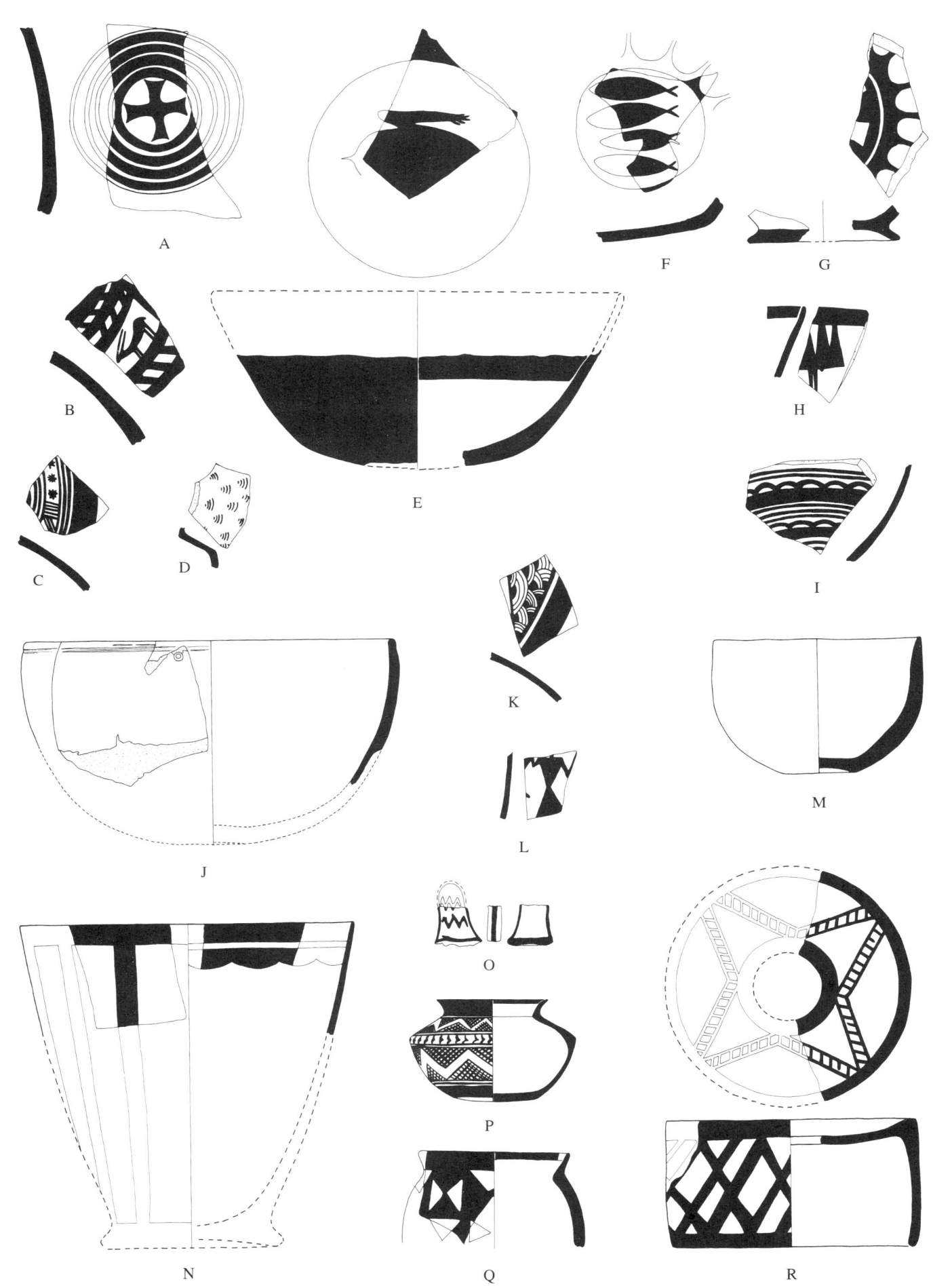

Figure 21. Various Types of Middle and Late Susiana Pottery. Scale 2:5

Figure 22. Various Types of Middle Susiana Pottery. Scale 2:5

	Field Number	Findspot	Elevation	Description
A	B 1334	M10:101	NA	Middle Susiana fine ware: Light greenish paste with no visible inclusion. Interior and exterior surfaces slipped. Greenish granular paint
B	B 1201	M10:101	NA	Middle Susiana standard ware: Orange buff paste with small grits inclusion. Creamy buff slip on the interior and exterior. Brown paint grading to dark brown, partly flaked off
C	B 1269	M10:101	NA	Middle Susiana reddish orange fine ware: Some visible grits. Possibly slipped. Reddish light brown paint
D	B 1206	M10:101	NA	Middle Susiana standard ware: Orange buff paste with some small grits. Exterior creamy buff slipped. Dark brown paint grading to black
E	B 1229	M9:101	NA	Middle Susiana fine ware: Light greenish buff paste with no visible inclusion. Exterior creamy buff slipped. Dark brown granulated paint grading to black
F	B 2024	K10:201	79.32	Middle Susiana fine ware: Dense yellowish buff paste with no visible inclusion. Creamy buff slipped. Dark brown paint laid down in many horizontal strokes, edges of which are still visible
G	B 1119	L10:103	78.72	Middle Susiana fine ware: Dense greenish buff paste with no visible inclusion. Overfired and somewhat warped. Probably slipped. Dark brown paint, grading to greenish brown
H	B 1012	NA	NA	Middle Susiana fine ware: Greenish buff paste with no visible inclusion. Creamy buff slipped. Black paint grading to brown where thinner
I	B 1241	M10:101	NA	Middle Susiana standard ware: Light orange paste grading to buff with some grits included. Exterior and interior surfaces are creamy buff slipped. Flaky dark brown paint
J	B 1015	NA	NA	Middle Susiana fine ware: No visible inclusion. Light creamy slip on both sides. Greenish brown paint
K	B 2025	K10:201	79.32	Middle Susiana fine ware: Yellowish buff paste with no visible inclusion. Creamy buff slip all over. Black paint
L	B 1230	M9:101	NA	Middle Susiana fine ware: Light greenish buff paste with no visible inclusion. Slipped all over. Dark brown to black granular paint
M	B 1243	M10:101	NA	Middle Susiana standard ware: Light orange paste with some small grits included. Yellowish creamy slip all over. Reddish orange paint

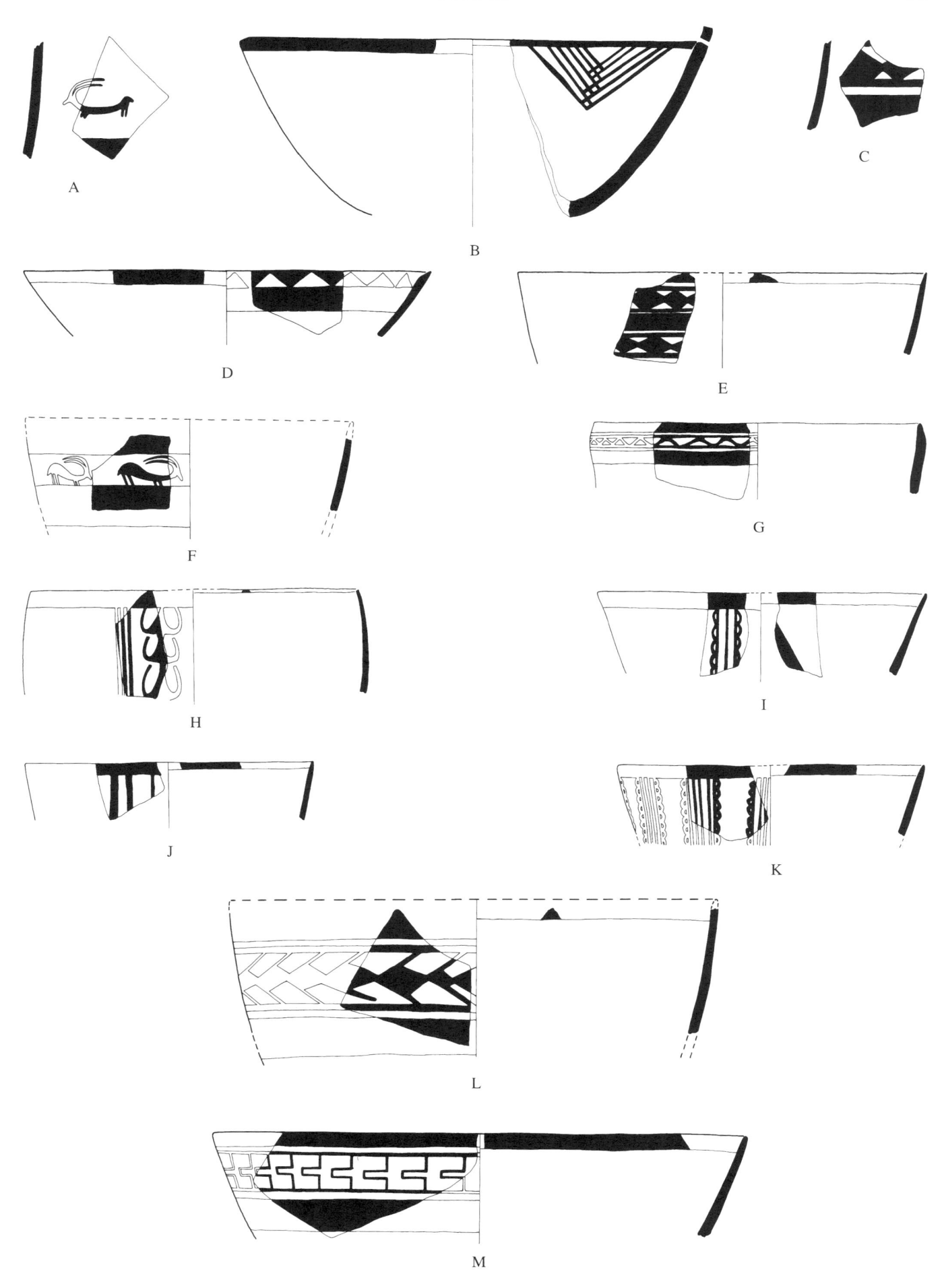

Figure 22. Various Types of Middle Susiana Pottery. Scale 2:5

Figure 23. Formative Susiana Pottery: Straw-tempered Soft Ware. Scale 2:5

	Field Number	Findspot	Elevation	Description
A	CB 192	S.T.	77.50	Straw-tempered soft ware: Gray-on-red ware. Core abruptly changing to reddish buff (2 mm thick). On exterior, grayish paint on red, burnished. Some grits and chaff visible
B	B 1131	M10:103	77.44	Straw-tempered soft ware: Orange buff ware. Light gray core with chaff tempering. Interior is smoothed and has orange wash. Exterior is smoothed and somewhat mottled with traces of orange wash. Reddish brown paint
C	CB 193	S.T.	77.50	Straw-tempered soft ware: Buff/black ware. The firing technique and clay chemicals have produced the odd division of the ware into half black on the interior and half buff on the exterior. Straw tempered, well fired. Exterior surface is smoothed, straw face
D	CB 187	S.T.	77.20	Straw-tempered soft ware: Greenish buff ware. Chaff tempered. Exterior burnished gray, interior grayish buff. Maroon paint
E	B 1134	M10:103	75.70	Straw-tempered soft ware: Lip and body fragment of tan ware. Heavy chaff tempering. Both surfaces are smoothed. Light brown to orange paint. Probably burnished
F	CB 191	S.T.	75.70	Straw-tempered soft ware: Buff ware. Chaff tempered, porous and friable. Reddish buff slip all over. Red paint
G	CB 212	S.T.	75.60	Straw-tempered soft ware: Warm buff ware. Straw tempered, straw face, friable. Both surfaces have yellow-brown wash, the base is not covered
H	CB 190	L 1	76.10–75.00	Straw-tempered soft ware: Buff ware. Chaff tempered, porous. Creamy buff slip all over, burnished with tightly applied horizontal strokes
I	CB 212	S.T.	75.50	Straw-tempered soft ware: Buff ware. Dark gray where thicker near the base. Straw tempered, straw face, lightly fired. Exterior mottled red. Traces of fugitive red paint or wash visible on the exterior
J	CB 215	S.T.	75.80	Straw-tempered soft ware: Warm buff ware. A 3 mm thick gray layer is formed on both surfaces. Chaff tempered. Red slip all over, burnished (visible burnishing strokes)
K	CB 224	S.T.	77.20	Straw-tempered soft ware: Buff ware. Gray core in base grading to warm buff towards the surface. Straw tempered, straw face. Exterior mottled red
L	B II-12	K10:203	78.55	Straw-tempered soft ware: Greenish buff, coarse ware. Straw tempered with straw imprints on both surfaces. Both surfaces are crackled. Exterior much rougher than interior with scrape marks all over
M	B II-22	L10:202	77.28	Straw-tempered soft ware: Buff ware. Gray core changing to yellowish buff towards the surface. Straw tempered, smoothed. Interior surface mostly orange, exterior mottled black, various buff shades and some orange. Both surfaces tend to flake away suggesting the application of a layer of fine clay (too thick to be slip or wash) with no straw. Surfaces are smoothed showing slight shine in spots. Perhaps originally more burnished than is preserved
N	CB 217	S.T.	76.00	Straw-tempered soft ware: Buff ware. Dense gray core sandwiched between two (2 mm thick) layers of light red clay. Straw tempered, straw face. Burnished all over
O	B 2152	L10:203	77.32	Straw-tempered soft ware: Light brownish buff ware. Abundant chaff tempering. Surface is smoothed and was perhaps originally covered with a thin layer of clay. Color of the surface is mottled ranging from light brownish buff to orange

Figure 23. Formative Susiana Pottery: Straw-tempered Soft Ware. Scale 2:5

Figure 24. Formative Susiana Pottery: (A–B, D, I–M) Smeared-painted Ware, (C, E–H) Orange Buff Plain Ware, (N–O) Black-on-Cream Painted Ware, (P–Q, S–T) Maroon-on-Cream Painted Ware, (R) Red-slipped Straw-tempered Ware, and (U–V) Maroon-on-Red Painted Ware. Scale 2:5

	Field Number	*Findspot*	*Elevation*	*Description*
A	B 2175	L10:207	76.47	Smeared-painted ware: Chaff and grit tempered. Interior is covered with a light brownish buff slip; exterior smoothed, low burnished with visible stokes. Surface covered with light maroon to orangish slip over which paint is splashed
B	B 1130	M10:103	76.30	Smeared-painted ware: Gray core. Chaff tempered. Interior smoothed, exterior burnished with dark paint, splashed and smeared on surface
C	CB 228	S.T.	76.20	Orange buff plain ware: Pale gray core sandwiched by thin (1 mm) light red layers. Chaff tempered. Exterior and interior are covered with maroon slip and highly burnished
D	CB 240	S.T.	76.20	Smeared-painted ware: Chaff tempered. Light maroon slip/wash all over. Deep maroon paint is smeared on the highly burnished surface. Plain where paint bubbles burst. The vessel seems to have originally had a pouring lip and a handle
E	CB 237	S.T.	76.20	Orange buff plain ware: Grayish core changing to buff. Chaff tempered. Light maroon slip all over. Deep maroon paint, highly burnished
F	CB 208	S.T.	76.50	Orange buff plain ware: Grayish core grading to buff towards the surface. Chaff tempered. Red wash smeared all over with visible finger marks. Burnished
G	CB 227	S.T.	76.50	Orange buff plain ware: Gray core sandwiched between two thin (2 mm) buff layers. Chaff tempered. Maroon slip/wash all over, burnished
H	CB 239	S.T.	76.55	Orange buff plain ware: Gray core sandwiched between two (1.5 mm) buff layers. Chaff tempered. Maroon slip/wash. Highly burnished all over
I	CB 209	S.T.	76.20	Smeared-painted ware: Dark gray core sandwiched between two thin pale red and buff layers (ext. 1 mm and int. 2 mm thick). Interior pale red, exterior warm buff. Chaff and straw tempered. Fine mica included. Brown paint, presumably applied with fingers, smeared on the surface. Burnished.
J	B 1096	NA	NA	Smeared-painted ware: Gray core changing to buff. Straw tempered. Rough interior. Orange buff wash on exterior over which red pain is applied, presumably with fingers, burnished
K	CB 210	L13	74.80	Smeared-painted ware: Gray core sandwiched by two (2 mm thick) layers of warm buff. Chaff tempered. Creamy buff slip with maroon paint, presumably applied with fingers. Crackled face
L	CB 216	S.T.	76.30	Smeared-painted ware: Gray core changing to buff. Chaff tempered. Bricky red slip all over. Smeared red paint on exterior. Burnished interior and exterior
M	CB 226	L1	76.10–75.00	Smeared-painted ware: Light gray core sandwiched between two (1 mm thick) pale red layers. Straw tempered. Paint is smeared with fingers (finger impressions are visible)
N	B 1116	M10:102	NA	Black-on-cream painted ware: Pink buff ware. Chaff tempered. Cream slipped. Both surfaces are smoothed. Dark brown paint. Burnished
O	CB 211	S.T.	77.00–76.95	Black-on-cream painted ware: Pink buff ware. Chaff tempered. Cream slipped and burnished all over. Thin dark paint, mostly eroded
P	CB 218	L2	75.60	Maroon-on-cream painted ware: Orange buff ware. Chaff tempered. Exterior motley buff/pale red, slipped. Maroon paint thinly applied, mostly eroded
Q	CB 236	L1	76.10–75.00	Maroon-on-cream painted ware: Orange buff ware. Warm buff ware. Chaff and occasional grits included. Creamy buff slip. Maroon paint, burnished. Crackled face. Maroon wash all over
R	CB 219	L2	75.60	Red-slipped straw-tempered ware: Pale red ware. Chaff tempered. Light red slipped. Dark paint (mostly eroded), burnished. Crackled face
S	CB 235	L1	76.10–75.00	Maroon-on-cream painted ware: Orange buff ware. Warm buff ware. Chaff and occasional grit included. Creamy buff slip. Maroon paint, burnished. Maroon wash on the interior. Crackled face
T	CB 234	L2	75.60	Maroon-on-cream painted ware: Orange buff ware. Dense gray core sandwiched between two (2 mm thick) reddish buff layers. Straw tempered. Warm buff slipped. Maroon paint, burnished
U	CB 233	L1	76.10–75.00	Maroon-on-red painted ware: Interior half of core light gray, exterior half of core reddish buff. Chaff tempered. Interior pale red slip, exterior orange-red slip. Maroon paint, burnished to shine, no visible strokes
V	CB 232	L1	76.10–75.00	Maroon-on-red painted ware: Core: interior half light gray, exterior half pale reddish buff. Chaff tempered. Interior pale red slip, exterior orange-red slip. Maroon paint, burnished to shine, no visible strokes

POTTERY 57

Figure 24. Formative Susiana Pottery: (A–B, D, I–M) Smeared-painted Ware, (C, E–H) Orange Buff Plain Ware, (N–O) Black-on-Cream Painted Ware, (P–Q, S–T) Maroon-on-Cream Painted Ware, (R) Red-slipped Straw-tempered Ware, and (U–V) Maroon-on-Red Painted Ware. Scale 2:5

Figure 25. Archaic Susiana 0 Pottery: Maroon-on-Cream Painted Ware. Scale 2:5

	Field Number	*Findspot*	*Elevation*	*Description*
A	CB 196	S.T.	76.80	Maroon-on-cream painted ware: Dark gray core sandwiched between a 4 mm reddish buff on the inside and a 2 mm reddish buff on the outside. Straw tempered. Cream slip/wash all over. Deep maroon paint. Burnished (the paint is shinier than the body)
B	CB 197	S.T.	76.85	Maroon-on-cream painted ware: Grayish buff core. Straw tempered. Cream slipped outside. Dark maroon paint. Inside all burnt black presumably as a result of secondary use
C	CB 198	S.T.	76.80	Maroon-on-cream painted ware: Grayish buff core sandwiched between (2–3 mm thick) pale red layers. Chaff tempered. Cream slip/wash exterior. Maroon paint, burnished

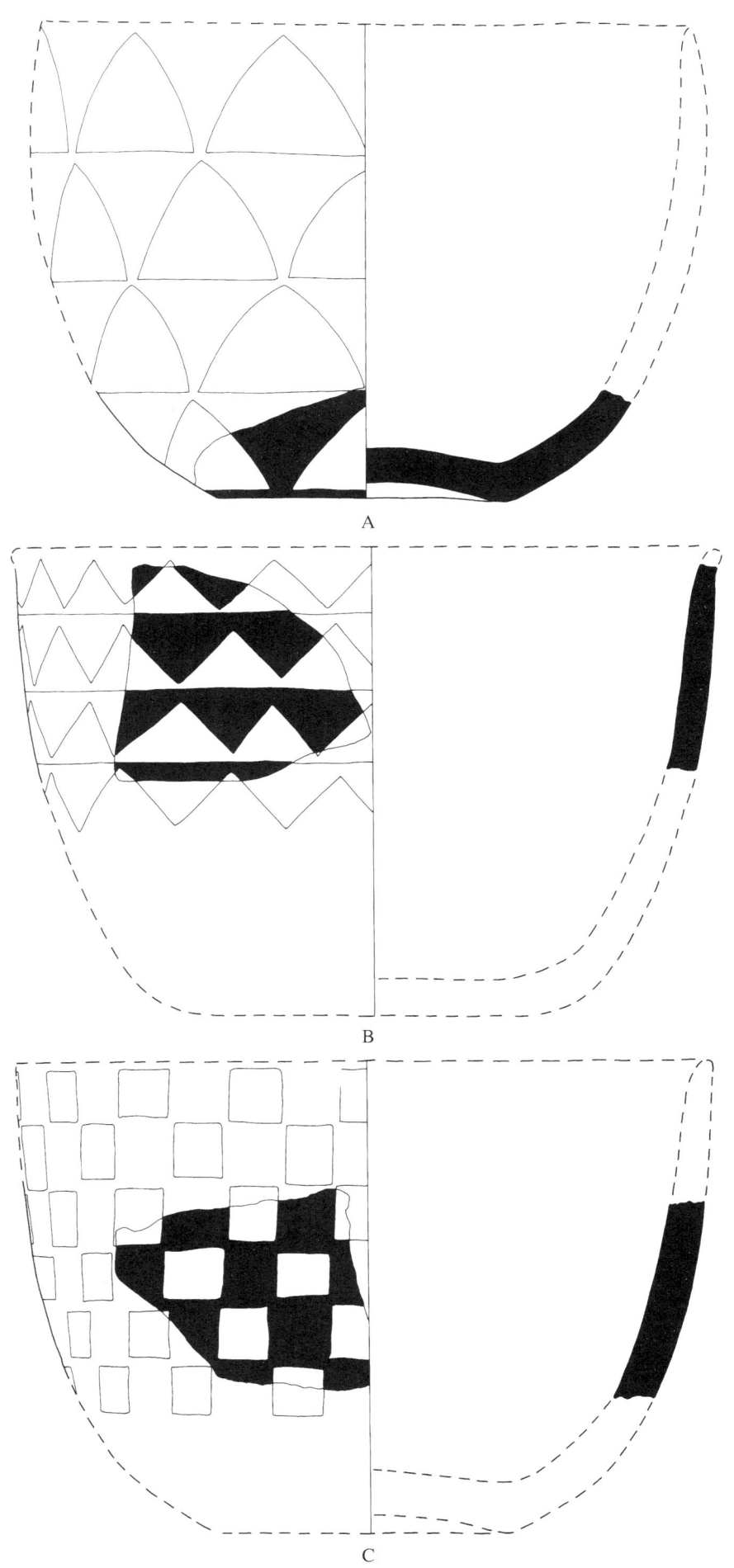

Figure 25. Archaic Susiana 0 Pottery: Maroon-on-Cream Painted Ware. Scale 2:5

Figure 26. Various Archaic Susiana Pottery Types: (A–B, D, F) Maroon-on-Cream Painted Ware, (C, E, G–H) Black-on-Cream Painted Ware, and (I–L) Broad Band-painted Ware. Scale 2:5

	Field Number	Findspot	Elevation	Description
A	CB 207	S.T.	77.20	Maroon-on-cream painted ware: Dark gray core. Chaff tempered. Cream slip all over. Maroon paint, highly burnished
B	CB 203	L1	76.10–75.00	Maroon-on-cream painted ware: Dark gray core sandwiched between two (2–3 mm thick) layers of warm buff on the interior and pale red on the exterior. Chaff tempered. Cream slipped all over. Maroon paint, burnished
C	B I-16	M10:102	77.37	Black-on-cream painted ware: Orange buff ware. Light orange buff core grades to grayish buff towards the surface. Dense chaff tempered. Slipped. Interior surface light orange buff, exterior surface mottled gray, light orange to yellow buff and tan. Black paint. Originally both sides were burnished but only traces remain due to salt encrustation. Chaff face where eroded
D	CB 202	S.T.	77.20	Maroon-on-cream painted ware: Gray core sandwiched between two (2 mm thick) layers of pale red. Chaff and straw tempered. Cream slipped all over. Maroon paint, burnished
E	CB 205	L13	74.80	Black-on-cream painted ware: Buff ware. Dark gray core sandwiched between two (1–2 mm thick) buff layers. Chaff tempered. Cream slip all over. Jet black paint, highly burnished. Intrusive
F	CB 238	L13	74.80	Maroon-on-cream painted ware: Thin gray core. Chaff tempered. Pale red slip all over. Deep maroon paint, the painted area is burnished. Intrusive
G	CB 204	L1	76.10–75.00	Black-on-cream painted ware: Orange buff ware. Dark gray core sandwiched between two (2 mm thick) layers of pale red. Chaff tempered. Light orange buff slipped, red spots on the exterior. Thin black paint
H	CB 206	S.T.	77.20	Black-on-cream painted ware: Grayish buff ware. Creamy buff exterior and interior. Cream slip. Thin dark brown paint. Both surfaces crackled
I	BI-1053	M10:101	NA	Broad band-painted ware: Orange buff ware. Light gray core grading to yellow ochre. Dense paste with scattered small cavities. Deep maroon paint spreading out as orange film over the unpainted areas at the edges of painted bands. Burnished on both surfaces
J	B I-14	M10:102	77.37	Broad band-painted ware: Buff ware. Core slightly gray where thicker. Dense, straw tempered. No discernible slip, but smoothed (self slipped?). Thin black paint, burnished. Chaff face on the lower interior where eroded. Mended in antiquity with rivets and bitumen
K	B I-15	M10:102	77.37	Broad band-painted ware: Buff ware. Gray core grading to tan. Chaff tempered. Friable paste and porous. Surfaces badly worn. Traces of burnishing are visible on the surface. Black paint
L	B I-13	M10:102	77.37	Broad band-painted ware: Buff ware. Light brownish core, pale gray where thicker. Straw tempered. Rather dense paste. Interior surface color varies from yellow-orange to bright rose-orange. Exterior surface mottled from tan to orange. Both sides are burnished. Thin, deep shiny maroon paint. The broad band has many trickles

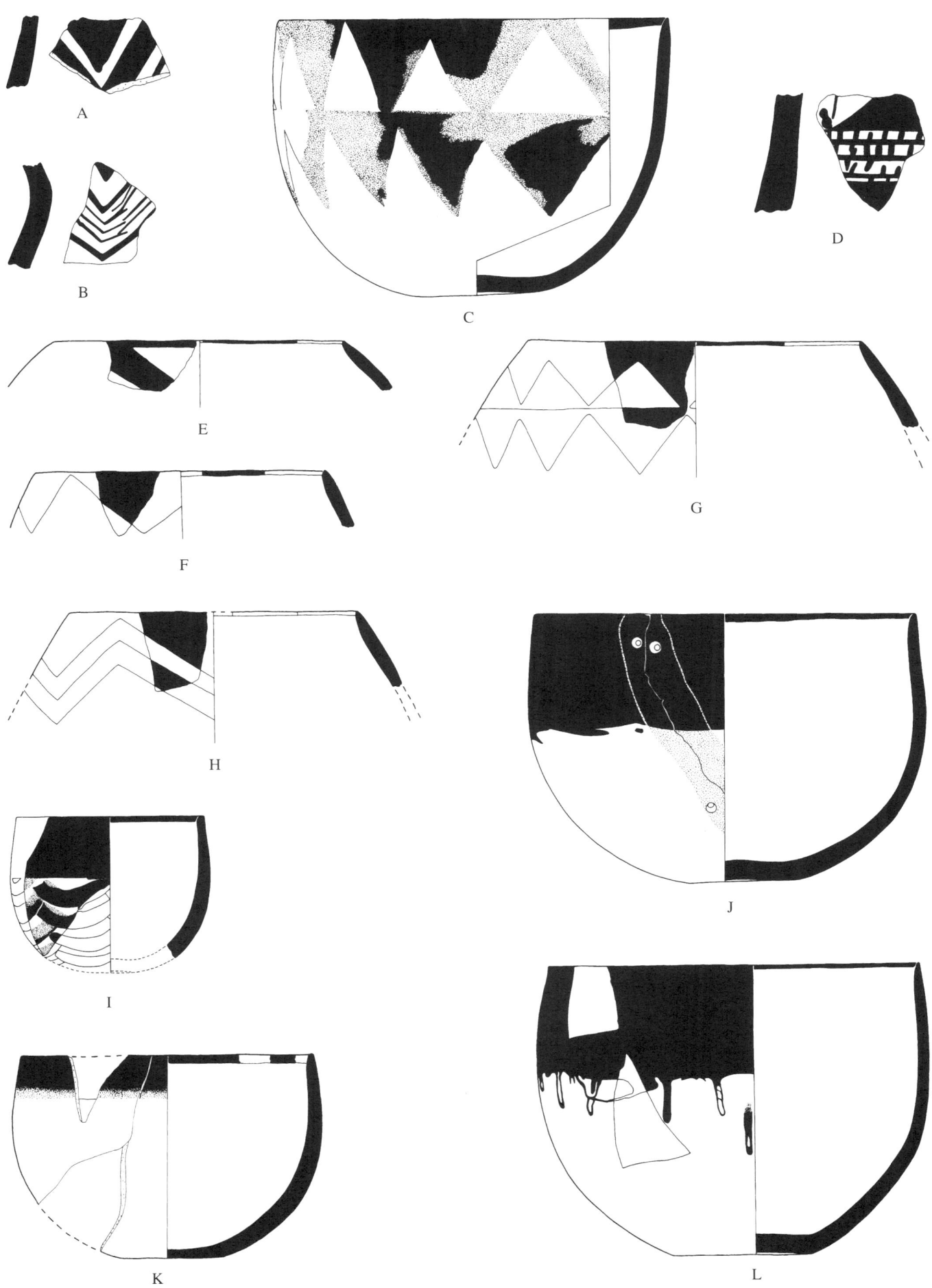

Figure 26. Various Archaic Susiana Pottery Types: (A–B, D, F) Maroon-on-Cream Painted Ware, (C, E, G–H) Black-on-Cream Painted Ware, and (I–L) Broad Band-painted Ware. Scale 2:5

Figure 27. Archaic Susiana Pottery: Painted-burnished Variant Ware. Scale 2:5

	Field Number	Findspot	Elevation	Description
A	B 1041	NA	NA	Painted-burnished variant ware: Buff ware. Brownish core grading to light orange. Chaff tempered. Interior somewhat smoothed, exterior light orange slipped. Red paint, burnished
B	B 1041	NA	NA	Painted-burnished variant ware: Buff ware. Gray core, chaff tempered. Yellowish buff slip all over. Red paint, burnished
C	B 1100	M10:102	NA	Painted-burnished variant ware: Buff ware. Orange buff core, gray where thicker. Straw tempered. Thick brownish paint, burnished
D	CB 231	L1	76.10–75.00	Painted-burnished variant ware: Buff ware. Grayish buff core, straw tempered. Thick bricky red slipped. Dark paint, burnished. Straw face where surface eroded
E	CB 195	S.T.	77.10	Painted-burnished variant ware: Buff ware. Dark gray core grading to warm buff. Chaff tempered. Warm buff slipped. Some reddish smudges on the exterior. Thin red paint, burnished
F	CB 189	L1	76.10–75.00	Painted-burnished variant ware: Buff ware. Warm buff core, chaff and grit tempered. Deep red slipped. Dark brown paint
G	B 2089	L10:203	77.63	Painted-burnished variant ware: Buff ware. Dense grayish buff core. Straw tempered with occasional grits. Cream slip on exterior. Shiny black paint grading to brown where thin
H	B 1095	L10:106	78.31	Painted-burnished variant ware: Buff ware. Orange buff core, gray where the paste is thicker. Heavily straw tempered. Smoothed interior and exterior surfaces. Brownish paint, probably burnished
I	CB 230	L1	76.10–75.00	Painted-burnished variant ware: Buff ware. Dense, some fine chaff included. Dark brown paint, burnished
J	B 2112	L10:204	77.92	Painted-burnished variant ware: Buff ware. Heavily chaff tempered. Both surfaces are smoothed and slipped. Exterior surface is mottled ranging from yellow to light orange in parts. Dark brown paint
K	B 1138	L10:106	78.31	Painted-burnished variant ware: Buff ware. Brownish buff to gray core. Chaff tempered. Both surfaces are smoothed. Thick and granular dark paint, burnished
L	B 1137	L10:103	78.46	Painted-burnished variant ware: Buff ware. Dense orange buff paste. Chaff tempered with occasional grits. Both surfaces are smoothed. Brown paint, burnished
M	CB 194	S.T.	77.10	Painted-burnished variant ware: Buff ware. Dark gray core changing to warm buff towards the surface. Fine chaff tempered. Exterior warm buff slipped with reddish smudges. Thin red paint, slightly burnished
N	B I-19	L10:103	78.00	Painted-burnished variant ware: Buff ware. Dense black core where thicker and reddish brown close to the surface. Straw tempered. Yellowish cream slip on the exterior. Chocolate brown paint, lower part of the body mottled cream, orange, and gray

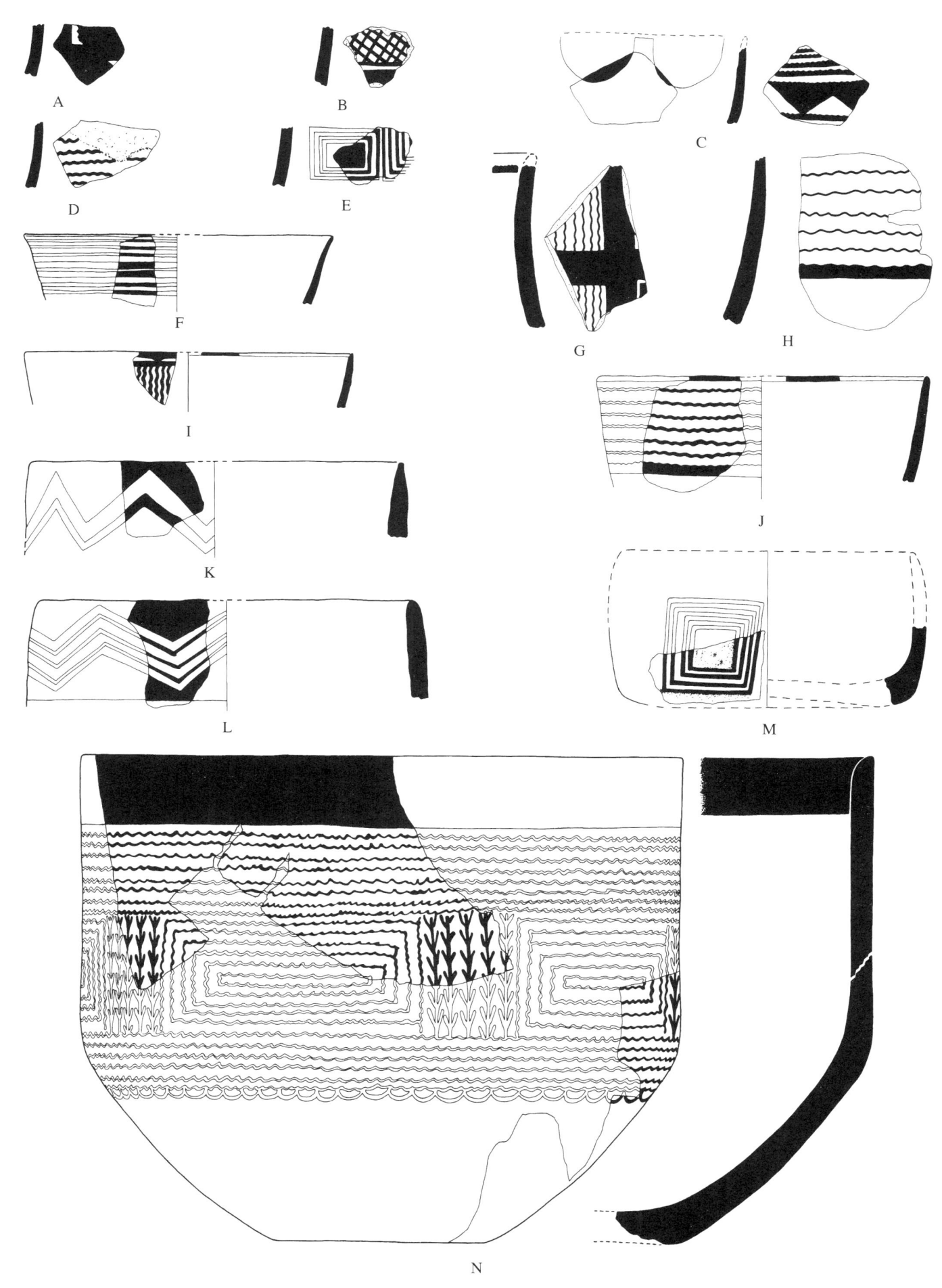

Figure 27. Archaic Susiana Pottery: Painted-burnished Variant Ware. Scale 2:5

Figure 28. Archaic Susiana Pottery: Painted-burnished Variant Ware. Scale 2:5

	Field Number	Findspot	Elevation	Description
A	B 2031	L10:201	78.73	Painted-burnished variant ware: Buff ware. Dense brownish buff core. Fine chaff tempered. Light buff slip(?) on the exterior. Black paint, burnished
B	B 2143	L10:203	78.02	Painted-burnished variant ware: Buff ware. Gray core grading to brownish buff. Chaff tempered. Mottle surface ranging from light brownish buff to orange. Dark paint, burnished
C	B II-31	L10:203	77.85	Painted-burnished variant ware: Buff ware. Orange buff core with gray spots. Chaff tempered. Possibly slipped. Dark paint, burnished all over
D	B 2144	L10:203	78.02	Painted-burnished variant ware: Buff ware. Gray core. Chaff tempered. Mottled orange surface. Dark paint, burnished
E	B II-23	L10:206	77.67	Painted-burnished variant ware: Buff ware. Light grayish to yellowish core. Straw tempered. Exterior slightly mottled light greenish cream buff with some orange or yellowish patches. Dark paint, mostly eroded, burnished
F	B 2145	L10:203	78.02	Painted-burnished variant ware: Buff ware. Light brownish core. Chaff tempered. Exterior mottled ranging from light brownish to orange. Dark paint, burnished
G	B II-32	L10:203	78.02	Painted-burnished variant ware: Buff ware. Gray core changing to orange-red close to surface. Straw tempered. Dark paint, mostly abraded, burnished

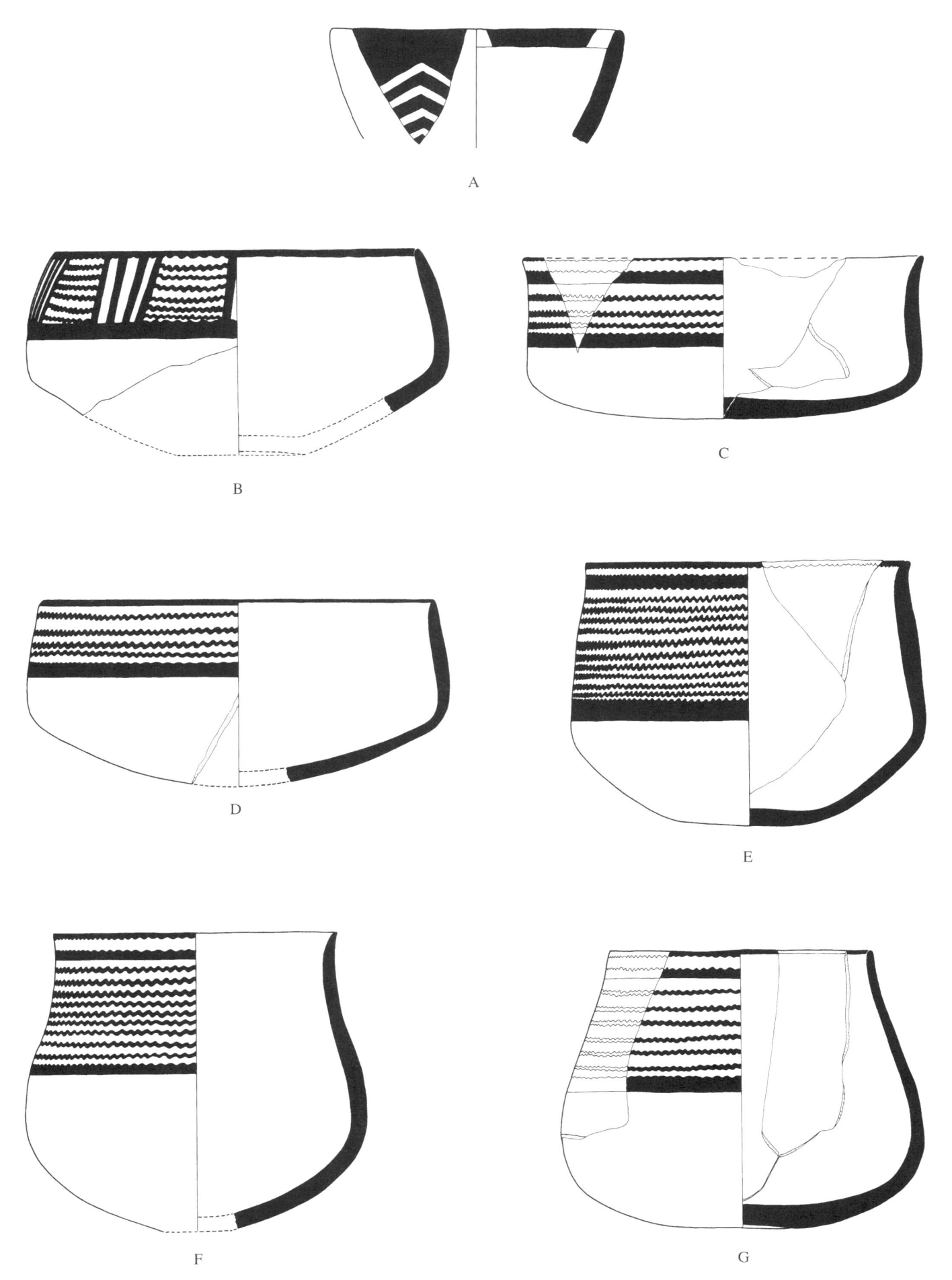

Figure 28. Archaic Susiana Pottery: Painted-burnished Variant Ware. Scale 2:5

CHAPTER 7
SMALL OBJECTS

In addition to pottery, Chogha Bonut yielded a variety of small objects made of stone, clay, bone, and shell. The most numerous were the clay figurines of humans and animals.

CLAY SPINDLE WHORLS

Three baked-clay spindle whorls were recovered from the Middle Susiana level (fig. 37:E–G).

CLAY HUMAN FIGURINES

As in the basal levels at Chogha Mish (Delougaz and Kantor 1996, p. 258), and at Chogha Bonut, the human figurines predominate in the Aceramic, Formative, and Archaic 0 phases. The elaborate "naturalistic" human figurines of Chogha Mish Archaic Susiana 1 phase (Delougaz and Kantor 1996, pl. 237), with decorated lower part (skirt?), were absent from Chogha Bonut, a further indication that Chogha Bonut had been abandoned before the beginning of the Archaic Susiana 1 phase. The human clay figurines from Chogha Bonut can be divided into three major categories: T-shaped figurines, figurines with abbreviated anatomical features, and highly abstract figurines. They are usually made of well levigated clay with no visible inclusions. Most of the figurines are well baked, but few unbaked examples also exist.

T-SHAPED FIGURINES

These figurines basically consist of an elongated ovoid base, from the center of which rises a narrow thorn-like projection (fig. 30:A–C; pl. 18:A–D, F). Often, incisions demarcate the head and/or suggest its highly abstract facial features. The most elaborate example (fig. 30:A) is decorated with fingernail impressions on the lower body and on the face. The head is tilted upward with what seems to represent a "chignon." Facial features are not very clear; imprints may represent either eyes and/or mouth. Fingernail impressions on the base (fig. 30:A, C) could have been an attempt to show some sort of clothing, although this may be too realistic an interpretation.

Because of the highly abstract and specific shape of these figurines we may consider them culture specific, the occurrence of which at widely scattered sites in the Near East may be more than coincidental.[25] T-shaped figurines are an excellent characteristic of the early Neolithic period providing a link with the contemporary sites in the Zagros Mountains, the Iranian central plateau, and northern Mesopotamia. In Deh Luran, a large number of these figurines have been found; the majority come from the early phases of Tappeh Ali Kosh and Chogha Sefid. At Tappeh Ali Kosh, they are reported from both Ali Kosh and Mohammad Jaffar phases, corresponding chronologically with those found at Chogha Bonut. Crude examples of T-shaped figurines are also found at Tappeh Sang-e Chakhmaq in the western part of the Iranian central plateau.

FIGURINES WITH ABBREVIATED ANATOMICAL FEATURES

Examples of figurines with abbreviated anatomical features are more "naturalistic" in the sense that an attempt is made at representing unmistakable anatomical and facial features (fig. 30:D–F, pl. 18:E). One figurine (fig. 30:D) consists of a head and torso with the lower part broken. Thin incised lines outline the head, eyes, brows, and possibly arms; on the back, similar lines show presumably hair and shoulder muscles. Another is a well-baked figurine of a female (fig. 30:E, pl. 18:E), represented in a sitting position. The head and lower legs are missing, but the genitalia are prominently indicated with a lump of clay bearing crisscross incisions. The third example is an almost complete

---

25. Chogha Mish (Delougaz and Kantor 1996, pp. 258–59, pl. 236:F–G) and Tappeh Tuleii (Hole 1974, fig. 15:F–K) in Susiana; Tappeh Ali Kosh (Hole, Flannery, and Neely 1969, fig. 98) and Chogha Sefid (Hole 1977, fig. 91:G–N) in Deh Luran; Sarab (Broman Morales 1990, pl. 15:T–AB) and Jarmo (Broman Morales 1983, fig. 164:7a–11) in the Zagros Mountains; and Tappeh Sang-e Chakhmaq (Masuda 1974, fig. 3:10, 12) in the Iranian central plateau.

unbaked figurine (fig. 30:F), made and shaped from a single lump of clay. The face consists of a protrusion with a slightly elongated tip, suggesting the nose. At the point where the neck joins the torso, the clay is pushed out, presumably to form ears. No arms or legs are indicated, but the base is slightly widened, perhaps to allow the object to sit on a flat surface.

OTHER ABSTRACT FIGURINES

If the other figurines are in fact human representations (fig. 30:G–L), they are of highly abstract style. In fact, except for one (fig. 30:H), where incisions and punctated marks suggest facial features, the rest are not easily distinguishable as human forms. One is presumably the lower part of a human figurine decorated with punctated marks (fig. 30:G), resembling the Archaic Susiana 1–2 "skirted" female figurines from Chogha Mish (Delougaz and Kantor 1996, pl. 237), although this is by no means certain. Others may very well be tokens (fig. 30:I–J, particularly I). Some (fig. 30:K–L) resemble similar objects from Jarmo considered by Broman Morales to be human figurines (1983, fig. 167:5–10).

Related to the figurines is a group of highly abstract finger-shaped objects made of both clay and stone (fig. 32). They are variously considered figurines,[26] mullers,[27] cylindrical-pestle-and-rolling handstones, conical-pestle-and-rolling-handstones,[28] clay cones and rubbing stones,[29] rubbing rods,[30] and tokens.[31]

ANIMAL FIGURINES

Animal figurines are represented throughout the entire sequence (fig. 31). They are made of clay with or without chaff inclusion and are baked. They are less varied and anatomically more realistic and less abstract than the human figurines. Unlike the animal figurines from Sarab, Çayönü,[32] Chogha Sefid,[33] and Jarmo,[34] those from Chogha Bonut's early Neolithic levels lack a number of anatomical details that would help identify them as certain species. The exception is figure 31:K, although it is by no means certain what species it represents. In this example, the eyes and the mouth are indicated by deep incisions and the head is comparatively more realistic than the others. Below the neck, the body is stretched to a wide panel and marked by three incisions, presumably suggesting hoofs or claws; the hind legs are missing. Except for one example (fig. 31:A) that may represent a "bird," the rest of the assemblage seems to represent some sort of quadruped with short, down-curved tail.

BONE OBJECTS

The soil at Chogha Bonut is particularly saline, compared with a number of other ancient sites in its vicinity. Since their excavation, bones and artifacts made of bone were never in good shape and often would crumble to the touch or were covered with thick layers of salt and/or chunks of salt crystal. Bone pieces that were covered with salt crystal and did not disintegrate when removed were soaked for forty-eight hours in water. Using a dental pick and/or wooden stylus, we then removed as much of the salt crystal as was possible without damaging the piece. Even so, most pieces were reduced to a powder during the cleaning process. Therefore, the present repertoire of Chogha Bonut bone objects (fig. 35) should not be interpreted as representative of the whole assemblage. The few bone artifacts that were found and could be rescued consist of spatulae, needles, reamers, awls, and perforators, made presumably from the distal end of sheep/goat metapodial, and a long, flat tool with two holes at the same end (fig. 35:A).

---

26. Broman Morales 1983, 1990.
27. Hole 1977, p. 218, fig. 87:E–H.
28. Hole, Flannery, and Neely 1969, p. 183, fig. 183:G–J, M–P.
29. Voigt 1983, p. 181, pl. 35:E–F, fig. 102:A.
30. Shimabuku 1996, p. 269, pls. 243–44.
31. Schmandt-Besserat 1992, p. 29.
32. Broman Morales 1990, pls. 19–21.
33. Hole 1977, fig. 89.
34. Broman Morales 1983, figs. 146–55.

SHELL OBJECT

Only one artifact made of shell was found at Chogha Bonut (fig. 33:C–D). This striking object was recovered from Middle Susiana debris pushed to the edge of the mound by the bulldozer in M10:201. It is a shell pendant that can be identified as a very simple rendering of a bucranium with down-curving horns. The obverse side is shiny; the reverse somewhat convex and dull. The two presumably suspension holes are carefully drilled from the dull, convex side.

STONE OBJECTS

TOOLS

A limited number of stone tools were found at Chogha Bonut. They consist of a mace-head (pl. 16:F), rubbing stones or mortars (pls. 15:G, 16:C), pestles (fig. 34:H; pl. 15:E, H–J), pounders (fig. 34:C; pl. 15:A–D, F), "whetstones" (fig. 34:B, D–E), hoes (fig. 34:G; pl. 16:G), celts (fig. 34:I), "sinkers/loom weights" (fig. 34:A, F), and scraper or adze (pl. 16:H). Except for a few pounders that were found in primary contexts, the majority of the stones are from disturbed layers and features. Even so, the absence of grinding stones and the limited types of tools in the assemblage is surprising; this may be an accident of discovery and not the actual representation of the stone tool assemblage at Chogha Bonut, bearing in mind the limited area of excavation.

MISCELLANEOUS

In addition to stone tools, two figurines (pl. 17:F, L), a ring or spacer (pl. 17:Q), and fragments of bracelets (pl. 17:T–U) and vessels (fig. 29; pl. 17:V–W) were recovered.

Figure 29. Stone Vessel Fragments. Scale 2:5

	Field Number	Findspot	Elevation	Description
A	B 2063	L11:203	78.24	Stone vessel base fragment. Color ranges from white to gray and grayish brown. Much yellow stain on the interior. Smoothed
B	CB 68	L1	76.10–75.00	Stone vessel lip and body fragment. Surface color beige with some light brown spots. Chisel and fine scraping marks on the exterior. Very smooth
C	CB 69	L30	74.10	Alabaster stone vessel lip and body fragment. Very smooth, no visible scrapping marks
D	B 2015	K11:202	78.97	Off-white stone vessel fragment. Exterior surface rough to the touch
E	CB 70	L30	74.10	Grayish stone vessel fragment. Horizontal chisel marks on the exterior
F	B 2096	K9:203	79.16	Body and beaded rim fragment of off-white stone vessel. Exterior rough to the touch
G	CB 67	L21	74.25	Alabaster stone vessel fragment. Very smoothed surfaces with no visible chisel marks

71

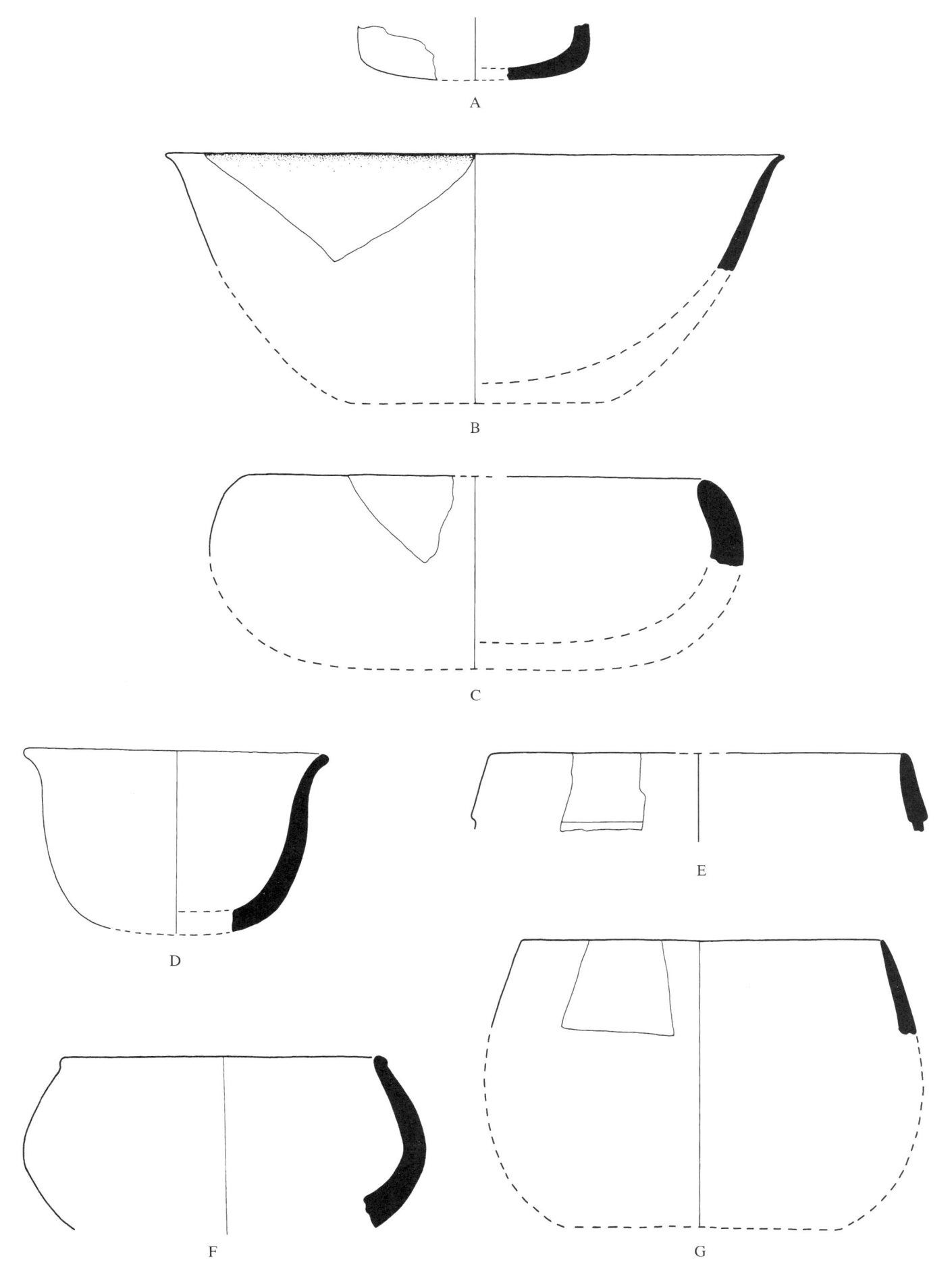

Figure 29. Stone Vessel Fragments. Scale 2:5

Figure 30. Anthropomorphic Figurines. Scale 1:1

	Field Number	Findspot	Elevation	Description
A	B II-1	K10:208	78.77	Top, side, and front views of a T-shaped figurine decorated with fingernail impressions on the lower body and face. The head is tilted upward with a "chignon." Facial features not clear; imprints may be interpreted as either eyes and/or mouth. Light gray clay, slightly baked with no visible inclusion
B	CB 3	L1	76.10–75.00	Two-thirds of a T-shaped figurine. Well-baked gray clay with no visible inclusion. Head and face are emphasized by a depression on the back and projection on the front
C	B 2163	L10:201	78.03	Two-thirds of a T-shaped figurine. Well-baked orange buff clay with no visible inclusion. Grooves cut into "base" running front to center and angling upward slightly. There is also a slight groove at the point where neck meets the base. A small groove line runs down the neck; the head seems slightly uplifted with a defined outline. There appears to be a hair- or head-piece form, as indicated in the back and side views. Very smooth
D	B 2072	L10:204	77.92	Head and upper torso fragment of a clay figurine. Very fine beige to brown color clay with no visible inclusion. Well baked. Some black stains on the back. Thin incised lines, in front, outline the head, eyes, brows, and possibly arms; on the back, the thin incised lines show presumably hair and shoulder muscles
E	B 2165	L9:202	78.68	Fragment of a female figurine of well-baked brownish clay. Figure seems to be represented in a sitting position. Broken lower part revealing the technique used in making the two round leg sections separately. The genitalia are indicated with a lump of clay with crisscross incisions
F	B 2099	L11:203	77.75	Unbaked clay figurine of orange buff clay with no visible inclusion in the form of what seems to be a human-like figure. Distinctive nose or face protrusion, as well as lumps on "shoulders" possibly indicating ears. Smooth surface
G	CB 9	F20/L23	74.22	Fragment of a baked clay "figurine." Mottled dark gray with fine chaff. Decorated with fingernail impressions and punctations
H	CB 22	F14	74.75	Well-baked "finger-shaped" figurine fragment. Dark gray clay with some fine chaff. The projecting upper part may be an attempt to indicate head. Facial features are probably represented by incision and punctated marks below the projection
I	CB 28	F14	74.75	A fragment of either a token or a finger-shaped clay figurine. Well baked, dark buff clay with no visible inclusion
J	CB 13	L13	74.80	Fragment of a well-baked clay figurine. Warm buff paste with no visible inclusion. Two appendages on either side may represent anatomical parts
K	CB 53	L11	75.00	Front, side, and back views of a baked clay finger-shaped figurine. Gray paste with no visible inclusion. Fingernail impressions all over
L	CB 48	F14	74.75	Baked clay figurine. Light gray paste with no visible inclusion. The oval-shaped body is mounted by a series of elongated lumps of clay indicating, perhaps, "hair" and facial features in a highly abstract form

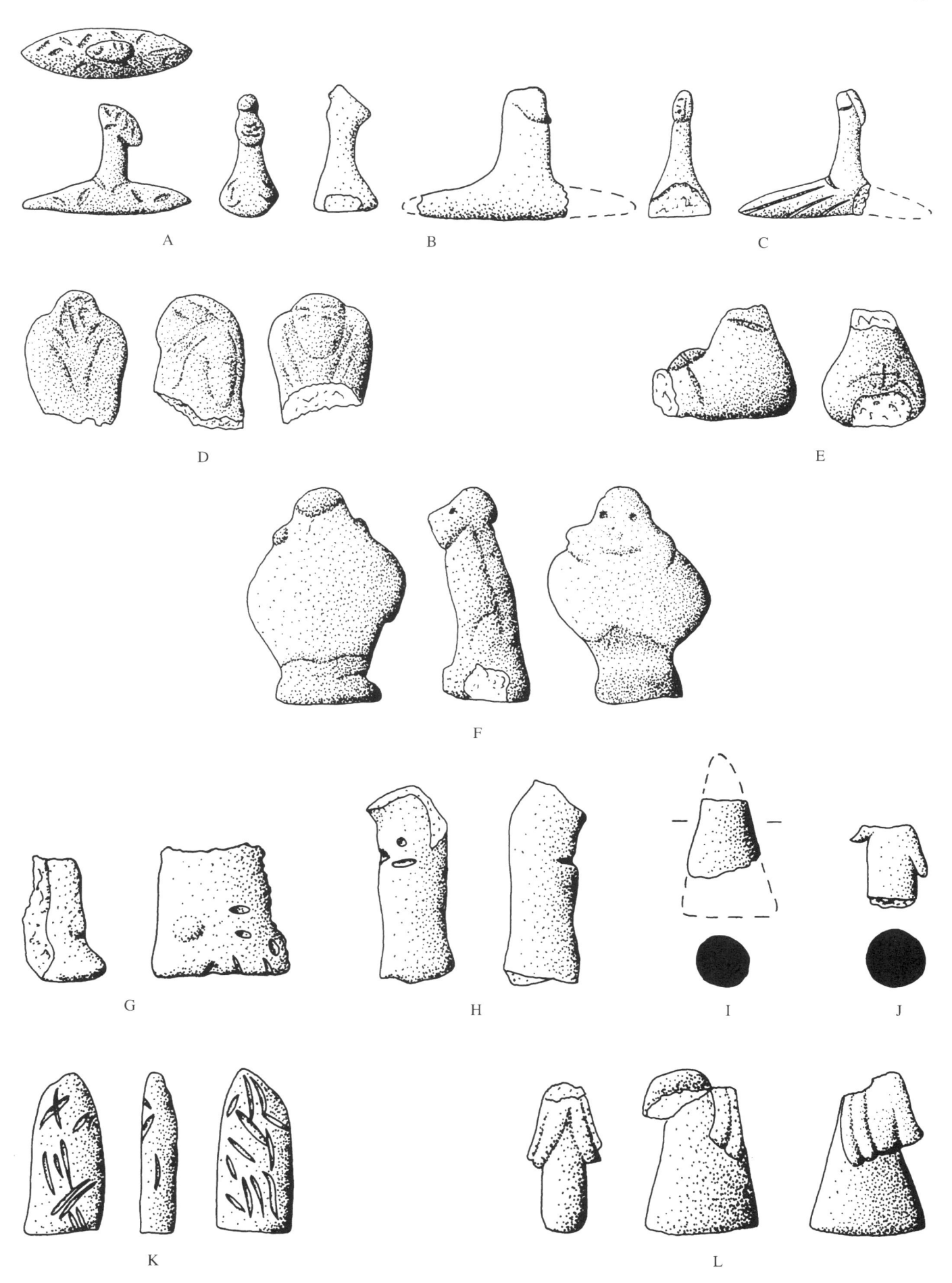

Figure 30. Anthropomorphic Figurines. Scale 1:1

Figure 31. Animal Figurines. Scale 1:1

	Field Number	Findspot	Elevation	Description
A	CB 18	F14	74.75	Top and side views of a well-baked clay "bird" figurine. Dark gray clay with some fine chaff. Impressions of fingers, made presumably while shaping the clay, are still visible on the body
B	CB 47	L21	74.25	Baked clay animal figurine. Grayish buff clay with no visible inclusion. Surface mottled gray, buff
C	CB 14	L13	74.80	Baked clay animal figurine fragment. Light gray clay with no visible inclusion
D	B 2066	L10:203	78.24	Top and bottom view of a baked clay animal figurine. Brownish buff clay with no visible inclusion. Black stain on one side. Original tail appears to have been broken
E	CB 46	L21	74.25	Section and side views of a baked clay animal figurine. Grayish buff clay with no visible inclusion
F	CB 59	F15	74.70	Well-baked clay animal figurine. Gray paste with some fine chaff. Smoothed surface
G	CB 8	S.T.	73.80–73.60	Baked clay animal figurine. Reddish buff clay with some fine chaff. Mottled orange buff surface. Part of the tail preserved
H	CB 21	F14	74.75	Front, side, and back views of a well-baked clay animal figurine. Dark gray clay with no visible inclusion
I	CB 19	F14	74.75	Front and side views of a well-baked clay animal figurine. Warm buff clay with some fine chaff
J	CB 20	F14	74.75	Side and back views of a well-baked clay animal figurine. Warm buff clay with no visible inclusion
K	B 2097	L11:203	77.75	Front and side views of an unbaked clay animal figurine. Light orange buff clay with no visible inclusion. Representation of a crouching animal with distinctive slit-type eyes and mouth

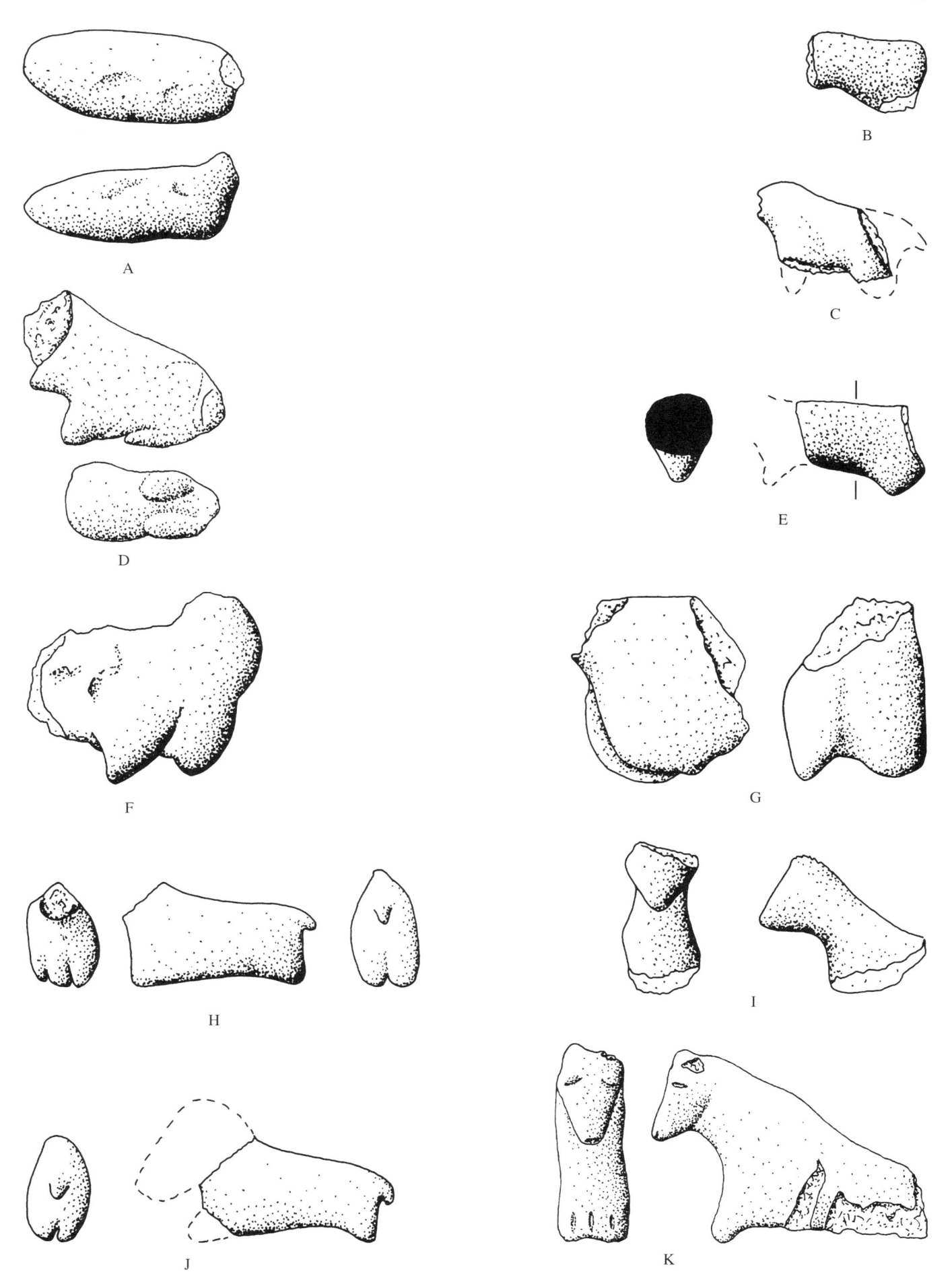

Figure 31. Animal Figurines. Scale 1:1

Figure 32. Abstract Figurines/Tokens. Scale 1:1

	Field Number	Findspot	Elevation	Description
A	CB 121	F23/L24a	74.32–74.22	Finger-shaped baked clay figurine. Buff clay with no visible inclusion
B	CB 55	L11	75.00	Finger-shaped baked clay figurine. Light gray clay with no visible inclusion. Top and bottom broken
C	CB 72	S.T.	75.60–75.40	Biconical-shaped baked clay figurine. Light gray paste with no visible inclusion. This type is distinguished from cone-shaped tokens by the prominent skirting lower part and tapering upper part, presumably intended to represent the neck
D	CB 25	F14	74.75	Baked clay finger-shaped figurine. Warm buff paste with no visible inclusion. The widening of the lower part may have allow the piece to sit on a flat surface
E	CB 30	F14	74.75	Finger-shaped baked clay figurine. Light buff paste with no visible inclusion. Concave widened base
F	CB 45	L21	74.25	Finger-shaped baked clay figurine. Light gray buff paste with no visible inclusion. Concave base
G	CB 52	F14	74.75	Finger-shaped baked clay figurine. Dark gray paste with no visible inclusion. Concave base
H	CB 123	F16/L19	74.75–74.65	Fragment of a finger-shaped stone figurine. Dark gray stone. Very smooth
I	CB 103	F15	74.70	Finger-shaped baked clay figurine. Light gray paste with no visible inclusion
J	CB 44	L21	74.25	Finger-shaped baked clay figurine. Warm buff paste with no visible inclusion. Flat base
K	CB 23	F14	74.75	Finger-shaped baked clay figurine. Dark gray paste with no visible inclusion. Concave base
L	CB 43	L21	74.25	Finger-shaped baked clay figurine. Orange buff paste with no visible inclusion. Concave base
M	CB 54	L11	75.00	Finger-shaped baked clay figurine. Dark gray paste with no visible inclusion. Smooth face
N	CB 26	F14	74.75	Finger-shaped baked clay figurine. Grayish buff paste with no visible inclusion. Both ends broken
O	CB 5	L1	76.10–75.00	Finger-shaped stone figurine. Limestone? Lower part is separated by a ridge
P	CB 42	S.T.	73.60–73.40	Roughly pyramid-shaped baked clay figurine. Light gray paste with no visible inclusion. Concave base
Q	CB 4	F15	74.70	Tubular baked clay figurine. Warm buff paste with no visible inclusion. A snake-like appliqué runs the length of the main shaft with broken ends
R	CB 2	S.T.	77.20	Finger-shaped baked clay figurine. Gray paste with some fine chaff. The surface is smoothed and ranges in color from light gray to dark gray to buff. Base broken
S	CB 1	S.T.	75.00	Front and side views of a finger-shaped stone figurine. Gray stone, polished
T	CB 138	F34	74.00	Bell-shaped stone figurine. Dark gray stone, polished. Base broken
U	CB 27	F14	74.75	Finger-shaped baked clay figurine. Grayish buff paste with no visible inclusion. Base broken
V	CB 17	F14	74.75	Finger-shaped baked clay figurine. Light gray paste with some fine chaff

SMALL OBJECTS 77

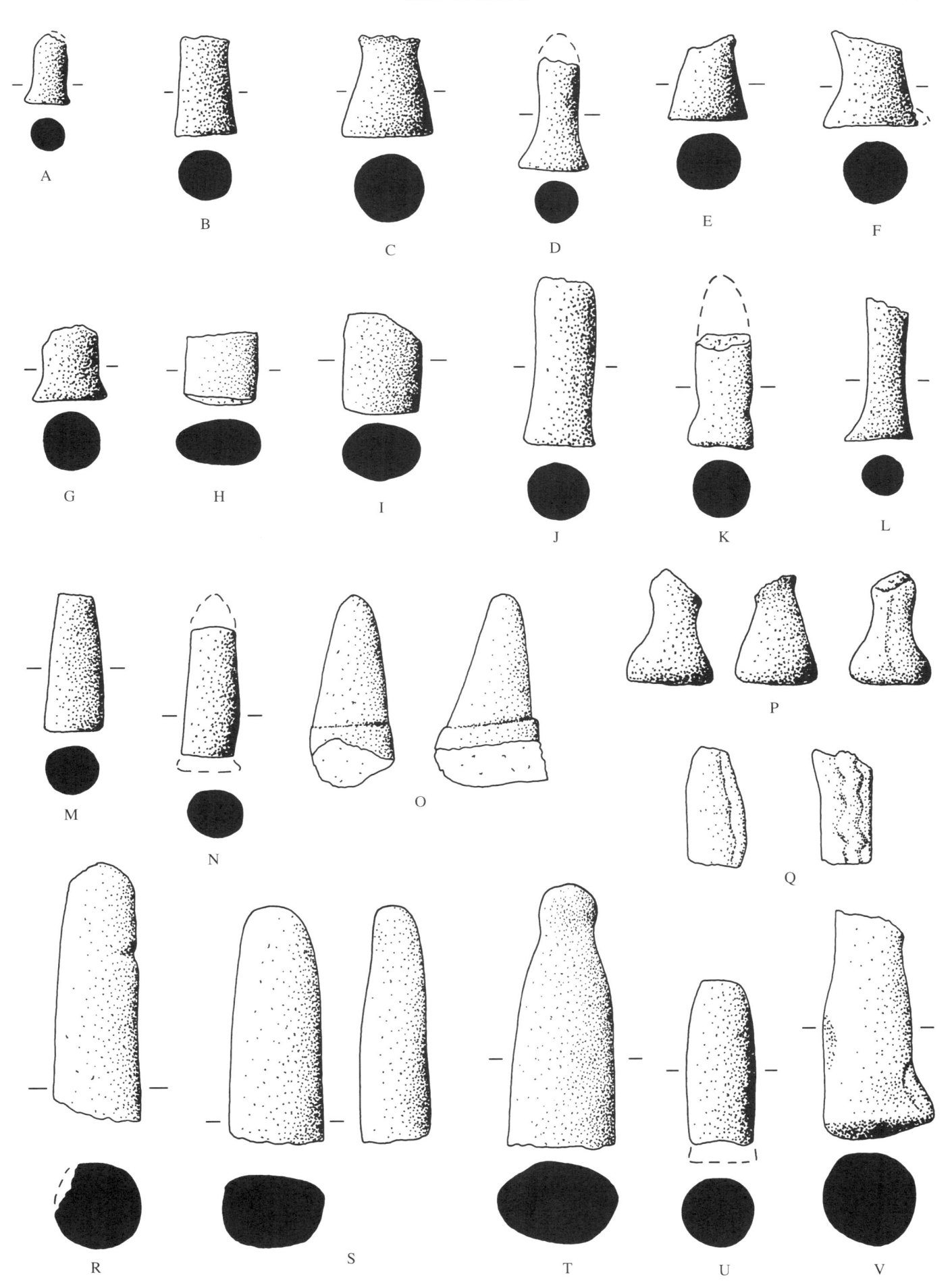

Figure 32. Abstract Figurines/Tokens. Scale 1:1

Figure 33. Various Stone, Shell, and Clay Objects. Scale 1:1

	Field Number	Findspot	Elevation	Description
A	CB 62	F14	74.75	Fragment of a stone bracelet. Veined off-white stone. Well smoothed, no tool marks
B	CB 63	F14	74.75	Stone ring/spacer. Alabaster. Very smooth surface
C	B II-25	M10:201	NA	"Bucranium" shell pendant with two perforations drilled from dull convex side. Shiny side slightly convex
D	B II-25	M10:201	NA	Back view of C
E	CB 65	F22/L24	74.25	Fragment of a stone bracelet. Gray stone, very smooth
F	CB 150	L39	73.30–73.20	Baked clay bead. Warm buff clay with no visible inclusion
G	CB 125	F27/L33	74.05	Baked clay bead. Grayish buff paste with no visible inclusion
H	CB 112	F14	74.75	Lump of unbaked clay with mat impression
I	CB 186	F23/L24a	74.20	Fragment of a baked clay bead. Warm buff paste with no visible inclusion
J	CB 143	F34	74.00	Fragment of a stone object (sinker?). Gray stone, polished
K	CB 115	L27	74.15	Lump of clay with reed impression. Mottled warm buff clay with some straw. Probably accidentally baked

SMALL OBJECTS

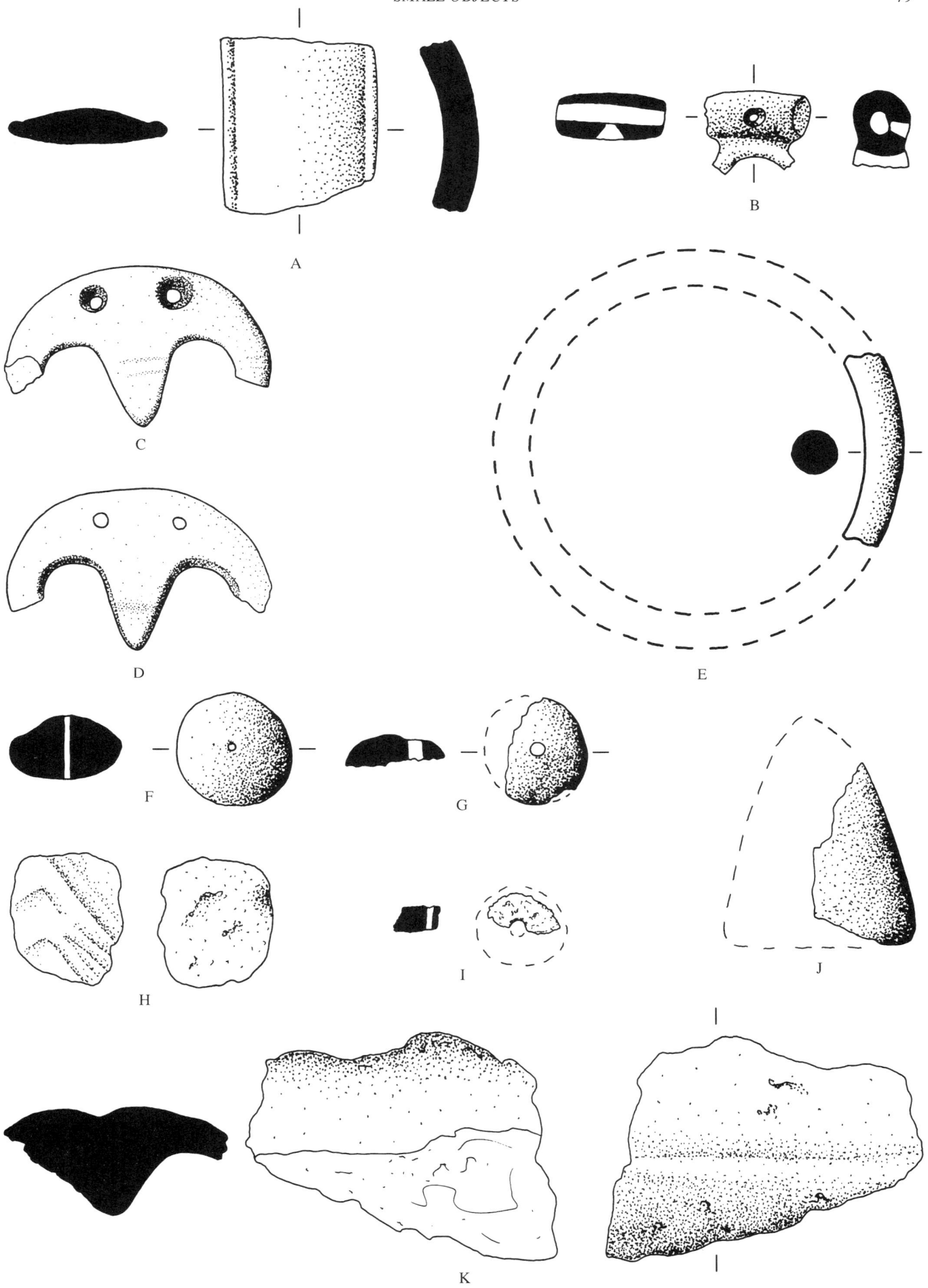

Figure 33. Various Stone, Shell, and Clay Objects. Scale 1:1

Figure 34. Various Stone Objects. Scale 1:1

	Field Number	Findspot	Elevation	Description
A	CB 172	S.T.	73.40–73.20	Fragment of a stone "sinker" or loom weight. Gray stone
B	B 2239	L10:203	77.63	Roundish stone object (whetstone?) with a trough-like slit in the middle. Stone color is mottled ranging from light gray to medium dark gray with some brownish spots
C	CB 181	S.T.	76.80–76.60	Conglomerate stone pounder, with sunken poles
D	B I-5	NA	NA	Perforated dense black stone object (whetstone?). Smoothed and polished all over. Hole appears to be bored from the two sides, concentric bore marks visible on the perforation
E	B I-8	M10:101	NA	Whetstone? Light gray
F	CB 177	L1	76.10–75.00	Grayish limestone "sinker" or loom weight. Smoothed
G	B I-11	M10:102	NA	Hoe made of greenish gray sandstone. Chipping on tang probably assisted hafting. Broad semi-circular blade with few slight chips at cutting edge
H	B I-9	L11:104	78.21	Pestle of greenish gray sandstone. One end convex. Rather smoothly shaped by hammering, but not completely circular. A few chips on the flat end
I	CB 178	L1	76.10–75.00	Celt of gray sandstone. Very smooth and polished. Part of the handle broken. A few chips on the blade

SMALL OBJECTS

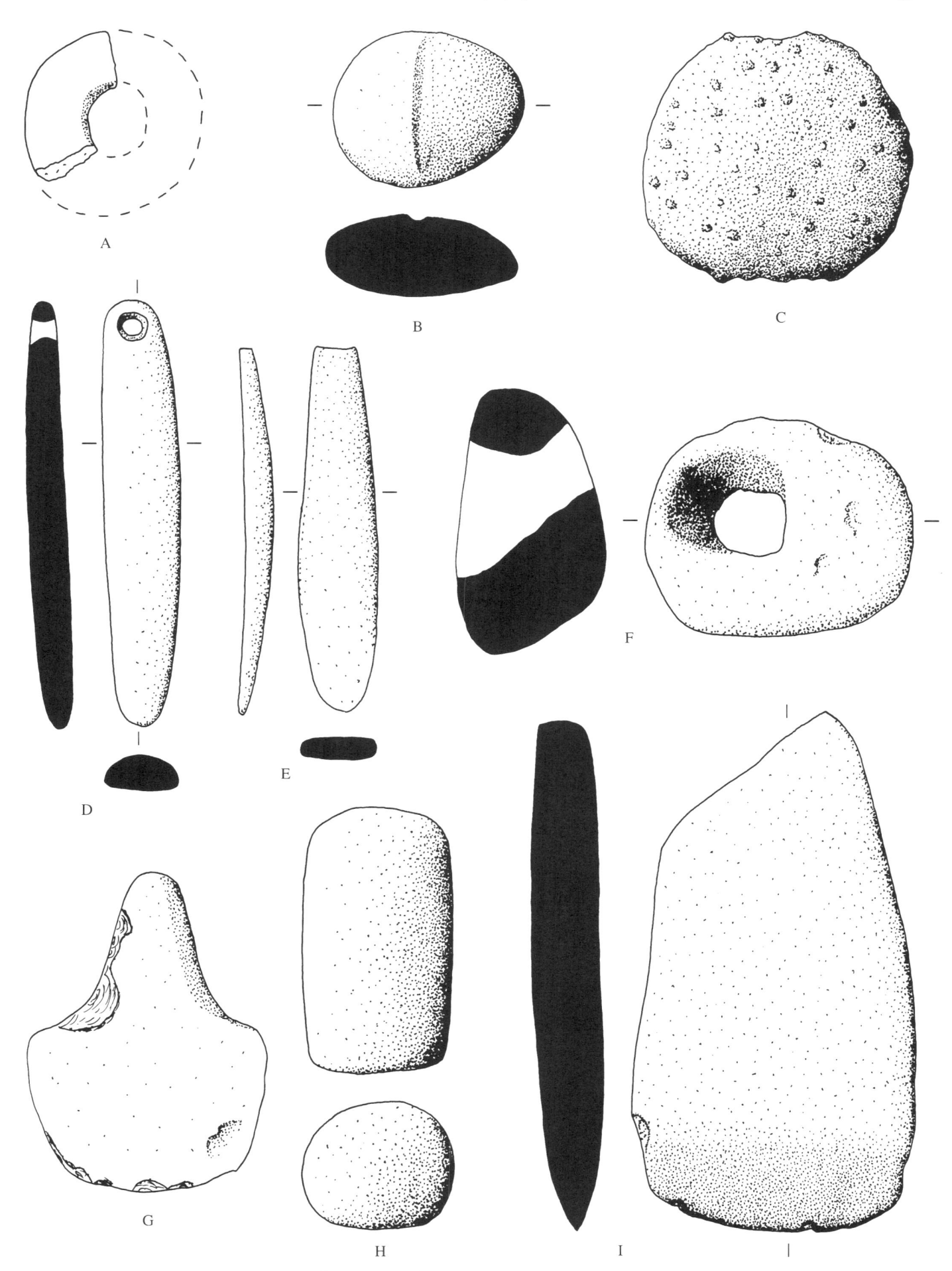

Figure 34. Various Stone Objects. Scale 1:1

Figure 35. Various Bone Objects. Scale 1:1

	Field Number	Findspot	Elevation	Description
A	B II-9	K10:205	79.28	Bone tool made of rib with one intact and one broken perforation. Drilled from one side. Very evenly shaped. Both sides highly polished
B	B II-6	K10:203	79.32	Bone needle. Very carefully shaped. Sharp, intact tip. Surface shiny
C	B I-3	K10:204	79.12	Bone "spatula," probably made from a rib. Polished all over, particularly at pointed end
D	B 2011	K11:201	79.38	Fragment of a bone "awl." Polished all over
E	B 2257	J9:202	78.79	Bone "awl." Polished near the tip
F	B II-7	K10:202	77.42	Bone "awl." Polished all over
G	B II-8	K10:205	79.28	Bone "awl." Polished all over

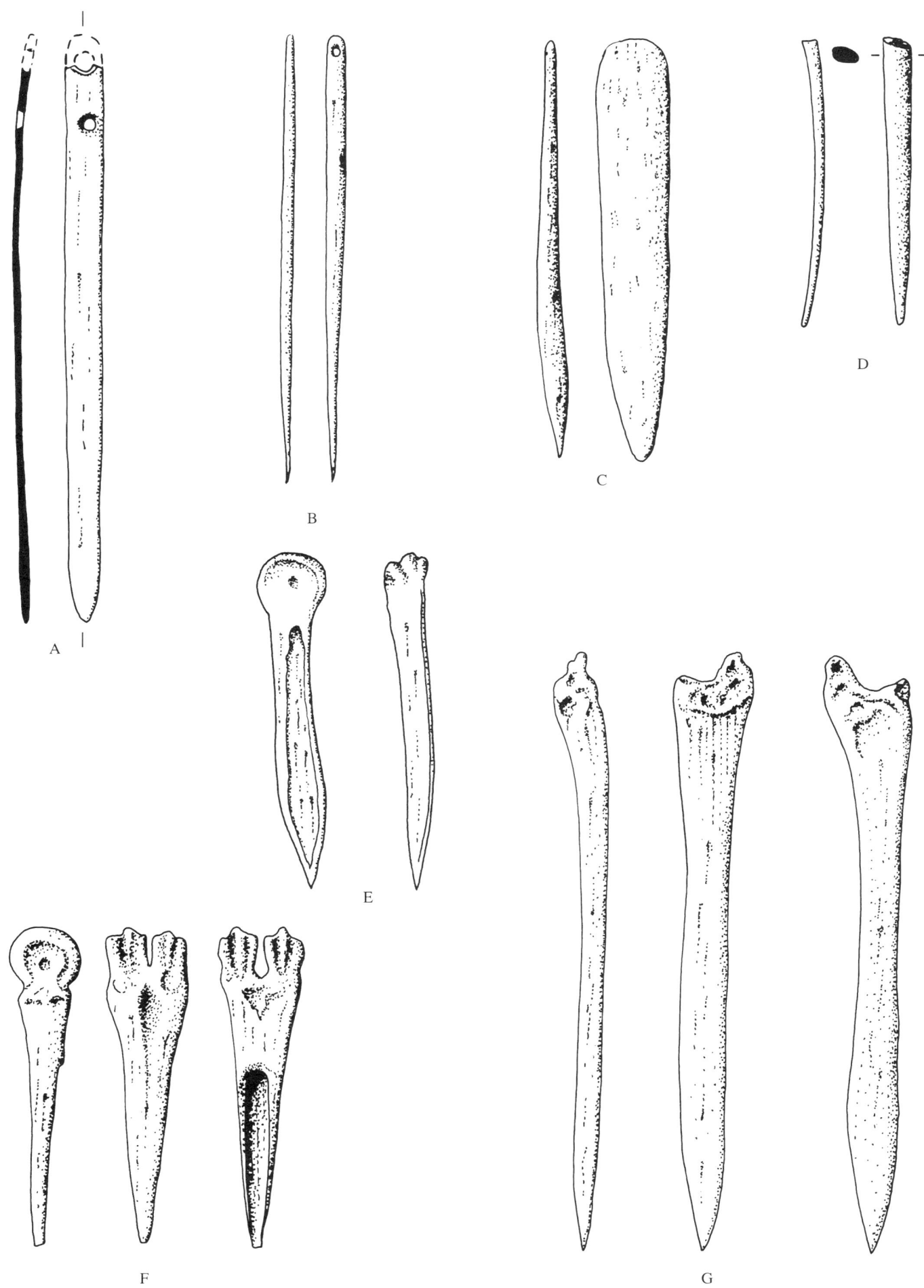

Figure 35. Various Bone Objects. Scale 1:1

CHAPTER 8
ADMINISTRATIVE TECHNOLOGY
INTRODUCTION

The domestication of some species of animals and plants in the Near East ushered in a widespread settled agricultural way of life that presented stronger economic and social pressure for a personal, if not interpersonal, mnemonic notation system that was not necessary for the fluid hunting-gathering Upper Palaeolithic communities, although, as Marshack (1972a, 1972b) argues, abstract notation systems may have existed even in the Aurignacian and Magdalian periods in Europe.[35] Marshack (1972b, p. 825) notes that such a system need not be formal, representing actual numbers, rather "… an informal tradition whose basic system is the accumulation of sets and subsets, but the precise form or style of the accumulation was not culturally determined except in general terms." The first appearance of simple clay tokens, as noted by Schmandt-Besserrat (1992), seems to have coincided with the time period considered as the beginning of agriculture in the Near East. Only relatively recently were these objects systematically analyzed and interpreted as tokens (fig. 36) for numerical notation.[36]

The early Neolithic clay tokens are of simple shapes and have a wide geographic distribution in the Near East. They occur in the Levant (e.g., Beisamoun, Jericho), Jordan (e.g., Beidha, Ain Ghazal), Syria (e.g., Mureybet, Tell Aswad), Anatolia (e.g., Çayönü, Çan Hassan, and Demircihüyük),[37] Iraq (e.g., Jarmo, Maghzaliyah, M'lefaat), Iran (e.g., Ganj Darreh, Tappeh Asiab, Tappeh Ali Kosh, Chogha Mish, and Zagheh), and Turkmanestan (e.g., Anau, Jeitun).[38] We do not know if these tokens developed in one particular region and then spread throughout the Near East. The system of notation represented by clay tokens, however, need not have developed only once or in one particular locus. The fact that the human brain is hard-wired to seek patterns and to organize them into some sort of manageable form, and the shared exigencies of daily life may have led to the parallel development of simple mnemonic methods of recording numerical data with notches on a stick, a collection of pebbles, or with a collection of variously shaped clay objects that were easy to make, store, carry, and count.

MIDDLE SUSIANA PERIOD

The most interesting component of the administrative technology at Chogha Bonut is the collection of small rectangular plaques of kneaded clay in the shape of "tablets." All the sides were flattened, but only one was "used" by making imprints on it. In two cases these "tablets" bear irregularly placed fingernail imprints (fig. 37:C–D), in a third, fingernail imprints and one round impression (fig. 37:B), and in a fourth, a rather regular arrangement of dots (pl. 20:A–B).

The horn-like object of baked clay (pl. 18:G) may also be considered as a record-keeping device. The possibility that this object was part of a statue of an animal is rejected because a horn at least 22.5 cm in size would have belonged to an almost life-size statue, examples of which appeared only much later in the archaeological record. The horn-like object has four finger-impressed depressions on one side and eight smaller imprints on the other. Although no object of comparable shape has so far been reported from elsewhere and the context of the horn-like object was mixed, we tentatively consider it as a part of Middle Susiana administrative technology at Chogha Bonut.

The lump of well-kneaded, well-baked clay in the shape of an apple turnover (fig. 37:A) may have had a similar function. The top is narrowed and evenly impressed with eight finger impressions on each side. The bottom is rather uneven, but smoothed, with two shallow depressions.

That these objects were quite carefully made in order to be imprinted implies that the marks had some meaning for those who made them. Thus, we may consider the clay plaques as primitive tablets and the marks on them, despite their seeming irregularity, as experiments in the making of records. In other words, we have here an early stage of a development that ultimately led to the complex economic documents of the Protoliterate period.

---

35. For critical review of Marshack's thesis, see Davidson 1993; King 1973; Rosenfeld 1971.
36. For a full treatment of these objects, see Schmandt-Besserat 1977a, 1978, 1992.
37. Baykal-Seeher and Obladen-Kauder 1996.
38. For comprehensive bibliographic references, see Schmandt-Besserat 1992.

Figure 36. Various Types of Tokens. Scale 1:1

	Field Number	Findspot	Elevation	Description
A	CB 220a	F14	74.75	Round baked clay token, slightly fired. Found together with CB 220b-e
B	CB 220e	F14	74.75	Round baked clay token, slightly fired
C	CB 220d	F14	74.75	Round baked clay token, slightly fired
D	CB 220c	F14	74.75	Round baked clay token, slightly fired
E	CB 220b	F14	74.75	Round baked clay token, slightly fired
F	CB 40	L21	74.25	Round baked clay token. Dark gray with rough crackled surface
G	CB 33	F14	74.75	Spherical baked clay token. Light gray surface with cloth impression on one side
H	CB 16	L13	74.80	Spherical baked clay token. Dark gray surface
I	CB 34	F14	74.75	Spherical baked clay token. Buff surface
J	CB 35	F14	74.75	Spherical baked clay"token" with one side flattened. Light gray color
K	CB 15	L13	74.80	Dome-shaped baked clay token with concave base. Grayish buff
L	CB 60	L21	74.25	Spool-shaped baked clay token. Light gray. Concave base and top
M	CB 169	S.T.	73.60–73.40	Finger-shaped baked clay token. Grayish buff color
N	CB 37	F14	74.75	Button-shaped baked clay token or "seal." Warm buff, eroded base
O	CB 38	F14	74.75	Button-shaped baked clay token. Light gray. Concave base
P	CB 124	F16/L19	74.75–74.65	Plano-convex-shaped baked clay token, or tip of a finger-shaped figurine. Buff surface
Q	CB 50	F14	74.75	Plano-convex-shaped baked clay sealing/token. Dark gray surface. Mat impression on the bottom
R	CB 51	F14	74.75	Plano-convex-shaped baked clay token. Light gray surface. Smoothed
S	CB 61	L21	74.21	Conical baked clay token. Grayish buff paste with no visible inclusion. Flat base
T	CB 222	F14	74.75	Slightly baked clay conical token. Warm buff paste with no visible inclusion. Smooth surface. Base broken
U	CB 24	F14	74.75	Front, side, and back views of a baked clay conical token. Light gray paste with no visible inclusion
V	CB 57	L30	74.10	Pyramid-shaped baked clay token. Grayish buff paste with no visible inclusion
W	CB 56	F19/L22	74.22	Pyramid-shaped baked clay token. Grayish buff paste with no visible inclusion. Concave base
X	CB 29	F14	74.75	Cone-shaped baked clay token. Light gray buff paste with no visible inclusion. Concave base
Y	CB 12	L13	74.80	Cone-shaped baked clay token. Dark gray clay. Concave base
Z	CB 71	S.T.	75.60–75.40	Cone-shaped baked clay token. Warm buff clay with no visible inclusion. Flat base
AA	CB 11	L13	74.80	Cone-shaped baked clay token. Grayish buff clay with no visible inclusion. Flat base
BB	CB 32	F14	74.75	Button-shaped baked clay token. Warm buff clay with no visible inclusion. Rough top, smooth base
CC	CB 36	F14	74.75	Button-shaped baked clay token. Grayish buff paste with no visible inclusion. Rough base
DD	CB 39	S.T.	74.40–74.20	Disc-shaped baked clay token. Dark gray clay with no visible inclusion. Concave top and bottom
EE	CB 58	S.T.	73.20–73.00	Disc-shaped baked clay token. Light gray paste with no visible inclusion. Rough top, smooth base
FF	CB 220g	F14	74.75	Disc-shaped baked clay token. Light gray clay with no visible inclusion. Smooth surface
GG	CB 221	F14	74.75	Disc-shaped baked clay token. Light gray clay with no visible inclusion. Fingernail impressions on top
HH	CB 223	F14	74.75	Crescent-shaped baked clay token. Warm buff clay with no visible inclusion. Smooth surface
II	CB 6	L1	76.10–75.00	Ovoid baked clay token. Warm buff paste with no visible inclusion
JJ	CB 133	L30	74.10	Disc-shaped stone token. Gray stone, smooth surface
KK	CB 7	L1	76.10–75.00	Ovoid baked clay token. Warm buff paste with no visible inclusion
LL	CB 64	L2	75.60	Ovoid baked clay token. Warm buff paste with no visible inclusion

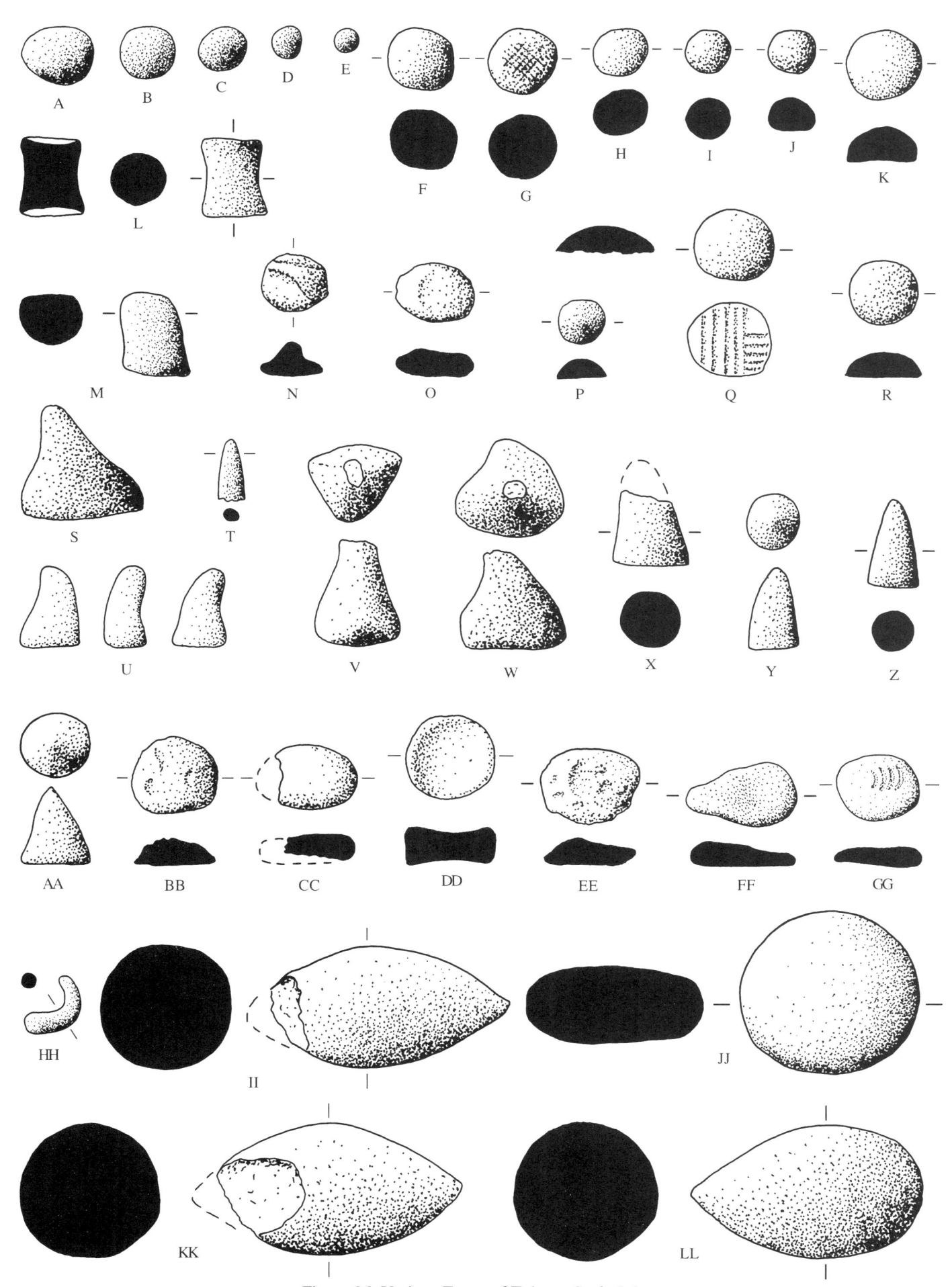

Figure 36. Various Types of Tokens. Scale 1:1

Based on the following, the three objects illustrated in figure 36:II, KK–LL are included herein as tokens. These clay oval-shaped objects occur in many archaeological contexts from the Levant to the Iranian plateau and from the early stages of the Neolithic to at least the end of the Protoliterate period. In most places in the Near East the objects are more or less the same size and shape, and they are made from fine clay and are slightly baked. The objects are commonly known as "missiles," presumably ammunition for slings. Their shape, however, is not suitable for a projectile (as my own experiment with some replica examples indicated) because the two pointed ends prevent the object from following a straight trajectory (see also Stout 1977 for similar results). Moreover, it seems to be too much coincidence that almost all Near Eastern prehistoric communities that used such objects would adhere for several millennia to the same shape and size, unless they represented some sort of standard object whose function we can only guess.

ARCHAIC, FORMATIVE, AND ACERAMIC PERIODS

A number of clay and stone objects illustrated in figure 32 are similar in shape to the conical clay tokens illustrated in figure 36:X–Z. Though the clay examples of this type may very well be part of the token assemblage, it is difficult to assume those made of stone had the same function because of the difficulty and time-consuming nature of carving and shaping stone objects when clay is so readily available. We therefore have presented them as abstract figurines, though this is by no means certain.

Figure 37. (A–D) Administrative Devices and (E–G) Spindle Whorls. Scale 1:1

	Field Number	Findspot	Elevation	Description
A	B II-30	L11:204	77.81	Baked clay object (a counter?). Warm buff clay with no visible inclusion. Two shallow holes on the uneven base. The top is shaped by eight pairs of evenly spaced finger-impressed depressions
B	B II-27	K10:205	79.22	"Tablet." Rectangular mass of kneaded reddish brown clay with mica particles. Two sides convex, one flattened, the other destroyed anciently. Bottom side uneven and rough. Upper side smoothed with round imprint and a number of fingernail impressions
C	B II-26	K10:205	79.28	"Tablet." Lump of rectangular kneaded clay. Warm buff clay with no visible inclusion. Top and bottom convex, sides are smoothed. String-like impression on one side; fingernail impressions on top
D	B II-28	K10:205	79.22	Mass of rectangular kneaded brownish clay with no visible inclusion. Two opposite sides are flattened, probably by fingers. Other sides convex. Upper surface smoothed; lower surface rough with what may be a circular imprint at one corner. Fingernail imprints scattered on top
E	B 2064	K10:207	78.43	Middle Susiana baked clay spindle whorl. Very fine greenish clay with some scattered small grits. Dark brown paint. Abstract "flying bird" filling motif between vertical zigzags
F	B 2087	J10:201	79.53	Atypical Middle Susiana baked clay spindle whorl. Rather coarse greenish buff paste with some small grits. Dark brown paint
G	B 2058	L9:201	78.47	Middle Susiana dome-shaped baked clay spindle whorl. Greenish buff paste with scattered small grits. Dark brown paint

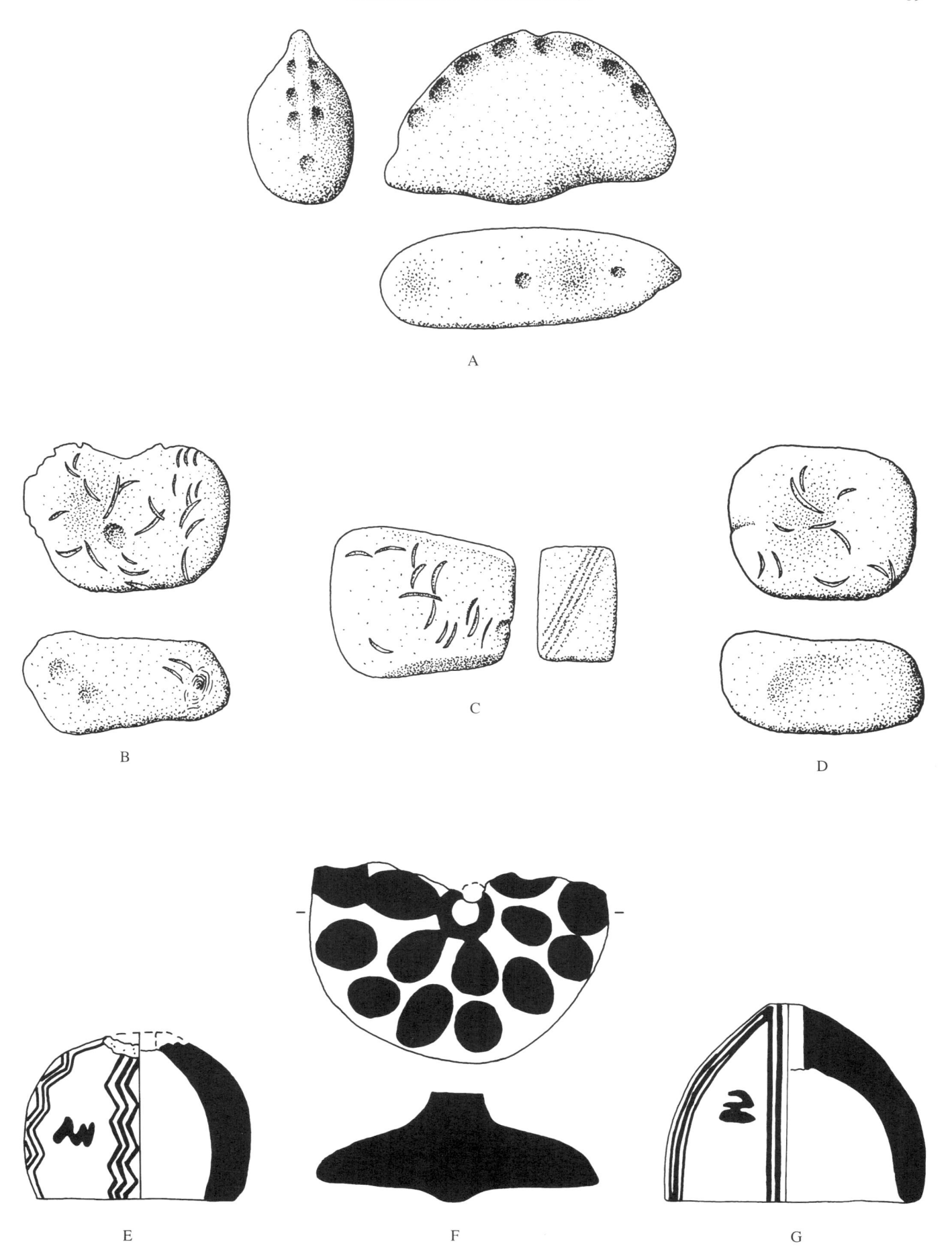

Figure 37. (A–D) Administrative Devices and (E–G) Spindle Whorls. Scale 1:1

CHAPTER 9
CHIPPED STONE INDUSTRY
INTRODUCTION

Analysis of the chipped stone industry of Chogha Bonut by a specialist would have provided much insight into the nature and stage in the development of this industry. Such an analysis is absent from this publication because we could not transfer the objects as a loan and thus they were unavailable to the interested specialists. Since our priority is to make available the data as soon as possible, we present herein a rudimentary and formal analysis of the chipped stone industry with examples of the assemblage so that the interested reader is able to reach his or her own conclusion. The index of all blades and flint cores in table 4 was produced in Iran by our student staff member Mr. Abbas Moqaddam, to whom I am very grateful for taking so much of his personal time in meticulously preparing it.

As with almost all early Neolithic sites in Iran and northern Mesopotamia, the chipped stone industry at Chogha Bonut is present throughout the Aceramic and Formative periods of occupation. Flint blades are the most numerous objects found in Chogha Bonut's Aceramic and early ceramic periods. Nevertheless, the number of pieces recovered is small relative to other early Neolithic sites, despite careful sifting. This is perhaps due to chance discovery and may not reflect the size of the chipped stone industry at the site. Based on the available evidence, three groups of blades and two groups of blade cores are distinguished, each consisting of a number of types according to their size, shape, and formal attributes. The criteria for typological division are not based on the specific functions of the tools because of the uncertainty inherent in assigning specific function to objects that may well have overlapping functions, and because formal geometric attributes represent a specific and/or general function of the tool. Figures 38–41 and plates 16 and 25:A represent all the types found at Chogha Bonut, and table 4 provides detailed descriptions of all types, so that readers will be able to come to their own conclusions as to the functions of the types represented.

The criteria used to distinguish the groups and the types within each group are based on geometric attributes and size of individual pieces. The whole assemblage is divided into four groups: 1) micro-blades (under 4 cm long), 2) blades with straight bulbar surface, 3) blades with curved bulbar surface, and 4) blade cores. Each group is then divided into several types based on attributes such as the shape of the bulb of percussion, number of ridges, presence or absence of retouch, and the presence of retouch on left, right, or both edges. To be consistent and to avoid arbitrary assignment of left or right to edges, the end (narrower point, opposite the bulb of percussion) of the blade is used as the guide and is illustrated pointing down. The round or straight shape of the end of blades could also be used as an additional criterion to subdivide the types, but since in specimens with straight or diagonal ends it is not always certain whether the end was intentionally shaped or unintentionally as a result of breakage, this criterion was not considered.

GROUP 1: MICRO-BLADES (FIG. 38)

Type 1 (fig. 38:A–F)

This type has a triangular bulb of percussion with one back ridge and no retouch.

Type 2 (fig. 38:G–X)

This type has either a very regular or somewhat irregular trapezoidal bulb of percussion and no retouch.

Type 3 (fig. 38:Y–Z)

This type has a triangular bulb of percussion and its left edge is retouched.

Type 4 (fig. 38:AA–DD)

This type has a trapezoidal bulb of percussion and the left edge is retouched.

Type 5 (fig. 38:EE–GG)

Similar to Type 1 but its left edge is retouched.

Type 6 (fig. 38:HH–II)

Similar to Type 4 but the specimens have retouch on their right edge.

Type 7 (fig. 38:JJ)

Similar to Type 1 with retouch on both edges.

Type 8 (fig. 38:KK–NN)

Similar to Type 2 with retouch on both edges.

GROUP 2: BLADES WITH STRAIGHT BULBAR SURFACE (FIG. 39)

Type 1 (fig. 39:A)

Examples of this group are rare; they consist of blades with plain edges and triangular bulb of percussion.

Type 2 (fig. 39:B–G)

This type consists of blades with no retouch, trapezoidal bulb of percussion, and two or more ridges. Two (fig. 39:F–G) are trapezoidal only on the narrow side.

Type 3 (fig. 39:H)

This is also a rare type; examples have retouch on the left edge and the bulb of percussion is triangular.

Type 4 (fig. 39:I–N)

Similar to Type 5 but differs from it in having retouch on the right edge.

Type 5 (fig. 39:O)

Save for the retouch on the right edge, this rare type is almost identical to Type 3.

Type 6 (fig. 39:P–R)

This type includes pieces similar to Type 4, but with retouch on the right, rather than left edge.

Type 7 (fig. 39:S–W)

This type has retouch on both edges with triangular bulb of percussion.

Type 8 (fig. 39:X–BB)

This type, too, has retouch on both edges, but the bulb of percussion is trapezoidal.

GROUP 3: BLADES WITH CURVED BULBAR SURFACE (FIG. 40)

The bulb of percussion on the examples assigned to this group is usually narrow and sometimes both ends are relatively sharp. They differ from the previous groups in that their bulbar face or reverse is curved. As in Groups 1 and 2, examples of this group can be divided into the following types:

Type 1 (fig. 40:A–F)

The examples of this type exhibit no retouch and they have either one or more ridges.

Type 2 (fig. 40:G–L)

The retouched left edge is characteristic of this type. The blades are rectangular, trapezoidal, or irregular in section.

Type 3 (fig. 40:M–Q)

Similar to Type 2, except the retouch is on the right edge of the blades.

Type 4 (fig. 40:R–T)

This type has two retouched edges but otherwise is similar to the previous types in this group.

GROUP 4: BLADE CORES (FIG. 41)

This group consists of bullet-shaped and tongue-shaped blade cores.

Type 1: Bullet-shaped blade cores (fig. 41:A–W, BB)

These cores consist of small to medium size conical cores, the platforms of which are either round (fig. 41:H), somewhat oval (fig. 41:U), or slightly square (fig. 41:W). Their colors predominantly range from red and maroon to brown, but gray, off-white, green, and dark gray also occur. The platforms usually have a concave surface where blades were struck.

Type 2: Tongue-shaped blade cores (fig. 41:X–AA)

These cores are not as frequent as those of Type 1. These cores are relatively larger than those of Type 1 and seem to be limited to the lower levels of Chogha Bonut; none were found in Formative levels.

Table 4. List of Flint Blades, Obsidian Blades, and Blade Cores by Type and Findspot[39]
A. Micro-blades less than 2 cm long

Findspot	Plain	Retouched	Backed (ridges)	Atypical	Color
L1	—	2	2	—	Light gray
L1	—	2	2	—	Cream
L1	—	2	1	—	Cream
L1	—	2	2	×	Maroon
L1	—	2	2	—	Light gray
L1	—	2	1	—	Beige
L1	×	—	1	—	Light brown
L1	×	—	—	×	Maroon
L1	—	2	2	—	Maroon
L1	—	2	2	—	Maroon
L1	—	2	2	×	Maroon
L1	—	2	3	—	Maroon
L1	—	2	1	—	Maroon
L1	—	1	1	—	Maroon
L1	—	2	1	—	Maroon
L1	×	—	1	×	Light red
L1	—	2	2	—	Maroon
L1	—	1	2	—	Gray
L1	×	—	2	×	Maroon
L1*	—	1	1	—	Greenish gray
L1*	—	2	1	—	Greenish gray
L1*	—	2	1	—	Greenish gray
L1*	—	2	1	×	Greenish gray
L1*	—	2	1	×	Greenish gray
L1*	—	2	1	—	Greenish gray
L2	—	2	1	—	Maroon
L2	—	?	1	—	Light brown
L2	—	2	2	—	Chocolate brown
L2	—	1	1	×	Chocolate brown
L2	—	1	1	×	Chocolate brown
L2	—	2	1	—	Gray
L2	—	2	1	—	Chocolate brown
L2	—	2	?	—	Light brown
L2	—	2	1	—	Light brown
L2	—	1	2	—	Light brown
L10	—	1	1	—	Gray
L10	×	—	—	×	Light maroon
L13	—	1	2	×	Chocolate brown
L13	—	2	1	—	Chocolate brown
L13	—	1	1	—	Chocolate brown
L13	—	2	2	—	Chocolate brown
L13	—	2	2	—	Chocolate brown
L13	—	1	1	—	Maroon

---

39. L = layer, F = feature, * = obsidian, S.T. = stratigraphic trench (1996), D.T. = deep trench (1996).

Table 4. List of Flint Blades, Obsidian Blades, and Blade Cores by Type and Findspot (*cont.*)
A. Micro-blades less than 2 cm long (*cont.*)

Findspot	Plain	Retouched	Backed (ridges)	Atypical	Color
L13	—	1	2	×	Maroon
L13	—	2	—	—	Maroon
L13*	—	1	1	×	Blackish gray
L13*	—	2	1	—	Blackish gray
L13	—	2	1	×	Gray
L13	—	2	2	—	Gray
L13	—	1	2	—	Blackish gray
L13	—	1	1	—	Blackish gray
L13	—	2	1	—	Blackish gray
L13	—	2	1	—	Blackish gray
L13	—	1	1	—	Blackish gray
L13	—	2	2	—	Blackish gray
L13	—	2	2	—	Brown
L13	—	2	1	—	Maroon
L13	—	2	1	—	Maroon
L13	—	2	2	—	Maroon
L13	—	2	1	—	Gray
L13	—	2	1	—	Light brown
L13	—	2	1	—	Chocolate brown
L13	—	2	2	—	Chocolate brown
L13	—	1	1	×	Blackish gray
L13	—	2	2	—	Warm pink
L13	—	2	1	—	Warm pink
L13	—	2	1	—	Chocolate brown
L13	—	2	1	—	Gray
L13	—	2	1	—	Chocolate brown
L13	—	1	—	×	Maroon
L13	—	1	1	—	Off-white
L13	—	2	2	—	Gray
L13	—	2	1	—	Maroon
L13	—	2	1	—	Maroon
L13	—	2	1	—	Maroon
L13	—	2	2	—	Gray
L13	—	2	1	—	Chocolate brown
L13	—	2	1	—	Pink
F14	—	2	2	—	Maroon
F14	—	2	2	—	Chocolate brown
F14	—	2	2	—	Chocolate brown
F14	—	2	2	—	Chocolate brown
F14	—	2	2	—	Maroon
F14	—	2	2	—	Maroon
F14	—	2	1	—	Off-white
F14	—	2	1	—	Maroon
F14	—	2	1	—	Maroon
F14	—	1	2	—	Light gray
F14	—	1	1	×	Brown
F14	—	1	1	—	Maroon
F14	—	2	2	—	Brown
F14	—	2	2	—	Chocolate brown
F14	—	2	2	—	Maroon
F14	—	1	2	—	Brown
F14	—	1	1	—	Chocolate brown
F14	—	1	2	—	Maroon
F14	—	1	2	—	Maroon
F14	—	1	2	—	Chocolate brown
F14	—	1	1	—	Blackish gray
F14	—	1	1	—	Maroon
F14	—	2	1	—	Gray
F14	—	2	2	—	Maroon
F14	—	2	3	—	Brown

Table 4. List of Flint Blades, Obsidian Blades, and Blade Cores by Type and Findspot (*cont.*)
A. Micro-blades less than 2 cm long (*cont.*)

Findspot	Plain	Retouched	Backed (ridges)	Atypical	Color
F14	×	—	1	—	Brown
F14	—	2	2	—	Off-white
F14	—	2	2	—	Light gray
F14	—	1	1	—	Red
F14	—	1	2	—	Gray
F14	—	1	2	—	Red
F14	—	2	1	—	Off-white
F14	—	1	1	—	Chocolate brown
F14	—	2	1	—	Red
F14	—	2	2	—	Blackish gray
F14	×	—	1	—	Chocolate brown
F14	—	2	2	—	Red
F14	—	2	1	—	Red
F14	—	2	2	—	Pink
F14	—	2	1	—	Dark red
F14	—	2	1	—	Gray
F14	—	1	2	—	Gray
F14	×	—	1	×	Brown
F14	—	1	1	—	Off-white
F14	—	2	2	—	Red
F14	—	2	1	—	Gray
F14	—	2	1	—	Red
F14	—	2	2	—	Maroon
F14	—	2	1	—	Maroon
F14	—	1	1	—	Maroon
F14	—	1	1	—	Chocolate brown
F14	—	2	1	—	Gray
F14	—	2	2	—	Gray
F14	—	2	2	—	Maroon
F14	—	1	1	—	Red
F14	—	1	1	—	Maroon
F14	—	1	1	—	Dark red
F14	—	2	1	—	Gray
F14	—	2	2	—	Dark red
F14	—	1	1	—	Gray
F14	×	—	1	×	Maroon
F14	—	1	1	—	Blackish gray
F14	—	1	1	×	Red
F14	—	1	1	—	Gray
F14	×	—	—	×	Gray
F14	—	1	1	—	Chocolate brown
F14	—	2	2	—	Creamy white
F14	—	2	1	—	Creamy white
F14	—	2	2	—	Maroon
F14	—	1	1	—	Dark cream
F14	—	1	1	×	Pink
F14	—	2	2	—	Off-white
F14	—	2	1	—	Light brown
F14	—	1	1	—	Maroon
F14	×	—	—	×	Light brown
F14	—	2	2	—	Maroon
F14	—	1	1	—	Maroon
F14	—	1	1	—	Maroon
F14	—	2	1	—	Brown
F14	—	2	2	—	Maroon
F14	—	1	1	—	Red
F14	—	1	1	—	Chocolate brown
F14	—	2	1	—	Chocolate brown
F14	—	2	1	—	Maroon
F14	—	1	2	—	Maroon

Table 4. List of Flint Blades, Obsidian Blades, and Blade Cores by Type and Findspot (*cont.*)
A. Micro-blades less than 2 cm long (*cont.*)

Findspot	Plain	Retouched	Backed (ridges)	Atypical	Color
F14	—	1	2	—	Brown
F14	—	1	1	—	Dark brown
F14	—	1	1	—	Red
F14	—	1	1	—	Red
F14	—	2	2	—	Maroon
F14	—	2	2	—	Brown
F14	—	2	1	—	Dark red
F14	—	2	1	—	Chocolate brown
F14	—	1	2	—	Chocolate brown
F15	—	1	1	—	Off-white
F15	—	2	1	—	Blackish gray
F15	—	2	2	—	Red
F15	—	2	1	—	Maroon
F15	—	2	1	—	Blackish gray
F15	—	2	1	—	Light red
F15	—	1	2	—	Off-white
F15	—	2	2	—	Gray
F15	—	2	1	—	Maroon
F15	—	1	1	—	Off-white
F15	—	2	2	—	Brown
F15	—	2	1	—	Off-white
F15	—	1	1	—	Blackish gray
F15	—	1	1	—	Maroon
F15	—	1	2	—	Gray
F15	—	2	2	—	Dark brown
F15	—	2	1	—	Light gray
F15	—	2	1	—	Dark brown
F15	—	1	1	×	Dark brown
L21	—	1	2	—	Gray
L21	—	1	2	—	Maroon
L21	—	1	2	—	Blackish gray
L21	—	2	1	—	Cream
L21	—	2	2	—	Maroon
L21	—	2	2	—	Gray
L21	—	2	1	—	Dark red
L21	—	2	2	—	Blackish gray
L21	—	2	2	—	Maroon and white
L21	—	2	2	—	Maroon
L21	—	2	1	—	Gray
L21	—	2	2	—	Maroon
L21	—	1	1	—	Gray
L21	—	2	2	—	Dark brown
L21	—	1	1	—	Dark brown
L21	—	2	2	—	Gray
L21	—	2	2	—	Pink
L21	—	2	2	—	Dark brown
F20/L23	—	2	2	—	Chocolate brown
F20/L23	—	2	1	—	Gray
F20/L23	—	2	1	—	Off-white
F20/L23	×	—	—	×	Cream
F22/L24	—	2	—	—	Maroon
F23/L24a	×	—	1	—	Blackish gray
F23/L24a	—	2	1	—	Blackish gray
F23/L24a	×	—	—	×	Brown
F23/L24a	—	2	1	—	Brown
F23/L24a	—	2	2	—	Gray
F23/L24a	—	2	1	—	Gray
L27	—	2	2	—	Brown
L27	—	2	2	—	Light brown
L27	—	2	1	—	Maroon

Table 4. List of Flint Blades, Obsidian Blades, and Blade Cores by Type and Findspot (*cont.*)
A. Micro-blades less than 2 cm long (*cont.*)

Findspot	Plain	Retouched	Backed (ridges)	Atypical	Color
L27	—	2	2	—	Chocolate brown
L27	—	1	1	—	Brown
L27	—	2	1	—	Chocolate brown
L27	—	1	2	—	Dark red
L30	—	2	1	—	Dark brown
L30	—	2	2	—	Maroon
L30	—	1	2	—	Maroon
L30	—	1	2	—	Dark brown
L30	—	1	1	—	Blackish gray
L30	—	2	1	—	Maroon
L30	—	1	1	—	Maroon
L30	—	1	1	—	Gray
F31	×	—	—	×	Light brown
F31	—	1	1	×	Dark brown
F31	—	1	1	×	Blackish gray
F31	×	—	—	×	Cream
F31	—	2	2	—	Maroon
F31	—	2	2	—	Dark brown
F31	—	2	2	—	Cream
F31	—	2	2	—	Blackish gray
F31	—	2	1	×	Maroon
F26/L32	—	2	2	—	Maroon
F26/L32	—	2	2	—	Blackish gray
F26/L32	—	2	2	—	Blackish gray
F27/L33	—	2	1	—	Maroon
F27/L33	—	2	1	—	Red
F27/L33	—	2	2	—	Cream
F27/L33	—	2	1	—	Maroon
F34	×	—	1	×	Blackish gray
F34	—	1	1	—	Dark brown
F34	—	2	2	—	Cream
F34	—	1	2	—	Blackish gray
F34	—	1	2	—	Maroon
F34	—	2	1	—	Chocolate brown
F34	×	—	1	—	Dark brown
F34	—	2	1	—	Off-white
F34	—	2	1	—	Hunter green
F34	×	—	2	—	Blackish gray
F34	—	1	1	—	Blackish gray
F34	—	2	1	—	Maroon
F34	—	2	2	—	Maroon
L35* (D.T.)	—	2	1	—	Greenish gray
L35* (D.T.)	×	—	2	—	Dark gray
L35* (D.T.)	—	2	1	—	Blackish gray
L37 (D.T.)	—	1	1	—	Blackish gray
L37 (D.T.)	—	2	2	—	Blackish gray
S.T. el. 77.60–77.20	—	2	1	—	Cream
S.T. el. 77.60–77.20	—	2	2	—	Maroon
S.T. el. 77.60–77.20	—	1	1	—	Blackish gray
S.T. el. 77.60–77.20	—	2	1	—	Maroon
S.T. el. 77.80–75.40	—	2	1	—	Blackish gray
S.T. el. 77.75	—	2	2	—	Brown
S.T. el. 77.75	—	1	2	—	Gray
S.T. el. 75.80–75.60	—	2	1	—	Maroon
S.T. el. 75.80–75.60	—	2	2	—	Maroon
S.T. el. 75.80–75.60	—	2	2	—	Maroon
S.T. el. 75.80–75.60	—	2	2	—	Cream
S.T. el. 75.80–75.60	—	2	1	—	Green
S.T. el. 75.80–75.60	—	2	1	—	Maroon
S.T. el. 75.80–75.60	—	2	2	—	Brown

Table 4. List of Flint Blades, Obsidian Blades, and Blade Cores by Type and Findspot (*cont.*)
A. Micro-blades less than 2 cm long (*cont.*)

Findspot	Plain	Retouched	Backed (ridges)	Atypical	Color
S.T. el. 75.80–75.60	—	2	1	—	Maroon
S.T. el. 75.80–75.60	—	2	1	—	Maroon
S.T. el. 75.80–75.60	—	2	2	—	Maroon
S.T. el. 75.80–75.60	—	2	1	—	Red
S.T. el. 75.80–75.60*	—	2	1	—	Greenish gray
S.T. el. 75.80–75.60	×	—	1	—	Maroon
S.T. el. 75.80–75.60	—	2	1	—	Maroon
S.T. el. 75.80–75.60	—	2	1	—	Gray
S.T. el. 75.80–75.60	—	2	1	—	Maroon
S.T. el. 75.80–75.60	—	2	1	—	Dark brown
S.T. el. 75.80–75.60	—	2	1	—	Brown
S.T. el. 75.80–75.60	—	2	2	—	Maroon
S.T. el. 75.80–75.60	—	2	2	—	Red
S.T. el. 75.80–75.60	—	2	2	—	Maroon
S.T. el. 75.80–75.60	—	2	1	—	Dark brown
S.T. el. 75.80–75.60	—	2	1	—	Maroon
S.T. el. 75.80–75.60	—	2	2	—	Maroon
S.T. el. 75.80–75.60	—	2	1	—	Dark brown
S.T. el. 75.80–75.60	—	2	1	—	Chocolate brown
S.T. el. 75.80–75.60	—	2	1	—	Pink
S.T. el. 75.80–75.60	—	2	1	—	Maroon
S.T. el. 74.50–74.40	—	2	2	—	Maroon
S.T. el. 74.40–74.20	—	2	2	—	Maroon
S.T. el. 74.40–74.20	—	2	2	—	Dark brown
S.T. el. 74.40–74.20	—	2	1	—	Chocolate brown
S.T. el. 74.40–74.20	—	2	1	—	Maroon
S.T. el. 74.40–74.20	—	2	1	×	Maroon
S.T. el. 74.40–74.20	—	2	1	—	Maroon
S.T. el. 74.40–74.20	—	2	1	—	Pink
S.T. el. 74.40–74.20	—	2	2	—	Dark brown
S.T. el. 74.40–74.20	—	2	1	—	Brown
S.T. el. 74.40–74.20	—	2	1	—	Brown
S.T. el. 74.40–74.20*	—	1	1	×	Blackish gray
S.T. el. 74.40–74.20	—	2	2	×	Maroon
S.T. el. 75.80–75.60	—	2	2	—	Maroon
S.T. el. 75.80–75.60	—	2	2	—	Red
S.T. el. 75.80–75.60	—	2	2	—	Maroon
S.T. el. 75.80–75.60	—	2	1	—	Dark brown
S.T. el. 75.80–75.60	—	2	1	—	Maroon
S.T. el. 75.80–75.60	—	2	2	—	Maroon
S.T. el. 75.80–75.60	—	2	1	—	Dark brown
S.T. el. 75.80–75.60	—	2	1	—	Chocolate brown
S.T. el. 75.80–75.60	—	2	1	—	Pink
S.T. el. 75.80–75.60	—	2	2	—	Maroon
S.T. el. 75.80–75.60*	—	2	2	—	Red
S.T. el. 75.80–75.60	—	2	2	—	Maroon
S.T. el. 75.80–75.60	—	2	1	—	Dark brown
S.T. el. 75.80–75.60	—	2	1	—	Maroon
S.T. el. 75.80–75.60	—	2	2	—	Maroon
S.T. el. 75.80–75.60	—	2	1	—	Dark brown
S.T. el. 75.80–75.60	—	2	1	—	Chocolate brown
S.T. el. 75.80–75.60	—	2	1	—	Pink
S.T. el. 74.20–74.00	—	2	1	—	Brown
S.T. el. 73.60–73.40	—	2	1	—	Brown
S.T. el. 73.60–73.40	—	2	2	—	Chocolate brown
S.T. el. 73.40–73.20	—	1	1	—	Maroon
S.T. el. 73.40–73.20	—	2	2	—	Blackish gray
S.T. el. 73.40–73.20	—	2	2	—	Maroon

Total: 335

Table 4. List of Flint Blades, Obsidian Blades, and Blade Cores by Type and Findspot (*cont.*)
B. Micro-blades 2–4 cm long

Findspot	Plain	Retouched	Backed (ridges)	Atypical	Color
L1	—	1	2	×	Gray
L1	×	—	1	—	Dark brown
L1	—	2	2	—	Maroon
L1	×	—	1	×	Maroon
L1	—	2	2	—	Light brown
L1	—	1	1	—	Dark brown
L1	—	2	2	—	Light brown
L1	—	2	2	—	Light gray
L1	—	1	2	—	Hunter green
L1	—	2	1	—	Cream
L1*	—	1	1	×	Greenish gray
L1*	—	2	2	—	Greenish gray
L1*	—	2	2	—	Greenish gray
L1	—	2	2	—	Maroon
L1	×	—	—	×	Dark red
L1	—	2	1	—	Maroon
L1	—	2	1	—	Light brown
L1	—	1	1	×	Light brown
L1	—	2	1	—	Dark brown
L1	—	1	2	—	Chocolate brown
L1	—	1	1	×	Brown and purple
L1	—	1	1	×	Maroon
L1	—	2	—	×	Dark brown
L1	—	1	1	×	Maroon
L1	—	2	1	×	Maroon
L1	—	1	1	×	Dark red
L2	—	2	1	—	Off-white
L2	—	2	1	×	Gray
L2	×	—	1	×	Gray
L10	—	1	1	×	Chocolate brown
L13	—	2	1	—	Chocolate brown
L13	—	1	1	—	Chocolate brown
L13	—	2	2	×	Light brown
L13	—	2	1	×	Chocolate brown
L13	—	2	1	—	Chocolate brown
L13	—	1	1	—	Maroon
L13	—	2	1	—	Maroon
L13	—	2	2	—	Blackish gray
F14	—	2	2	—	Pink
F14	×	—	1	×	Tan
F14	—	2	1	—	Cream
F14	—	2	1	—	Cream
F14	—	1	1	—	Dark cream
F14	—	2	2	—	Greenish cream
F14	—	2	1	—	Greenish cream
F14	—	2	1	—	Dark cream
F14	—	2	1	—	Cream
F14	—	1	1	×	Maroon
F14	—	1	1	×	Maroon
F14	—	2	1	—	Chocolate brown
F14	—	2	1	—	Chocolate brown
F14	—	2	1	—	Dark brown
F14	—	2	1	—	Maroon
F14	—	2	1	—	Brown
F14	—	1	1	—	Maroon
F14	—	1	1	×	Maroon
F14*	—	2	2	—	Blackish gray
F14	—	1	2	—	Maroon
F14	—	1	1	×	Maroon
F14	—	2	1	—	Maroon

Table 4. List of Flint Blades, Obsidian Blades, and Blade Cores by Type and Findspot (*cont.*)
B. Micro-blades 2–4 cm long (*cont.*)

Findspot	Plain	Retouched	Backed (ridges)	Atypical	Color
F14	—	1	1	×	Brown
F14	—	2	1	—	Brown
F14	—	2	1	—	Dark brown
F14	—	2	1	—	Light brown
F14	—	1	1	—	Light red
F14	—	2	2	—	Dark brown
F14	—	1	1	—	Maroon
F14	—	2	2	—	Maroon
F14	—	1	2	—	Maroon
F14	—	2	1	×	Maroon
F14	—	2	1	×	Dark red
F14	—	2	1	—	Maroon
F14	—	2	1	—	Dark brown
F14	—	1	1	—	Maroon
F14	—	2	1	×	Dark brown
F14	—	2	1	—	Chocolate brown
F14	×	—	1	×	Dark brown
F14	—	2	1	—	Dark red
F14	—	2	2	—	Chocolate brown
F14	—	2	1	×	Dark brown
F14	—	1	1	—	Maroon
F14	—	2	1	—	Chocolate brown
F14	—	2	1	—	Brown
F14	—	1	1	—	Dark brown
F14	—	1	1	×	Brown
F14	—	1	2	×	Dark brown
F15	—	2	2	—	Light brown
F15	—	2	1	—	Pink
F15	—	2	1	—	Off-white
F15	—	1	1	×	Buff
F15	—	2	1	—	Off-white
F15	—	2	2	—	Dark brown
F15	—	2	1	—	Chocolate brown
F15	—	2	2	—	Gray
F15	—	2	2	—	Maroon
F15	—	2	2	—	Maroon
F15	—	2	1	—	Chocolate brown
F15	—	2	1	—	Maroon
F15	—	2	2	—	Dark brown
F15	—	1	1	—	Dark brown
F15	—	2	1	—	Dark brown
F15	—	1	1	—	Dark brown
F15	—	1	1	—	Blackish gray
F15	—	1	1	—	Maroon
F15	—	1	1	×	Dark red
F15	—	2	1	—	Dark red
F15	—	1	1	×	Maroon
F15	—	1	1	×	Gray
F15	×	—	1	×	Gray
F15	—	2	1	—	Buff
L21	—	2	1	×	Gray
L21	—	2	2	—	Light gray
L21	—	1	2	—	Brown
L21	—	2	1	—	Light gray
L21	—	2	1	—	Brown
L21	—	2	1	—	Brown
L21	—	2	1	—	Light brown
L21	—	1	1	—	Brown
L21	—	2	2	—	Blackish gray
L21	—	2	1	—	Gray and white

Table 4. List of Flint Blades, Obsidian Blades, and Blade Cores by Type and Findspot (*cont.*)
B. Micro-blades 2–4 cm long (*cont.*)

Findspot	Plain	Retouched	Backed (ridges)	Atypical	Color
L21	—	1	1	×	Blackish gray
L21	—	1	1	×	Brown
L21	—	1	1	—	Gray and white
L21	—	2	1	×	Gray
L21	—	2	2	—	Light gray
L21	—	2	1	×	Gray
L21	—	1	—	×	Blackish gray
L21	—	1	1	×	Blackish gray
L21	—	2	1	×	Dark brown
L21	—	2	1	—	Cream
L21	—	1	2	—	Dark brown
L21	—	2	1	—	Gray
L21	—	1	2	—	Blackish gray
L21	—	1	1	×	Maroon
L21	—	1	1	—	Maroon
L21	—	2	1	—	Maroon
L21	—	2	1	—	Maroon
L21	—	2	1	—	Gray
L21	—	1	1	×	Maroon
L21	—	2	1	×	Chocolate brown
L21	—	1	1	×	Maroon
L21	—	1	1	—	Brown
L21	—	2	1	—	Chocolate brown
L21	—	2	1	×	Maroon
L21	—	2	1	—	Dark brown
L21	×	—	1	×	Maroon
L21	—	1	1	×	Maroon
L21	—	1	1	×	Maroon
L21	—	2	1	—	Blackish gray
L21	—	2	2	—	Blackish gray
L21	×	—	—	×	Maroon
L21	—	1	1	×	Red
L21	×	—	—	×	Maroon
L21	×	—	—	×	Pink
L21	—	1	1	×	Light brown
L21	×	—	—	×	Dark brown
L21	×	—	—	×	Light gray
L21	×	—	—	×	Chocolate brown
L21	×	—	—	×	Blackish gray
L21	×	—	—	×	Maroon
L21	—	1	1	×	Dark brown
L21	—	1	—	×	Brown
L21	—	1	1	×	Dark brown
L21	×	—	1	×	Maroon
L21	—	1	1	×	Maroon
L21	×	—	1	×	Blackish gray
L21	—	1	—	×	Blackish gray
L21	—	2	1	×	Blackish gray
L21	—	1	1	×	Brown
L21	—	1	1	×	Cream
L21	—	1	1	—	Maroon
L21	—	1	2	×	Dark brown
L21	—	1	2	—	Blackish gray
L21	—	2	2	—	Cream
L21	×	—	—	×	Off-white
L21	—	1	—	×	Chocolate brown
L21	—	1	—	×	Chocolate brown
L21	—	1	1	×	Light red
L21	—	2	1	—	Blackish gray
L21	—	2	1	—	Dark brown

Table 4. List of Flint Blades, Obsidian Blades, and Blade Cores by Type and Findspot (*cont.*)
B. Micro-blades 2–4 cm long (*cont.*)

Findspot	Plain	Retouched	Backed (ridges)	Atypical	Color
L21	×	—	—	×	Blackish gray
F20/L23	—	2	1	—	Cream
F20/L23	—	1	1	×	Blackish gray
F22/L24	—	2	1	—	Cream
F22/L24	—	2	1	—	Cream
F24/L25	—	2	1	—	Maroon
L27	—	1	1	—	Cream
L27	—	2	1	—	Light brown
L27	—	2	1	—	Cream and brown
L27	—	2	1	—	Maroon
L27	—	1	2	—	Dark brown
L27	—	1	2	—	Maroon
L27	—	2	1	—	Orange red
L27	—	2	1	—	Dark brown
L27	—	1	1	—	Dark brown
L27	—	2	1	—	Gray
L27	—	2	1	—	Dark brown
L27	—	2	1	—	Maroon
L27	—	1	1	—	Gray and white
L27	×	—	2	—	Light brown
L30	—	1	—	×	Cream
L30	—	2	1	—	Chocolate brown
L30	—	2	2	—	Blackish gray
L30	—	2	1	—	Cream
F31	—	2	2	—	Maroon
F31	—	1	1	—	Cream
F31	—	2	2	—	Light brown
F31	—	2	1	—	Off-white
F31	—	2	1	—	Maroon
F31	—	2	1	—	Maroon
F31	—	2	1	—	White
F31	—	2	1	—	Buff
F31	—	2	2	—	Maroon
F31	—	2	2	×	Cream
F31	—	1	1	×	Maroon
F31	—	2	1	×	Dark brown
F26/L32	—	2	1	—	Gray
F26/L32	—	1	2	—	Dark brown
F26/L32	—	2	1	—	Maroon
F27/L33	—	2	1	—	Brown and buff
F27/L33	—	2	2	—	Cream
F27/L33	—	2	2	—	Maroon
F34	—	1	1	×	Dark buff
F34	—	1	1	×	Dark brown
F34	—	1	1	×	Gray
F34	—	1	1	—	Dark buff
F34	—	2	1	—	Maroon
F34	—	2	1	—	Brown
F34	—	2	1	×	Light brown
F34	—	2	2	—	Maroon
F34	—	2	1	×	Blackish gray
F34	—	2	2	—	Blackish gray
F34	—	2	2	—	Maroon
F34	—	2	1	—	Maroon
F34	×	—	1	×	Maroon
F34	—	1	2	—	Maroon
F34	—	2	2	×	Maroon
F34	—	2	1	×	Light brown
F34	—	2	1	—	Maroon
F34	—	2	1	×	Dark brown

Table 4. List of Flint Blades, Obsidian Blades, and Blade Cores by Type and Findspot (*cont.*)
B. Micro-blades 2–4 cm long (*cont.*)

Findspot	Plain	Retouched	Backed (ridges)	Atypical	Color
F34	—	2	1	—	Gray
F34	×	—	1	×	White
F34	—	2	1	×	Gray
L35 (D.T.)	—	2	1	—	Maroon
L35 (D.T.)	—	2	1	—	Chocolate brown
L35 (D.T.)	—	2	1	—	Maroon
L35 (D.T.)	—	2	2	—	Maroon
L35 (D.T.)	—	2	1	—	Maroon
L35 (D.T.)	—	2	1	—	Maroon
L35 (D.T.)	—	2	2	—	Maroon
L35 (D.T.)	—	2	2	×	Gray
L35 (D.T.)	—	2	2	—	Brown
L35 (D.T.)	—	2	1	—	Chocolate brown
S.T. el. 77.60–77.20*	—	2	2	—	Greenish gray
S.T. el. 77.60–77.20*	—	2	2	—	Greenish gray
S.T. el. 77.60–77.20*	—	2	2	—	Greenish gray
S.T. el. 76.80–76.20	—	1	1	×	Brown
S.T. el. 75.80–75.60	—	2	1	—	Maroon
S.T. el. 75.80–75.60	—	1	1	—	Pink
S.T. el. 75.80–75.60	—	2	1	—	Dark brown
S.T. el. 75.80–75.60	—	2	1	—	Maroon
S.T. el. 75.80–75.60	—	2	1	—	Black
S.T. el. 75.80–75.60	—	2	1	—	Cream
S.T. el. 75.80–75.60	—	2	1	—	Maroon
S.T. el. 75.80–75.60	—	2	1	—	Gray
S.T. el. 75.80–75.60	—	2	1	—	Gray
S.T. el. 75.80–75.60*	×	—	—	×	Greenish gray
S.T. el. 75.80–75.60*	×	—	2	—	Greenish gray
S.T. el. 75.60–75.40	—	2	2	—	Black
S.T. el. 75.60–75.40	—	2	2	—	Chocolate brown
S.T. el. 74.70–74.50	—	2	1	—	Black
S.T. el. 74.70–74.50	—	2	2	—	Gray
S.T. el. 74.40–74.20	×	—	1	×	Maroon
S.T. el. 74.40–74.20	—	2	1	—	Maroon
S.T. el. 74.40–74.20	×	—	1	×	Gray
S.T. el. 74.40–74.20	—	2	1	—	Pink
S.T. el. 74.40–74.20	—	1	1	×	Chocolate brown
S.T. el. 74.40–74.20	—	1	1	—	Maroon
S.T. el. 74.40–74.20	—	1	?	—	Pink
S.T. el. 74.40–74.20	—	2	1	—	Dark brown
S.T. el. 74.40–74.20	—	2	2	—	Maroon
S.T. el. 74.40–74.20	—	2	2	—	Brown
S.T. el. 74.20–74.00	—	2	2	—	Brown
S.T. el. 74.20–74.00	—	1	?	×	Cream
S.T. el. 74.20–74.00	—	2	2	—	Maroon
S.T. el. 74.00–73.80	—	1	1	—	Maroon
S.T. el. 74.00–73.80	—	2	2	×	Off-white
S.T. el. 73.80–73.60	—	2	1	—	Pink
S.T. el. 73.80–73.60	—	2	2	—	Brown
S.T. el. 73.80–73.60	—	2	2	—	Maroon
S.T. el. 73.80–73.60	—	1	—	×	Cream
S.T. el. 73.60–73.40	×	—	1	×	Cream
S.T. el. 73.60–73.40	—	2	1	×	Maroon
S.T. el. 73.60–73.40	—	2	1	—	Maroon
S.T. el. 73.60–73.40	—	2	1	—	Brown
S.T. el. 73.60–73.40	—	2	2	×	Cream
S.T. el. 73.40–73.20	—	1	1	—	Maroon
S.T. el. 73.40–73.20	—	2	2	—	Cream
S.T. el. 73.40–73.20	—	2	1	—	Gray
S.T. el. 73.40–73.20	—	2	2	×	Maroon

Table 4. List of Flint Blades, Obsidian Blades, and Blade Cores by Type and Findspot (*cont.*)
B. Micro-blades 2–4 cm long (*cont.*)

Findspot	Plain	Retouched	Backed (ridges)	Atypical	Color
S.T. el. 73.40–73.20	—	2	1	—	Cream
S.T. el. 73.00–72.85	—	2	1	—	Maroon
S.T. el. 73.00–72.85	—	2	1	×	Brown
S.T. el. 73.00–72.85	—	2	2	—	Hunter green
S.T. el. 73.00–72.85	—	1	1	×	Maroon

Total: 306

Table 4. List of Flint Blades, Obsidian Blades, and Blade Cores by Type and Findspot (*cont.*)
C. Blades 4–6 cm long

Findspot	Plain	Retouched	Backed (ridges)	Atypical	Color
L1	—	2	1	—	Maroon
L1	—	1	1	×	Maroon
L1	—	1	3	—	Chocolate brown
L1	—	1	2	—	Light gray
L1	—	2	1	—	Chocolate brown
L1	—	2	2	—	Off-white
L1	—	2	2	—	Maroon
L1	—	2	2	—	Chocolate brown
L1	—	2	1	—	Off-white
L1	—	2	2	—	Gray
L1	—	2	2	—	Gray
L1	—	1	1	×	Dark cream
L1	—	2	1	—	Maroon
L1	—	2	1	—	Off-white
L1	—	1	2	—	Gray
L1	—	1	1	×	Brown
L1	—	2	1	×	Maroon
L1	—	2	1	—	Gray
L1	—	1	1	×	Gray
L1	—	2	2	—	Chocolate brown
L1	—	2	2	—	Buff
L1	—	2	1	—	Light brown
L1	×	—	1	×	Off-white
L1	—	2	2	—	Off-white
L1	—	2	2	—	Buff
L1	—	2	2	—	Off-white
L1	—	2	1	—	Off-white
L1	—	2	1	—	Buff
L1	×	—	1	×	Maroon
L1	—	1	1	×	Maroon
L13	—	1	1	×	Maroon
L13	—	2	1	—	Maroon
L13	—	2	1	—	Chocolate brown
L13	—	1	1	—	Off-white
L13	—	1	2	—	Pink
L13	—	2	1	—	Chocolate brown
L13	—	2	1	×	Chocolate brown
L13	—	2	1	—	Chocolate brown
L13	—	1	1	×	Off-white
L13	—	2	1	—	Chocolate brown
L13	—	1	2	—	Chocolate brown

Table 4. List of Flint Blades, Obsidian Blades, and Blade Cores by Type and Findspot (*cont.*)
C. Blades 4–6 cm long (*cont.*)

Findspot	Plain	Retouched	Backed (ridges)	Atypical	Color
L13	—	2	1	—	Off-white
L13	—	2	1	—	Off-white
F14	—	2	2	—	Chocolate brown
F14	—	2	2	—	Off-white
F14	—	1	1	×	Cream
F14	×	—	1	—	Dark brown
F14	—	2	1	—	Chocolate brown
F15	×	—	1	×	Gray
F15	—	2	1	—	Gray
F15	—	2	1	—	Gray
F15	×	—	1	×	Off-white
F15	×	—	1	×	Chocolate brown
F15	×	—	1	—	Blackish gray
F15	—	2	2	—	Blackish gray
F15	—	2	1	—	Gray
F15	×	—	1	×	Dark brown
F15	—	1	1	×	Blackish gray
F15	—	1	—	×	Dark brown
F15	×	—	—	×	Blackish gray
F15	—	2	2	—	Gray
F15	—	2	1	—	Gray
F15	×	1	—	×	Gray
L21	—	2	1	—	Maroon
L21	—	1	—	×	Blackish gray
L21	—	2	1	—	Pink
L21	—	1	1	—	Maroon
L21	—	2	1	×	Maroon
L21	—	2	1	×	Blackish gray
L21	—	2	1	×	Light green
L21	×	—	—	×	Blackish gray
L21	—	2	2	×	Chocolate brown
L21	×	—	—	×	Dark brown
L21	×	—	1	—	Blackish gray
L21	—	1	1	×	Dark brown
L21	×	—	—	—	Brown
L21	×	—	1	×	Chocolate brown
L21	—	2	1	—	Red
L21	—	2	1	—	Brown
L21	—	2	2	—	Red
L21	—	2	1	×	Blackish gray
L21	—	1	1	×	Dark brown
L21	—	2	2	—	Blackish gray
L21	—	1	1	×	Chocolate brown
L21	—	1	1	×	Dark red
L21	—	2	1	—	Dark red
L21	×	—	—	×	Dark brown
L21	—	2	1	—	Brown
L21	—	2	2	—	Off-white
F20/L23	×	—	—	×	Blackish gray
F20/L23	×	—	—	×	Blackish gray
F20/L23	×	—	—	×	Blackish gray
F20/L23	—	2	2	—	Blackish gray
F20/L23	—	1	1	—	Blackish gray
F22/L24	×	—	—	—	Blackish gray
F22/L24	×	—	—	—	Maroon
F22/L24*	×	—	—	×	Greenish gray
F23/L24a	—	1	1	—	Brown
F23/L24a	—	2	2	—	Maroon
F23/L24a	—	2	1	—	Cream
F23/L24a	—	2	1	×	Blackish gray

Table 4. List of Flint Blades, Obsidian Blades, and Blade Cores by Type and Findspot (*cont.*)
C. Blades 4–6 cm long (*cont.*)

Findspot	Plain	Retouched	Backed (ridges)	Atypical	Color
F23/L24a	—	2	1	—	Red
F23/L24a	×	—	—	—	Maroon
F24/L25	×	—	—	×	Dark brown
F24/L25	—	1	1	—	Chocolate brown
F24/L25	—	1	1	—	Chocolate brown
F24/L25	—	2	2	—	White
F24/L25	—	1	2	—	Chocolate brown
F24/L25	—	2	1	—	Blackish gray
F24/L25	—	2	2	—	Gray
F24/L25	—	2	2	—	Chocolate brown
L27	—	1	1	—	Chocolate brown
L27	—	1	2	—	Blackish gray
L27	—	2	1	—	Off-white
L27	—	2	1	×	Dark brown
L27	—	2	2	—	Gray
L27	—	1	1	—	Red and white
L27	—	1	1	×	Cream
L27	—	2	2	—	Light brown
L27	—	1	1	—	Maroon
L27	—	1	1	—	Maroon
L27	—	2	1	—	Gray
L27	—	2	2	—	Buff
L27	×	—	—	×	Dark brown
L27	—	2	1	—	Gray
L27	—	1	2	—	Dark brown
L27	—	2	1	—	Dark brown
L27	—	1	—	×	Dark brown
L27	×	—	—	×	Light brown
L27	—	2	1	—	Cream
L27	—	2	1	—	Chocolate brown
L27	—	2	1	—	Cream
L27	—	2	2	—	Off-white
L27	—	2	1	—	Maroon
L27	—	2	1	—	Cream
L27	—	2	1	—	Brown
L27	—	2	2	—	Dark brown
L27	—	1	1	×	Dark brown
L27	×	—	—	×	Maroon
L30	—	2	2	—	Chocolate brown
L30	×	—	—	×	Brown
L30	—	2	2	—	Cream
L30	—	1	1	×	Hunter green
L30	—	1	1	—	Blackish gray
L30	—	1	1	—	Buff
L30	—	1	2	—	Light brown
L30	—	2	1	—	Dark brown
L30	—	2	2	—	Cream
L30	—	2	2	—	Dark brown
L30	—	1	1	×	Chocolate brown
L30	—	1	2	—	Gray
L30	—	2	2	—	Maroon
L30	—	1	1	—	Maroon
L30	—	2	1	—	Dark brown
L30	—	1	1	—	Dark brown
L30	—	2	1	—	Cream
L30	×	—	—	×	Maroon
L30	—	1	1	—	Dark buff
L30	—	2	1	—	Cream
L30	—	2	1	—	Maroon
L30	—	2	1	×	Dark brown

Table 4. List of Flint Blades, Obsidian Blades, and Blade Cores by Type and Findspot (*cont.*)
C. Blades 4–6 cm long (*cont.*)

Findspot	Plain	Retouched	Backed (ridges)	Atypical	Color
L30	—	2	1	—	Blackish gray
L30	—	2	1	—	Blackish gray
L30	—	2	2	—	Cream
L30	—	2	1	—	Cream
L30	—	2	1	—	Cream
L30	—	2	1	×	Brown
L30	—	2	1	—	Brown
L30	—	1	1	×	Maroon
L30	—	2	1	—	Gray
L30	—	2	2	—	Maroon
L30	—	2	1	—	Brown
L30	—	2	1	—	Chocolate brown
L30	—	2	1	×	Dark brown
L30	—	2	2	—	Maroon
L30	—	2	1	—	Cream
L30	—	2	1	—	Maroon
L30	—	2	2	—	Chocolate brown
L30	—	2	1	—	Maroon
L30	—	2	2	—	Maroon
L30	×	—	—	×	Maroon
L30	—	1	2	—	Dark brown
L30	—	2	1	—	Maroon
L30	—	2	1	—	Chocolate brown
L30	—	1	1	×	Blackish gray
L30	—	2	1	—	Dark red
L30	—	2	2	—	Dark brown
L30	×	—	—	×	Maroon
L30	—	1	1	—	Dark brown
L30	—	1	1	×	Gray
L30	—	2	2	—	Brown
L30	—	1	1	×	Gray
L30	—	2	1	—	Blackish gray
L30	—	1	1	×	Light brown
L30	—	2	1	—	Cream
L30	—	2	1	—	Maroon
L30	—	2	1	—	Chocolate brown
L30	—	2	1	—	Brown
L30	—	2	1	—	Maroon
L30	—	1	3	—	Maroon
L30	—	2	1	—	Brown
L30	—	1	2	—	Brown
L30	—	2	1	—	Brown
L30	×	—	1	×	Gray
L30	—	2	1	×	Light brown
L30	—	2	1	—	Dark red
L30	—	2	1	×	Blackish gray
L30	—	1	1	—	Brown
L30	—	2	1	—	Cream
L30	—	1	1	—	Brown
L30	—	2	1	—	Brown
L30	—	2	2	—	Maroon
L30	—	2	—	×	Maroon
L30	—	2	2	—	Buff
L30	—	1	2	×	Blackish gray
L30	×	—	—	×	White
L30	—	1	1	×	Dark buff
L30	—	2	1	×	White
L30	—	2	2	—	Gray
L30	—	2	—	×	Chocolate brown
L30	—	2	1	—	Brown

Table 4. List of Flint Blades, Obsidian Blades, and Blade Cores by Type and Findspot (*cont.*)
C. Blades 4–6 cm long (*cont.*)

Findspot	Plain	Retouched	Backed (ridges)	Atypical	Color
L30	—	2	2	—	Cream
L30	—	1	1	—	Maroon
L30	—	2	1	—	Dark brown
L30	—	1	1	×	Cream
L30	—	1	1	×	Cream
F31	×	—	—	×	Gray
F31	×	—	—	×	Gray
F31	—	2	—	×	Cream
F31	—	1	1	—	Light brown
F31	—	2	—	×	Chocolate brown
F31	—	2	1	×	Maroon
F31	×	—	2	×	Gray
F31	—	2	2	—	Gray
F31	—	2	1	—	Cream
F31	—	2	2	—	Chocolate brown
F31	—	2	2	—	Chocolate brown
F31	—	2	1	—	Gray
F31	—	2	1	—	Chocolate brown
F31	×	—	—	×	Light red
F31	×	—	1	×	Chocolate brown
F31	—	1	1	—	Dark red
F31	×	—	1	×	Blackish gray
F31	—	2	2	—	Dark brown
F31	—	1	—	×	Brown
F31	—	2	1	—	Pink
F31	—	2	1	—	Maroon
F31	—	2	2	—	Maroon
F31	—	2	2	—	Cream
F31	—	2	1	×	Blackish gray
F31	—	2	2	—	Blackish gray
F31	—	1	—	×	Mustard yellow
F31	—	2	1	—	Chocolate brown
F31	—	1	1	—	Cream
F31	—	1	1	—	Cream
F27/L33	—	1	—	×	Chocolate brown
F27/L33	—	1	1	—	Cream
F27/L33	—	2	2	—	Gray
F27/L33	—	2	1	—	Maroon
F27/L33	—	2	2	—	Gray
F27/L33	—	1	1	—	Dark brown
F27/L33	—	2	2	—	Gray
F27/L33	—	2	1	—	Maroon
F27/L33	—	2	1	×	Dark brown
F34	—	2	1	×	Dark brown
F34	—	2	1	—	Brown
F34	—	2	1	—	Dark brown
F34	—	2	1	—	Dark brown
F34	—	2	3	—	Maroon
F34	—	2	1	—	Dark brown
F34	—	2	1	×	Cream
F34	—	2	2	—	Dark brown
F34	—	1	1	—	Pink
F34	—	2	1	—	Cream
F34	—	2	1	×	Pink
F34	×	—	1	×	Maroon
F34	—	1	1	—	Maroon
F34	—	2	2	—	Gray
F34	—	2	2	—	Off-white
F34	—	2	1	—	Gray
F34	×	—	1	—	Blackish gray

Table 4. List of Flint Blades, Obsidian Blades, and Blade Cores by Type and Findspot (*cont.*)
C. Blades 4–6 cm long (*cont.*)

Findspot	Plain	Retouched	Backed (ridges)	Atypical	Color
F34	—	1	1	—	Blackish gray
F34	—	2	1	—	Gray
F34	—	2	1	×	Blackish gray
F34	—	1	1	×	Gray
F34	—	2	1	—	Brown
F34	—	2	1	—	White
F34	—	2	1	—	Blackish gray
F34	—	1	1	×	Blackish gray
F34	—	2	1	—	Off-white
F34	—	1	—	×	Blackish gray
F34	—	2	1	—	Blackish gray
F34	—	2	1	—	Off-white
F34	—	2	2	—	Cream
F34	—	2	1	—	Cream
L35 (D.T.)	—	2	2	—	Maroon
L35 (D.T.)	—	2	2	—	Maroon
L35 (D.T.)	—	2	1	—	Cream
L35 (D.T.)	—	2	1	—	Maroon
L35 (D.T.)	—	2	1	—	Dark brown
L35 (D.T.)	—	2	2	—	Chocolate brown
L35 (D.T.)	—	2	2	—	Maroon
L35 (D.T.)	—	2	1	—	Gray
L35 (D.T.)	—	2	1	—	Blackish gray
L35 (D.T.)	—	2	1	—	Blackish gray
L35 (D.T.)	—	2	2	—	Blackish gray
L35 (D.T.)	×	—	—	×	Brown
L35 (D.T.)	—	1	1	—	Cream
L35 (D.T.)	—	2	1	—	Brown
L35 (D.T.)	—	2	1	—	Gray
L35 (D.T.)	—	2	1	×	Maroon
L37 (D.T.)	—	2	1	—	Brown
L37 (D.T.)	—	2	1	—	Brown
L37 (D.T.)	—	1	1	—	Maroon
L37 (D.T.)	—	2	1	—	Hunter green
L37 (D.T.)	—	2	2	—	Blackish gray
L37 (D.T.)	—	2	1	×	Maroon
L37 (D.T.)	—	2	—	×	Dark brown
L37 (D.T.)	—	2	2	—	Maroon
L39 (D.T.)	—	1	2	—	Maroon
S.T. el. 77.60–77.20	—	2	3	—	Gray
S.T. el. 77.60–77.20	—	2	1	×	Dark brown
S.T. el. 77.60–77.20	—	2	1	—	Maroon
S.T. el. 76.80–76.20	—	2	1	—	Chocolate brown
S.T. el. 75.90–75.70*	—	2	2	—	Greenish gray
S.T. el. 75.90–75.70	—	2	1	—	Brown
S.T. el. 75.70–75.50	—	2	2	×	Gray
S.T. el. 75.70–75.50*	—	2	1	—	Greenish gray
S.T. el. 75.70–75.50*	—	2	2	—	Greenish gray
S.T. el. 75.70–75.50	—	2	1	×	Cream
S.T. el. 75.70–75.50	—	2	1	—	Maroon
S.T. el. 75.70–75.50	—	2	2	—	Gray
S.T. el. 75.70–75.50	—	2	1	×	Chocolate brown
S.T. el. 75.70–75.50	—	2	1	—	Cream
S.T. el. 75.70–75.50	—	2	1	—	Maroon
S.T. el. 75.50–75.30	—	1	—	×	Light brown
S.T. el. 75.50–75.30	—	2	1	—	Maroon
S.T. el. 75.50–75.30	—	1	1	—	Maroon
S.T. el. 75.50–75.30	—	1	1	×	Gray
S.T. el. 75.50–75.30	—	2	1	—	Maroon
S.T. el. 75.50–75.30	—	2	2	—	Dark brown

Table 4. List of Flint Blades, Obsidian Blades, and Blade Cores by Type and Findspot (*cont.*)
C. Blades 4–6 cm long (*cont.*)

Findspot	Plain	Retouched	Backed (ridges)	Atypical	Color
S.T. el. 75.50–75.30	—	1	1	×	Maroon
S.T. el. 75.50–75.30	—	2	1	—	Gray
S.T. el. 75.50–75.30	—	2	—	×	Maroon
S.T. el. 75.50–75.30	—	2	2	—	Maroon
S.T. 290–310	—	1	1	×	Gray
S.T. el. 74.70–74.50	—	2	1	—	Maroon
S.T. el. 74.50–74.40	—	2	2	—	Hunter green
S.T. el. 74.70–74.60	—	2	2	—	Cream
S.T. el. 74.70–74.50	—	2	1	—	Maroon
S.T. el. 74.70–74.50	—	2	1	—	Mustard yellow
S.T. el. 74.40–74.20	—	2	1	—	Brown
S.T. el. 74.20–74.00	×	—	—	×	Buff
S.T. el. 74.20–74.00	×	—	—	×	Brown
S.T. el. 74.20–74.00	—	1	1	×	Chocolate brown
S.T. el. 74.20–74.00	—	2	1	—	Brown
S.T. el. 74.20–74.00	—	1	1	—	Brown
S.T. el. 74.20–74.00	—	2	1	—	Gray
S.T. el. 74.20–74.00	—	2	2	—	Blackish gray
S.T. el. 74.20–74.00	—	2	2	—	Maroon
S.T. el. 74.20–74.00	—	2	?	×	Dark brown
S.T. el. 74.20–74.00	—	1	2	—	Dark brown
S.T. el. 74.20–74.00	—	2	1	—	Brown
S.T. el. 74.20–74.00	—	2	1	—	Maroon
S.T. el. 74.00–73.80	—	2	1	—	Brown
S.T. el. 74.00–73.80	—	2	1	—	Gray
S.T. el. 74.00–73.80	—	2	2	—	Blackish gray
S.T. el. 74.00–73.80	—	2	2	—	Maroon
S.T. el. 74.00–73.80	—	1	1	×	Dark brown
S.T. el. 74.00–73.80	×	—	—	×	Dark brown
S.T. el. 74.00–73.80	—	1	—	×	Dark brown
S.T. el. 74.00–73.80	×	—	—	×	Cream
S.T. el. 74.00–73.80	—	2	1	—	Cream
S.T. el. 74.00–73.80	—	2	1	—	Cream
S.T. el. 74.00–73.80	—	2	1	—	Chocolate brown
S.T. el. 74.00–73.80	—	2	1	—	Blackish gray
S.T. el. 74.00–73.80	—	2	1	—	Blackish gray
S.T. el. 74.00–73.80	—	2	1	—	Hunter green
S.T. el. 74.00–73.80	—	2	1	×	Cream
S.T. el. 74.00–73.80	—	2	1	—	Dark brown
S.T. el. 74.00–73.80	—	2	1	—	Gray
S.T. el. 74.00–73.80	—	2	1	—	Cream
S.T. el. 74.00–73.80	—	1	—	×	Maroon
S.T. el. 73.80–73.60	—	2	1	—	Cream
S.T. el. 73.60–73.40	—	1	—	×	Gray
S.T. el. 73.60–73.40	×	—	—	×	Hunter green
S.T. el. 73.60–73.40	—	2	1	—	Maroon
S.T. el. 73.60–73.40	—	1	2	—	Maroon
S.T. el. 73.40–73.20	—	2	2	—	Maroon
S.T. el. 73.40–73.20	—	2	1	—	Pink
S.T. el. 73.40–73.20	—	2	1	—	Brown
S.T. el. 73.00–72.85	—	2	1	—	Blackish gray
S.T. el. 73.00–72.85	—	2	1	—	Maroon
S.T. el. 73.00–72.85	—	1	1	—	Gray
S.T. el. 73.00–72.85	—	1	1	×	Hunter green
S.T. el. 73.00–72.85	—	1	1	—	Cream
S.T. el. 73.00–72.85	×	—	—	×	Maroon
S.T. el. 73.00–72.85	×	—	—	×	Dark brown
S.T. el. 73.00–72.85	×	—	—	×	Dark brown

Total: 439

Table 4. List of Flint Blades, Obsidian Blades, and Blade Cores by Type and Findspot (*cont.*)
D. Blades 6 cm and longer

Findspot	Plain	Retouched	Backed (ridges)	Atypical	Color
L27	—	2	2	—	Blackish gray
L30	—	2	2	—	Gray
L30	—	2	2	—	Brown
L30	—	2	1	—	Gray
L30	—	2	2	—	Cream
F27/L33	—	2	2	—	Cream
F34	—	2	?	×	Cream
F34	—	2	2	—	Cream
F34	—	2	1	×	Maroon
F34	—	1	2	—	Dark brown
F34	—	1	1	—	Dark brown
F34	×	—	1	—	Maroon
F34	×	—	1	—	Maroon
F34	×	—	1	×	Maroon
F34	×	—	—	×	Dark brown
F34	—	2	2	—	Hunter green
F34	—	2	2	—	Off-white
F34	—	2	2	—	Blackish gray
F34	—	2	1	—	Gray
F34	—	2	2	—	Hunter green
F34	—	2	2	—	Gray
F34	—	1	1	—	Gray
F34	—	2	1	—	Dark brown
F34	—	2	1	—	Cream
F34	—	1	1	—	Cream
F34	—	1	1	—	Chocolate brown
F34	—	1	?	×	Blackish gray
L39	—	2	2	—	Dark brown
S.T. el. 77.60–77.20	—	2	2	—	Cream
S.T. el. 76.80–75.40	—	1	1	—	Gray
S.T. el. 75.60–75.40	—	2	2	—	Buff
S.T. el. 74.70–74.50	—	2	2	—	Dark brown
S.T. el. 74.70–74.50	—	2	1	—	Maroon
S.T. el. 74.50–74.40	—	2	1	—	Blackish gray
S.T. el. 74.40–74.20	—	2	2	—	Blackish gray
S.T. el. 73.60–73.40	×	—	1	×	Blackish gray
S.T. el. 73.60–73.40	—	1	1	—	Gray
S.T. el. 73.40–73.20	—	2	1	—	Cream
S.T. el. 73.00–72.85	—	2	2	—	Gray
S.T. el. 73.00–72.85	—	2	2	—	Buff
S.T. el. 73.00–72.85	—	2	2	—	Cream

Total: 41

Table 4. List of Flint Blades, Obsidian Blades, and Blade Cores by Type and Findspot (*cont.*)
E. Bullet-shaped Blade Cores

Findspot	Length cm	Diameter cm	Geometric Platform	Irregular Platform	Color
L1	5	2.5	—	×	Cream
L1	4	1.5	×	—	Maroon
L13	6.5	4.5	—	×	Maroon
F14	4	1.5	×	—	Maroon
F14	3.5	1.3	×	—	Gray
F14	3	1.2	×	—	Dark red
F14	3	1.5	×	—	Red
F14	3	1	×	—	Light red
F14	3	1.7	—	×	Gray
F14	?	2	×	—	Chocolate brown
F15	3.2	1.5	×	—	Maroon
F15	3.6	1.7	×	—	Brown
F15	3.5	1.8	—	×	Gray
F15	3	2.5	—	×	Brown
F16/L19	3	2.5	—	×	Dark red
L21	4.5	4	—	×	Maroon
L21	4	1.8	×	—	Blackish gray
L21	3.4	0.7	×	—	Dark brown
L21	3	1	×	—	Light brown
L21	3.5	0.6	×	—	Gray
L21	4.3	2.8	×	—	Maroon
L21	5	3	×	—	Light brown
L21	4.5	2.9	—	×	Maroon
L27	2.3	1.7	×	—	Maroon
L30	3	1.2	×	—	Brown
L30	4.3	2.3	—	×	Chocolate brown
L30	2.9	1.4	×	—	Dark brown
L30	3.9	2.4	×	—	Blackish gray
L30	2.5	2	×	—	Maroon
F31	6.5	2.4	×	—	Cream
F31	3.1	0.8	—	×	Maroon
F31	3.7	3.5	—	×	Maroon
F31	3.5	2.5	—	×	Dark buff
F31	4	2.1	—	×	Blackish gray
F27/L33	3.1	1.9	—	×	Chocolate brown
F27/L33	2.5	3.4	?	?	Chocolate brown
F27/L33	2.8	0.7	×	—	Maroon
F34	3.6	1.4	×	—	Maroon
F34	2.7	1.4	×	—	Maroon
F34	2.9	1.9	×	—	Dark brown
F34	2.4	2.1	—	×	Brown
F34	3.2	1.2	×	—	Maroon
F34	2.6	1.2	×	—	Brown
F34	3	1.5	×	—	Cream
F34	4.1	2.7	—	×	Maroon
F34	?	4	—	×	Maroon
L35 (D.T.)	4	1.5	×	—	Brown
L37 (D.T.)	3.2	1.3	×	—	Maroon
L37 (D.T.)	3.9	1.2	×	—	Dark brown
L37 (D.T.)	3.2	2.9	—	×	Chocolate brown
L37 (D.T.)	3.5	3.4	—	×	Maroon
S.T. el. 77.60–77.20	3.7	2	×	—	Chocolate brown
S.T. el. 77.60–77.20	2	1.5	—	×	Maroon
S.T. el. 74.50–74.40	2.2	1.3	×	—	Maroon
S.T. el. 74.20–74.00	3.4	1.2	×	—	Brown
S.T. el. 74.20–74.00	3.1	1	×	—	Pink
S.T. el. 74.20–74.00	2.9	2.6	—	×	Dark brown
S.T. el. 74.20–74.00	5.6	2.6	—	×	Blackish gray
S.T. el. 74.20–74.00	3	1.3	—	×	Chocolate brown

Table 4. List of Flint Blades, Obsidian Blades, and Blade Cores by Type and Findspot (*cont.*)
E. Bullet-shaped Blade Cores (*cont.*)

Findspot	Length cm	Diameter cm	Geometric Platform	Irregular Platform	Color
S.T. el. 74.00–73.80	3.6	1.8	×	—	Gray
S.T. el. 73.80–73.60	5.1	2.7	×	—	Maroon
S.T. el. 73.60–73.40	2.9	2.7	—	×	Maroon
S.T. el. 73.40–73.20	3.1	3	—	×	Cream
S.T. el. 73.40–73.20	4.1	3.1	—	×	Maroon
S.T. el. 73.40–73.20	2.9	1.2	×	—	Maroon
S.T. el. 73.40–73.20	2.9	1.4	×	—	Maroon
S.T. el. 73.20–73.00	3.1	1.4	×	—	Speckled cr.
S.T. el. 73.20–73.00	2.9	0.9	×	—	Dark brown
S.T. el. 73.00–72.85	2.4	2	—	×	Maroon
Total	69				

114 EXCAVATIONS AT THE PREHISTORIC MOUND OF CHOGHA BONUT, KHUZESTAN, IRAN

Figure 38. Various Types of Flint Micro-Blades. Scale 1:1

	Field Number	Findspot	Elevation	Description
A	CB 155c	S.T.	76.80–76.60	Dark gray stone, no retouch. Triangular section, flat back
B	CB 139b	F 34	74.00	Grayish beige stone, no retouch. Triangular section, flat back
C	CB 79	F8/L10	75.10	Dark gray stone, no retouch. Obtuse-angled section, flat back
D	CB 105b	L21	74.25	Translucent creamy beige stone, no retouch. Triangular section, flat back
E	CB 145a	L35	74.00–73.80	Brown stone, no retouch. Triangular section, flat back
F	CB 164b	S.T.	74.20–74.00	Dark gray stone, no retouch. Triangular section, flat back
G	CB 81	L11	75.00	Chocolate flint stone, no retouch. Trapezoidal section, flat back
H	CB 174b	S.T.	73.40–73.20	Dark brown stone, no retouch. Trapezoidal section, flat back
I	CB 158b	S.T.	75.60–75.40	Greenish gray obsidian blade, no retouch. Trapezoidal section, flat back
J	CB 105c	L21	74.25	Dark brown stone, no retouch. Trapezoidal section, flat back
K	CB 130a	F15	74.70	Grayish stone, no retouch. Trapezoidal section, flat back
L	CB 91	F14	74.75	Grayish cream stone, no retouch. Trapezoidal section, flat back
M	CB 130b	F15	74.70	Dark maroon stone, no retouch. Trapezoidal section, flat back
N	CB 146a	L35	73.80–73.60	Dark gray obsidian blade, no retouch. Trapezoidal section, flat back
O	CB 128	F27/L33	74.05	Cream gray stone, no retouch. Trapezoidal section, flat back
P	CB 115	L27	74.15	Dark brown microlith, no retouch. Trapezoidal section, flat back
Q	CB 174d	S.T.	73.40–73.20	Dark-speckled gray stone, no retouch. Trapezoidal section, flat back
R	CB 74	L1	76.10–75.00	Chocolate brown stone, no retouch. Trapezoidal section (irregular), flat back
S	CB 166a	S.T.	74.00–73.80	Chocolate brown stone, no retouch. Triangular section, flat back
T	CB 158a	S.T.	75.80–75.60	Greenish gray obsidian blade, no retouch, flat back
U	CB 168a	S.T.	73.80–73.60	Dark gray stone, no retouch. Trapezoidal section, flat back
V	CB 104	F24/L25	74.20	Dark brown stone, no retouch. Trapezoidal section, flat back
W	CB 149a	L39	73.30–73.20	Deep maroon stone, no retouch. Trapezoidal section, flat back
X	CB 159d	S.T.	74.70–74.50	Gray stone, no retouch. Trapezoidal section, flat back
Y	CB 176b	S.T.	73.00–72.85	Veined, reddish brown stone, one edge retouched. Triangular section, flat back
Z	CB 134b	L30	74.10	Chocolate flint stone, one edge retouched. Triangular section, flat back
AA	CB 139a	F34	74.00	Brown stone, one edge retouched. Trapezoidal section, flat back
BB	CB 134c	L30	74.10	Dark gray stone, one edge retouched. Trapezoidal section, flat back
CC	CB 134a	L30	74.10	Beige stone, one edge retouched. Trapezoidal section, flat back
DD	CB 159a	S.T.	74.70–74.50	Chocolate brown stone, one edge retouched. Trapezoidal section, somewhat curved back
EE	CB 162b	S.T.	74.40–74.20	Light brown stone, one edge retouched. Triangular section, flat back
FF	CB 180d	S.T.	73.60–73.40	Grayish beige stone, one edge retouched. Triangular section, slightly curved back
GG	CB 174a	S.T.	73.60–73.40	Gray stone, one side retouched. Triangular section, flat back
HH	CB 152b	F31	74.08	Chocolate flint microlith, one side retouched. Trapezoidal section, flat back
II	CB 171b	S.T.	73.60–73.40	Deep maroon stone, one edge retouched. Trapezoidal section, slightly curved back
JJ	CB 154c	S.T.	77.20	Greenish gray stone, both edges retouched. Triangular section, slightly curved back
KK	CB 153c	S.T.	77.20	Greenish gray obsidian blade, both edges retouched. Triangular section, flat back
LL	CB 148a	S.T.	77.20–77.00	Dark brown stone, both edges retouched. Triangular section, flat back
MM	CB 73	L1	76.10–75.00	Greenish gray obsidian blade, both edges retouched. Trapezoidal section, flat back
NN	CB 148b	L35	73.60	Light brown stone, both edges retouched. Trapezoidal section, curved back

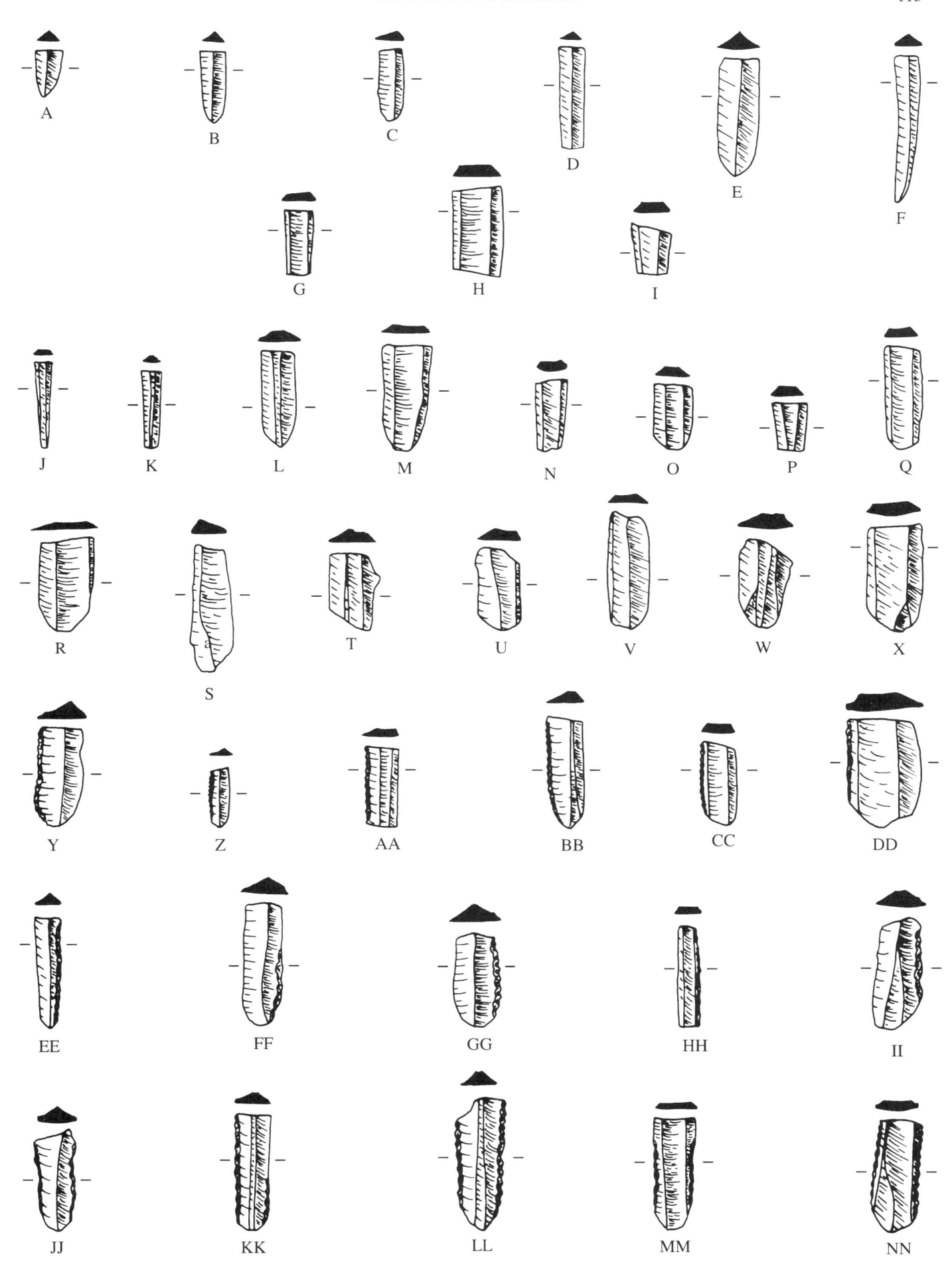

Figure 38. Various Types of Flint Micro-Blades. Scale 1:1

Figure 39. Various Types of Flint Blades with Straight Bulbar Surface. Scale 1:1

	Field Number	Findspot	Elevation	Description
A	CB 166c	S.T.	73.60–73.40	Black stone, no retouch. Triangular section, flat back
B	CB 162a	S.T.	74.40–74.20	Dark gray stone, no retouch. Trapezoidal section, flat back
C	CB 149b	L39	73.30–73.20	Dark brown stone, no retouch. Trapezoidal section, flat back
D	CB 107a	L21	74.25	Dark gray stone, no retouch. Trapezoidal section, flat back
E	CB 140d	F34	74.00	Bright maroon stone, no retouch. Flat back
F	CB 141a	F34	74.00	Grayish green stone, no retouch. Triangular section, flat back
G	CB 152c	F31	74.08	Chocolate brown stone, no retouch. Triangular section, flat back
H	CB 92	F14	74.75	Dark brown stone, one edge retouched. Triangular section, flat back
I	CB 107b	L21	74.25	Dark gray stone, one edge retouched. Triangular section, flat back
J	CB 146b	L35	73.80–73.60	Gray stone, one edge retouched. Triangular section, flat back
K	CB 96	F14	74.75	Fine grain grayish green stone, one edge retouched. Trapezoidal section, curved back
L	CB 75	L1	76.10–75.00	Gray speckled creamy stone, one edge retouched. Trapezoidal section, slightly curved back
M	CB 108	L21	74.25	Light gray stone, one edge retouched. Trapezoidal section, flat back
N	CB 157b	S.T.	75.60–75.40	Beige stone, one edge retouched. Trapezoidal section, flat back
O	CB 131a	F15	74.70	Red speckled yellowish stone, one edge retouched. Triangular section, flat back
P	CB 78	F8/L10	75.10	Chocolate brown stone, one edge retouched. Flat back
Q	CB 135a	L30	74.10	Fine grain tan stone, one edge retouched. Trapezoidal section, flat back
R	CB 106a	L21	74.25	Dark gray stone, one edge retouched. Trapezoidal section, flat back
S	CB 135b	L30	74.10	Gray stone, both edges retouched. Triangular section, flat back
T	CB 174e	S.T.	73.00–72.85	Light gray stone, both edges retouched. Triangular section, flat back
U	CB 140c	F34	74.00	Brown stone, both edges retouched. Triangular section, flat back
V	CB 159c	S.T.	74.70–74.50	Chocolate brown stone, both edges retouched. Triangular section, flat back
W	CB 176a	S.T.	73.00–72.85	Dark (shaded) and gray stone, both edges retouched. Obtuse-angled section, flat back
X	CB 84	L13	74.80	Gray stone, both edges retouched. Trapezoidal section, flat back
Y	CB 135c	L30	74.10	Dark gray stone, both edges retouched. Trapezoidal section, flat back
Z	CB 141b	F34	74.00	Light gray stone, both edges retouched. Trapezoidal section, flat back
AA	CB 161d	S.T.	74.90–74.70	Grayish cream stone, both edges retouched. Trapezoidal section, flat back
BB	CB 93	F14	74.75	Dark gray stone, both edges retouched. Trapezoidal section, flat back

CHIPPED STONE INDUSTRY 117

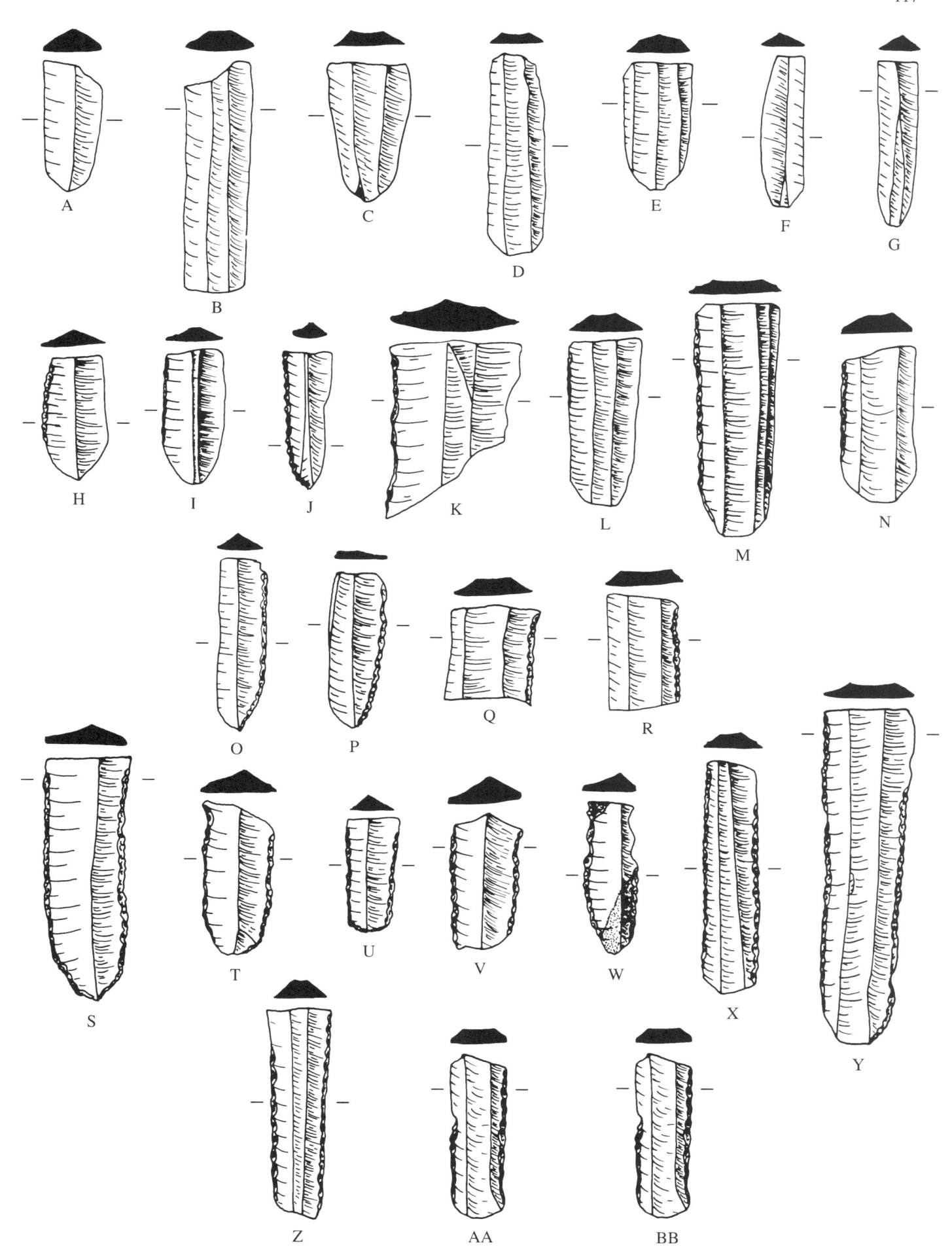

Figure 39. Various Types of Flint Blades with Straight Bulbar Surface. Scale 1:1

Figure 40. Various Types of Flint Blades with Curved Bulbar Surface. Scale 1:1

	Field Number	Findspot	Elevation	Description
A	CB 176g	S.T.	73.00–72.85	Gray stone, no retouch, sharp edges
B	CB 122	F23/L24a	74.20	Dark maroon stone, no retouch, sharp edges with shin
C	CB 145c	L35	74.00–73.80	Brown stone, no retouch, sharp edges
D	CB 129b	F27/L33	74.05	Dark gray stone, no retouch, sharp edges with shin
E	CB 161e	S.T.	74.50–74.30	Chocolate brown stone, no retouch, sharp edges with shin
F	CB 119b	L27	74.15	Yellowish tan stone, no retouch
G	CB 166f	S.T.	74.00–73.80	Dark beige stone, one edge retouched
H	CB 166e	S.T.	74.00–73.80	Gray stone, one edge retouched
I	CB 176h	S.T.	73.00–72.85	Deep maroon stone, one edge retouched with slight shin
J	CB 157a	S.T.	75.60–75.40	Dark gray flint blade, one edge retouched
K	CB 140a	F34	74.00	Maroon stone, one edge retouched
L	CB 171f	S.T.	73.60–73.40	Beige stone, one edge retouched
M	CB 114	F22/L24	74.25	Gray stone, one edge retouched
N	CB 119a	L27	74.15	Translucent gray stone, one edge retouched with shin
O	CB 107c	L21	74.25	Chocolate brown flint blade, one edge retouched, slight shin
P	CB 168b	S.T.	73.80–73.60	Beige stone, one edge retouched
Q	CB 180b	S.T.	73.20–73.00	Pale maroon stone, one edge retouched
R	CB 131b	F15	74.70	Dark gray stone, both edges retouched, slight shin on both edges
S	CB 118	L27	74.15	Dark gray stone, both edges retouched
T	CB 183b	S.T.	77.20	Dark brown stone, both edges retouched

CHIPPED STONE INDUSTRY

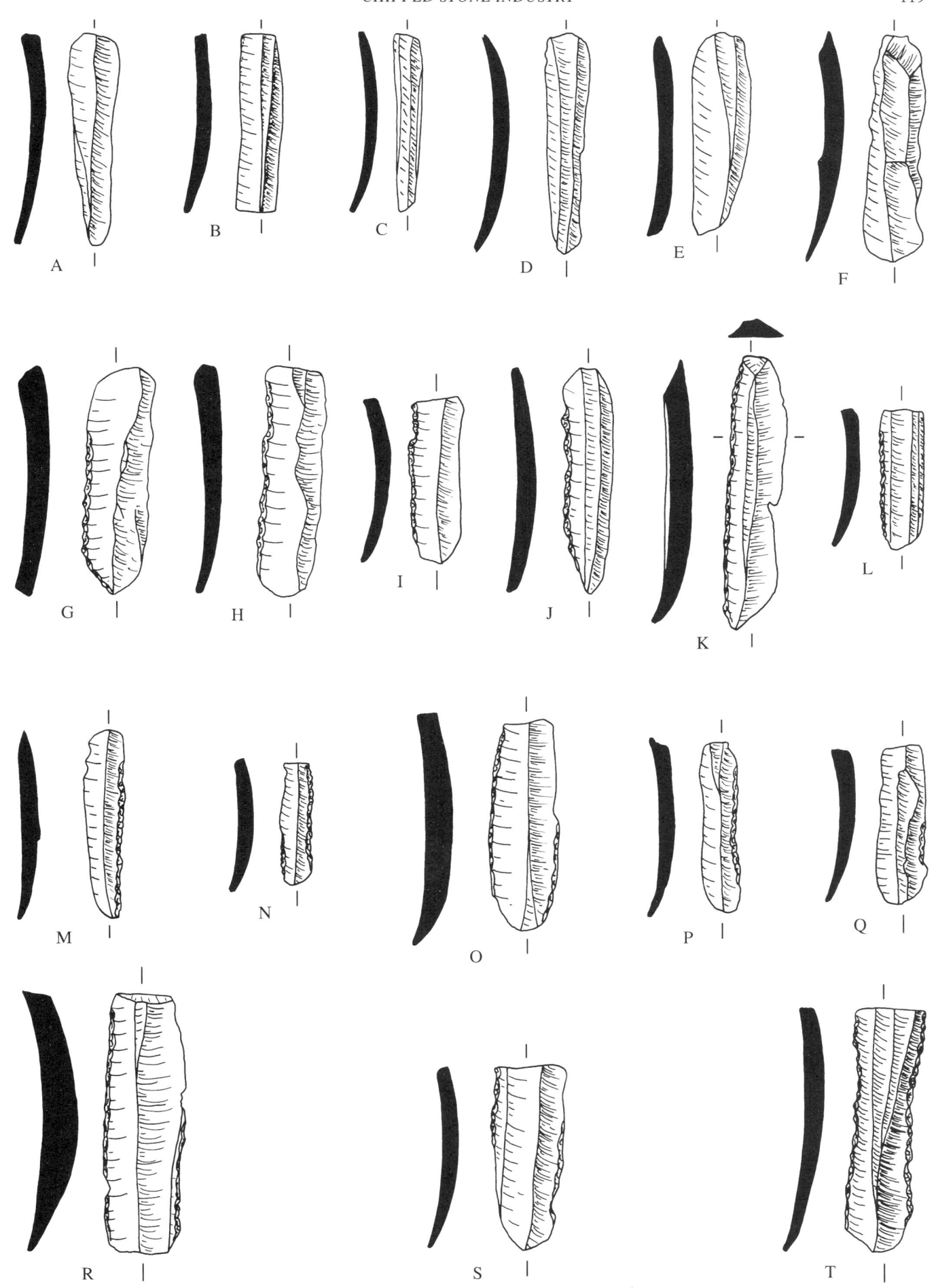

119

Figure 40. Various Types of Flint Blades with Curved Bulbar Surface. Scale 1:1

Figure 41. Bullet-shaped and Tongue-shaped Flint Blade Cores. Scale 1:1

	Field Number	Findspot	Elevation	Description
A	CB 127	F27/L33	74.05	Dark brown bullet-shaped flint core
B	CB 110	L21	74.20	Light gray bullet-shaped flint core
C	CB 173a	S.T.	73.40–73.20	Chocolate brown bullet-shaped flint core
D	CB 163b	S.T.	74.20–74.00	Chocolate brown bullet-shaped flint core
E	CB 100	F14	74.75	Chocolate brown bullet-shaped flint core
F	CB 132b	F15	74.70	Grayish brown bullet-shaped flint core
G	CB 136c	L30	74.10	Light beige bullet-shaped flint core
H	CB 160	S.T.	74.50–74.30	Chocolate brown bullet-shaped flint core
I	CB 111	L21	74.25	Dark gray/black bullet-shaped flint core
J	CB 89	L13	74.80	Dark beige bullet-shaped flint core
K	CB 144b	L35	74.00–73.80	Chocolate brown bullet-shaped flint core
L	CB 136b	L30	74.10	Chocolate brown bullet-shaped flint core
M	CB 179b	S.T.	73.20–73.00	Speckled gray bullet-shaped flint core
N	CB 147	L36	73.60–73.40	Dark brown bullet-shaped flint core
O	CB 163a	S.T.	74.20–74.00	Yellow mustard bullet-shaped flint core
P	CB 142b	F34	74.00	Grayish beige bullet-shaped flint core
Q	CB 76	L1	76.10–75.00	Chocolate brown bullet-shaped flint core
R	CB 109	L21	74.25	Dark brown bullet-shaped flint core
S	CB 98	F14	74.75	Chocolate brown bullet-shaped flint core
T	CB 132a	F15	74.70	Dark gray bullet-shaped flint core
U	CB 144a	L35	74.00–73.80	Grayish beige bullet-shaped flint core
V	CB 179a	S.T.	73.20–73.00	Grayish black bullet-shaped flint core
W	CB 170	S.T.	73.60–73.40	Chocolate brown tongue-shaped flint core
X	CB 151a	F31	74.05	Gray tongue-shaped flint core
Y	CB 169	S.T.	73.80–73.60	Chocolate brown tongue-shaped flint core
Z	CB 77	L1	76.10–75.00	Grayish cream tongue-shaped flint core
AA	CB 182	S.T.	77.20–77.00	Veined grayish purple tongue-shaped flint core
BB	CB 142a	F34	74.00	Chocolate brown tongue-shaped flint core

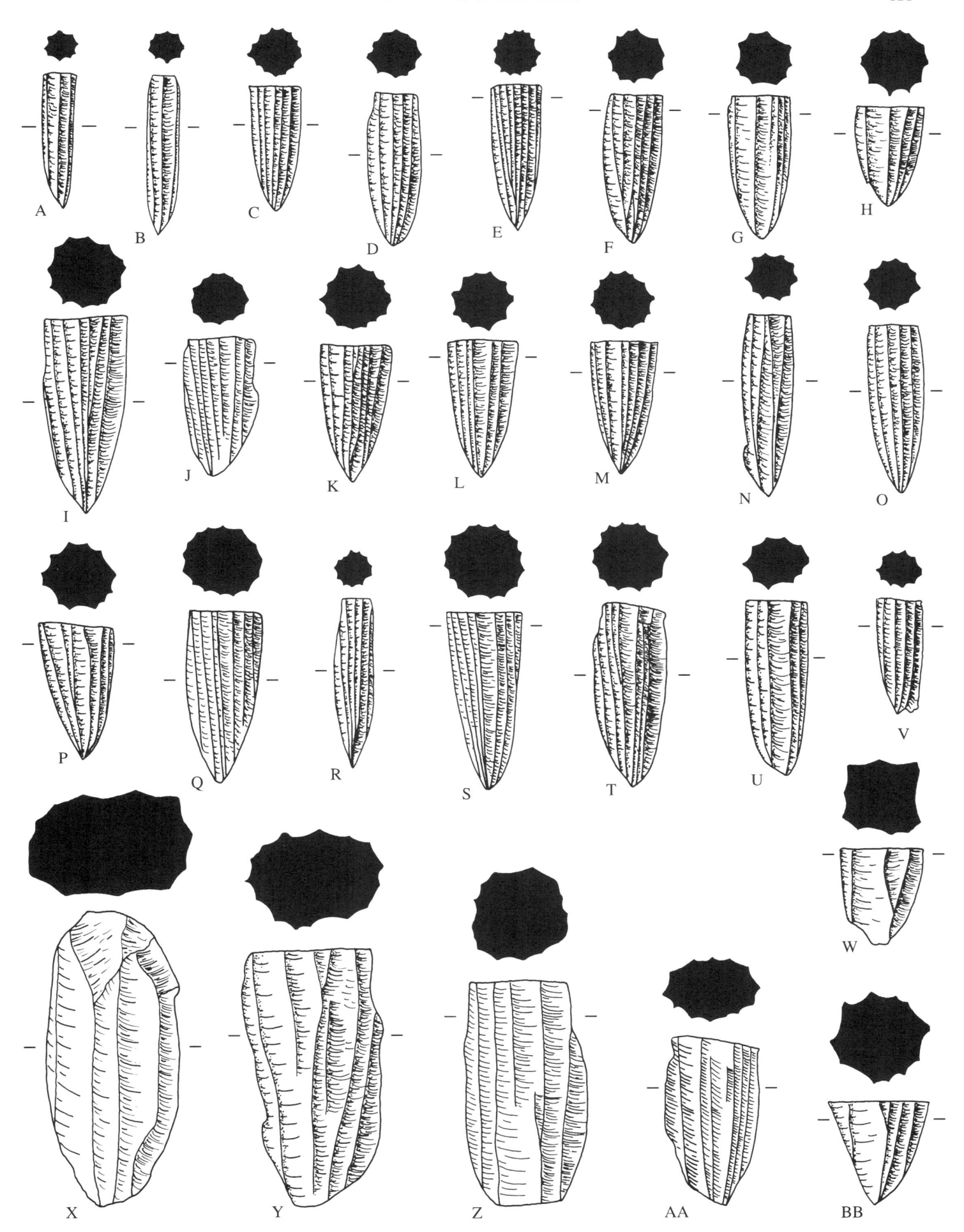

Figure 41. Bullet-shaped and Tongue-shaped Flint Blade Cores. Scale 1:1

CHAPTER 10
PLANT REMAINS FROM THE 1996 EXCAVATION
Naomi F. Miller

Twenty-four archaeobotanical samples from Chogha Bonut were submitted to the Museum Applied Science Center for Archaeology (MASCA) Ethnobotanical Laboratory (tables 5–6) for analysis. The samples came from Aceramic to Formative Susiana levels (8000–6000 B.C.), the earliest settlement in Susiana (Alizadeh 1997a, 1997b, and pers. comm.).

SAMPLING AND FLOTATION

Samples were taken when dry-sieving in the field suggested charred remains would be recovered in at least moderate quantities. The contents of fire pits were floated in their entirety. Up to one-fifth of large features and layers were also taken, but soil volume was not recorded. Charred material was retrieved through manual flotation. Soil was poured into 1 mm mesh and immersed in the water; then it was gently stirred. Floating material was collected with a metal spoon. The soil remaining in the mesh (heavy fraction) was spread on newspaper to dry. Anything visible with a magnifying glass that was burnt or looked like a seed was added to the sample (Alizadeh 1997b).

CHARACTER OF THE ASSEMBLAGE

During laboratory analysis in Philadelphia, it became clear that the samples lacked both small and large particles. The only charred items that passed through a 1 mm mesh were a few broken fragments. Despite careful retrieval attempts, it is possible that the most minute particles, including seeds, were not seen, and therefore missed, during flotation; if excavation and sampling continue, it should be possible to check this. There were no items larger than 4.75 mm, either. As these are hard to miss with any flotation method, it is safe to conclude that none were preserved in the samples examined.

Wood charcoal fragments of any size were scarce. Ordinarily, this suggests wood was unavailable as fuel. Tappeh Ali Kosh, for example, had no wood charcoal (Helbaek 1969). Unlike Chogha Bonut, however, it did have thousands of small seeds, probably from the main alternative fuel of southwestern Iran, animal dung (Miller 1996). The absence of such tiny seeds at Chogha Bonut could mean animals ate no small-seeded plants, but it could just mean that the flotation method discriminated against small items.

Most of the deposits had very low densities of material. This is particularly the case for the large "occupational debris" samples from Layer 30 and Feature 34 (fig. 15). Even the smaller fire pit samples had little material, with the exception of Feature 26/Layer 32, which may represent *in situ* burning. It is unfortunately fairly common that hearths and fire pits have few remains because they were probably swept and cleaned periodically in antiquity. Building collapse, too, tends to have low density of remains because any charred trash remains are diluted by the melted mudbricks. Finally, a number of the deposits were relatively close to the modern surface, where periodic wetting and drying could help destroy the delicate charred remains.

TAXA

The range of types of taxa recovered is relatively small (table 7). Most of the material comes from cereals, primarily barley (*Hordeum vulgare*) and emmer wheat (*Triticum dicoccum*), but also einkorn (*T. monococcum*) and bread/hard wheat (*T. aestivum/durum*). Lentil (*Lens*) seems to be part of the crop assemblage as well. In addition to the cultivated plants, seeds of several wild and weedy taxa were seen, notably leguminous types, grasses, and a few others.

Table 5. Inventory of Flotation Samples from 1996 Excavation

Sample no.	Provenance	Description	Period
CB 1	L3	Occupational debris	Aceramic
CB 2	L13	Occupational debris	Aceramic
CB 3	F14	Living surface	Aceramic
CB 4	L21	Occupational debris	Aceramic
CB 5	L30	Occupational debris	Aceramic
CB 6	F34	Living surface	Aceramic
CB 7	F1/L4	Fire pit	Aceramic
CB 8	F4/L7	Fire pit	Aceramic
CB 9	F5/L8	Fire pit	Aceramic
CB 10	F7	Living surface	Aceramic
CB 11	F19/L22	Fire pit	Aceramic
CB 12	F20/L23	Fire pit	Aceramic
CB 13	F22/L24	Fire pit	Aceramic
CB 14	F24/L25	Fire pit	Aceramic
CB 15	F26/L32	Fire pit	Aceramic
CB 16	L35 (D.T.)	Ashy/organic layer	Aceramic
CB 17	L37 (D.T.)	Ashy/organic layer	Aceramic
CB 18	S.T. el. 75.70	Fire pit	Formative
CB 19	S.T. el. 75.70–75.60	Occupational debris	Formative
CB 20	S.T. el. 75.60	Occupational debris	Formative
CB 21	S.T. el. 73.30	Black ash deposit	Aceramic
CB 22	Square M10	NA	Aceramic
CB 23	Square M10	NA	Aceramic
CB 24	Square M10	NA	Aceramic

CEREALS

Most of the cereals occur as fragments. For that reason, weights rather than counts are recorded. Due to the low number of whole grains, it is not possible to calculate a reasonable weight per grain. Nevertheless, to get an idea of relative numbers, a typical charred grain weighs about 0.01 gm or a bit less. No cereal rachis fragments were seen.

Barley

Barley is one of the two most important identified types, occurring in fifteen samples with total weight of just over 0.40 gm. A few of the grains appear to be twisted. Although sometimes grains of the two-row type (*Hordeum vulgare* var. *distichum*) get distorted by charring, twistedness may also be an indication that six-row barley (*H. vulgare* var. *hexastichum*) is present (see Helbaek 1969, p. 392). Ethnographic analogy suggests that in the areas where both wheat and barley grow, barley is grown primarily as a fodder plant. First, barley straw is more nutritious than wheat straw. Second, it tends to be more drought-tolerant than wheat, although six-row barley needs more water and is more likely to be irrigated than the two-row type. And third, because the glume (husk) is fused to the grain by a layer of cells, milling is more difficult. When barley is consumed by humans, it is frequently sprouted and made into beer.

Wheat

In contrast to barley, wheat tends to be preferred by humans for food. It is easier to process than barley, though some wheats (emmer, einkorn) are not free-threshing. Nevertheless, compared to barley, people tend to be more willing to risk losing some of the crop to drought or to expend the effort to irrigate it.

Emmer wheat (*Triticum dicoccum*) is the second important type in the Chogha Bonut assemblage, occurring in fifteen samples with a total weight of about 0.42 gm. Some of the emmer grains here are relatively long, and others are not; few are whole and measurable. Emmer is perhaps the first domesticate, but it originated in the Levantine Corridor (van Zeist 1986). It did not take long for it to travel along the Taurus-Zagros arc toward Tappeh Ali Kosh, where wheat was present from the beginning and the most prominent cereal in the Mohammad Jaffar phase (Helbaek 1969). The presence of wheat at Chogha Bonut in the Aceramic Susiana period shows that it had made its way from the Levant even earlier than previously documented.

Table 6. Miscellaneous Non-botanical Items

Sample no.	Provenance	Description	Item(s)
CB 2	L13	Occupational debris	Charred dung, > 2 mm: present
CB 3	F14	Living surface	Two red chert chips
CB 6	F34	Living surface	Charred dung, > 2 mm: 0.35 gm
CB 9	F5/L8	Fire pit	Chert chip
CB 11	F19/L22	Fire pit	Fish vertebra
CB 22	Square M10	NA	Red micro-blade
CB 23	Square M10	NA	Indeterminate charred material

Einkorn

Einkorn (*Triticum monococcum*) is a minor component of the assemblage, and as might be the case for Tappeh Ali Kosh (cf. Helbaek 1969, p. 403), it may not have been a crop in its own right, but a weedy contaminant.

There are a few grains that have tentatively been identified as hard wheat (*Triticum durum*). Unlike the grains designated as emmer, these grains are blunt at the distal end and widest at the base. They also tend to be shorter and plumper than the emmer grains. Although the grains of hard wheat and bread wheat (*Triticum aestivum*) are not distinguishable on morphological grounds alone, bread wheat probably did not evolve until ca. 6000 B.C. (Zohary and Hopf 1993), so the grains here are probably a tetraploid hard wheat.

PULSES AND OTHER LEGUMES

Pulses are members of the pea or legume family (Fabaceae) cultivated for their large, edible seeds. It is not clear that the Chogha Bonut legumes were cultivated because they are so small. A few seeds are probably lentil (*Lens*), but they could be wild, with diameters of 1.8, 2.0, and 2.4 mm. Tappeh Ali Kosh also had a few lentils.

More numerous is a heterogeneous type that I have designated "*Pisum/Vicia/Lathyrus*" (pea/vetch/grasspea). The seeds are fairly round and average 2.1 mm in diameter (n = 166, range 1.5–3.0 mm; fig. 42). These are small compared to the peas at Çayönü (average > 4.0 mm; van Zeist and de Roller 1991/1992), and it is likely that they are from wild plants. That they were intentionally collected, however, is likely because they predominate in F26/L32 (table 5, CB 15).

Prosopis ("shauk" in Arabic) is a non-pulse legume. Mostly it occurs in fragmentary form, so weight is recorded in table 7. F24/L25 (table 5, CB 14) had two whole seeds which weighed 0.03 gm + fragments. It would have been

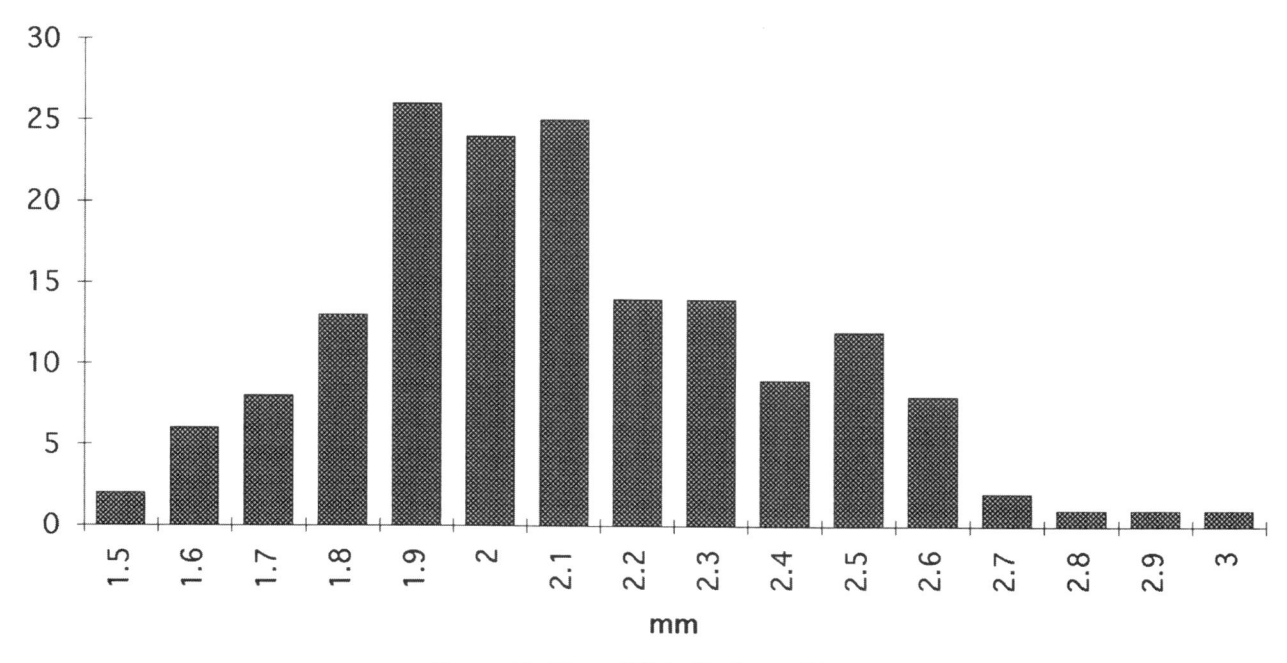

Figure 42. *Pisum/Vicia/Lathyrus* Diameter

Table 7. Plant Remains from Chogha Bonut

PROVENANCE	L3	L13	L21	L30	L34	F1/L4	F4/L27	F5/L8	F7	F14	F19/L22	F20/L23
CB	1	2	4	5	6	7	8	9	10	3	11	12
Soil Volume (liters)	NA	NA	NA	NA	NA	4.6	1	5.2	58	NA	13	11
Seed (gm, >2mm)	0.13	0.28	—	+	0.13	0.02	—	—	0.03	0.78	0.06	0.02
Charcoal (gm, >2mm)	—	+	—	—	—	—	—	—	—	—	+	+
CEREAL												
Hordeum (gm)	0.03	0.06	—	+	0.05	—	—	—	—	0.15	0.01	—
Triticum dicoccum (gm)	0.02	0.03	+	—	0.02	—	—	—	0.01	0.18	0.02	0.01
T. monococcum (gm)	+	—	—	—	0.01	—	—	—	—	—	+	—
T. durum (gm)	0.03	0.04	—	—	—	—	—	—	—	0.01	—	—
Triticum sp. (gm)	0.02	0.06	—	—	—	+	+	+	0.02	0.25	0.05	—
Cereal (gm)	0.06	0.18	+	+	—	0.02	—	—	+	0.45	0.01	0.02
FABACEAE												
Cf. *Lens*	—	—	—	—	—	—	—	—	—	—	—	—
Pisum/Vicia/Lathyrus	—	—	—	—	—	—	1	—	—	1	—	—
Prosopis (gm)	—	—	—	—	0.09	—	—	—	—	—	—	—
Pulse, indet.	—	+	—	—	—	—	—	—	+	—	—	—
WILD AND WEEDY												
Cf. *Liliaceae*	—	—	—	—	—	—	—	—	—	—	—	—
Aegilops	—	—	—	—	—	—	—	—	—	—	—	—
Cf. *Avena*	—	—	—	—	—	—	—	—	—	—	—	—
Cf. *Lolium*	—	—	—	—	—	—	—	—	—	—	—	—
Poaceae	1	2	—	—	—	—	—	—	—	—	1	—
Unknown	—	—	—	—	—	—	—	—	—	—	—	—

PROVENANCE	F22/L24	F24/L25	F26/L32	L35	L37	S.T.	S.T.	S.T.	S.T.	M:10	M:10	M:10
CB	13	14	15	16	17	18	19	20	21	22	23	24
Soil Volume (liters)	12	19	4.6	30	30	60	60	60	60	NA	NA	NA
Seed (gm, <2 mm)	0.02	0.18	0.56	0.07	0.02	+	0.02	0.02	0.08	0.07	0.06	0.03
Charcoal (gm, >2 mm)	—	—	+	—	—	—	—	—	0.01	—	—	—
CEREAL												
Hordeum (gm)	—	0.01	0.01	0.02	—	—	0.01	+	0.02	0.01	0.02	+
Triticum dicoccum (gm)	0.01	—	—	0.02	—	—	—	0.02	0.03	0.01	0.02	0.02
T. monococcum (gm)	—	+	—	—	—	—	—	—	—	—	—	—
T. durum (gm)	—	—	—	—	—	+	—	—	—	—	—	—
Triticum sp. (gm)	—	0.02	—	0.02	0.02	—	+	—	0.04	0.03	—	—
Cereal (gm)	0.03	0.04	0.02	0.04	0.01	0.01	+	0.02	0.06	—	0.04	0.01
FABACEAE												
Cf. *Lens*	—	—	2	—	—	—	—	—	—	1	—	—
Pisum/Vicia/Lathyrus	—	33	177	—	—	—	—	—	—	3	—	4
Prosopis (gm)	—	0.04	+	—	—	—	—	—	0.01	—	0.02	—
Pulse, indet.	—	—	—	—	—	—	—	—	—	—	—	—
WILD AND WEEDY												
Cf. *Liliaceae*	—	—	—	—	—	—	—	—	—	—	—	1
Aegilops	—	—	—	1	—	—	—	—	—	—	—	—
Cf. *Avena*	—	—	—	—	—	—	—	—	—	—	—	1
Cf. *Lolium*	—	—	—	—	—	—	—	—	—	—	1	—
Poaceae	—	—	—	—	1	—	—	—	1	—	—	—
Unknown	—	—	2	—	—	—	—	—	—	—	—	—

NA = Information not available

part of the natural vegetation in Susiana. Present in small numbers from the beginning of the sequence at Tappeh Ali Kosh, Helbaek (1969) suggested *Prosopis* expanded with agricultural disturbance.

WILD AND WEEDY PLANTS

A few wild grasses (*Poaceae*) were seen: *Aegilops* (goat-face grass), cf. *Avena* (wild oat), *Lolium* (ryegrass), and indeterminate grasses. Two seeds, possibly of the lily family (*Liliaceae*), resemble *Ornithogalum* (van Zeist and Bakker-Heeres 1982, fig. 24:9), and there are a couple of unknown types.

INTERPRETATION

Chogha Bonut lies in an area that today is without trees, but that would naturally have steppe or savanna vegetation (cf. Zohary 1973). The site seems to be at about the 250 mm precipitation isohyet (British Naval Intelligence 1944, fig. 46), the borderline for successful rainfall agriculture in the Near East (i.e., for wheat and barley cultivation). As Hole (1987, p. 91) points out, "In wet years, grains can be grown without irrigation on nearly every part of the [Susiana] plain, but with even simple irrigation, agriculture success is greatly enhanced." Precipitation increases from southwest to northeast, and Chogha Bonut is at the northeastern edge of Susiana, which may explain why the early settlers established the village there.

Several aspects of the plant remains are consistent with this picture. First, the near absence of wood charcoal strongly suggests that wood did not grow nearby; recovery methods were quite adequate for the retrieval of wood charcoal. A similar situation occurred at Tappeh Ali Kosh, where Helbaek (1969, p. 387) reports "no carbonized wood … and bits and pieces of reed seem to indicate that the fuel was reed and stems of other herbaceous plants of the marshy environ." For a variety of reasons explained elsewhere, I think the fuel included animal (i.e., sheep or goat) dung at Tappeh Ali Kosh (Miller 1996), but the source of Chogha Bonut's fuel is not yet established.

If the assemblage recovered accurately reflects the range of charred material deposited in antiquity, we can consider several explanations:

a. The seeds are remnants of dung fuel, and animals were fed barley, wheat, and large-seeded legumes. This does not seem likely because even in areas where animals are thought to have been foddered with cultigens, one usually encounters a wider range of types.

b. The seeds are remains of crop-processing debris (see Hillman 1984), thrown into a fire as trash. This is plausible, but why, then, are there no fuel or rachis remains?

c. The seeds are remnants of accidentally burned food stores, dispersed in settlement trash. If this were the case, there should be more trash in general, and other charred remains mixed in, as, for example, at Çayönü (van Zeist and de Roller 1991/1992).

If the charred seed assemblage originated in dung fuel, we could begin to identify certain agricultural practices. For example, if cultivated fodder was provided to the herds, we would expect to see relatively high proportions of barley relative to wheat (Miller 1997). If animals were sent out to graze on the steppe, as seems likely at Tappeh Ali Kosh (Miller 1996), high proportions of wild and weedy seeds relative to cereals would be expected. If, as may be the case, we are missing the small seeds, we cannot test these ideas.

POTENTIAL FOR FURTHER RESEARCH

Despite the disappointing recovery rate achieved to date, it would be well worth maintaining the sampling program if excavation continues. To maximize the quantity of plant remains for effort expended, hearth and pits should all be sampled (ca. 10–20 liters) as should ash deposits and other places where charred material is seen. Other occupational layers should be sampled as well, and 10 liter samples should be sufficient to determine if there are plant remains.

Some of the questions we can reasonably hope to answer with plant remains include:

1. What does the charred assemblage (seeds and wood) tell us about food, fodder, and the agro-pastoral economy?
2. Does the assemblage change through time? The remains are still too scanty to tell, but with sufficient material we can consider evidence for changes in land use practices through:
    a. Proportions of crop plants
    b. Introduction of new types
    c. Introduction or spread of wild plants
    d. Fuel types (possibly reflecting deforestation)

CHAPTER 11

PRELIMINARY PHYTOLITH ANALYSES

Arlene Miller Rosen

Two sediment samples from Chogha Bonut were analyzed for preliminary indications of the preservation and amount of phytoliths at the site. The results showed that phytoliths are abundant, with both single-cell and multi-cell forms represented.

The two samples from Chogha Bonut come from different archaeological contexts and levels (fig. 43). Sample CB-97-1 was collected from the base of the Deep Trench in Square M10. It is described as a broadly distributed 30 cm thick black organic sediment. Sample CB-97-2 is from Layer 30, an occupation surface, possibly a courtyard in Square M10.

METHODS

A sub-sample consisting of up to 5 gm of sediment was sieved through a 0.25 mm mesh and treated with 1 N HC1 to remove pedogenic carbonates. The samples were then washed and clays dispersed by soaking them for twenty-four hours in distilled water and treating them with a saturated solution of sodium pyrophosphate. Clays were then pipetted off after settling fine sand and silt for one hour in an 8 cm high column of water. Organic matter was removed by burning in a muffle furnace at 500° C for two hours. The remaining sediment was floated in a heavy density liquid, sodium polytungstate adjusted to a density of 2.3 specific gravity, in order to separate the opaline silica bodies from the quartz and heavy minerals. The suspense was pipetted off, washed, dried, and mounted in entellen. About 500 phytoliths were counted at 400×, using a polarizing microscope.

RESULTS

The phytoliths occur in two general categories. One of these is the single-cell phytolith that forms when a single plant epidermis cell is encased in silica while still in the living plant. These forms consist of the more traditionally described phytolith shapes such as the saddles, cones, bilobes (also known as dumbells), and rondels which are indicative of monocotyledon families and sub-families. As such they are also indicative of general environmental conditions around the site. Plant parts such as stems versus seed husks can also be distinguished from these forms by the epidermal long cells that tend to be smooth-sided in stems and highly wavy or dendritic in the floral parts and seed husks. This distinction provides a tool for the estimation of seasonality, with floral and husk forms dominant in the spring. Large numbers of husk phytoliths in agricultural sites are also indicative of high intensity seed processing and use.

Monocot phytoliths also occur as multi-cell forms or silica skeletons. These consist of suites of adjacent cells sometimes numbering in the hundreds. Recent experiments have shown that in semi-arid environments, the number of cells per silica skeleton increases in phytoliths from irrigated cereals or those cultivated in naturally moist alluvial soils. Dry-farming cereals produce silica skeletons with smaller numbers of silicified cells (Rosen and Weiner 1994). This technique can be used at agricultural sites to assess farming technology.

Phytoliths from dicotyledons (woody plants and shrubs) are usually less diagnostic, allowing us to determine only that the form came from either the wood and bark of a woody plant or on the other hand the leaf of such a plant.

SINGLE-CELL PHYTOLITHS

Within the category of single-cell phytoliths (table 8), the *bilobe* and *cross* forms are generally found in the panicoid grass sub-family. This sub-family of grasses contains genera that favor warm-damp environmental conditions, but also reed grasses such as *Arundo* sp. and *Phragmites* sp. that grow within slow-moving perennial streams, canals, and in areas with high water tables. The sub-family of pooid grasses produces the *rondel* phytolith form. These genera are usually found in cooler regions with rainfall over about 300 mm per annum. Wheat and barley are also included within this group. Other significant phytolith forms include the *saddles* that can occur in chloridoid grasses but

Table 8. Phytolith Counts and Percentages

Sample	CB-97-1 No.	%	CB-97-2 No.	%
SINGLE–CELLS				
Long (Leaf/Stem)	96	27.7	95	26.9
Long (Floral)	135	38.9	119	33.7
Papillae	7	2.0	2	0.6
Hairs	5	1.4	2	0.6
Bulliform	23	6.6	36	10.2
Keystone	4	1.2	10	2.8
Crenates	1	0.3	1	0.3
Bilobes	22	6.3	39	11
Crosses	0	0.0	2	0.6
Rondels	23	6.6	20	5.7
Saddles	14	4.0	14	4.0
Cones	8	2.3	8	2.3
Starch	1	0.3	0	0.0
Tracheids	0	0.0	3	0.8
Single Polyhedron	6	1.7	1	0.3
Jigsaw Puzzle	0	0.0	1	0.3
Block	2	0.6	0	0.0
TOTAL	347		353	
MULTIPLE CELLS				
Leaf/Stem	36	21.7	59	41.8
Unidentifiable Husk	18	10.8	5	3.5
Wheat Husk	41	24.7	9	6.4
Barley Husk	30	18.1	0	0.0
Setaria Husk	0	0.0	0	0.0
Stipa Husk	1	0.6	0	0.0
Aegilops	1	0.6	1	0.7
Wild Grass Husk	3	1.8	3	2.1
Cyperus Type	2	1.2	1	0.7
Phragmites Leaf	8	4.8	17	12.1
Phragmites Stem	5	3.0	37	26.2
Juncus(?)	3	1.8	0	0.0
Cereal Straw	1	0.6	1	0.7
Awn	8	4.8	0	0.0
Panicoid Leaf/Steam	7	4.2	6	4.3
Polyhedrons	2	1.2	2	1.4
TOTAL	166		141	

are also produced in great number by *Phragmites* sp. The cone-shaped phytolith form is commonly produced in sedges and is also usually indicative of marshes, irrigation canals, and other moist micro-environments.

Figure 45 displays the percentages of phytoliths according to grass and sedge sub-families. The pooids, sedges, and saddles are equally represented in both samples. The pooid-type phytoliths are probably derived from cereals and crop weed grasses. One difference between the two samples, however, is the number of panicoid-type phytoliths, with a much larger percentage in CB-97-2. This high percentage is probably a function of intensive use of reed grasses such as *Arundo* and *Phragmites* within this particular archaeological context.

Another notable point evident from these two samples is the occurrence of very high percentages of phytoliths from the long-cells of husks. In both archaeological contexts they far outnumber the phytoliths from stems and leaves.

Although cereal husks are locations of high phytolith yields, in most Near Eastern archaeological sites phytoliths from the stems and leaves of a variety of grasses usually outnumber the phytoliths from husks. At Chogha Bonut the very high percentages of husk phytoliths suggest intensive production and consumption of grains in these locations.

MULTI-CELL PHYTOLITHS

Unlike single-cell phytoliths, multi-cell forms are more readily identifiable to genus because of their suites of different cell types (table 8). Therefore, it is possible to distinguish between the husks of wheat, barley, and a variety of weed grasses as well as some reeds, sedges, and palms. As the number of reference samples expands, the quantity of identifiable silica skeletons will also increase. In the Chogha Bonut samples multi-cell forms are abundant. The percentages of select multi-celled forms are displayed in figure 46.

The most notable characteristic of sample CB-97-1 is the high percentage of wheat (*Triticum* sp.) and barley (*Hordeum* sp.) phytoliths with a dominance of wheat (fig. 44). Sample CB-97-2 contains no barley and only a small number of wheat-husk phytoliths. In contrast to sample CB-97-1, sample CB-97-2 is dominated by the stems and leaves of common reed (*Phragmites* sp.) and a very high percentage of leaves and stems from unidentifiable grasses (fig. 43).

In wheat husk phytoliths, the number of cells per silica skeleton was analyzed to determine if the wheat was cultivated in moist alluvium or possibly with the assistance of some form of irrigation. Figure 47 shows the percentages of silica skeletons ranging in size from two cells to over ten adjacent silicified cells. Over twenty percent of the wheat husk silica skeletons from Chogha Bonut have greater than ten cells per phytolith. This distribution is similar to phytoliths produced in wheat cultivated by irrigation or floodwater farming in the northern Negev Desert. It is possible, then, that the wheat at Chogha Bonut was cultivated in soils that were naturally moist from floodwater, or that the inhabitants of the site were actively engaged in some form of water manipulation.

DISCUSSION

The two samples from Chogha Bonut have distinctly different phytolith profiles. The main contrasts include the dominance of common reeds (*Phragmites* sp.) in CB-97-2 versus the prevalence of wheat and barley husks in CB-97-1. Phragmites is both an indicator of ethno-botanical uses of the plant and suggestive of micro-environments in the site vicinity. The large reeds are commonly used to build brush fences for animal pens and courtyards, which is consistent with the archaeological interpretation of Square M10, Layer 30 as a possible courtyard area. The young shoots and leaves are also used as fodder for cattle and other herd animals. If cattle dung was employed as fuel, then large numbers of Phragmites phytoliths could end up on living surfaces in the vicinity of hearths.

Large numbers of reed phytoliths also suggest that there were locations of high water tables, or slow-moving streams near the settlement. This moist environment would have been a productive locale for cereal cultivation as well. The large numbers of silica skeletons from wheat and barley, and copious numbers of cells per individual silica skeleton suggest that the inhabitants of the site utilized these moist areas for cultivation of cereals. The abundance of cereal husk phytoliths from the deep trench (CB-97-1) implies that this archaeological layer could be a midden deposit or perhaps threshing floor.

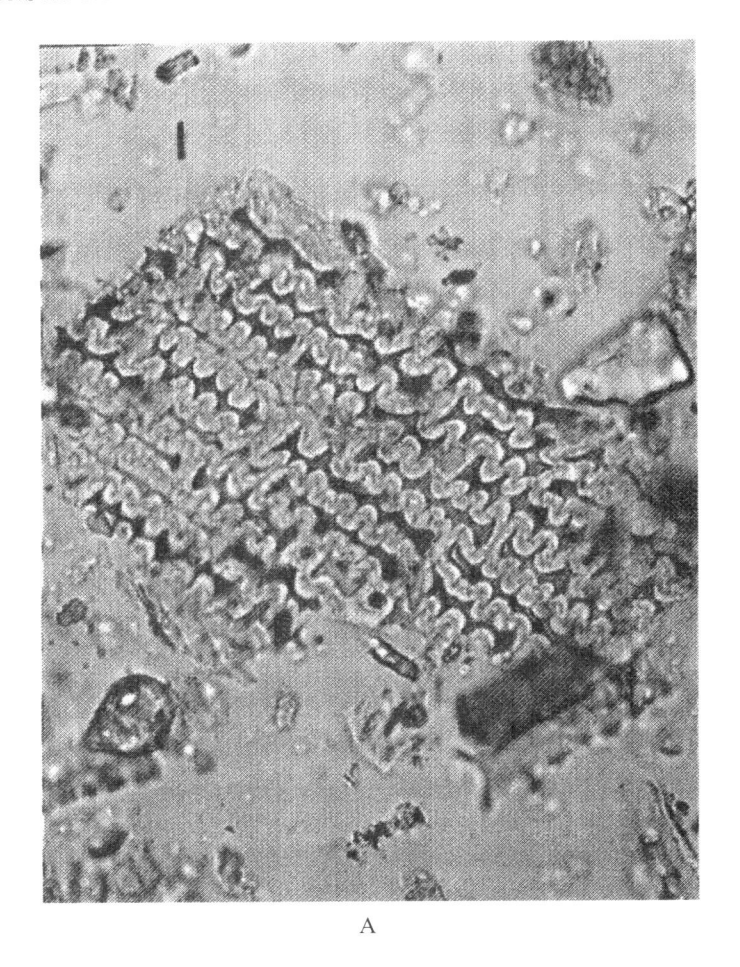

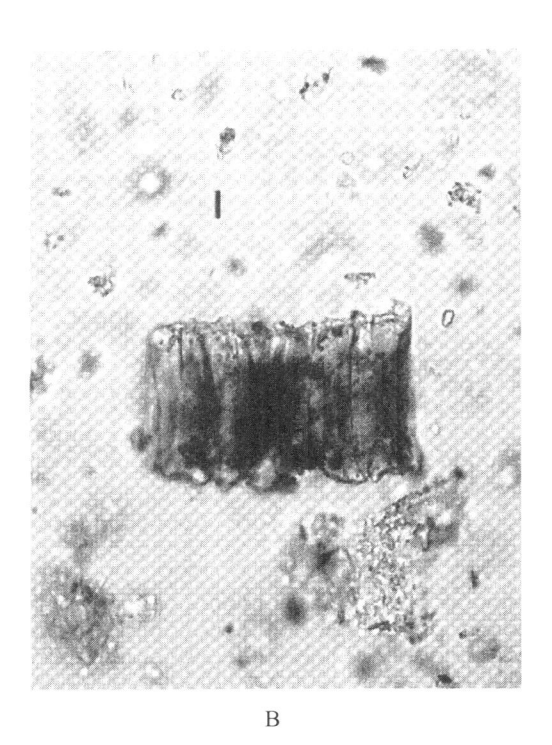

Figure 43. (A) CB-97-2 Phytolith of *Phragmites* sp. Stem and
(B) CB-97-1 Phytolith from *Phragmites* sp. Leaf

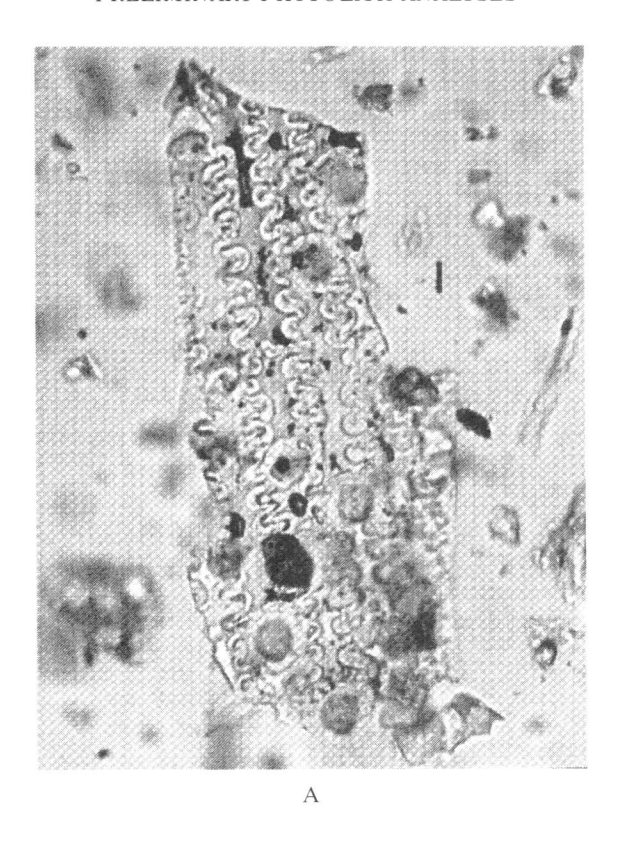

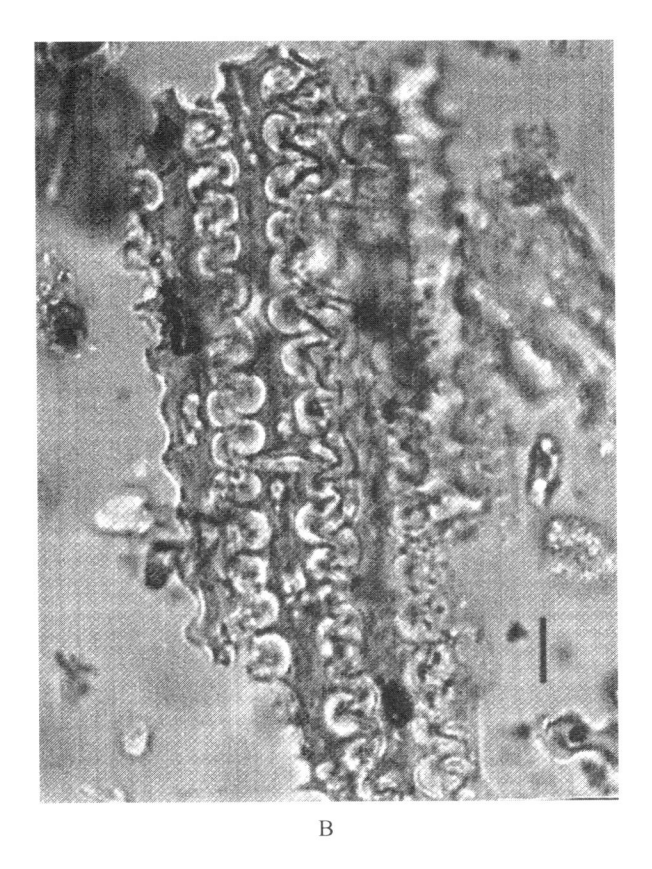

Figure 44. (A) CB-97-1 Wheat Husk Phytolith and (B) CB-97-1 Barley Phytolith

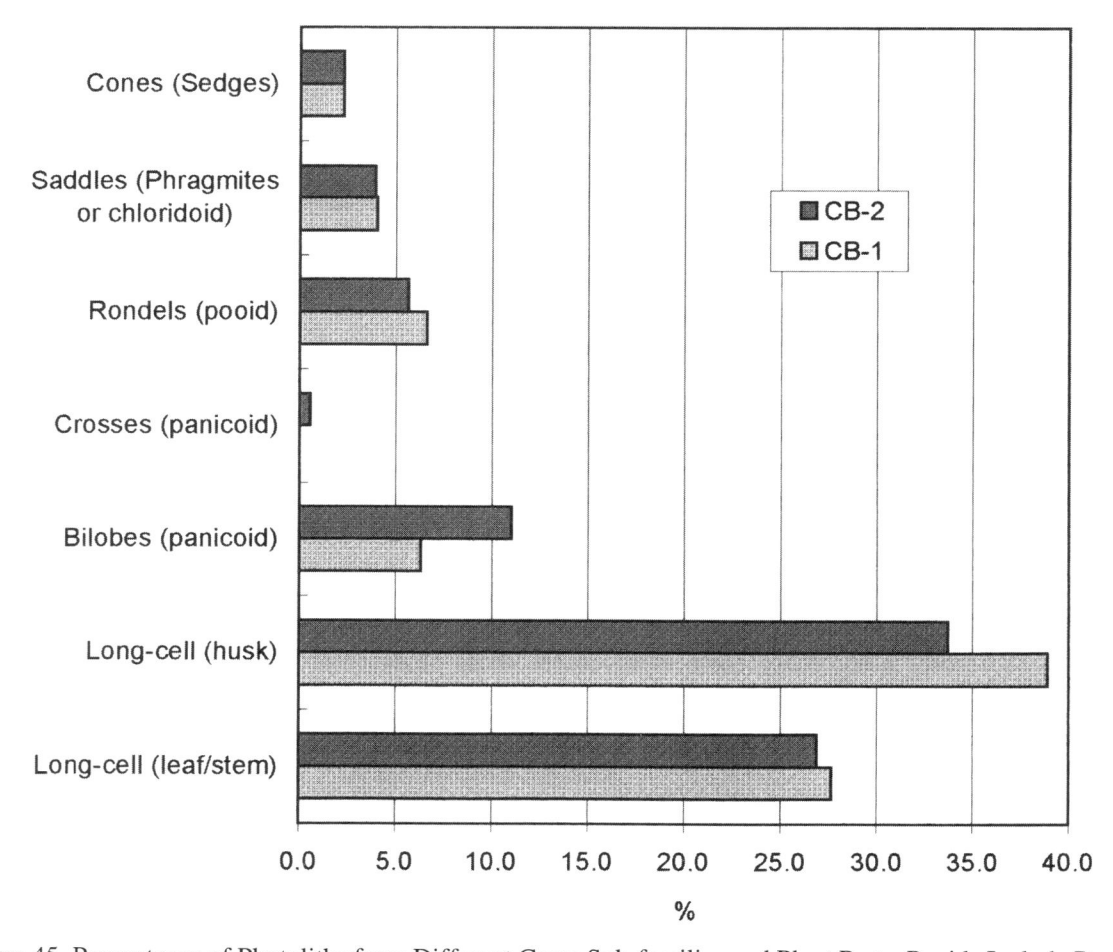

Figure 45. Percentages of Phytoliths from Different Grass Sub-families and Plant Parts. Pooids Include Rondels and Panicoids Include Crosses and Bilobes. Cones Are Associated with Cyperaeceae (sedges) and Saddles Are Found in Both Chlorides and Phragmites Reed Grasses

Chogha Bonut, 1997

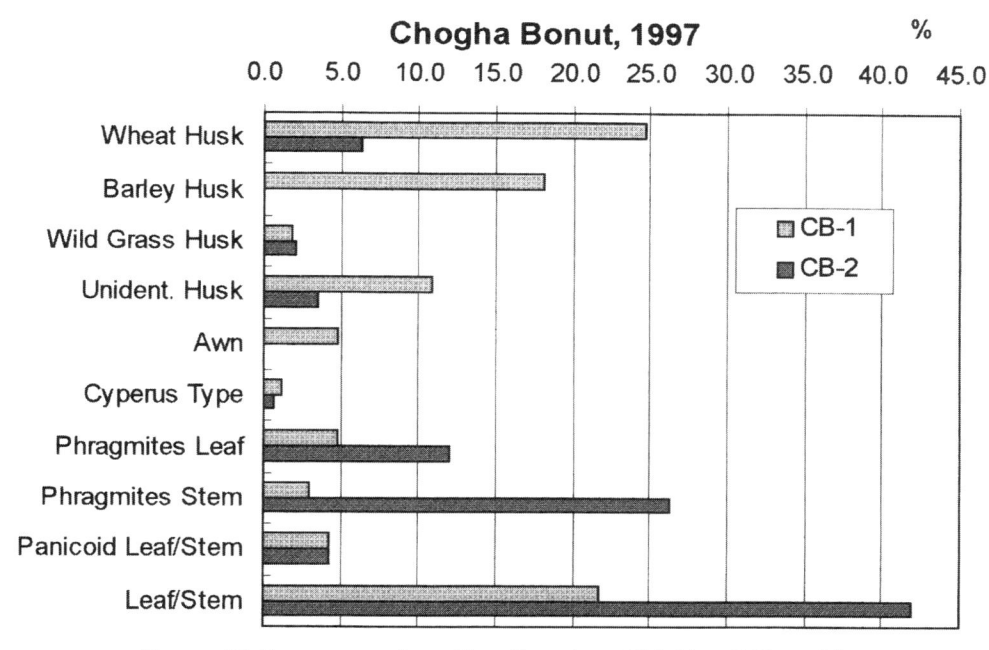

Figure 46. Percentages from Two Samples of Multi-cell Phytoliths

Chogha Bonut, 1997
CB-97-1; Wheat

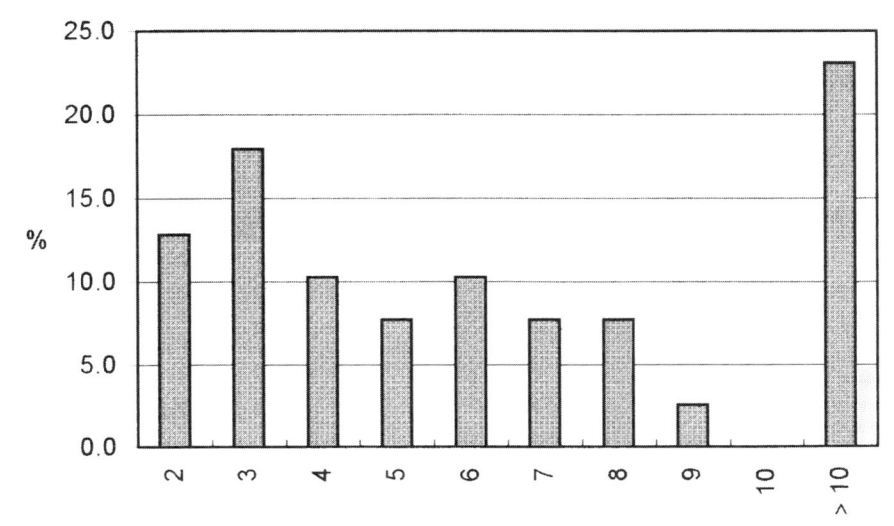

Figure 47. Percentage of Cells Per Silica from Wheat Husk Phytoliths

CHAPTER 12

FIRST REPORT ON FAUNAL REMAINS

Richard W. Redding

Although several excavations of aceramic Neolithic sites have been undertaken on the Susiana plain in southwestern Iran, no faunal studies have been published. The nearest published aceramic fauna is from Tappeh Ali Kosh on the Deh Luran plain. Hence, the sample of faunal remains from Chogha Bonut is an important resource representing a critical period in the evolution of human subsistence behavior in southwestern Iran. It represents the end of the transition from hunting and gathering to food production and the early development of village life. For these reasons I would like to thank Dr. Abbas Alizadeh for the opportunity to examine the fauna and the Iranian Cultural Heritage Organization for allowing the material to be loaned.

QUANTIFYING THE DATA: MEASURING ABUNDANCE

NISP (number of identified specimens) is used to establish species ratios that I assume to be a measure of abundance between two taxa. The use of NISPs as measures of abundance, particularly absolute abundance, has a number of problems and requires a number of assumptions. I am not trying to present a formal defense of this approach here; however, for individuals not familiar with the state of archaeozoology, I offer a few comments justifying its use.

Important analyses of methods for quantifying species abundance include Grayson (1984), Chase and Hagaman (1986), and Ringrose (1993). All of these authors have criticized the use of NISPs to estimate relative abundance. Grayson (1984, pp. 94–96) argues that MNIs (minimum number of individuals) or NISPs cannot provide a valid estimate of taxonomic abundance. I certainly agree with Grayson's arguments concerning the problem of aggregation with MNIs and would not use this measure to provide an estimate of relative abundance. However, as Grayson (ibid., p. 96) notes, this is not a problem with NISPs. Grayson argues that NISPs cannot provide a robust measure of abundance because they represent the maximum number of individuals and we do not know how an estimate of maximum number of individuals relates to actual abundance. Chase and Hagaman (1986, p. 82) present a mathematically based analysis of a number of estimates of abundance. They argue that NISPs are biased by differences between taxa in recovery rate of elements, number of skeletal parts, and degree of fragmentation. Ringrose finds fault with the use of NISP as an indicator of taxonomic abundance for three reasons. First, as with Chase and Hagaman, Ringrose notes that some taxa have more bones than others and, hence, they are overrepresented. Second, some animals reach the site whole and others do not, and those reaching the site whole are overrepresented. Third, Ringrose notes that using NISP as an estimate of abundance overlooks that 125 fragments are counted the same whether they are from one or 125 animals.

The first point I would like to make is that all of these individuals work with faunas from sites occupied by hunter-gatherers. Of 132 references cited by Ringrose, only four are the work of individuals working with the remains of food producers. Faunal assemblages derived from sites occupied by food producers are qualitatively different from sites occupied by hunter-gatherers. At sites that were inhabited by food producers the faunal samples are much larger and result from more intensive deposition. For example, 500 identifiable bone fragments from a hunter-gatherer site might have been deposited over hundreds if not thousands of years; while 500 identifiable fragments at a site occupied by food producers may represent one week's garbage. At the site of Sharafabad a 1.5 meter wide excavation in a garbage pit that was four meters deep and four meters wide yielded 1,177 limb and skull fragments from sheep, goats, pigs, and cattle. This four meter deep deposit, a twenty percent sample of the entire pit, represents human subsistence behavior over only two years (Wright, Miller, and Redding 1980; Wright, Redding, and Pollock 1989).

Certainly the faunal remains recovered from a site have been subjected to a series of cultural filters and preservational processes. Hence, the faunal remains may provide a data set biased by a number of filters and processes. The more similar the taxa and the more similarly they are used the more likely the filters and processes act uniformly across a site and may be ignored, or by examining changes in ratios between taxa rather than counts or percentages the effect of the filters and processes may be canceled out. Also, the more similar the taxa the less likely the difference between them in NISP is biased by differences in number of skeletal parts. And, finally, the more similar the taxa and the more similarly they are used the less likely the difference between them in NISP is biased by differences in fragmentation or differences in rates of return of fragments to the site.

Ringrose's third criticism that using NISP as an estimate of abundance overlooks that 125 fragments are counted the same whether they are from one or 125 animals is only a problem if one is estimating absolute abundance. If one is using NISPs to estimate relative abundance then as long as the average number of fragments per animal is similar for the two taxa then a ratio of NISPs reflects relative use.

Grayson is correct in asserting that NISPs represent the maximum number of individuals and we do not know how an estimate of maximum number of individuals relates to actual abundance. But NISP does reflect the actual abundance of a taxon in archaeological samples and ratios between NISPs for different taxa must reflect the relative rate of inclusion of the taxa in the sample. The question becomes what such ratios represent. I maintain that such ratios reflect consumption and, if bias related to physiology, transport, and consumption can be factored out, these may be used to reconstruct the relative proportions of each taxon in the herds/flocks from which the animals consumed were drawn.

I use NISP to calculate species ratios primarily for the sheep, goats, cattle, and gazelle. These ratios provide an estimate of the relative use of different taxa. I compare these ratios for Chogha Bonut with ratios derived from a baseline model. It is temporal and geographic changes in these ratios that contain information on human subsistence behavior. In such comparisons of recovery rates, number of skeletal parts and fragmentation largely cancel out. If any of these factors create problems it is recovery rates, but these, when recognized, may be considered in developing explanations for differences between ratios.

As an additional point I note that it is apparent in regional and site studies that estimates of relative abundance based on NISP exhibit patterns (e.g., Redding 1981). If patterns are identified in the faunal data they may be the result of biasing forces, but as an initial research position I would argue that patterns in the data are more likely to be explained by spatial and temporal variation in subsistence strategies and tactics used by the inhabitants of the site or sites. If this position is incorrect, then over time we will find that serious discrepancies exist between explanations or models of human subsistence we develop and the data. Even if the empirically identified patterns prove to be the result of biasing processes, by using the approach advocated above we should gain insight into and learn to identify where and how the biasing agencies effect faunal samples. This will help us in compensating for their effects.

Another assumption I make is that all of the faunal material recovered is the result of human subsistence behavior. Evidence of carnivore gnawing is present but at relatively low levels. Given the manner in which faunal material accumulates in residential areas of village and larger sites that are occupied by food producers, bias introduced by carnivore activity should be a minor problem. The problem with sites such as Chogha Bonut is determining what percentage of the faunal material is not the result of human activity rather than what proportion of the fauna is the result of human activity.

METHODOLOGY

The recording system used by the excavators employed layers and features. The faunal remains were collected into bags. Each bag was tagged with layers and feature information. I recorded the faunal remains by bag and, hence, in my data book, which is organized by layers and features, some pages have identical designations reflecting that they record the fauna material from the same layers and feature but different bags.[40] Animal bone fragments from all layers were collected by hand during picking and troweling. This may introduce a slight bias in the samples due to under-representation of small elements (e.g., carpals and tarsals).

The unit of analysis used in this report is the layers and features. All tables present counts (NISP) of the material recovered totaled by layers and features. All bags were treated in the same fashion. The following describes my standard process, parts of which may or may not be applicable to Chogha Bonut (e.g., only two fish fragments were recovered). First the sample is sorted into four piles: fish, reptile, bird, and mammal. Fish material is divided into identifiable to at least genus and not identifiable to genus. The material that is not identifiable to at least genus is divided into four categories; cranial, vertebrae, post-cranial but not vertebrae, and unidentifiable. Material in each category is counted and weighed. Material identifiable to genus is identified and each element is weighed. The reptile material is identified to taxa and each piece is weighed independently except for carapace fragments that are weighed as a group. Bird bones that are identifiable to genus are counted and weighed independently. Bird remains that can not be identified to genus are counted and weighed by the categories limb, vertebra, and unidentifiable. Mammal bones that are

---

40. A copy of the data books is available upon request.

identifiable to at least the level of the genus are weighed independently. The remaining mammal bones are sorted into the following categories; large limb, medium limb, small limb, large rib, medium rib, large skull, medium skull, large vertebrae, medium vertebrae, teeth, and unidentifiable. The material in each of these categories is counted and weighed.

Measurements are taken, whenever possible, on identifiable, unburnt mammal fragments from adult individuals. In general, measurements are taken as described by Angela von den Driesch (1976) and her abbreviations are used in the text and tables. A few additional measurements were taken. Two that are commonly taken are the diameters of the inner and outer articular surfaces of the distal metapodials: abbreviated in the text and tables as IS and OS respectively. These measurements, described in Hole, Flannery, and Neely (1969, pp. 269–71), are used to calculate a ratio that can separate metapodials of sheep, goat, and gazelle.

MATERIAL FROM CHOGHA BONUT

The faunal remains from Chogha Bonut were, generally, in very good condition. Some of the remains were encased in a gypsum/calcite cemented matrix that was only minimally removed in this initial analysis. Only two fragments exhibited any evidence of carnivore gnawing and no carnivore remains were recovered in the samples. This suggests that bias introduced by the activity of dogs is minimal. One bone of a porcupine (Hystrix indica) was recovered but it was from the uppermost layer of the site and was clearly a recent intrusion. No evidence of porcupine gnawing was found on the remains. A number of fragments showed marks characteristic of rodent gnawing. Only a few fragments were burnt and the majority of these were unidentifiable fragments. These data suggest that burning was the result of fragments of bones ending up in fire pits and that roasting of meat was not systematically practiced.

CLASS OSTEICHTHYES (FISH)

Only two fish fragments were recovered at Chogha Bonut. Both are vertebrae and are from one of the lowest layers of the stratigraphic trench (S.T. el. 73.80–73.60). They both appear to represent a cyprinid, a number of which are common at present in the rivers, streams, canals, and sloughs of the Susiana plain. Based on this faunal sample from Chogha Bonut fish were not an important resource.

CLASS REPTILIA (REPTILES)

Only a single fragment from Chogha Bonut could be identified as from a reptile. A carapace fragment from the Caspian terrapin (*Mauremys caspica*) was recovered from the lowest layer of the stratigraphic trench (S.T. el. 73.20–73.00). The Caspian terrapin is at present a common inhabitant of the rivers, streams, and canals on the Susiana plain. Caspian terrapins are known from almost every site on the Susiana plain for which we have faunal data. Terrapins are a good source of food, but based on the presence of only one fragment they were not an important resource.

CLASS AVES (BIRDS)

Birds at Chogha Bonut are represented by four fragments. A proximal ulna was recovered from Layer 1, a disturbed deposit. A mandible fragment was identified in the material from Feature 15 (fig. 13B). Two fragments were recovered from Layer 30. One of these was a pelvis fragment and the other a carpometacarpus. The carpometacarpus is from a cormorant (Phalacrocorax carbo). The cormorant is a common winter visitor to the Susiana plain where it fishes along the major rivers. During the winter of 1971 and 1973, large numbers could be observed just below the barrage south of Dezful.

CLASS MAMMALIA (MAMMALS)

Mammals are represented by 643 fragments that could be identified to at least the level of the genus. Another 1,230 fragments could only be identified as mammal and in some cases to region of the body (e.g., limb, rib, vertebra, skull, tooth). These fragments are not included in this report but will be dealt with in the final report.

Equus sp. An equid is represented in the Chogha Bonut sample by ten fragments. These fragments are presented by body part and by layer and feature in table 9. The species represented by the material is most likely the wild half ass or onager, *Equus hemionus*. The onager was common in the Ali Kosh and Mohammad Jaffar phases at Tappeh Ali Kosh (Hole, Flannery, and Neely 1969, p. 295). Measurements were taken on three of the fragments and are presented in table 14. Measurements on the distal metacarpal compare well with measurements on modern and archaeological onagers but are also similar to measurements on modern asses (*Equus asinus*) (Hilzheimer 1941, p. 13). Two equid fragments provided fusion data. A proximal femur was in the process of fusing when the animal was killed indicating an onager about thirty-six to forty-two months of age. A distal metapodial was fused suggesting that the animal was more than sixteen months of age when killed. Onagers are a good source of meat and were probably hunted occasionally or killed when encountered by the inhabitants of Chogha Bonut. However, onagers were not a major meat source.

Sus scrofa. The pig is represented in the Chogha Bonut samples by six fragments. These fragments are presented by body part and by layer and feature in table 9. The sample is too small to provide any reliable information on age structure, sex ratio, and body part distribution. This with the absence of any measurable molar teeth makes it impossible at present to determine whether the Chogha Bonut pigs were domestic or wild. Pigs were common in the Ali Kosh phase at Ali Kosh (Hole, Flannery, and Neely 1969, p. 295). Flannery determined that the pigs from Tappeh Ali Kosh were hunted, wild animals. Given the low number of pig fragments at Chogha Bonut this is probably the case at this site also. Wild pigs were probably killed when encountered but not systematically hunted. Three fragments provide data on age structure. A distal radius was unfused indicating the pig was killed before thirty-six to forty-two months of age. A calcaneum was unfused indicating the animal was killed before twenty-four to thirty months. And, a fused second phalanx is evidence of a pig killed after attaining twelve to fifteen months of age. Two fragments were measured and the measurements are provided in table 14.

Bos sp. Cattle are represented in the Chogha Bonut sample by forty-five fragments. These fragments are presented by body part and by layer and feature in table 9. The critical question with regard to the cattle is whether they are domestic or wild. The measurements for the cattle fragments are presented in table 14. The astragalus with a length of 60.3 mm is clearly from a domestic animal. It is only slightly larger than the astragalus from a modern cow from Luristan (Hole, Flannery, and Neely 1969, p. 305). It is smaller than domestic cattle at Tappeh Sabz and Ras al-'Amiya (Hole, Flannery, and Neely 1969, p. 305). On the other hand the second and third phalanges all fall in the range of wild cattle from Tappeh Ali Kosh (Hole, Flannery, and Neely 1969, p. 305). Several fragments, while not measurable, support the mixed nature of the cattle from Chogha Bonut. A huge stylohyoid fragment was recovered from Layer 27 along with an unfused distal metapodial from Layer 30 that must have been from wild animals. Either the cattle at Chogha Bonut were in the process of domestication or the inhabitants of Chogha Bonut were hunting wild cattle while, at the same time, maintaining some domestic cattle. Given the extremes in size I think the latter is more likely. A small number of domestic cattle were being kept at Chogha Bonut, probably as an insurance resource (perhaps for milk?), while wild cattle were hunted.

Nine fragments provide data on the age structure of the animals consumed. Four fused second phalanges provide evidence of cattle that must have been more than twenty-four months in age. A fused proximal tibia was from an animal at least forty-eight months old. A fused proximal radius provides evidence of an animal that was at least sixteen months. An unfused distal metapodial is from an animal less than twenty-six months. And, an unfused first phalanx is from an animal less than sixteen months.

The percentage of limb fragments from non-meat bearing elements is 84.8%. If whole animals were being returned to the site the percentage should be 70%. The non-meat bearing limb fragments are slightly overrepresented in the sample.

Clearly, cattle were consumed at Chogha Bonut and formed an important source of meat, hides and, probably, bone. We do not know if the domestic livestock was milked.

Ovis-Capra. Sheep and goats are represented by 282 fragments in the sample from Chogha Bonut. The distribution of sheep-goat fragments is presented by body part and layer and feature in tables 10 and 11. These tables also include the counts of sheep-goat elements that could be identified as either sheep or goat. Based on these numbers the ratio of sheep to goats consumed is 0.60:1. This low ratio of sheep to goats is unusual in latter phases in southwestern Iran but is in accord with the dominance of goats in the aceramic levels of Tappeh Ali Kosh (Hole, Flannery, and Neely 1969, p. 271).

Fusion data for the sheep-goat material is provided in table 12. The survivorship data suggests that about half of the animals slaughtered were less than two years of age and about half were older than two years. This is not the pattern of survivorship produced by hunting and is in fact rather unusual. The sexed fragments indicate that females slaughtered exceed the number of males slaughtered by 2:1 (see tables 10 and 11). That females occur more frequently among the slaughtered animals is also unusual.

The body part data are summarized in tables 10 and 11. The percentage of non-meat bearing fragments in the sample of limb fragments is 48.4%. The expected percentage if whole animals were being butchered on the site is

70%. Clearly, non-meat bearing limb elements are underrepresented in the sample. This is probably due to the lack of screening of deposits but certainly needs to be looked at in future excavations.

Again the critical question is whether the sheep and goats at Chogha Bonut were wild or domestic. A goat horn core from Feature 31 is from a domestic animal. Given the sex ratios and age structures and how they do not fit with models of hunting wild sheep-goats it is likely that we are dealing with domestic herds.

The unusual age structure and sex ratio for the sample of sheep-goat material is similar to the winter deposits in the Uruk phase pit at Tappeh Sharafabad, located just south of Dezful (Wright, Miller, and Redding 1980). The split age structure represents the slaughter of young males just prior to and during the breeding season in order to open resources for newborn kids and lambs, and the slaughter of older females who have not become pregnant or who had exhibited unfavorable traits. As we go further into the breeding season the sex ratio becomes increasingly biased towards females. I would suggest that the deposits sampled at Chogha Bonut are from the winter, probably January through April. This view is supported by the small number of neonate fragments, representing newborns, that were found in the material.

Herds of goats with a small number of sheep were kept by the inhabitants of Chogha Bonut. They were kept for their meat and probably hides (see the discussion of gazelle presented below). It is not known whether the milk of the sheep/goats was consumed.

Gazella subgutturosa. The goitered-gazelle is represented by 216 fragments. The distribution of these fragments by body part, level, and feature is presented in tables 10 and 11. Based on two horn cores, the species of gazelle present at Chogha Bonut is the goitered gazelle, *Gazella subgutturosa*. This taxon is found around the Susiana plain at present and was found at Tappeh Ali Kosh (Hole, Flannery, and Neely 1969, p. 294).

The fusion data for the gazelle are presented in table 13. Not surprisingly the survivorship looks like what one would expect from a hunted population — a small number of young animals and a lot of old animals.

The distribution of body parts is rather unusual (see tables 10 and 11). The percentage of limb fragments from non-meat bearing elements is 82.9%. The percentage expected if whole animals were being butchered on the site is 70.0%. Clearly, non-meat bearing elements are overrepresented in the sample. This is particularly apparent in several samples that had large numbers of gazelle foot elements recovered in articulated condition (e.g., Features 21, 31, and S.T. el. 73.80–73.60). These may represent hide processing areas where the hides of gazelles were scraped and conditioned and accompanying foot bones discarded.

Gazelles were hunted by the inhabitants of Chogha Bonut. They were an important source of meat and possibly hides.

Ursus arctos. The brown bear is represented by a central tarsal from Layer 30. The brown bear is an inhabitant of the Zagros Mountains but is not known from the Susiana plain. It is likely that the brown bear was obtained in the mountains behind Chogha Bonut and the element or some portion containing it was transported to Chogha Bonut. The importance of this find is that it indicates that the inhabitants of Chogha Bonut probably traveled into the mountains.

Hystrix indica. A single fragment from a porcupine was recovered from Layer 1. It is not discolored and is probably a late (recent) intrusion. Porcupines are common burrowers on archaeological sites on the Susiana plain.

Tatera indica. The giant Indian gerbil is represented by various body parts and one nearly complete skeleton. It is found in F9/L12 (1 fragment), Feature 14 (2), Layer 27 (2), Feature 31 (74), Feature 34 (1), and lost provenance (3). These occurrences do not appear to be recent intrusions and based on similar discoloration are as old as the deposits that contain them. Hence, it is likely that the area around Chogha Bonut supported the giant Indian gerbil during the Aceramic period. This is important because the area does not support this gerbil at present and instead supports the Sundevall's jird (*Meriones crassus*). This suggests that the area around Chogha Bonut was much wetter in the Aceramic period — so damp that grasses (Gramineae) grew there nearly year round. Indeed, the area could have been irrigated. If not, then the area would have been ideal for dry farming.

DISCUSSION

The occupants of Chogha Bonut were herders of cattle, sheep, and goats and hunters of gazelle, pig, and cattle. The ratio of sheep-goat to cattle is 6.3:1. This is not unexpected in a system based on herding and dry farming of cereals prior to the introduction of intensive farming. It is not meaningful to compare this ratio to Tappeh Ali Kosh as Flannery identifies all the Tappeh Ali Kosh cattle as wild (Hole, Flannery, and Neely 1969, p. 264).

The ratio of sheep-goats to gazelle for Chogha Bonut is 1.3:1. For Tappeh Ali Kosh the ratio is 1.66:1 in the Mohammad Jaffar phase, 2.1:1 for the Ali Kosh phase, and 3.0:1 for the Buz Murdeh phase (ibid., p. 264).

Even more basic is the rank order for Chogha Bonut and Tappeh Ali Kosh, which is identical. Sheep and goats are most common followed by gazelle, onager, cattle, and pig.

CONCLUSION

We can draw a number of conclusions based on the samples from the excavations at Chogha Bonut:

1. Domestic sheep and goats were herded with goats dominating the flocks.
2. A small number of domestic cattle were kept.
3. Gazelles were hunted and hides processed at the site.
4. Wild cattle and pigs were hunted.
5. Based on the sheep-goat and bird data, the site was probably seasonally occupied with the inhabitants on the site during the winter and early spring.
6. The area was much wetter than today with grasses present nearly year round.

These conclusions are tentative and require larger samples to test. What can not be doubted is the importance of adequately analyzed faunal samples from this critical period in the evolution of human subsistence in southwestern Iran.

Table 9. NISP for Mammal Taxa Other than Gazella, Ovis, and Capra Presented by Body Part and Provenance

Provenance	Equus sp. Other	MB	NMB	Bos sp. Other	MB	NMB	Sus scrofa Other	MB	NMB	Ursus	Tatera	Hystrix
L1	1	—	1	2	1	2	—	—	—	—	—	1
L13	2	—	—	1	—	1	—	—	—	—	1	—
F14	1	—	—	—	—	1	—	—	—	2	—	—
F15	—	—	—	—	1	—	—	—	—	—	—	—
F11/L16	—	—	—	—	1	—	—	—	—	—	—	—
L21	—	—	—	—	—	2	—	—	—	—	—	—
L27	—	—	—	3	—	1	1	—	—	—	2	—
L30	—	—	2	2	1	7	—	—	—	1	—	—
F31	—	—	—	3	—	4	—	—	—	—	74	—
F27/L33	—	—	—	—	—	5	—	—	—	—	—	—
F34	—	—	—	—	—	—	—	—	—	—	1	—
L35 (D.T.)	—	—	—	—	—	—	—	—	2	—	—	—
Lost	—	—	—	1	—	1	—	—	—	—	—	—
Lost	—	—	—	—	—	—	—	—	—	—	3	—
S.T. el. 74.70–74.50	—	—	—	—	—	—	1	—	—	—	—	—
S.T. el. 74.40–74.20	—	1	—	—	—	1	—	—	—	—	—	—
S.T. el. 74.20–74.00	—	—	—	—	—	2	—	—	—	—	—	—
S.T. el. 74.00–73.80	—	—	1	—	1	1	—	—	—	—	—	—
S.T. el. 73.60–73.40	—	—	—	—	—	—	—	1	—	—	—	—
S.T. el. 73.40–73.20	—	—	—	—	—	—	—	—	1	—	—	—
S.T. el. 73.20–73.00	1	—	—	—	—	—	—	—	—	—	—	—
Subtotal	5	1	4	12	5	28	2	1	3			
Total		10			45			6		1	83	1

Table 10. NISP for Gazelle, Sheep, and Goat for Square M10
Presented by Body Part and Provenance

Level	Gazella sp. Other	Gazella sp. MB	Gazella sp. NMB	Ovis-Capra Other	Ovis-Capra MB	Ovis-Capra NMB	Ovis	Capra	Male	Female
L1	4	2	4	5	13	5	—	1	1	1
L3	—	—	48	—	1	—	—	1	—	1
F1/L4	—	—	—	—	2	—	—	—	—	—
F4/L7	1	3	—	1	3	12	2	—	—	—
L13	—	2	2	3	7	3	2	—	1	2
F14	—	1	2	1	4	12	2	2	—	—
F15	—	1	6	1	3	1	1	1	—	—
F11/L16	—	1	—	3	—	—	—	—	—	—
F16/L19	1	—	—	1	—	1	—	—	—	—
L21	1	3	20	5	4	2	—	—	—	—
F19/L22	—	—	—	—	1	—	—	—	—	1
F23/L24a	—	—	1	—	—	—	—	—	—	—
L27	—	—	—	3	3	5	—	3	—	—
L30	1	5	9	7	16	27	3	13	—	—
F31	2	2	18	3	5	8	2	5	—	1
F26/L32	—	—	1	—	—	1	—	1	—	—
F27/L33	—	2	1	8	7	8	1	—	—	1
F34	—	—	—	1	—	—	—	—	—	—
L35 (D.T.)	—	1	—	1	1	1	1	1	—	1
L35 (D.T.)	—	—	—	—	1	1	—	—	—	—
Lost	—	1	5	7	17	8	—	4	1	2
Lost	—	—	—	—	1	1	—	—	—	—
Subtotal	10	24	117	50	89	96				
Total		151			235		14	32	3	10

Table 11. NISP for Gazelle, Sheep, and Goat for the 1996 Stratigraphic Trench
Presented by Body Part and Level

Level	Gazella sp. Other	Gazella sp. MB	Gazella sp. NMB	Ovis-Capra Other	Ovis-Capra MB	Ovis-Capra NMB	Ovis	Capra	Male	Female
el. 77.40	—	2	—	2	3	1	1	—	—	—
el. 76.00–75.80	—	—	—	1	2	2	1	1	—	—
el. 75.10–74.90	—	—	—	—	1	1	1	—	—	—
el. 74.90–74.70	—	—	—	—	—	1	—	—	—	—
el. 74.70–74.60	—	2	1	—	1	—	—	—	1	—
el. 74.60–74.40	1	—	—	—	—	2	1	—	—	—
el. 74.40–74.20	—	2	—	—	2	1	—	—	—	—
el. 74.20–74.00	—	—	3	1	1	—	—	—	—	—
el. 74.00–73.80	3	—	1	—	1	1	—	—	—	—
el. 73.80–73.60	—	2	42	—	—	—	—	—	—	—
el. 73.60–73.40	—	—	—	1	4	4	—	—	—	—
el. 73.40–73.20	1	1	—	1	3	2	1	—	1	—
el. 73.20–73.00	2	1	1	—	3	5	—	1	—	—
Subtotal	7	10	48	6	21	20				
Total		65			47		5	2	2	0

Table 12. Fusion Data for Ovis-Capra Bones

Group	Age of Fusion (months)	Element	Fused	Fusing	Unfused	Group Index
I	8–10	Scapula	1	0	1	
		Distal humerus	5	0	0	
		Proximal radius	4	0	0	
	Group total		10	0	1	90.1
II	16	Proximal phalanx	24	0	3	
	Group total		24	0	3	88.0
III	24	Distal metapodial	8	1	12	
		Distal tibia	5	0	0	
	Group total		13	1	12	51.9
IV	36	Distal radius	3	0	3	
		Proximal femur	4	0	1	
		Calcaneum	4	0	3	
	Group total		11	0	7	72.2
V	42	Proximal humerus	1	0	2	
		Distal femur	3	0	1	
		Proximal tibia	1	0	2	
		Ulna	1	0	1	
	Group total		6	0	6	50.0

Table 13. Fusion Data for Gazella Bones

Group	Age of Fusion (months)	Element	Fused	Fusing	Unfused	Group Index
I	8–10	Scapula	3	0	0	
		Distal humerus	6	0	0	
		Proximal radius	0	0	0	
	Group total		9	0	0	100.0
II	16	Proximal phalanx	62	0	1	
	Group total		62	0	1	98.4
III	24	Distal metapodial	6	0	3	
		Distal tibia	1	0	1	
	Group total		7	0	4	63.6
IV	36	Distal radius	0	0	1	
		Proximal femur	4	0	0	
		Calcaneum	3	0	0	
	Group total		7	0	1	87.5
V	42	Proximal humerus	0	0	0	
		Distal femur	2	0	2	
		Proximal tibia	1	0	0	
		Ulna	2	0	0	
	Group total		5	0	2	71.4

Table 14. Measurements (in mm) for Bones

Equus sp.

Upper second molar	L 28.3	—	B 27.3	—
Distal metapodial	Bd 39.4	—	Dd 28.1	—
First phalanx	Bp 37.0+	—	—	—

Sus scrofa

Fourth metacarpal	Bp 16.0	—	Dp 16.1	—
Second phalanx	Bp 14.2	Dp. 14.2	GL 25.6	Bd 12.1

Bos sp.

Upper first molar	L 31.2	—	B 17.1	—
Astragalus	GLl 60.3	Glm -	Bd -	—
2nd+3rd carpal	B 51.6	D 43.4	—	—
2nd+3rd tarsal	B -	D 48.3	—	—
Second phalanx	Bp	Dp	GL	Bd
	30.3	—	—	—
	40.3	44.9	50.9	37.5
	34.3	—	48.9	30.0
Third phalanx	DLS	LD	—	—
	87.0	—	—	—
	90.0	65.0	—	—

Ovis-Capra

Axis	DC 180.0, 15.3, 12.7, 12.2, 9.3	—	—	—
Scapula	GLp 28.3	—	—	—
Distal humerus	Bd 28.5, 23.5	—	—	—
Proximal radius	Bp 32.8, 30.5	—	—	—
Distal radius	Bd 30.8	—	—	—
Distal femur	Bd 33.5	—	—	—
Proximal tibia	Bp 39.6	Dp 39.8	—	—
Distal tibia	Bd 23.1	Bd 18.0	—	—
Calcaneum	GL 55.2	—	—	—
Astragalus	GLl	GLm	Bd	—
	25.7	24.3	17.0	—
	—	28.5	—	—
	—	23.1	—	—
	—	26.0	—	—
	29.9	27.7	19.6	—
	29.3	27.3	19.1	—
	—	25.0	—	—
First phalanx	Bp	Dp	GL	Bd
	12.6	15.1	37.2	12.7
	12.1	14.8	37.2	11.8
	16.8	18.1	44.0	—
	11.7	13.8	—	11.8
	—	—	—	12.3
	11.7	—	35.1	—
	13.2	15.3	36.7	—
	11.1	14.1	36.3	11.3
	11.0	14.0	35.3	—
	11.1	14.1	33.8	10.6
	9.4	13.6	—	—
	12.0	14.8	34.6	11.2
	12.6	15.3	36.4	12.3
	—	—	34.4	11.9
Second phalanx	12.7	12.7	22.7	9.9
	—	—	—	7.4

Table 14. Measurements (in mm) for Bones (*cont.*)

Ovis-Capra (*cont.*)

Second phalanx (*cont.*)	10.9	11.8	23.3	8.1
	10.3	—	—	7.7
	14.4	—	22.9	11.7
	11.5	—	—	—
	11.8	—	—	10.1
Third phalanx	GL 24.6	—	—	—

Gazella sp.

Scapula	Glp 27.3, 29.7	—	—	—
Distal humerus	Bd	BT	—	—
	25.2	22.7	—	—
	25.5	24.1	—	—
	25.9	24.1	—	—
	25.7	—	—	—
	26.7	23.9	—	—
Proximal radius	Bp 24.1	—	—	—
Distal tibia	Bd	Dd	—	—
	21.2	18.6	—	—
	19.5	16.8	—	—
Astragalus	GLl	GLm	Bd	—
	26.2	24.4	15.4	—
	25.6	23.3	15.5	—
	25.6	23.4	15.8	—
	—	23.3	16.7	—
	—	23.5	14.5	—
	23.9	22.7	14.8	—
	—	20.8	—	—
First phalanx	Bp	Dp	GL	Bd
	9.5	13.4	—	—
	10.1	12.6	—	—
	9.5	13.3	—	—
	9.6	13.1	39.2	8.7
	9.6	13.3	38.8	8.2
	9.6	13.4	39.0	8.5
	9.4	13.9	40.6	8.6
	9.9	13.6	—	—
	10.1	14.1	37.2	8.7
	10.5	14.0	42.3	8.5
	10.4	14.3	43.5	9.0
	9.4	13.7	41.4	8.8
	9.6	13.7	40.2	8.6
	9.9	13.0	37.0	8.7
	10.3	13.9	—	—
	10.4	—	—	—
	—	—	—	9.0
	—	—	—	8.8
	—	—	—	7.7
	7.9	11.9	36.7	7.1
	7.0	—	—	—
	9.7	13.1	35.4	—
	9.3	12.8	35.2	8.2
	9.1	11.0	38.1	8.5
	—	—	—	8.3
	—	—	—	8.1
	10.0	13.6	—	—
	10.1	13.5	35.9	8.3
	10.6	14.5	—	—
	—	—	37.0	—

Table 14. Measurements (in mm) for Bones (*cont.*)

Gazella sp. (*cont.*)

First phalanx (*cont.*)	11.1	14.2	—	9.0
	10.1	13.8	36.8	8.9
	—	—	—	9.1
Second phalanx	8.2	10.0	20.2	—
	8.5	11.4	19.3	7.5
	8.5	11.6	19.6	7.2
	8.5	11.5	19.7	7.4
	—	—	—	7.4
	8.3	12.2	19.8	7.6
	9.1	11.0	22.0	7.5
	8.5	11.8	20.5	7.5
	9.3	11.8	22.0	7.6
	9.1	12.6	21.5	7.8
	8.8	11.6	20.5	7.5
	9.3	12.0	21.4	7.9
	8.7	11.0	21.2	7.4
	9.3	12.2	22.0	8.0
	—	—	—	7.5
	9.2	11.9	—	—
	9.2	12.6	22.0	—
	8.6	—	—	7.4
	7.5	10.3	18.0	6.2
	7.2	10.1	17.9	5.8
	8.3	11.6	20.0	7.7
	8.2	10.7	20.5	6.8
	8.3	10.2	—	—
	7.9	9.9	18.0	6.7
	—	—	—	7.8

Third phalanx: GL 22.1, 25.1, 24.7, 25.0, 23.5, 21.4, 24.7, 24.6, 24.8, 24.6, 25.6, 25.9, 29.4, 24.5, 23.2, 23.6, 23.9, 25.6, 21.8, 20.6, 22.7, 26.4, 24.5, 24.1, 25.6, 23.4, 22.9, 24.7

APPENDIX 1
RADIOCARBON DATING OF THE SUSIANA SEQUENCE FROM CHOGHA BONUT

We collected more than fifty samples from a number of features and layers at Chogha Bonut for radiocarbon dating. Due to budgetary constraints, we submitted only seven samples of organic ash taken from the Aceramic (6 samples) and Formative (1 sample) levels at Chogha Bonut (table 15). In addition, we selected and submitted three organic samples from the Early Middle Susiana, Early Susiana, and Archaic Susiana levels at Chogha Mish for radiocarbon analysis (table 16). The samples were analyzed by Accelerator Mass Spectrometry (AMS) technique at Groningen and Beta Analytic, Inc., in Miami, Florida.

Five out of seven dates obtained are internally consistent and correspond to dates reported for contemporary periods from other sites. The dates obtained from samples Beta-104553 and 104554 of 10,980 B.P. and 41,930 B.P. are obviously too high; perhaps the samples were contaminated with a secondary deposit and/or the presence of fossil fuel.

The calendric dates estimated for the Aceramic period range from 7500 B.C. (basal level) to 6600 B.C., fitting very well with the dates obtained from similar sites, especially Tappeh Ali Kosh in the Deh Luran plain, northwest of Susiana (Hole 1987, table 3). The estimated date for the aceramic periods of Buz Murdeh and Tappeh Ali Kosh ranges from 7500 to 6000 B.C. (Hole, Flannery, and Neely 1969, pp. 331–41). 6000 B.C. as the terminal date for the aceramic sequence presents some chronological problems since the Mohammad Jaffar phase and long periods of Archaic, Early Susiana, and Middle Susiana (in Hole's terminology, Jaffar, Sefid, Surkh, Chogha Mami Transitional, Sabz, Khazineh, Mehmeh, Bayat, and Farukh phases) with deep stratified deposits span a comparatively shorter time range. But such observations need not be of major concern as radiocarbon dates obtained from archaeological sites continue to be controversial. In the future, we may be able to use radiocarbon dates to anchor our absolute chronological discussions of archaeological periods when we can no longer arbitrarily discern radiocarbon dates as too old or too young.

Table 15. List of Radiocarbon Dates from Chogha Bonut

Laboratory No.	Provenance	Type of Sample	B.P. 5568 hl	B.C.: 95% Probability
Beta-104552	L39 (D.T.)	Organic Sediment	8,270+/-100	7505–7025
Beta-104553	Layer 13	Organic	10,980+/-100	—
Beta-104554	S.T. (76.10) Formative Susiana	Organic	41,930+/-1,000	—
Beta-104555	Feature 28	Charred Material	8,070+/-50	7065–6975
Beta-106164	L39 (D.T.)	Charred Material	8,170+/-60	7310–7015
Beta-106165	F26/L32	Charred Material	8,020+/-50	7040–6705
Beta-106166	Feature 14	Charred Material	7,950+/-50	7015–6615

RADIOCARBON DATING OF THE SUSIANA SEQUENCE FROM CHOGHA MISH

Except for one radiocarbon date (Delougaz and Kantor 1996, p. 323) for the Protoliterate period, no other absolute dates are available from prehistoric levels at Chogha Mish. To fill this gap and to provide an absolute chronological link between the Archaic Susiana 0 phase at Chogha Bonut and Archaic Susiana 1 phase at Chogha Mish, we submitted to Beta Analytic three samples obtained from the sixth, eighth, and ninth seasons of excavations at Chogha Mish.

As noted in table 16, sample no. Beta-106168 came from Square S18:902, dated by the pottery to the Early Middle Susiana, contemporary with the Ubaid 2 (Haji Mohammad) period in southern Mesopotamia. The calibrated date of 5590–5435 B.C. seems to fit the general chronological position of the Early Middle Susiana. The calibrated date of 5605–5450 B.C. for the Early Susiana sample Beta-106169 is only a bit higher than that obtained for the Late Middle Susiana sample. This sample came from Square P22:629, but the absolute depth where this sample was taken is unknown to us, and given the closeness of its date to that of the Early Middle Susiana sample, we can imagine that it was taken from the terminal phase of the Early Susiana period. The third sample was obtained from Square S22:823, dated by ceramics to the Archaic Susiana period. The calibrated radiocarbon date of 7480–7075 B.C. seems to be much higher compared with the dates obtained for the Aceramic and Formative Susiana periods at Chogha Bonut.

Table 16. List of Radiocarbon Dates from Chogha Mish

Laboratory No.	Provenance	Type of Sample	B.P. 5568 hl	B.C.: 95% Probability
Beta-106168	S18:902 Middle Susiana	Charred Material	6,610+/-50	5590–5435
Beta-106169	P22:629 Early Susiana	Charred Material	6,660+/-50	5605–5450
Beta-106167	S22:823 Archaic Susiana	Charred Material	8,300+/-60	7480–7075

APPENDIX 2
INDEX OF FEATURES AND LAYERS FROM THE 1996 SEASON

Feature/Layer	Description
Layer 1	Topsoil and bulldozed and redeposited earth
Layer 2	Erosion deposit
Layer 3	Tiny striated deposit surrounded by bulldozed debris
Feature 1/Layer 4	Small fire pit filled with ash and some cracked rocks
Layer 5	Not used
Feature 3/Layer 6	Round hole (post hole?) next to a fire pit (F5/L8) filled with loose dirt mixed with some ash
Feature 4/Layer 7	Large, but badly preserved fire pit (mostly under the west balk) filled with loose ash and cracked rocks
Feature 5/Layer 8	Badly preserved fire pit filled with loose ash and some cracked rocks
Feature 6/Layer 9	Round hole (post hole?) to the north of a fire pit (F5/L8) filled with loose dirt and some ash
Feature 7	Burnt and beaten earth surface
Feature 8/Layer 10	Pit mostly destroyed by bulldozer and possibly by a 1978 trench
Layer 11	Occupational debris
Feature 9/Layer 12	Pit from presumably the Middle Susiana period (contained only Middle Susiana and earlier pottery) dug to an unknown depth. The filling dirt was clayish and contained little and sometimes no material
Layer 13	First fairly well-preserved occupational deposit below Layer 11 stretching the entire eastern half of Square M10
Feature 10/Layer 15	Large round fire pit on the southwest of Square M10 filled with loose dirt and dark ashes mixed with small cracked rocks
Feature 11/Layer 16	Small, badly-preserved round fire pit immediately south of F10/L15, filled with loose dirt and ash — mostly under the south balk
Feature 12/Layer 17	Horseshoe-shaped fire pit filled with dark ash and loose brownish dirt. No rocks were discovered from this feature
Feature 13/layer 18	Horseshoe-shaped fire pit filled with loose dirt and partially preserved; half of the pit is under the west balk
Feature 14	Beaten earth surface with a number of fire pits, clusters of rocks, tokens, and figurines
Feature 15	Beaten surface similar to F14. The southeastern corner of this surface was heavily damaged by extensive animal and root holes. On the northwestern section were a cluster of rocks mixed with light gray ash and numerous flint blades and debitage
Feature 16/Layer 19	Apparently a large fire pit, most of which is under the west balk and filled with loose ash
Feature 17/Layer 20	Large circular fireplace pit with loose dark ash and brownish dirt mixed with a few small cracked rocks. Part of the fire pit is under the north balk
Feature 18	Beaten earth surface with fire pits and patches of hard white dirt in between the fire pits
Layer 21	Occupational debris consisting of brownish to yellowish and off-white dirt mixed with some pebbles, bones, and flint blades
Feature 19/Layer 22	Large oval-shaped fire pit (partly under the south balk) filled with loose dark gray ashes mixed with some bones, flint blades, and cracked rocks
Feature 20/Layer 23	Circular fire pit partially destroyed by animal/root holes and another fire pit (F23/L24a)
Feature 21	Beaten earth surface
Feature 22/Layer 24	Fire pit almost completely destroyed by animal/root hole
Feature 23/Layer 24a	This fire pit was first thought to be part of F20/L23, but further clearing revealed a separate construction cut into F20/L23
Feature 24/Layer 25	Large circular shallow fire pit filled with dark ashes mixed with flint blades and a few clay objects
Feature 25/Layer 26	Oval-shaped fire pit with some cracked rocks on the bottom

Index of Features and Layers from the 1996 Season (*cont.*)

Feature/Layer	Description
Layer 27	Accumulation of loose brownish dirt mixed with lumps of perhaps accidentally burnt clay, bones, rocks, flint blades, and debitage
Feature 28	Beaten earth with patches of loose gray deposit, traces of rain-deposited sediment, bones, horns, ash, reed impressions, and red ochre
Layer 29	Most probably an extension of F28, but a bit thicker and darker
Layer 30	Brownish dirt with little material, perhaps part of L29
Feature 31	Occupational level consisting of scattered ash, brown dirt, small riverine pebbles, bones, and some flint blades
Feature 26/Layer 32	Large circular fire pit filled with loose gray ash and cracked rocks
Feature 27/Layer 33	Small circular fire pit
Feature 34	Partly excavated occupational debris consisting of greenish tan dirt and some light gray ashes mixed with bones and flint blades
Layer 35 (D.T.)	Loose greenish soil with streaks of dark ash
Layer 36 (D.T.)	Clayish deposit with very little archaeological material
Layer 37 (D.T.)	Thick streaky layer of dark ash
Layer 38 (D.T.)	Clayish deposit with very little archaeological material
Layer 39 (D.T.)	Thick streaky layer of dark ash

APPENDIX 3
INDEX OF LOCI FROM THE 1976/77 AND 1977/78 SEASONS

As noted in the *Preface*, the abrupt and unexpected end to the Chogha Mish Project of the Oriental Institute in 1978/79 resulted in the loss of some important data gathered from both Chogha Mish and Chogha Bonut. As a result, there are a number of gaps in the stratigraphic information obtained in the course of the 1976/77 and 1977/78 seasons of excavations at Chogha Bonut. In this appendix, we have made every effort to present detailed descriptions of the available data on a number of loci presented in this volume. The following is by no means a comprehensive index of all the loci that appear on the top plans and/or described in the text. Ideally, we would have preferred to include a comprehensive list of objects found in each locus, but that information is scanty and, in any case, such information, when available, is indicated in the descriptive tables of objects.

J8:202

J8:202 is directly north of J9:203 W and J9:207. Apparently a rectangular room. Here there was ca. 30 cm of bulldozer debris, and the locus was heavily disturbed by animals burrows.

J9:201

J9:201 is a rather large, irregular, elongated stone pebble pavement directly west of K9:201. The locus is a high standing ridge of earth piled up by the bulldozer, with many Middle Susiana sherds. Parts of the stones were covered by a thin layer of mud plaster that could have been secondarily deposited because of the deterioration of the nearby walls of Buildings I and II. Below this level, reddish soil and a slab of yellow brown hard soil with black ashy material was found.

J9:206

J9:206 is a rectangular room directly north of J9:205, bordered on the west by J9:207. Tops of walls were encountered immediately below bulldozer debris. A floor was discovered at el. 78.31.

J9:207

J9:207 is a small rectangular room north of J9:204. Preserved tops of walls were found at el. 78.88. The bottom of excavation was reached at el. 78.24. The base of the walls lies at el. 78.17. The tops of the walls appeared approximately 50 cm below the bulldozer debris.

J9:209

J9:209 is one of the main rooms of Building I. The locus consists of a rather large L-shaped room in the northern part of the structure. To the north, it is bordered by J9:201 (pebble pavement) and to the south by J10:206 and J9:210. The eastern walls are better preserved than the western walls. On the middle of the east side of the locus some low partition walls were built against the higher standing eastern wall of J9:210. A buttress was used in the corner of the wall near the doorway of J9:210.

J9:210

J9:210 is a rectangular room with its north-south axis on the northwest side of Building I. A clear doorway into room J9:209 is preserved in the northern wall.

J10:202

J10:202 is an apparently roughly rectangular room directly west of J10:209. The southern wall has a raised squarish projection or pillar in the middle and the wall is to the west and east of the pillar.[41] The top of this feature is at el. 78.93. At el. 78.49 a floor was uncovered, the western part of which was orange grayish showing traces of fire.

---

41. No drawing or photograph of this feature was available, hence its absence from the plan.

J10:203

J10:203 is apparently a room-like enclosure; the preserved tops of the walls appeared immediately below the bulldozer debris at el. 78.97. The bright soil is soft with no special features.

J10:204

J10:204 is a very small, irregular, rectangular room bordered on the north by J10:20. The tops of the north, east, and south walls are preserved. The top of the south wall is covered by a fragmentary pebble pavement of probably a later phase. No doorway was found. A badly preserved floor of mud plaster and beaten earth was recovered at el. 78.71.

J10:206

J10:206 is a rectangular room on an east-west orientation in the middle of Building I. The locus was divided into east and west. Floors are preserved at el. 78.61–63. The border consists of a thin and low north-south wall. This wall, only 11–13 cm above the floor, is much lower than the surrounding walls. No entrance was discovered. On the eastern side of the locus, clear doorways were recovered in both the east-west walls that form the northern and southern walls of the locus, providing passage from J9:209 into J10:207 and the other kiln areas in the southern side of the central structure.

J10:207

J10:207 is a fairly rectangular room on a north-south orientation of the southernmost part of Building I. The entrance is through the north side and leads from J10:206 E. At the southern end there is a kiln of typical ovoid shape, separated from a similar one in J10:208 by means of a short north-south partition wall. The kiln is mounted on a rather high platform made of light brown straw-tempered clay. Directly opposite the partition wall, there is a similar short wall ending in what appears to be a buttress.

J10:208

J10:208 is a rectangular room in the southwest of Building I. To the north, it is bordered by J10:206 W, to the south by J10:209. At the south side of the locus, adjoining the east-west oriented south wall, there is a typical oval shaped kiln that was constructed on a platform. The preserved top of the slightly incurving walls of the kiln was found at ca. el. 79.80, rising only a few centimeters above the floor of the kiln, showing that the kiln was domed. The floor consisted of a minimum of three hard-packed burnt clay and straw layers. The stoke hole was located at its north side, but this is not clear. A large quantity of ash was discovered on the north side of the platform, another indication of the presence of the stoke hole on that side. The platform rests on a series of ash layers and floors, some 10 cm thick.

J10:209

J10:209 is a rectangular enclosure south of Building I. The main features are two kilns. The westernmost kiln rests upon a pisé platform as does the kiln in J10:208. The stoke hole is located in the east wall. The preserved top is at el. 79.22, and the floor is at el. 79.19. The walls are covered with reddish brown clay mixed with straw and gypsum flecks. The floor consists of hard dark reddish brown to black burnt clay.

On the east, the second smaller kiln was found. Roughly circular, its stoke hole faces west. The walls were built against the southern and eastern walls of the area. The tops of the walls are preserved at el. 79.38; the floor is at ca. el. 79.10. Enough of the wall was preserved to indicate curvature of the dome. Below the burnt layers of clay, a sherd bedding was found. The area between the two kilns was filled with ash.

J10:211

J10:211 is apparently a fairly regular mudbrick floor in front of and contiguous with a rectangular room to its west. The top of the floor was found at ca. el. 78.55.

K8:201

Most of K8:201 is an area that was heavily disturbed by the bulldozer. On the northern slope, just below the bulldozed level, stumps of walls were seen but not explored. Between the highest preserved level and the wall stumps, a thick layer of ash underlaid the surface deposit.

K9:201

K9:201 is a circular structure made of pisé wall and plastered with a hard coat of mud. The bottom is at el. 79.35.

K9:201–202

K9:201 is a large circular structure. Directly below bulldozed debris was the trace of a curving wall, the inner side of which was slightly leveled with plaster. The curving wall tapers out to west, southwest, and northeast. The entire interior face was plastered as its accumulation at the base of the wall indicates. Two courses of bricks were revealed, the top course was 11 cm thick. Immediately to the west of this installation, a ca. 85 × 40 cm patch of very dark brown material several centimeters deep was found. The interior material consisted of brownish earth mixed with bricky debris and soft brown earth. The floor was found at el. 79.35 sloping to 79.21. Underlying this, a similar structure, K9:202, was recovered. It was of roughly the same size and shape.

K9:202 is a kiln, partly destroyed by K9:201. The walls of this kiln consisted of an outer layer (15–25 cm thick) of light grayish pisé mixed with a large amount of gypsum, inside which is a layer (3–10 cm wide of mid to dark clay with three distinct linings) of hard (baked) clay. Four distinctive successive burnt floors were found inside the kiln.

K9:204

K9:204 is an elliptical pottery kiln made of pisé. The bottom elevation is not known.

K9:205

K9:205 is a rectangular room in Building IV with beaten earth floor at el. 78.49.

K9:206

K9:206 is a squarish room on the southeastern corner of Building IV, with a beaten earth floor mixed with gypsum. No doorways were found in the low preserved walls.

K9:207

K9:207 is an area east of Building IV consisting of a small pebble pavement at el. 78.22 and a fragmentary wall parallel to the eastern wall of K9:206. The pebbles were mostly fire cracked and blackened, one with a red ochre stain. This area is presumably the space between Building IV and another to its east, now completely destroyed by bulldozer.

K10:201

K10:201 is a mudbrick "platform" partly under kiln K10:204. It consisted of one layer of bricks measuring 37 × 20 × 9 and 41 × 23 × 10 cm. Below the bricks was a layer of ashy earth with traces of burning.

K10:202

K10:202 is a deep well, presumably dating to the Late Susiana 2 phase. The locus was excavated to a depth of 5.50 m, at which point work was stopped for safety reasons. The fill consisted of alternating soft gray earth and hard light brown clay. The bottom is at el. 74.25.

K10:203

K10:203 is a rectangular room of Building III. The walls are mud plastered. The east wall has a stone foundation, superimposed by at least five courses of mudbricks with dark mortar.

K10:204

K10:204 is an elliptical kiln paved with sherds. The bottom is at el. 79.13.

K10:204 S

NA

K10:205 E

NA

K10:209

K10:209 is a roughly oval-shaped kiln south of a similar kiln (K10:204) with rather irregular walls (10–40 cm thick and 40 cm high). Walls were made of hard clay pisé mixed with gypsum plaster flakes. The walls curve slightly inward, suggesting a domed structure. The floor consisted of a thin burnt black layer with an underlying sherd pavement at el. 79.10.

K10:211

K10:211 is a circular oven (kiln?) immediately north of K10:212 and south of kiln K9:204. The walls are made of mud mixed with straw. Several floor levels were uncovered, the topmost of which is hard and ca. 3–6 mm thick. Under this, two layers of burnt orange brown to black ashy soil including a sherd pavement were found. Below this a second hard fired floor similar to the topmost one was encountered. Below, one more burnt brown to gray soil layer and a second sherd pavement were found.

K10:212

K10:212 is a rectangular room of a building destroyed, perhaps in antiquity. The east wall consisted of two courses of bricks with a buttress in the middle. A narrow doorway was found in the southern wall. Patches of hard earth may have belonged to the original floor.

K11:202

K11:202 is a general area southwest of Building III. Traces of a floor were found at el. 79.00, over which a blackish ashy layer was found. Over this ashy deposit a greenish earth layer covers the area. Scattered in the area, presumably as a result of bulldozer destruction, were sherds of Late Middle Susiana type, a badly destroyed skull with some bones, mostly ribs and vertebrae, the skull of a child and some other long bones, chin bones, a jaw, one tooth, and few other skeletal fragments. The top of the skull was at el. 78.56. Located nearby were very badly preserved skeletal remains of an adult. If these bones belonged to individual graves, they must have been simple pits. Lower down, at el. 78.08 to the south of the child's skull, was found a circular hearth ca. 60 × 60 cm consisting of burnt fire-broken pebbles in a shallow hole dug into a hard gray clay or pisé floor of some Archaic/Formative structure now destroyed. More skull fragments were found in the area, indicating some sort of concentration of graves.

L9:201

L9:201 is a hard floor of yellowish brown and bricky texture reached at el. 77.30. Connected with this floor are several hearths, three consisting of fire-cracked pebbles mixed with loose soil in round depressions dug into the floor. In another, similar pebbles in a deep circular hole were found. Another is a squarish area of burnt soil with a few fire-cracked pebbles. On the side, long, cigar-shaped, finger-impressed mudbricks were found. The floor is flat and regular except for the northeastern part where it becomes bumpy and uneven, possibly the floor of a courtyard. A number of successive floors were found beneath the topmost one, all with circular fire pits. No plans or other information are available.

L9:202 N

L9:202 N is a rather confused area with scattered stones and what seem to be fragments of a mudbrick platform consisting of four roughly parallel bricks that rest on loose gray earth. A pile of bones ca. 10 cm deep and some complete teeth of presumably sheep/goat were discovered at the base of the platform. The western part of this area contained at least three small circular fire pits filled with ash and fire-cracked rocks as well as some large pebbles stained with red ochre and a number of flint tools.

L9:203

L9:203 is presumably an open area with at least two circular fire pits (only one could be located on the plan), filled with fire-cracked rocks. The fire pit was cut into a bricky floor/surface next to a large, rounded flattish stone, ca. 28 × 7 cm, with a red ochre stain. Two fragments of an apparent child's skull were found amid some scattered rocks to the east of the fire pit.

L10:202

L10:202 is a circular bin made of pisé. The bottom elevation is unknown.

L10:207

L10:207 is the interior of a squarish room dated to the Formative Susiana period. The floor was partially preserved and consisted of tightly packed pebbles and soft brownish black earth mixed with Formative period sherds. One course of finger-impressed bricks on the north side was all that remained of the wall. The eastern wall was much better preserved with its top at el. 77.48.

L10:203 S

L10:203 S is a rectangular room dated to the Formative Susiana period. The western part of the locus had been destroyed, but the eastern part consisted of a fragmentary floor made of beaten earth mixed with some sherds, pebbles, and few burnt spots.

L10:204

NA

L10:205

L10:205 is a rectangular room with walls made of long bricks. The presumed part of the floor shows signs of burning. The bottom is at el. 77.28.

L10:207

NA

L11:201

L11:201 consists of a small rectangular bin-like structure inside the eastern part of K11:201. The bin was constructed of very thin, irregular walls. The southern, eastern, and western walls were built against the plastered surface of the east-west wall of Middle Susiana Building III. The base of the bin was at el. 78.69.

L11:202

L11:202 is a patch of pebbles perhaps related to a very badly preserved wall made of long bricks (not located on the plan), on a greenish clay layer. Next to this patch of stones is a mudbrick "platform" (not located on the plan). The base of this feature was covered with a thick layer of mudbrick detritus, presumably belonging to a wall.

L11:203

NA

M8; M9; M10; M11

These areas were most heavily damaged by the bulldozer. The available records list the descriptions of a number of excavated loci, but they are excluded from the index because none of these loci could be located on the top plan.

INDEX OF GEOGRAPHICAL NAMES

Abadan	13
Abu Hureyra	10
Agha Jari Hills	13
Ahvaz	13–14
Ain Ghazal	85
Ali Kosh, Tappeh	5–9, 22, 45, 67, 85, 123–26, 137, 139–42, 149
Anatolia	1, 9, 85
Anau	85
Andimeshk	6
Asiab, Tappeh	5–6, 8, 85
Aswad, Tell	10, 85
Bakun, Tall-e	18
Beidha	85
Beisamoun	85
Bendebal	47
Çan Hassan	85
Çayönü	70, 85, 125–26
Chogha Bonut	1–9, 14–15, 17–28, 30, 33–35, 40, 43–47, 52, 67–69, 85, 91, 93, 123–27, 129, 131, 137–42, 149, 150, 153
Chogha Mami	6
Chogha Mish	1–2, 4, 6–8, 14, 19, 28, 43–45, 47–48, 67–68, 70, 85, 149–50, 153
Chogha Sefid	6, 8, 43, 45, 48, 67–68
Dar Khazineh	6, 21
Dawairij River	6
Deh Luran plain	2, 4–8, 43, 45, 47, 67, 137, 149
Demircihüyük	85
Dez River	4, 14
Dezful	13–14, 17, 139, 141
Dimcheh	14
Gachsaran	14
Ganj Darreh	5–6, 8–9, 22, 85
Gargar River	14
Haji Firuz	45
Hakalān	4
Hendijan River	14
Iran	1–2, 4–5, 8–9, 13, 19, 31, 45, 85, 91, 123, 137, 140, 142
Iranian central plateau	45, 67
Iraq	8, 13, 85
Jafarabad	47
Jarmo	6, 8–9, 45, 67–68, 85
Jarrahi River	14
Jeitun	45, 85
Jericho	10, 85
Jordan	1, 9, 85,
Karkheh River	4, 14
Karun River	14
Kermanshah	5
Khuzestan	6–7, 13–15, 21, 43, 47
Levant	9, 85, 124
M'lefaat	85
Maghzaliyah, Tell	85
Meimeh River	6
Mesopotamia	2, 4, 31, 67, 91, 149
Mianab region	45
Mureybet	10, 85
Nativ Hagdud	10
'Oueili, Tell el-	6
Parchineh	4
Persian Gulf	2, 13
Qabr-e Sheikheyn	47
Qara Su River	5
Qum	4
Ras al-'Amiya	140
Sabz, Tappeh	47, 140
Sang-e Chakhmaq, Tappeh	45, 67
Sarab	6, 8, 45, 67–68
Shaur River	14
Shush	14
Shushtar	13–15, 21, 45
Sialk, Tappeh	4, 45
Susa	1–2, 14, 45, 47
Susangerd	13
Syria	1, 9, 85
Taurus Mountains	124
Tehran	19
Tuleii, Tappeh	5–8, 14, 19, 43, 45, 48, 67
Turkmanestan	45, 85
Zagheh, Tappeh	45, 85
Zagros Mountains	1, 4–6, 9, 13–14, 21–22, 34, 45, 67, 124, 141

PLATES

Plate 1

(A) Staff of the 1996 Season of Excavation at Chogha Bonut. Standing (left to right): Hamidreza Tabrizian, Farhad Jafary, Abbas Alizadeh, Hasan Rezvani, Gabriel Nokandeh; (sitting): Abbas Moqadam, Quli Muhammadnezhad (village boy), Behruz Omrani; (B) the Late Haj Qapuni (our majordomo, sitting third from right) and His Extended Bakhtiari Family; and (C) (left to right): Ebrahim Kamali, Ali Qulami, and Quli Mohammadnezhad, Three Boys from the Village of Upper Bonut

Plate 2

(A) Panoramic View of Chogha Bonut, View West, (B) Panoramic View of Chogha Bonut, View East, and
(C) Test Trench at the Eastern Base of Chogha Bonut

Plate 3

(A) Square M10 Prior to Excavation, View Southeast, (B) Excavations in Square M10, View Northwest, and (C) Excavations in Square M10, View Southeast

Plate 4

A

B

(A) *In Situ* Dry-sieving in Square M10 and
(B) Members of the 1996 Expedition in the Process of Flotation at Susa Castle

Plate 5

(A) Straw-tempered Mudbrick Fragment from Aceramic Level in Square M10 (Scale ca. 1:3), (B) Piece of Red Ochre on Feature 28, and (C) an Early Neolithic Circular Fire Pit with Rocks in Feature 34

Plate 6

(A) Top View of Feature 28 Showing Articulated Sheep/Goat Legs and a Circular Fire Pit, (B) Close-up of Sheep/Goat Horn on Feature 28, and (C) Close-up of Articulated Sheep/Goat Legs and Horn on Feature 28

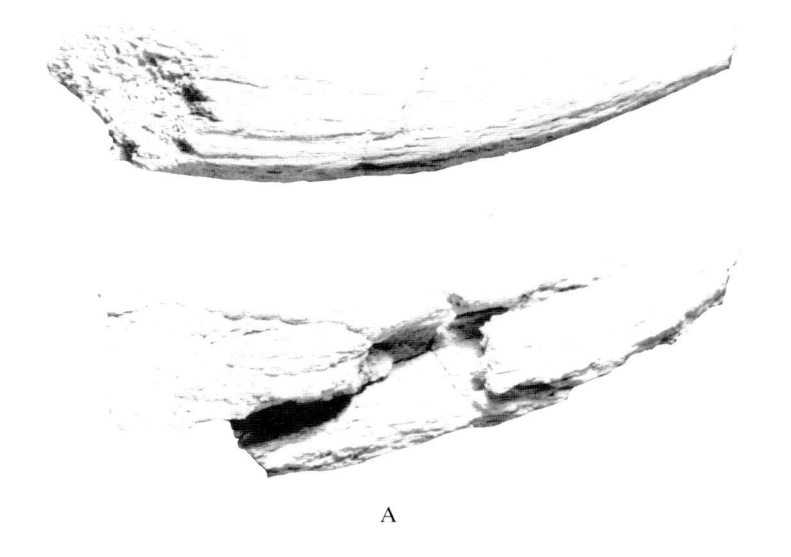

(A) Sheep/Goat Horns from Feature 28 (Scale 3:4) and (B) Top View of Feature 18 with Fire Pits and Root/Animal Holes

Plate 8

A

B

(A) Feature 31 Showing Patch of White Ash and Unexcavated Fire Pits, View West, and
(B) Features 31 and 34 with Southern Balk of Square M10, Showing Deep Trench

Plate 9

A

B

(A) View of the Stratigraphic Trench, View West, and (B) Northern Balk of Square M10

Plate 10

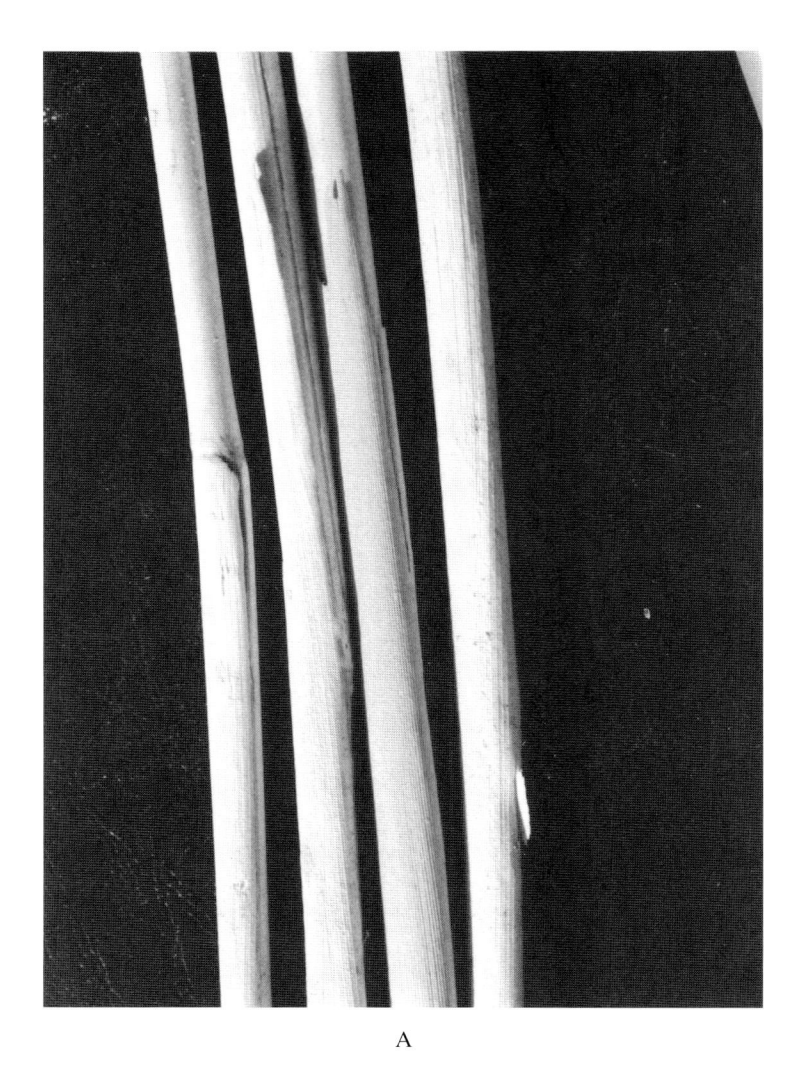

(A) Samples of Reeds from the Vicinity of Chogha Bonut and
(B) Reed Impressions on the Northwestern Corner of Feature 28

Plate 11

(A) Late Middle Susiana Building I, View South, and (B) Kiln J10:209 (foreground) and Building I, View East

Plate 12

A

B

(A) Late Middle Susiana Kilns in Building I, View South, and (B) Late Middle Susiana Kiln K10:209

Plate 13

A

B

(A) Late Middle Susiana Oven K10:205, View South, and
(B) Late Middle Susiana Circular Structure K9:201, View South

Plate 14

Long Cigar-shaped Mudbricks of Archaic Susiana 0 Building in L11, View East

Plate 15

	Field Number	Findspot	Elevation	Description
A	CB 241	L13	74.80	Pounder, sandstone, somewhat worn on the poles
B	CB 242	F14	74.75	Pounder, sandstone, uneven surface
C	CB 243	L1	76.10–75.00	Pounder, sandstone, uneven surface
D	CB 181	S.T.	76.80	Pounder, conglomerate stone, concave on both poles
E	CB 244	F31	74.05	Pestle(?), Limestone, very smooth surface
F	CB 245	L27	74.15	Pounder, blackish gray stone, smoothed
G	CB 246	L30	74.10–74.05	Rubbing stone (quern?), one side smooth and concave, one side rough
H	CB 247	F14	74.75	Pestle(?), blackish gray stone, rounded base
I	CB 248	F15	74.70	Pestle(?), sandstone, rounded base
J	CB 249	L21	74.25	Pestle(?), dark gray stone, both ends rounded

Various Stone Objects

Plate 16. Stone Objects and Bullet-shaped Flint Cores

	Field Number	*Findspot*	*Elevation*	*Description*
A	NA (Bonut 1978)	NA	NA	Bullet-shaped flint core. Scale ca. 2:5
B	NA (Bonut 1978)	NA	NA	Bullet-shaped flint core. Scale ca. 2:5
C	B I-4	L10:103	NA	Stone mortar. Marble(?). Interior with considerable traces of dark red pigment. Height 4.2 cm. Diameter 8.0–8.5 cm
D	NA (Bonut 1978)	NA	NA	Fragment of bullet-shaped flint core. Scale ca. 2:5
E	NA (Bonut 1978)	NA	NA	Flint core. Scale ca. 2:5
F	B II-14	K10:208	77.52	Mace-head, conglomerate stone. Bored from one end which has a marked flat rim ca. 3–4 mm wide. Highly polished. Height 7.6 cm. Diameter 5.5 cm
G	B II-21	K10:208	78.00	Stone hoe or scraper. Black stone with gray cortex. Obverse smooth, natural surface. Length 23.5 cm. Thickness 3.3 cm
H	B 2114	K10:205	78.93	Stone scraper or adze. Grayish green stone. Edges show sign of wear, smooth back. Scale ca. 2:5
I	NA (Bonut 1978)	NA	NA	Flint blade. Scale ca. 2:5
J	NA (Bonut 1978)	NA	NA	Flint blade. Scale ca. 2:5
K	NA (Bonut 1978)	NA	NA	Flint blade. Scale ca. 2:5

Plate 16

A

B

C

D

E

F

G

H

I

J

K

Stone Objects and Bullet-shaped Flint Cores

Plate 17. Various Small Clay Objects, Small Stone Objects, and Stone Vessel Fragments

	Field Number	Findspot	Elevation	Description
A	CB 28	F14	74.75	Fragment of either a token or a finger-shaped clay figurine. Well-baked dark buff clay with no visible inclusion
B	CB 26	F14	74.75	Finger-shaped baked clay figurine. Grayish buff paste with no visible inclusion. Both ends broken
C	CB 54	L11	75.00	Finger-shaped baked clay figurine. Dark gray core with no visible inclusion
D	CB 27	F14	74.75	Finger-shaped baked clay figurine. Grayish buff paste with no visible inclusion. Base broken
E	CB 2	S.T.	77.20	Finger-shaped baked clay figurine. Gray paste with some chaff. No visible inclusion, smoothed
F	CB 1	S.T.	75.00	Front and side views of a finger-shaped stone figurine. Gray stone, polished
G	CB 101	F14	74.75	Finger-shaped baked clay figurine, warm buff with some gray spots, no visible inclusion
H	CB 250	L21	74.25	Finger-shaped baked clay figurine, warm buff clay with no visible inclusion
I	CB 43	L21	74.25	Finger-shaped baked clay figurine. Orange buff paste with no visible inclusion. Concave base
J	CB 44	L21	74.25	Finger-shaped baked clay figurine. Warm buff paste with no visible inclusion. Flat base
K	CB 17	F14	74.75	Finger-shaped baked clay figurine. Light gray paste with some fine chaff
L	CB 5	L1	76.10–75.00	Finger-shaped stone figurine. Limestone? Lower part is separated by a ridge
M	CB 13	L13	74.80	Fragment of a well-baked clay figurine. Warm buff paste with no visible inclusion. Two appendages on either side may represent anatomical parts
N	CB 13	L13	74.80	Back view of M above
O	CB 48	F14	74.75	Baked clay figurine. Gray paste with no visible inclusion. The body is mounted by a series of elongated lumps of clay indicating perhaps "hair" and facial features in a highly abstract form
P	CB 48	F14	74.75	Another view of O above
Q	CB 63	F14	74.75	Stone "ring"/"spacer." Alabaster
R	CB 4	F15	74.70	Tubular baked clay figurine. Warm buff paste with no visible inclusion. A snake-like applique runs the length of the main shaft with broken ends
S	CB 3	L1	76.10–75.00	Two-thirds of a T-shaped figurine. Well-baked gray clay with no visible inclusion. Head and face are emphasized by a depression on the back and projection on the front
T	CB 62	F14	74.75	Fragment of a stone bracelet. Veined stone, smoothed, no tool marks
U	CB 65	F22/L24	74.25	Fragment of a stone bracelet. Gray stone, very smooth
V	CB 69	L30	74.10	Alabaster stone vessel fragment. Very smooth, no visible scraping marks
W	CB 68	L1	76.10–75.00	Stone vessel fragment. Beige stone with some light brown spots. Chisel and fine scraping marks on the exterior. Very smooth

Plate 17

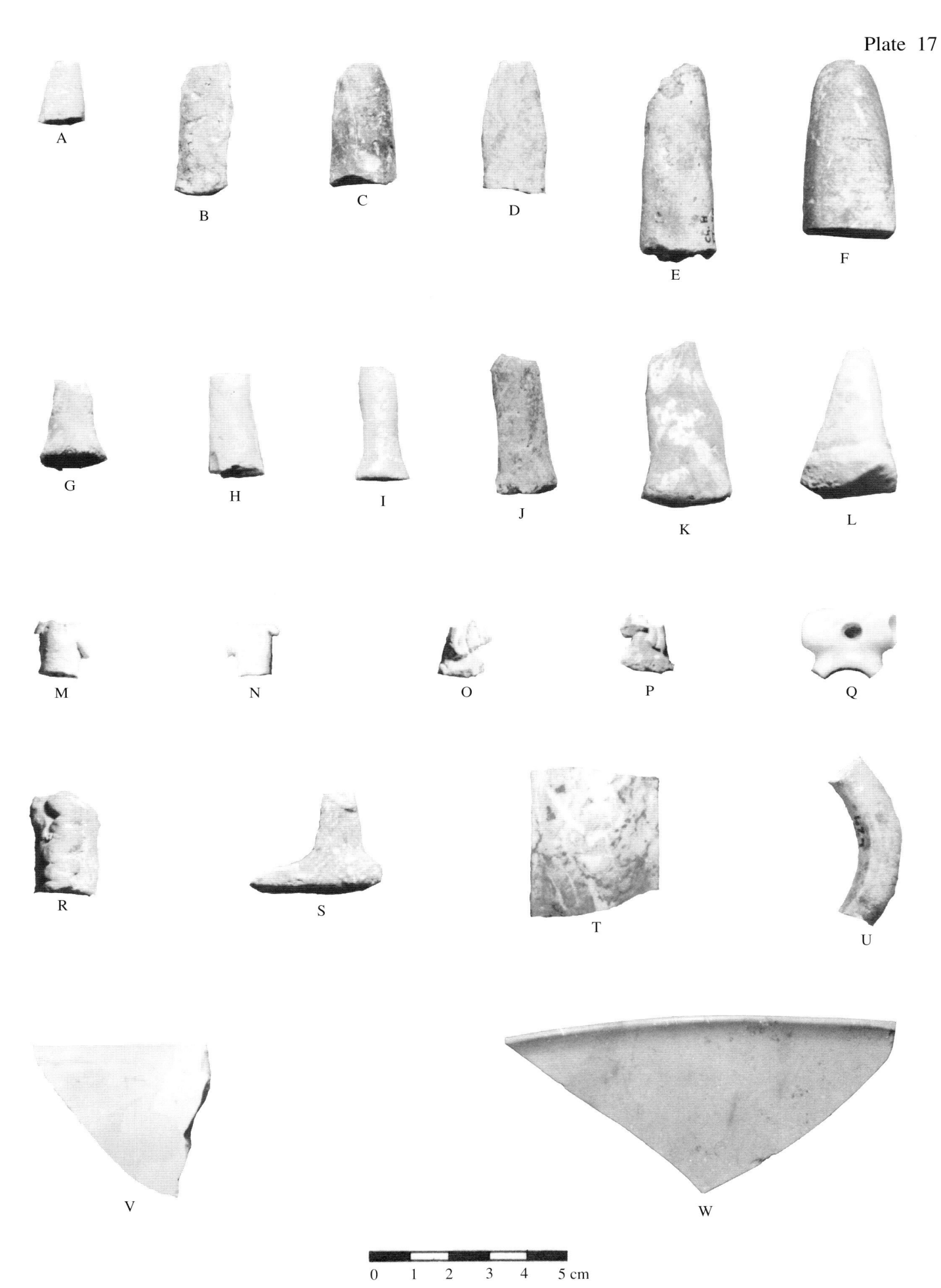

A B C D E F

G H I J K L

M N O P Q

R S T U

V W

0 1 2 3 4 5 cm

Various Small Clay Objects, Small Stone Objects, and Stone Vessel Fragments

Plate 18. Clay Figurines and Horn-like Clay Object

	Field Number	Findspot	Elevation	Description
A	NA (Bonut 1978)	NA	NA	Fragment of a baked clay T-shaped figurine. Warm buff clay with no visible inclusion. Few incised marks on the back. Length 3 cm
B	B 2118	J10:201	NA	Fragment of a baked clay T-shaped figurine. Grayish buff clay with light gray core, no visible inclusion. Length 2.3 cm
C	B 2128	L9:201	77.85	Base of a baked clay T-shaped figurine. Buff clay, few incised marks on the back. No visible inclusion. Length 2.2 cm
D	B 2038	NA	NA	Base of a baked clay T-shaped figurine. Grayish buff clay with no visible inclusion. Length 5 cm
E	B 2165	L9:202	78.68	Fragment of a female figurine of well-baked brownish clay. Figure seems to be represented in a sitting position. Broken lower part revealing the technique used in making the two round leg sections separately. The genitalia are indicated with a lump of clay with criss-cross incisions
F	B 2233	K11:202	78.06	Unbaked clay T-shaped figurine. Warm buff clay with no visible inclusion. The upright shaft extends from the base with slight bend. Scoring and incised marks on the base and "head." Height 3 cm
G	B 2060	K10:205	79.08	Horn-like baked clay object, perhaps counting device. Four finger imprints on one side and eight on the other. Coarse paste ranges in color from yellowish buff to grayish buff. Chaff tempered mixed with some grits. Length 22.5 cm

Plate 18

A

B

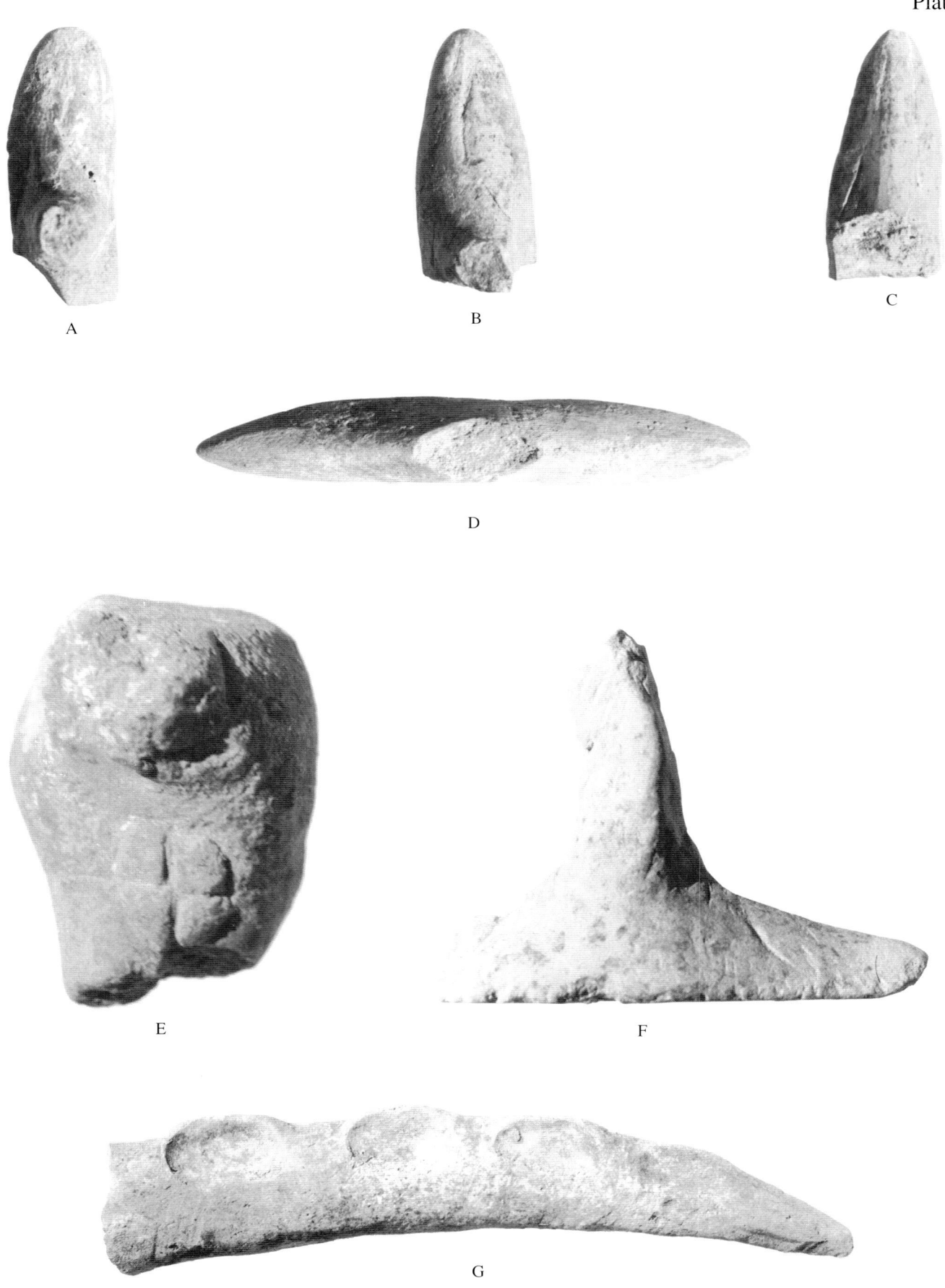

C

D

E

F

G

Clay Figurines and Horn-like Clay Object

Plate 19. Various Clay Tokens

	Field Number	Findspot	Elevation	Description
A	CB 36	F14	74.75	Button-shaped baked clay token. Grayish buff paste with no visible inclusion. Rough base
B	CB 251	L13	74.80	Bean-shaped sealing? Warm buff clay with no visible inclusion. Reed impression on one side
C	CB 38	F14	74.75	Button-shaped baked clay token. Light gray. Concave base
D	CB 32	F14	74.75	Button-shaped baked clay token. Warm buff clay with no visible inclusion. Rough top, smooth base
E	CB 50	F14	74.75	Plano convex-shaped baked clay sealing/token. Dark gray surface. Matt impression on the bottom
F	CB 36	F14	74.75	Back of A above
G	CB 251	L13	74.80	Back of B above
H	CB 38	F14	74.75	Back of C above
I	CB 32	F14	74.75	Back of D above
J	CB 50	F14	74.75	Back of E above
K	CB 16	L13	74.80	Spherical baked clay token. Dark gray surface
L	CB 34	F14	74.75	Spherical baked clay token. Buff surface
M	CB 220d	F14	74.75	Round baked clay token, slightly fired
N	CB 33	F14	74.75	Spherical baked clay token. Light gray surface with cloth impression on one side
O	CB 220a	F14	74.75	Round baked clay token, slightly fired. Found together with CB 220b–e
P	CB 16	L13	74.80	Back of K above
Q	CB 34	F14	74.75	Back of L above
R	CB 220d	F14	74.75	Back of M above
S	CB 33	F14	74.75	Back of N above
T	CB 220a	F14	74.75	Back of O above
U	CB 35	F14	74.75	Spherical baked clay token with one side flattened. Light gray color
V	CB 15	L13	74.80	Dome-shaped baked clay token with concave base. Grayish buff
W	CB 39	S.T.	74.40–74.20	Disc-shaped baked clay token. Dark gray clay with no visible inclusion. Concave top and bottom
X	CB 61	L21	74.21	Conical baked clay token. Grayish buff paste with no visible inclusion. Flat base
Y	CB 7	L1	76.10–75.00	Ovoid-shaped baked clay token. Warm buff paste with no visible inclusion. Compare Baykal-Seeher and Obladen-Kauder 1996, pp. 355–56, pl. 103: 1–12; Wilkinson, Monahan, and Tucker 1996, pp. 39–41, fig. 14: 1–4
Z	CB 6	L1	76.10–75.00	Ovoid-shaped baked clay token. Warm buff paste with no visible inclusion. Compare Baykal-Seeher and Obladen-Kauder 1996, pp. 355–56, pl. 103: 1–12; Wilkinson, Monahan, and Tucker 1996, pp. 39–41, fig. 14: 1–4

Plate 19

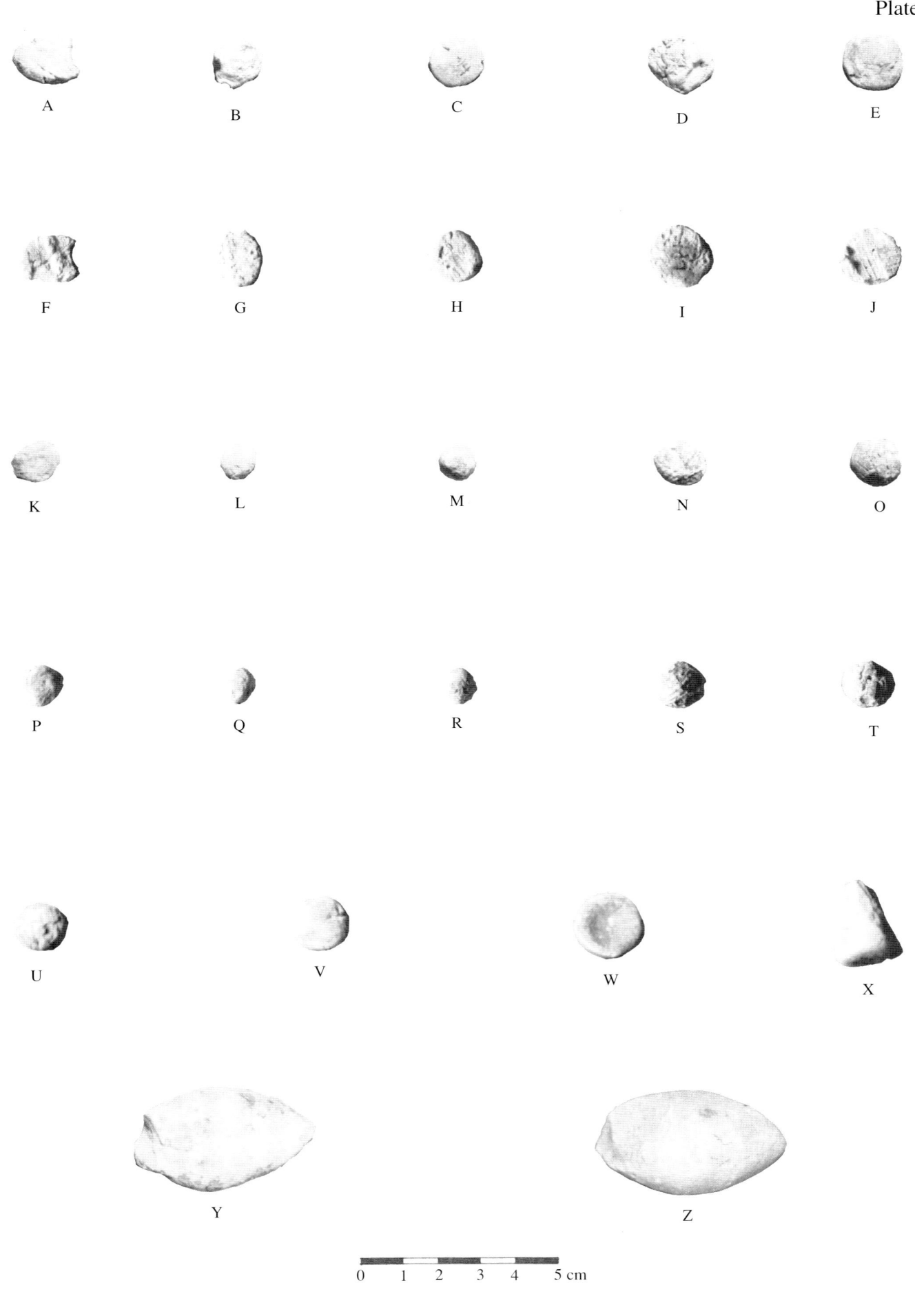

A	B	C	D	E
F	G	H	I	J
K	L	M	N	O
P	Q	R	S	T
U	V	W	X
Y	Z

0 1 2 3 4 5 cm

Various Clay Tokens

Plate 20

Plate 20. Late Middle Susiana Administrative "Tablets." Scale ca. 3:2

	Field Number	Findspot	Elevation	Description
A	B 2113	L10:203	77.40	Top view of B. Spherical lump of kneaded clay ("tablet") with no visible inclusion. Flattened on one side. Round impression on top center surrounded by punctated marks in an almost concentric pattern. Below the punctated marks, fingernail impression, see B
B	B 2113	L10:203	77.40	Side view of A above
C	NA (Bonut 1978)	NA	NA	Baked clay "tablet" with fingernail impressions

Plate 20

A

B

C

Late Middle Susiana Administrative "Tablets." Scale ca. 3:2

Plate 21. Various Types of Formative Susiana Pottery

	Field Number	Findspot	Elevation	Description
A	CB 212	S.T.	75.50	Straw-tempered soft ware: Buff ware. Dark gray core where thicker near the base. Straw tempered, straw face. Lightly fired. Exterior mottled red. Traces of fugitive red paint or wash visible on the exterior
B	CB 252	S.T.	75.60	Straw-tempered soft ware: Buff ware. Dark gray core where thicker. Straw tempered, straw face. Lightly fired. Exterior mottled red
C	CB 253	S.T.	75.55	Straw-tempered soft ware: Buff ware. Gray core, straw tempered, straw face. Mottled red and gray
D	CB 254	S.T.	75.65	Straw-tempered soft ware: Buff ware. Grayish buff core grading to brownish buff towards surface. Straw tempered, straw face, possibly red wash on the exterior
E	CB 209	S.T.	76.20	Smeared-painted ware: Dark gray core sandwiched between two thin pale red and buff layers (exterior 1 mm and interior 2 mm thick). Interior pale bricky exterior warm buff. Chaff and straw tempered. Fine mica included. Brown paint, presumably applied with fingers, smeared on the surface. Burnished
F	CB 255	S.T.	76.05	Smeared-painted ware: Gray core, straw tempered. Reddish brown wash smeared over the exterior
G	CB 256	S.T.	76.00	Smeared-painted ware: Gray core, straw tempered. Reddish brown wash smeared on the exterior
H	CB 257	S.T.	76.00	Smeared-painted ware: Pale gray core. Straw tempered. Uneven, vertical bands finger-painted(?) in light brown on the exterior
I	CB 210	L13	74.80	Smeared-painted ware: Gray core sandwiched by two (2 mm thick) layers of warm buff. Chaff tempered. Cream buff slip. Maroon paint, presumably applied with fingers. Crackled face. Intrusive
J	CB 258	S.T.	76.10	Smeared-painted ware: Gray core. Straw tempered. Reddish brown wash smeared on the exterior, mottled red and gray
K	CB 233	L1	76.10–75.00	Orange buff plain ware: Core: interior layer light gray, exterior layer reddish buff. Chaff tempered. Interior pale bricky red slip, exterior orange red slip. Maroon paint, burnished to shine
L	CB 232	L1	76.10–75.00	Orange buff plain ware: Same as K above
M	CB 204	L1	76.10–75.00	Orange buff plain ware: Dark gray core sandwiched between two (2 mm thick) layers of light red. Chaff tempered. Light orange buff slipped, red spots on the exterior. Thin black paint
N	CB 205	L13	74.80	Maroon-on-cream painted ware: Buff ware. Dark gray core sandwiched between two (1–2 mm thick) buff layers. Chaff tempered. Cream slip all over. Jet black paint, highly burnished. Intrusive
O	CB 206	S.T.	77.20	Maroon-on-cream painted ware: Buff ware. Grayish buff core where thicker. Creamy buff exterior and interior. Cream slipped. Thin dark brown paint; both surfaces crackled
P	CB 235	L1	76.10–75.00	Maroon-on-cream painted ware: Warm buff ware. Chaff and occasional grits included. Cream buff slip, maroon paint, burnished. Crackled face. Maroon wash all over
Q	CB 236	L1	76.10–75.00	Maroon-on-cream painted ware: Warm buff ware. Chaff and occasional grits included. Cream buff slip, maroon paint, burnished. Crackled face. Maroon wash all over
R	CB 211a	S.T.	77.00	Maroon-on-cream painted ware: Pink buff ware. Chaff tempered. Cream slipped and burnished all over. Thin dark paint, mostly eroded
S	CB 259	S.T.	76.90	Maroon-on-cream painted ware: Lip fragment. Straw-tempered brownish buff clay with gray core. Brown wash smeared and burnished
T	CB 211b	S.T.	76.95	Maroon-on-cream painted ware: Pink buff ware. Chaff tempered. Cream slipped and burnished all over. Thin dark paint, mostly eroded
U	CB 260	S.T.	76.90	Orange buff plain ware: Lip and body fragment. Gray core; straw tempered. Red wash on exterior, straw face
V	CB 238	L13	74.80	Orange buff plain ware: Lip and body fragment. Thin gray core. Chaff tempered. Pale red slip all over. Deep maroon paint, the painted area is burnished
W	CB 261	S.T.	76.90	Orange buff plain ware: Lip and body fragment of a closed form. Chaff tempered. Pale red clay with some calcite(?) particles. Red-orange wash all over, burnished
X	CB 240	S.T.	76.20	Smeared-painted ware: Chaff tempered. Light maroon slip/wash all over. Deep maroon paint is smeared on the highly burnished surface, plain where paint bubbles burst
Y	CB 262	S.T.	76.90	Orange buff plain ware: Lip and body fragment of a closed form. Chaff tempered ware. Pale red clay with some calcite particles. Red-orange wash all over, burnished
Z	CB 263	S.T.	76.90	Orange buff plain ware: Lip and body fragment of a closed form. Chaff tempered with some calcite(?) particles. Red-orange wash all over, burnished

Plate 21

0   2   5 cm

Various Types of Formative Susiana Pottery

Plate 22. Formative Susiana Straw-tempered Soft Ware. Scale 1:1

	Field Number	*Findspot*	*Elevation*	*Description*
A	NA (Bonut 1978)	M10	NA	Straw-tempered soft ware: Primitive coarse ware. Fragment of a body sherd formed against a basket. Not well baked, straw tempered
B	B 1123	M10:103	76.33	Straw-tempered soft ware: Coarse ware. Orange buff clay with light gray core, heavily chaff tempered
C	NA (Bonut 1978)	M10	NA	Straw-tempered soft ware: Coarse ware. Body fragment of straw-tempered soft ware. Light gray core, straw face
D	B 2188	L9:201	NA	Straw-tempered soft ware: Coarse buff ware. Base and body fragment of a straw-tempered. straw face soft ware. Both surfaces smoothed

Plate 22

A

B

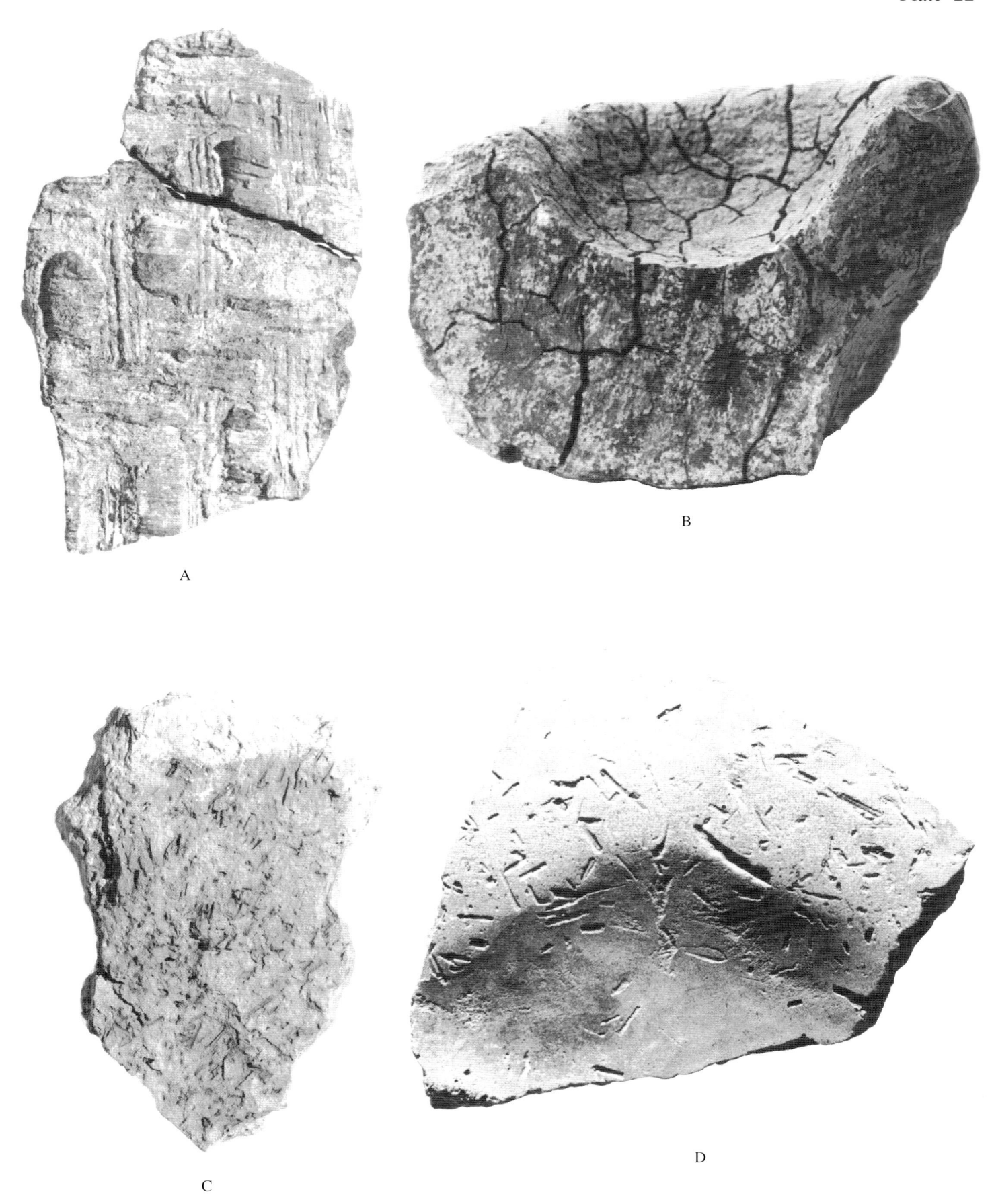

C

D

Formative Susiana Straw-tempered Soft Ware. Scale 1:1

Plate 23. Formative Susiana Smeared-painted Ware. Scale 1:1

	Field Number	Findspot	Elevation	Description
A	B 1060	M10:103	76.50	Smeared-painted ware: Body fragment, brownish buff clay with gray core. Staw tempered, surface yellowish ochre. Red paint smeared with fingers
B	B 1096	NA	NA	Smeared-painted ware: Orange buff ware. Gray core changing to buff. Straw tempered. Rough interior. Orange buff wash on exterior over which red paint is applied, presumably with fingers, burnished
C	B 2111	L10:202	76.00	Smeared-painted ware: Lip and body fragment. Light brown buff with light gray core. Straw tempered, smoothed. Reddish brown paint
D	NA (Bonut 1978)	NA	NA	Smeared-painted body sherd. Description not available

Plate 23

A

B

C

D

Formative Susiana Smeared-painted Ware. Scale 1:1

Plate 24. Archaic Susiana Painted-burnished Variant Ware. Scale 1:1

	Field Number	Findspot	Elevation	Description
A	B 2195	L10:206	77.47	Painted-burnished variant ware: Orange buff ware. Gray core, chaff tempered. Dark brown paint, burnished; the painted area is shinier
B	B 2107	L10:207	77.75	Painted-burnished variant ware: Orange buff ware. Gray core. Chaff tempered, mottled surface, burnished. Chaff face where eroded
C	B 2158	L10:204	77.90	Painted-burnished variant ware: Reddish buff ware. Gray core. Dense paste, chaff tempered. Brownish orange paint, burnished
D	B 2174	L10:203	77.46	Painted-burnished variant ware: Grayish buff ware. Buff core, chaff tempered. Light brown paint, burnished
E	B 2143	L10:203	78.02	Painted-burnished variant ware: Light brownish buff ware. Light gray core. Chaff tempered. Chaff face where eroded. Mottled surface. Light brown paint, burnished

Plate 24. Archaic Susiana Painted-burnished Variant Ware. Scale 1:1

Plate 25. (A) Flint Blades, (B–D) Painted-burnished Variant Ware, and (E–K) Maroon-on-Cream Painted Ware

	Field Number	*Findspot*	*Elevation*	*Description*
A	—	—	—	Various flint blades
B	CB 231	L1	76.10–75.00	Painted-burnished variant ware: Buff ware. Grayish buff core, straw tempered. Thick bricky red slip. Dark paint, burnished, straw face where surface eroded
C	CB 230	L1	76.10–75.00	Painted-burnished variant ware: Buff ware. Dense clay with some fine chaff. Dark brown paint, burnished
D	CB 264	S.T.	77.30	Painted-burnished variant ware: Buff ware. Base and body fragment. Straw tempered dark buff clay with some air pockets. Probably slipped. Brown paint, burnished
E	CB 200	S.T.	77.10	Maroon-on-cream painted ware: Lip and body fragment of a closed form (hole mouth). Straw and chaff tempered. Cream slipped. Light maroon paint; painted area burnished. The hole appears to have been closed with bitumen, lumps of which were still attached to the interior surface
F	CB 199	L1	76.10–75.00	Maroon-on-cream painted ware: Lip and body fragment of a straight-sided vessel with flaring rim. Straw and chaff tempered warm buff paste. Cream slipped. Maroon paint, highly burnished
G	CB 201	S.T.	77.00	Maroon-on-cream painted ware: Body fragment. Chaff tempered grayish buff core sandwiched by two layers of pale red clay. Cream slipped. Maroon paint, burnished, chaff face where slip is eroded
H	CB 197	S.T.	76.85	Maroon-on-cream painted ware: Grayish buff core. Straw tempered. Cream slipped outside. Deep maroon paint. Inside all burnt black presumably as result of secondary use
I	CB 265	S.T.	77.10	Maroon-on-cream painted ware: Body fragment. Chaff and straw tempered. Cream slipped. Maroon paint. Painted area burnished
J	CB 207	S.T.	77.20	Maroon-on-cream painted ware: Dark gray core. Chaff tempered. Cream slip all over. Maroon paint, highly burnished
K	CB 196	S.T.	76.80	Maroon-on-cream painted ware: Gray core sandwiched between a 4 mm reddish buff layer on the inside and a 2 mm reddish buff on the outside. Straw tempered. Cream slip/wash all over. Deep maroon paint. Burnished shinier than the body

Plate 25

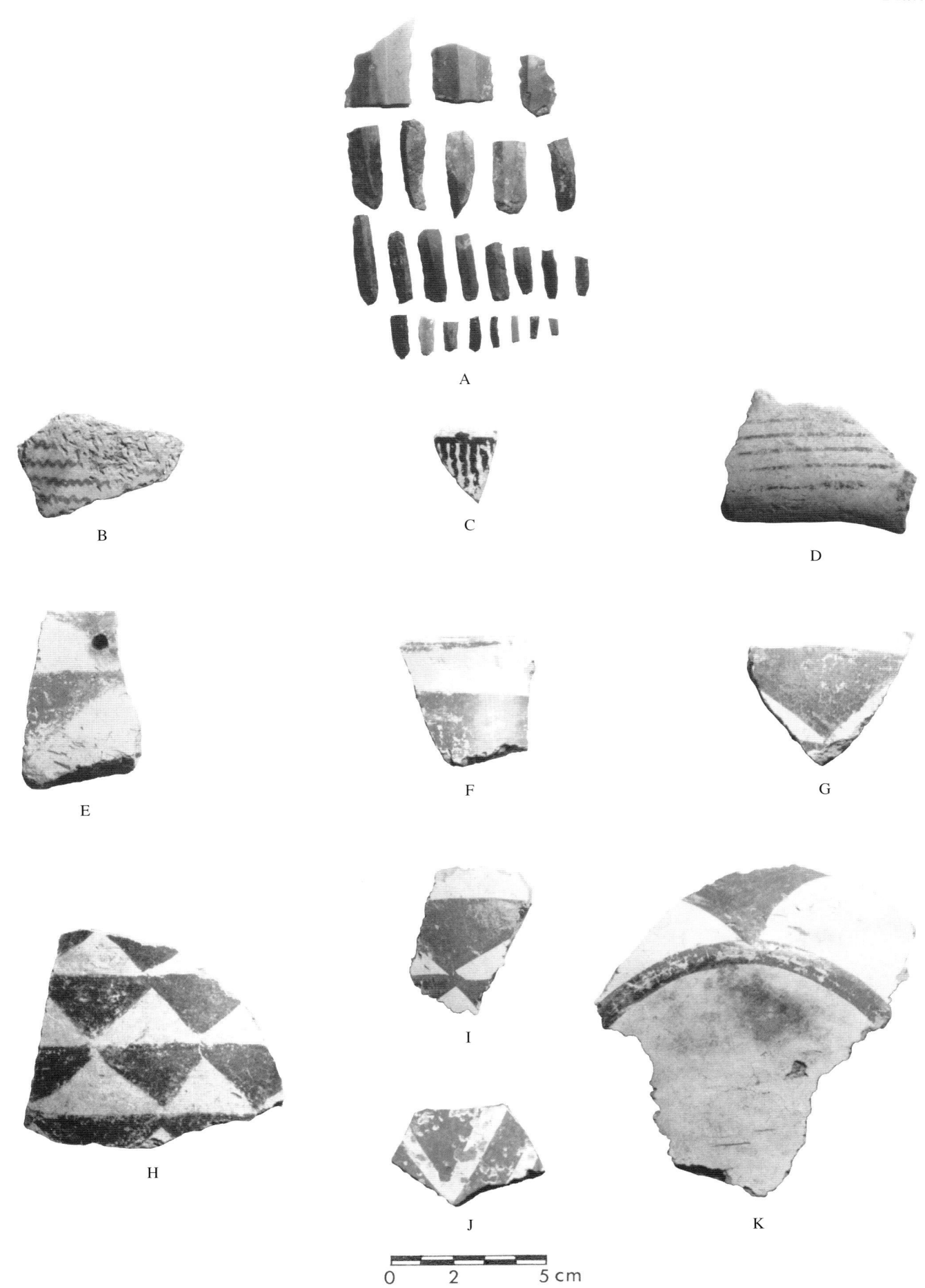

(A) Flint Blades, (B–D) Painted-burnished Variant Ware, and (E–K) Maroon-on-Cream Painted Ware

Plate 26. Late Middle Susiana and Late Susiana 2 Pottery

	Field Number	Findspot	Elevation	Description
A	NA (Bonut 1978)	NA	Surface	Late Middle Susiana standard buff ware: Kiln waster consisting of two painted bowls stuck together. This is an example of numerous such pieces found in and around kilns, and scattered all over the site. Scale ca. 1:2
B	B 1189	M10:102	NA	Late Middle Susiana standard buff ware: Interior of an open form decorated with perhaps a representation of mountain goat flanked by wavy lines, perhaps representing streams of water or cultivated fields. Greenish buff ware, some grits included in the paste, creamy buff slip all over. Greenish granular paint ingrained into the surface. Scale ca. 3:4
C	B 2253a–b	K10:202	77.80–76.17	Late Susiana 2 standard buff ware: Fine ware. Beaker fragment joining other fragments found in the Late Susiana well K10:202. Buff ware with no visible inclusion. Creamy buff slip all over. Dark paint. Scale ca. 3:4
D	NA (Bonut 1978)	NA	NA	Late Middle Susiana standard buff ware: Base fragment of open bowl with central motif of a turtle. Buff clay with some small grits inclusion. Creamy buff slipped. Dark paint. Scale ca. 1:2
E	B 1–2	NA	NA	Late Middle Susiana standard buff ware: Dense greenish buff paste with no visible inclusion. Surface color varies from greenish to yellowish buff. Olive green paint, slightly granular where thicker. Scale not known

Plate 26

A

B

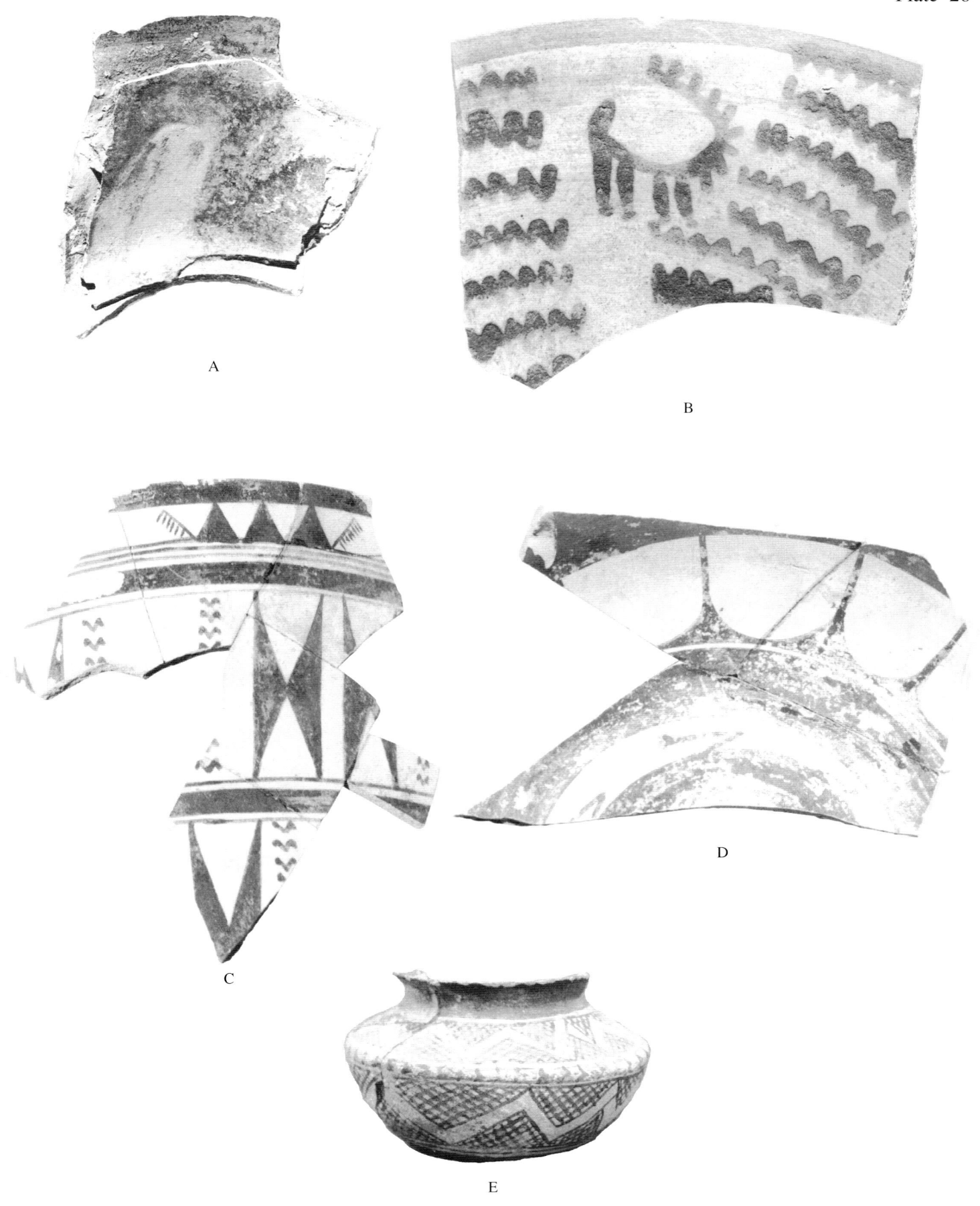

C

D

E

Late Middle Susiana and Late Susiana 2 Pottery. Scales (A, D) 1:2, (B–C) 3:4, and (E) Unknown